# THE GOLDEN AGE OF SOUTHERN CAMEROONS

# THE GOLDEN AGE OF SOUTHERN CAMEROONS

## Prime Lessons for Cameroon

*Anthony Ndi*

SPEARS MEDIA PRESS

Spears Media Press
Denver • Bamenda
7830 W. Alameda Ave, Suite 103 Denver, CO 80226

Spears Media Press publishes under the auspices of the Spears Media Association.

The Press furthers the Association's mission by advancing the frontiers of knowledge in education, learning, entertainment and research.

First Published 2016 by Spears Media Press
www.spearsmedia.com
info@spearsmedia.com
Information on this title: www.spearsmedia.com/thegoldenage

© Anthony Ndi 2016
All rights reserved.

No part of this publication may be reproduced, distributed, or transmitted in any form or by any means, including photocopying, recording, or other electronic or mechanical methods, without the prior written permission of the publisher, except in the case of brief quotations embodied in critical reviews and certain other noncommercial uses permitted by copyright law. For permission requests, write to the publisher, addressed "Attention: Permissions Coordinator," at the address below.

Ordering Information:
Special discounts are available on bulk purchases by corporations, associations, and others. For details, contact the publisher at any of the addresses above.

ISBN: 9781942876120 [Paperback]
ISBN: 9781942876151 [eBook]

Spears Media Press has no responsibility for the persistence or accuracy of urls for external or third-party internet websites referred to in this publication, and does not guarantee that any content on such websites is, or will remain, accurate or appropriate.

To Patriots, Posterity and Cameroonians of Goodwill

## Historical Quotes

*Those who do not remember their past are apt to repeat its errors*

*Not to know what happened before you were born is to remain forever a child*

# Contents

| | |
|---|---|
| *List of Figures* | xi |
| *List of Maps* | xi |
| *Acknowledgements* | xv |
| *Abbreviations and Acronyms* | xvii |
| *Foreword to the New Edition* | xxv |
| *Preface to the New Edition* | xxix |

**Chapter One** — 1
*Philosophical and Historical Concepts of the "Golden Age"*

**Chapter Two** — 33
*Legacies: Colonial, Christian and Indigenous*

**Chapter Three** — 77
*The Southern Cameroons: Character*

**Chapter Four** — 123
*The Emergence of a Genuine Democratic Culture*

**Chapter Five** — 151
*Decline of the FRC: Internal and External Factors*

**Chapter Six** — 185
*Violating the "Inviolable Federal Constitution"*

**Chapter Seven** — 229
*Ironic Outcome of Marginalisation: An Invincible Spirit*

**Chapter Eight** — 261
*The last Lines: Ahidjo-Biya Tussle*

| | |
|---|---|
| *Epilogue* | 279 |
| *Appendix I* | 291 |

| | |
|---|---|
| *Appendix II* | 297 |
| *Appendix III* | 299 |
| *Appendix IV* | 301 |
| *Appendix V* | 303 |
| *Interviews and Written Notes* | 311 |
| *Bibliography* | 315 |
| *Index* | 321 |

# List of Maps and Figures

## Maps
1. Cameroons 1922-1961   xxi
2. Federal Republic of Cameroon (1961-1972), showing the two states, West Cameroon (formerly Southern Cameroons) and East Cameroon (formerly the Republic of Cameroon).   xxii
3. Southern Cameroons Relief and Drainage   xxiii
4. West Cameroon (North West and South West Provinces) Political, 1961-1972   xxiv

## Figures
1. Mr. P M Kale   11
2. Dr. E M L Endeley   11
3. Mr. J N Foncha   11
4. Mr. N N Mbile   11
5. Mr. A N Jua   11
6. Mr. S T Muna   11
7. Malcolm Milne, Acting Commissioner   12
8. Kwame Nkrumah, being presented a carved elephant tusk by Mr. JN Foncha, newly elected PM of Southern Cameroons, February 1959   18
9. Dr Nnamdi Azikiwe   19
10. Prime Minister, JN Foncha and Fon Galega II of Bali, chat with Brigadier EJ Gibbons OBE, first Commissioner of Southern Cameroons.   21
11. Left, Mr. Ndeh Ntumazah; Right, Mr. A W Mukong. Founder and co-founder of the One Kamerun (OK) Party in Southern Cameroons in 1957   24
12. Dr. Djalal Abdoh, UN Plebiscite Commissioner for Southern Cameroons is the gentleman on the left with his left hand on his mouth. He is conferring with colleagues over the counting process.   26
13. Southern Cameroons Police on Parade   34
14. Left, HRH Fon Galega II of Bali Nyonga, Right, Chief J Manga Williams of Victoria. They Represented Southern Cameroons as Native Authorities (NA) in Nigerian Legislatures.   36
15. Hon SN Tamfu & the Fon of Tabenken about to fire den guns at a traditional celebration   42

## LIST OF MAPS AND FIGURES

16. The Governor General of Nigeria, H E, Sir James Robertson unveils Victoria Centenary Monument in 1958 — 44
17. Mr. John IE Foleng, a highly qualified young accountant. He worked in the Treasury Department, Buea. — 49
18. Bismarck Fountain, Buea — 57
19. Woermann, who together with Jantzen and Thormalen opened enormous agricultural estates in German Kamerun, precursors of the present day vast CDC plantations — 60
20. Left, Dr E M L Endeley and Bp. Peter Rogan; Right, St Francis' Teacher's Training College, Kumba. — 69
21. Top, St. Joseph's College Sasse, Buea opened in 1939, and the first secondary school in Southern Cameroons. It provided manpower for the civil service; bottom, Man O'War Bay, Victoria, where Bilingual Grammar School, Buea, the first Government Secondary School was originally opened in 1963 — 71
22a. Dr E M L Endeley & wife congratulate Mr. J N Foncha after CPNC defeat by KNDP and replacement by Foncha as Premier — 72
22b Left, J O Field, Commissioner of Southern Cameroons and right, HE Sir James Robertson, Governor General of Nigeria — 72
22c. Top, Prime Minister, A N Jua acquiring land for CCAST at Bambili, Bamenda; bottom, President Ahmadou Ahidjo being received in Buea, West Cameroon — 73
23. Dr. E M L Endeley: Leader of Government Business — 91
24. The Southern Cameroons Executive Council, 1958 — 95
25. The Foncha (KNDP) Government, 1959 — 97
26. Fon Achirimbi II of Bafut with Gerald Durrell — 102
27. The Southern Cameroons National Assembly in Session — 105
27a. Top, voters line up for Plebiscite vote; Bottom, Premier J N Foncha at a Press Conference after Plebisicite — 114
27b. Top, Bamenda All Party Conference 26-28 June 1961. Note Fon Galega II of Bali, Prominent among others; Middle Foncha, PM with Jua, Muna and Kemcha to his left; Note the presence of three British colonial officials in attendance including the Attorney General (It is repeatedly alleged that the British were not consulted or invited to the Bamenda all party conference nor to the Foumban Conference but they were present at both) — 115
27c. Top: some Southern Cameroons delegates to the Foumban Conference flew in by air from Tiko International Airport. Here at the Koutaba Military Airport, left to right are: ST Muna, PM Kemcha, Dr. EML Endeley and JN Foncha.

LIST OF MAPS AND FIGURES

Bottom: Delegates at the Foumban Conference in front of the sultan's palace: the three central figures are: President Ahmadou Ahidjo, JN Foncha and Sultan Njimoulouh. 116

27d. Top: Note, President Ahidjo in white, flanked by Charles Assale and Moussa Yaya on his right. Bottom: Inside the Conference Hall, Note Endeley and Foncha with microphones in front of them, flanked by Muna and Kemcha on the right with Jua and the Attorney General to the left 117

27e. Top: cross section of audience at the Foumban Conference; Middle: Prime Minister, JN Foncha decorated by Sultan Njimoulouh as Prime Minister, Charles Assale looks on Bottom: in the Conference Hall, sitting right to left are: the Attorney General, Jua, Foncha and Muna. 118

27f. Top left, Malcolm Milne, Deputy Commissioner of Southern Cameroons receives President Ahmadou Ahidjo at Tiko International Airport as he comes to preside over the independence day celebrations. Note Joseph Lafon in the background. Top right, Ahmadou Ahidjo presides over the independence celebrations in Buea. Bottom left, Independence Day celebration at Buea Mountain Hotel: The British Ambassador to Cameroon, C E King reads the Queen's speech. Bottom right; Governor General of Nigeria, Sir James Robertson, left, received by JO Field and JN Foncha 119

27g. Left, Endeley and wife; Top Right and bottom, Foncha and Ahidjo dance at the Independence celebration, Mountain Hotel Buea. 120

28. Mungo Bridge christened "Reunification Bridge" 125

29. Mr J N Foncha, Vice-President of the Federal Republic of Cameroon and Mr. A N Jua, PM of West Cameroon inspect Guard of Honour 129

30. SDO, Nick Ade Ngwa receives Federal Minister and his entourage from Yaoundé in Victoria, Fako Division 139

31. President Ahmadou Ahidjo being received in Buea, West Cameroon 143

32. Left, Zintgraff; Right HRH Fon Galega I of Bali. They undertook a blood pact, literally, drank each other's blood in a palm wine concoction as a sign of intimate friendship. 144

33. Like Mr. A N Jua and Mr. S T Muna, both Nzoh and Egbe were candidates for elections to key posts in the KNDP party at the 9th Convention, which sparked serious discords and dissent within the Party 159

34. From Left to right Hon. Ajebe-Sone, PM Augustine N Jua, SDO Ngwa and DO Mbuyonga during the PM's Official Visit to Muyuka 165

35. New Secretaries of State in the Jua Coalition Government (Messrs. Nsame, Tamfu

and Mbile). 168
36. Mgr. Ndongmo standing left of Pope Paul VI at the Vatican, Rome 171
37. Hon S T Muna seated second from left. 179
38. The Ahidjo Government, 1975; Front row from left to right: Messrs Ayissi Mvodo, Sadou Daoudou, Paul Biya, Ahmadou Ahidjo, Samuel Eboa, Enock Kwayeb and Emmanuel T Egbe. 182
39. Prime Minister, Charles Assale. 225
40. Copy of Ballot paper for the 1972 Referendum 228
41. Christian Cardinal Tumi; outspoken on issues of human rights and the marginalization of Anglophone Cameroonians. 231
42. Independence Day celebrations in Buea with Cecil King, the British Ambassador to Cameroon reading the Queens speech 239
43. André-Marie Mbida 249
44. The Green Tree Agreement; Presidents Paul Biya of Cameroon and Obasanjo of Nigeria shake hands as Kofi Anan, former Secretary General of the UN looks on 283
45. Plebiscite Results 297

# ACKNOWLEDGEMENTS

The origin and much of the content of this book resulted from practical discussions and consultations. I am therefore highly indebted to several institutions and individuals both at home and abroad for its production. I received assistance from the National Archives at Buea; the Archives and library of the Presbyterian Church in Cameroon (PCC), Buea; St. Thomas Aquinas Major Seminary (STAMS) library, Bambui; the Public Record Office, London; the Mill Hill Archives and Library, London and the Bodleian Library, Oxford. Furthermore, some persons generously allowed me the use of their personal libraries and archives. Still, many others, most of them "prime actors" in the narrative, freely gave me their precious time in personal interviews and group discussions. My gratitude to these though acknowledged in the bibliography and list of interviewees is far from satisfactory. I wish l could do more to express it.

Nonetheless, I must single out for mention a few of the people who have been most instrumental in this publication. These include Professor Richard Gray, Emeritus Professor of History, School of Oriental and African Studies, (SOAS) University of London, who gave me every encouragement to have the topic investigated into and published; Dr. Paul Gifford, Reader, SOAS, University of London, who read through the manuscript and made useful suggestions; Dr. Omer Weyi Yembe of the Cameroon GCE Board, who first suggested my elaboration of the topic and Mrs. Elizabeth M Chilver, a central "prime actress", who was very supportive in personal discussions, correspondence and the copious supply of useful material. In fact, she provided a stub for the book.

Others, who critically read the work, made fertile written or verbal comments include: Mons. Clemens Ndze, Messrs. Peter Nsanda Eba, a prime actor; David Ngiewi Asunkwan, a retired Senior Journalist and prime actor; Henry Fonge, Assistant Chief Examiner, General Certificate, Advanced Level; History; Stephen Nfor, London-based former CRTV journalist and Ms Mary-Tonia Ndi, recent graduate of the Catholic

## ACKNOWLEDGEMENTS

University of Central Africa, (UCAC), Yaoundé. Mr. Nicholas Ade Ngwa, Retired Principal Civil Administrator, who served both as Senior Tutor at Sasse, Education Officer and participated both in the political and administrative life of this country, was a marvellous source of firsthand information and encouragement. He graciously accepted to write the Foreword to this work; Barrister Luke Sendze another key player, especially in the "Ndongmo Affair," threw great insight into that epic trial and supplied invaluable material included in the Appendix. Mr. Cyril Ebu, a retired accountant, literally a "priest without orders", who missed priestly ordination by months, offered inside information about the Church as well as about the civil service, while Mr. John Mofor Ndi, was exceptionally enthusiastic and made available to me rare, invaluable documents and information. In short all of these were insiders and prime actors during the existence of the state of Southern Cameroons.

In the final analysis, however, it was Fr. George Nkuo's homily and the appointment of HE Chief Ephraim Inoni as Prime Minister and Head of Government that sparked the fire in me to further investigate and undertake this publication in the abiding faith and hope that change is inevitable and the ripe time for it is now.

Mr. Henry Bongbi of Maple Fair Graphics undertook the entire burden of putting the pieces together for this production with intermittent assistance derived variously from Mr. Leo Yuniwo Ndi, Mrs. Colette Nahsang Horatio-Jones, Mrs. Renee Mungo Nfor, and Mr. Cornelius Tfurndabi Tawong. My wife, Patience Ndi, bore my seclusions "patiently", and above all, proved to be a fairly reliable proof-reader. To each and every one of these noble souls I am heartily indebted and immensely grateful.

Anthony Ndi
Bamenda 20 April 2005

# Abbreviations and Acronyms

## *Chronological Nomenclature of "Cameroons*[1]

- German Kamerun, 1884-1915
- Cameroons Province, 1922-1949
- British Southern Cameroons, 1949-1954
- British Cameroons: this appellation referred to both British Southern Cameroons and British Northern Cameroons under colonial rule
- Southern Cameroons, 1954-61; then, West Cameroon, 1961-1972
- French Cameroon, also "French Cameroun" 1922-1960
- Republic of Cameroun also, "République du Cameroun", 1960-1961 and again, the entire territory after 1984`
- East Cameroun, (former French Cameroon) 1961-1972
- Federal Republic of Cameroon, FRC, 1961-1972
- United Republic of Cameroon, URC, 1972-1984
- République du Cameroun; Republic of Cameroon: (Former French Cameroon) 1960-61
- North West Province (NWP), 1972- 1984
- North West Region (NWR), 1984-Date
- South West Province (SWP), 1972-1984
- South West Region (SWR), 1984- Date

## *Civic Titles*
AO   Administrative Officer
EO   Education Officer
DO   District Officer
SDO  Senior Divisional Officer
CO   Colonial Office
NA   Native Authority, Native Administration
NC   Native Court, Native Council
NT   Native Treasury
IR   Indirect Rule

---

[1] *Cameroons* with an "S" is commonly used with :"The Southern Cameroons", "The Northern Cameroons" or British Southern Cameroons.

## Clerical Names and Titles

| | |
|---|---|
| BM | Basel Mission (1925-1957) |
| PCC | Presbyterian Church in Cameroon (1957 -1961 & 1984 – Date) |
| PCWC | Presbyterian Church in West Cameroon 1962 – 1972 |
| CBM | Cameroon Baptist Mission (1924 -1954) |
| CBC | Cameroon Baptist Convention (1954 – Date) |
| CBCWF | Cameroon Baptist Convention Women's Fellowship |
| CWF | Christian Women's Fellowship (PCC) |
| RCM | Roman Catholic Mission (1922 – 1972) |
| CM | Catholic Mission, (Popular within the Local Church since the 1970s) |
| CC | Catholic Church, (Same as above) |
| BAPEC | Bamenda Provincial Episcopal Conference comprising: The Archdiocese of Bamenda and the Dioceses of Buea, Kumbo and Mamfe |
| NECC | National Episcopal Conference of Cameroon |
| MHM | Mill Hill Missionary (Missionaries) |
| STAMS | St. Thomas Aquinas' Major Seminary (Bambui) |
| Bp | Bishop |
| Mgr | Mons. Monsignor |
| Mod | Moderator |
| Rev | Reverend |

## Political Parties and other Institutions: Evolution

| | |
|---|---|
| CWU | Cameroons Welfare Union; launched in 1939 in Victoria by Mr. G J Mbene |
| CYL | Cameroons Youth League; founded in 1940 in Lagos by Messrs P M Kale, E M L Endeley, NN Mbile, J N Foncha and some forty others |
| NCNC | National Congress of Nigeria and Cameroons; inaugurated in 1944 in Lagos by Messrs Nnamdi Azikiwe and Herbert Macaulay |
| UPC | *Union des Populations du Cameroun*: inaugurated in 1948 by Messrs Reuben Um Nyobe, Mayi Matip and others at Douala |

## ABBREVIATIONS AND ACRONYMS

| | |
|---|---|
| CNF | Cameroons National Federation; founded in 1949 by Dr. E M L Endeley, (It comprised some twenty Development Associations including the Bakweri Land Committee, J B K Dibongue's FCWU and the CDC-WU) |
| KUNC | Kamerun United National Congress; founded in 1951 by Nerius Namaso Mbile, JB Kum Dibongué and Ernest Ouandié in Kumba. (Note the UPC element within it in the guise of Ernest Ouandie) |
| KNC | Kamerun National Congress; resulted from the merger in 1953 of the KUNC and CNF leadership. |
| KPP | Kamerun People's Party; founded in 1953 by PM Kale and NN Mbile |
| KNDP | Kamerun National Democratic Party; founded in 1955 by Messrs JN Foncha and AN Jua. |
| OK | One Kamerun; formed in 1957 by Messrs Ndeh Ntumazah and Albert Mukong; literally, it was the Southern Cameroons version of the UPC |
| UC | Union Camerounaise; founded in 1958 by Ahmadou Ahidjo with the able assistance of Moussa Yaya in Garoua |
| KUC | Kamerun United Congress; inaugurated at Mamfe (and Kumba) |
| CPNC | Cameroon People's National Congress; merger of the KNC and KPP in June 1960 |
| CUC | Cameroon United Congress, formed after split from the KNDP in 1964 by Messrs ST Muna and Emmanuel Tabi Egbe |
| CNU | Cameroon National Union; merger in 1966 of all political parties in East and West Cameroon under President Ahmadou Ahidjo |
| AU | African Unity (evolution of the OAU) |
| OAU | Organisation of African Unity |
| ECOWAS | Economic Commission of West African States |
| NEPAD | New Partnership for African Development |
| PWD | Public Works Department |

***Other Abbreviations***

| | |
|---|---|
| GTC | Government trade centre (Ombe) |
| GTTC | Government Teachers Training Centre (Kumba, Kake) |
| TTC | Teacher Training Centre |
| PWD | Public Works Department |

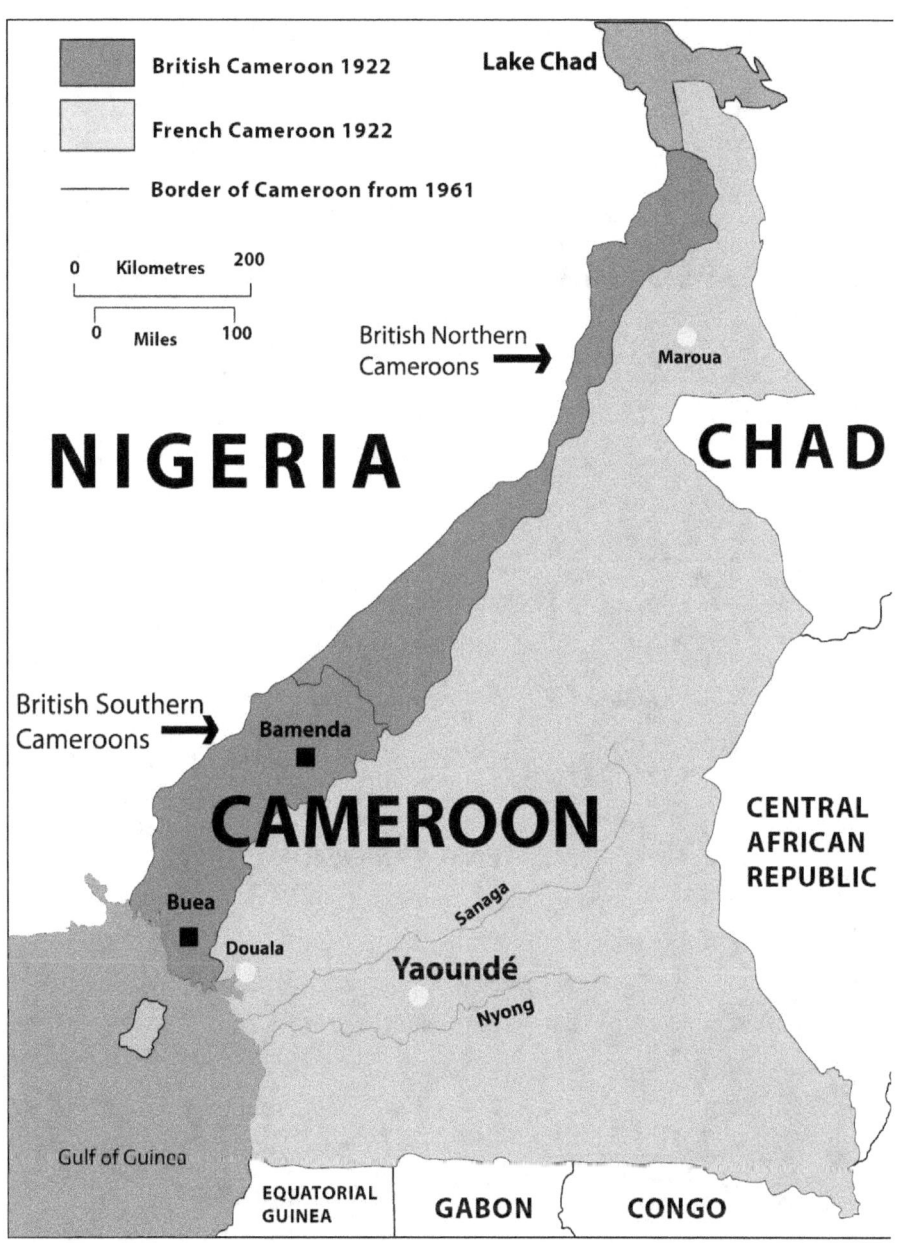

*Map 1. Cameroons 1922–1961*

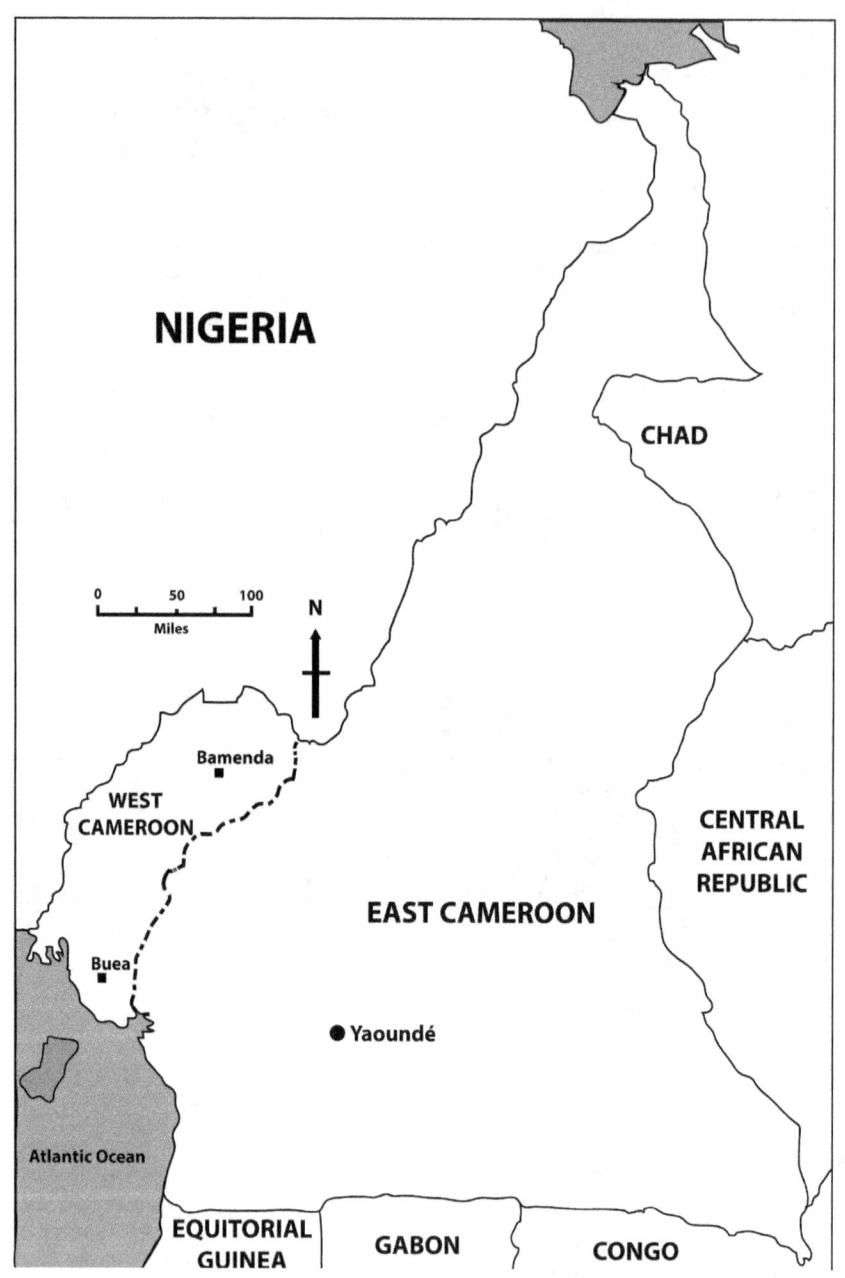

*Map 2. Federal Republic of Cameroon (1961-1972), showing the two states, West Cameroon (formerly Southern Cameroons) and East Cameroon (formerly the Republic of Cameroon).*

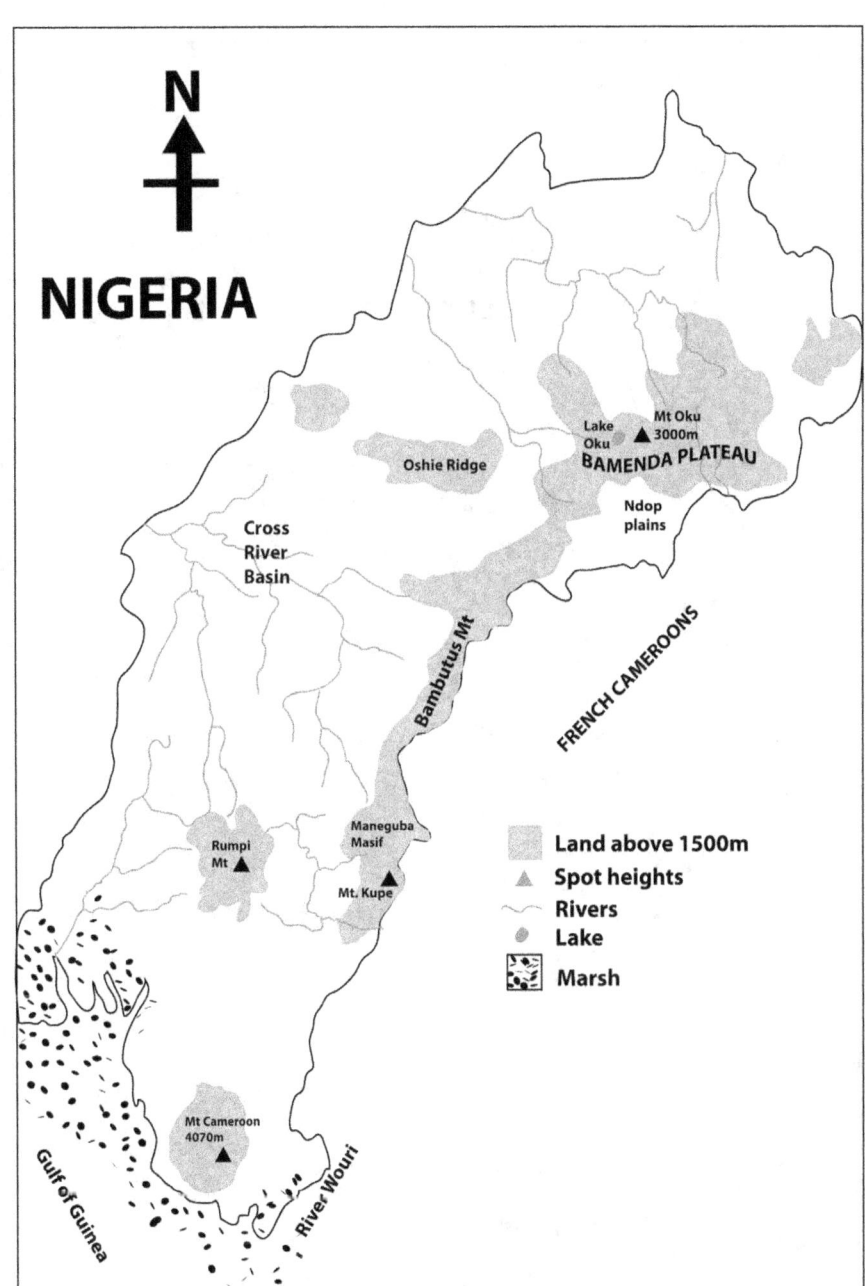

*Map 3. Southern Cameroons Relief and Drainage*

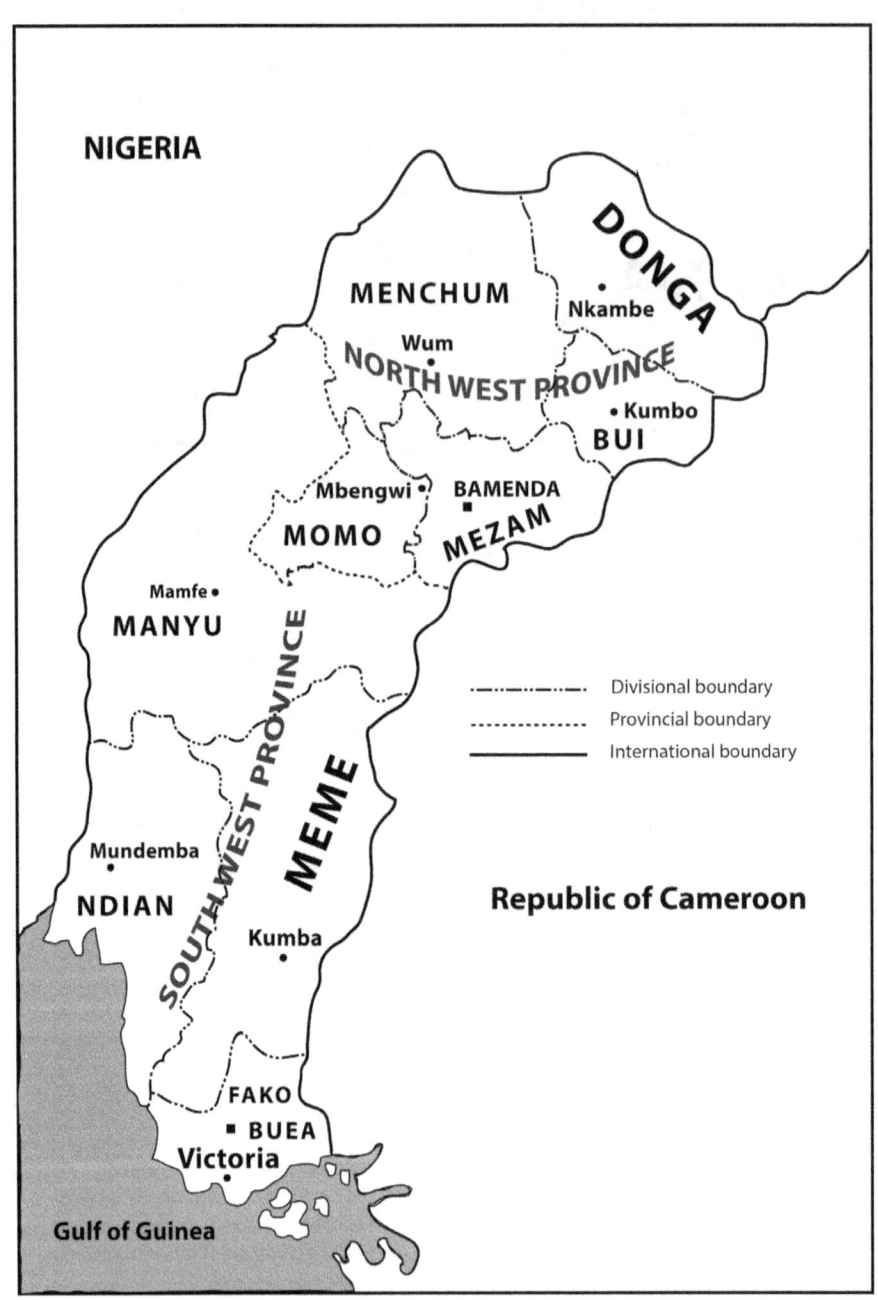

*Map 4. West Cameroon (North West and South West Provinces) Political, 1961-1972*

# FOREWORD TO THE NEW EDITION

Each generation writes its own history with hopes of understanding how and why things became the way they are. This is particularly true for Cameroon, a nation which has been affected by the major historical forces of slavery, colonialism, nationalism, tyranny, and neo-colonialism. Within the last two decades contemporary participants and historians alike have doubled efforts to understand the sources of many of Cameroon's contemporary challenges. The literature has addressed topics including ethnicity, youth culture, women and gender, corruption, poverty, education, religion, and the Anglophone Problem.

Much of the written work also has pointed to areas in need of urgent scholarly inquiry. Anthony Ndi's: *The Golden Age of Southern Cameroons: Prime Lessons for Cameroon* is consistent with that trend. It adds to the growing literature on Cameroon and also raises issues which require scholarly attention. The book places "Southern Cameroons" (contemporary North West and South West Regions of Cameroon) within a broader historical context and reminds readers that this region was once autonomous, vibrant and prosperous. The period from 1955-1965, Ndi argues, was the "peak" of the Golden Age in Southern Cameroons when "elections were comparatively free, fair, and transparent" (p.93). A chief beneficiary of "Anglo-Saxon liberal and democratic culture," Southern Cameroons promoted freedom of the press, civic responsibility, good governance, and socio-cultural progress. Christianity, the author maintains, was a vital part of the region's culture. Religion was an integral part of the educational system, and as such young people grew up with a strong sense of moral and social responsibility, which impacted indelibly on their adult life.

Institutions such as Cameroon Bank, the West Cameroon Marketing Board, and POWERCAM pointed to economic stability. Southern Cameroons was a progressive region, Ndi surmises. However, with the creation of a one party state in 1966, the Cameroon National Union (CNU), and the change from the Federal to United Republic of Cameroon six years later, things unraveled quickly in West Cameroon. Ahmadou Ahidjo, Cameroon's founding leader, deceived and manipulated leaders of Anglophone Cameroon. Prior to reunification of East and West Cameroon, Ahidjo had promised equality, respect, and integration of both regions on a strictly federal basis. However, after reunification he pursued policies which undermined the political, economic, and social development of West Cameroon and finally established a highly centralized oppressive unitary state. These adverse policies became fixtures on the nation's social and cultural landscape, and were continued by his successor, Paul Biya. The People of former Southern Cameroons were dismissed as "Biafrans," Anglo fools," and traitors. Southern Cameroonians or Anglophones became in essence a "colony" of East Cameroon. Ahidjo was indeed the undertaker of the "*Golden Age*" of Southern Cameroons.

In constructing the narrative the author delves into significant issues including the inability of Southern Cameroonian political leaders to form a united front against Ahidjo's policies, the role and perception of Ibos in the region, and the resurgence of political activism in Anglophone Cameroon. The study serves as a reminder of the painful cost and legacy of colonialism in contemporary African societies. Like other books, this one also draws attention to areas which need urgent scholarly attention. Critical biographies are needed on Southern Cameroons political leaders including John Ngu Foncha, Dr. Emmanuel L Endeley, Paul M Kale, Solomon T Muna, Augustine N Jua, Emmanuel T Egbe, and several others. It is surprising that three decades since Ahidjo stepped down from power; there is still no monograph on him by an Anglophone Cameroonian. While there is literature on aspects of Biya's policies, a complete biography on him is urgently needed. The role of and relationship between Cameroonians and Ibos prior to, during, and post "Golden Age" requires scholarly attention. Ndi is highly critical of British colonial administration in Southern Cameroons, especially in their policy of 'benign socio-economic neglect' and finally, their deliberate obstruction of its independence, a factor which is responsible for their present predicament. However, he appreciates the enriched and "domesticated" Anglo-Saxon culture of liberalism, democracy and self reliance inculcated through their colonial policy of Indirect Rule better known as "Native Administration". Deeply entrenched in the people, it has become a hybrid, imbedded culture from which they continue to draw strength and inspiration.

In summary, *The Golden Age of Southern Cameroons: Prime Lessons for Cameroon* will appeal to both the general and serious reader. It is a reminder that history matters. Southern Cameroons was once a vibrant, democratic, autonomous and prosperous state with enormous prospects for a brilliant future unfortunately shattered by Ahidjo's dictatorship. The greatest Anglophone frustration remains the penchant of the Francophone-led administration for violating every single accord reached with them including even the constitution. This is the reason why Ndi convincingly argues, the Anglophone clamour since 1972, has been for a return to the drawing board at Foumban in 1961. It certainly was not a perfect agreement but it remains the best option for a firm and united Cameroon, where Anglophones and Francophones would find space and unity in diversity, harmony and progress.

This book challenges the current generation of Anglophone Cameroonians to do their part and restore to the North West and South West Regions of Cameroon a sense of pride, dignity, and prosperity, which will not come on a platter of gold.

Julius A. Amin, PhD, *Professor of History*
The University of Dayton, Ohio, USA

# PREFACE TO THE NEW EDITION

The first edition of this book titled: *The Golden Age of Southern (West) Cameroon*, was locally published ten years ago in Bamenda, North West Region, Cameroon, a country with a poor reading culture. This is further worsened among the Anglophones by the fact that they constitute by far, a smaller population than their Francophone compatriots. For that reason, it is a well-established adage that if you want to preserve a secret, or to keep anything away from public knowledge in Cameroon, the safest place to do so is within the pages of a book. As proof of this, I encountered a friend recently, who argued fiercely and passionately about all that he thought went wrong with the 1961 Plebiscite and the subsequent Foumban Constitutional Conference, which he held accountable for all the Anglophone woes. Sadly, however, much of what he said did not square up with the facts on record, but was based on conspiracy theories, fallacies and sheer conjecture. In a bid to help him broaden his views so as to buttress his arguments on the topic, I politely suggested for him to read pertinent literature on the subject, notably the book by John Percival.[1] His reaction was typical: "How big is the book?" and next, "How many pages is it?" Needless to say I was greatly disappointed especially as he is popular and influential elite whose opinion is highly respected in the community because of his eloquence and forceful personality.

As pointed out, *The Golden Age of Southern (West) Cameroon* was published a decade ago with a little over one thousand copies. However, barely five years later, they had run out of stock in the few bookshops, where they were on sale with requests for more, even for use as a textbook

---

[1] John Percival, *The 1961 Cameroon Plebiscite, Choice Or Betrayal* (Langaa Research and Publishing CIG, Mankon, Bamenda) 2008.

in secondary schools and colleges. This was in spite of the fact that it had neither been formally launched nor publicly advertised anywhere; it simply passed from hand to hand or by word of mouth. Yet, there were those readers, who further requested if possible, for it to be translated into French given that our Francophone compatriots are either poorly informed, care little about who and what the Anglophones are or, much less, accept the existence of Anglophones as a unique polity within the country, or still more distressing recognise the legitimate existence of an "Anglophone problem".

## "Anglophones" or "Southern Cameroonians"

Many are those who regard the "Anglophones" or "Southern Cameroonians" and their complaints as something of a curiosity, a minority group like all the other ethnic groups in Cameroon; but generally as a sort of nuisance, an insatiable lot, who do not deserve any more attention than they already have been accorded. Consequently, the prevalent grievances about their: second class citizenship, marginalisation, assimilation and annexationist tendencies of Anglophone Southern Cameroonians by the ruling *Francophone elite* are simply incomprehensible, even to some of the top grade administrators and intellectuals. It is regrettable that with the passage of time especially after the 1972 debacle, memories have waned or have been so warped and politicised that Southern Cameroonians or Anglophones are increasingly regarded and equated with large ethnic groups elsewhere in the country on the basis of size requiring no extra attention than these others. Historically, this is sad and much like playing the ostrich over a nagging problem that cannot be ignored or wished away.

This attitude totally negates the indisputable, historical fact that *Southern Cameroons* enjoyed full internal autonomy or *Self-Government* for seven years; in actual fact, four long years ahead of *French Cameroon*, its size notwithstanding. For that matter, it had a vibrant House of Assembly, a House of Chiefs (or Senate), an independent Judiciary, an ideal Public Service with a government and ministers presided over by an Executive Prime Minister. Of equal, indelible significance is the process by which Southern Cameroons attained its political autonomy, which did not come on a platter of gold as every iota of its identity was critically contested.

Unfortunately, these facts are hardly done justice to in our national history. *Reunification*, the complicated process by which Southern Cameroons chose to join Republic of Cameroon was a massive international affair endorsed by the UN, the international community and sanctioned by over 70% of the electorate in a UN organised plebiscite, declared as exemplary; free, fair and transparent.

These are documented facts of history that cannot by any means or for any reason, simply be minimised or trampled on as they are bound bubble up and out sooner or later. The surprise therefore, is how the entire Federal Republic of Cameroon could have been made to vote in the 1972 referendum over an issue which ten years previously, in February 1961 had involved only a fifth or 20% of the entire Federal Republic of Cameroon. This is all the more embarrassing given that more than fifty years later, there still remain huge gaps about Anglophone, "Southern Cameroons" in the minds of the vast majority of the Francophones in the country. This sort of game cannot usher Cameroon as a modern democratic nation united not in "false" uniformity but in diversity far into a stable future in a world that daily shrinks into a global village in the face of modern technology and infusion of radical ideologies.

These issues were handled in the first edition and are further elaborated upon in the present volume, which for emphasis is titled: *The Golden Age of Southern Cameroons – Prime Lessons for Cameroon.* It was during the period of its *Golden Age,* that the foundation was laid for it to acquire the status of a Quasi Federal Territory within the Federation of Nigeria. Appellations of the North and South West have changed from Provinces to Regions but they are used interchangeably in this volume depending on whether reference is being made to the period before 12 November 2008, when the decree replacing the Provinces with Regions was promulgated, after, or even earlier when by a simple decree, the name reverted from the United Republic of Cameroon (URC) to the pre-reunification appellation "Republic of Cameroon" which French Cameroon adopted at independence in 1960.[2]

---

[2] See Article 1 of Decree No. 2008/376 of 12 Nov. 2008. Also, Emmanuel Y Sobseh, *Rethinking Citizenship, Politics and Governance in Cameroon,* Global Press, p.93 for the decree of 1984 which renamed the country reverting to the name French Cameroon

On the whole, this volume has extensively been enriched in quality and significantly enlarged in size to cater for areas which readers indicated needed amplification. This is precisely the case with the elaboration on the dubious role Britain played initially as the Mandatory and later as Trusteeship Authority over the Territory, its obstinate insistence to administer Southern Cameroons as an "integral" part of its Nigerian Colony from 1916 -1961 and, especially the role of Nigerians (Ibo) within that unfortunate arrangement. Consequently, additional light has been thrown on their function as the "black colonial masters" by proxy, for Britain in Southern Cameroons, one that backfired tremendously. However, the greatest significance in this edition is the additional chapter on the "Invincibility of the Southern Cameroons Spirit". This comes with an analysis of its anatomy, emphasising its indefatigability and prowess – the greater the suppression, exclusion or attempts at assimilation by the Francophone majority, the more resolute the spirit.

The Nigerians (Ibos) with British assistance had earlier tried this trick and failed woefully as ultimately, the Southern Cameroonian choice of re-unification with Republic of Cameroon, was practically a decisive sanction against Britain and Nigeria. Also exploited and added to the appendices are pertinent extracts of the declassified British secret papers especially those dealing with Southern Cameroons during the administration of Dr. John Ngu Foncha, 1959-1961, when the struggle towards the plebiscite was fiercest with the British covertly and openly backing the opposition KNC/KPP alliance and facilitating carpet crossings to topple the KNDP re-unificationist government. This unveils stinking filth about British colonial administration. That is why the enlarged product is not merely a revised edition but actually, a brand new edition renamed: *The Golden Age of Southern Cameroons: Vital Lessons for Cameroon*, which better reflects its new essence, content and outlook.

### "The Golden Age of the Southern Cameroons Civil Service"

It will be recalled that it was Rev. Father George Nkuo, then, Rector

---

adopted at independence in 1960.

of Buea Town Catholic Parish, Buea Diocese, whose rousing homily on the "Golden Age of the Southern Cameroons Civil Service," inexplicably read like pages taken out of the manuscript I had prepared for a volume with that title and impinged on the production of the first edition of this book ten years ago. It is amazing that barely one year later, precisely on 8 July 2006; he was elevated to the Episcopacy as Bishop of Kumbo, the Diocese, which sprang out of the famous Shisong Parish inaugurated by the Sacred Heart Missionaries in 1913.[3] Rev. Fr. George Nkuo in his inspiring sermon at the funeral of Late Mr. Ernest Kalla Lottin in Buea on Saturday 13 November 2004 graphically described him as belonging to: "The generation of civil servants, who despite their human failings had discipline; where people were paid for work done with commitment for our Fatherland, where corruption and embezzlement were heavily reduced", a nostalgic period, which the priest maintained could hardly be challenged as: "The *golden age* of the civil service in Cameroon". The image he recommended for the new generation of civil servants as typified by the life of Mr. Lottin, was that of people:

> Who cannot be bought; whose word is their bond; who put character above wealth; who possess opinion and a will; who are larger than their vocations; who do not hesitate to take chances.... who will be as honest in small things as in great things; who will make no compromise with wrong; whose ambitions are not confined to their own selfish desires; who will not say they do something because everybody else does it ...who are not ashamed to stand for the truth when it is unpopular; who can say 'no' with emphasis although the rest of the world says 'yes"[4]

---

[3] Shisong was the foundation of Roman Catholicism in the North West Region and ceed of the bitterest clashes between the Missionaries and their zealous followers on the one hand and the Traditional Establishment backed by the AOs on the other. The Diocese presently combines the ancient foundations of the faith as well as enormous areas of primary evangelisation, a good challenge to Bishop Nkuo, who apparently is equal to the task in bulldozing and breaking new grounds in primary evangelisation and development.

[4] Homily at the Funeral Mass of Pa Ernest Kalla Lottin at St. Anthony's Parish Church, Buea Town, Saturday 13/11/04 by Rev Fr. George Nkuo

Every syllable of the powerful homily seemed to strike a common cord with what I had separately and independently written. It was as if the priest and I had been reading from the same song sheet and he had torn the key note from my manuscript – all, far too providential to be regarded and dismissed as a mere coincidence. In fact, it was divine providence; a "mission" challenging me to bring out in a more elaborate and forceful manner, what I had written simply as a chapter in my book in case this seminal work never had a chance to be exposed for the benefit of posterity by anybody. It directly reminded me of Chinua Achebe's timeless novel: *Things Fall Apart*[5], and his apt observation on being interviewed on CNN, that it was a book waiting to be written if not by him, then by some other person.

Thus Shisong (Kumbo) is the foundation of the Catholic Church in Bamenda Division, precisely the entire North West Region at the time, which presently comprises two Dioceses and some eighty Catholic Parishes besides the numerous Fields and Congregations of the Presbyterian Church in Cameroon and the Cameroon Baptist Convention. Politically, it is one of the ten Regions of Cameroon comprising seven divisions administered by a governor with headquarters at Bamenda.

However, unlike the positive note on the elevation of Rev. Father George Nkuo to the Episcopate, the same thing cannot be said of His Excellency, Rt. Hon. Chief Ephraim Inoni, erstwhile Prime Minister, on the political plane. He raised great hopes, when he introduced the audacious '*Operation Antelope*' programmed to root out bribery and corruption which had become deeply entrenched in the civil service, where some dishonest workers dubiously earned multiple salaries and bled the government coffers white. This reform received universal acclamation and raised great expectations. Regrettably, not much seems to have changed while he himself fell victim to a new anti-corruption outfit, the National Anti-Corruption Commission (CAN) established by the government and, ironically, presently together with dozens of other high profiled government and parastatal officials is behind bars on alleged charges of

---

[5] The historical novel published in 1958 depicts the conflict and impact on Igbo society brought about British colonial rule and Christianity.

embezzlement of public funds. In fact, several more of these reforms have been instituted to fight the scourge of corruption in Cameroon since then, generally with feeble results as corruption has eaten deep into the core of the society and has become near indestructible.

## Southern Cameroons: Moral Fibre

History *per se* does not set out teach any specific lessons, but taken as the 'collective memory' or wisdom of a people and, a record of the good, the bad and the ugly, we can always extract whatever moral applies to our particular circumstance from it: what to emulate, to retain or to avoid and discard. In the course of this study for example, some startling points have come to light. Principally, it has established the reality that Southern Cameroons does undeniably have a unique, glorious past containing an authentic indigenous culture shaped by appreciable contributions from British and German colonial experiences greatly sanctified by Christian ethics from which enormous hope and inspiration could be drawn. Among the main actors both in the public and private sectors were heroes and heroines in the art of nation-building, noble characters whose lives could become role models. The substance of the much applauded "Anglo-Saxon" component, meaning specific British contributions to Cameroon culture was largely through the contributions of the voluntary agencies on which they relied.

The impact of missionary activity on the other hand was overwhelming, with Christian ethical values transcending and impacting on all aspects even on secular life. All over the Territory, the early Europeans, especially missionaries in their contacts with the people reported very high moral and ethical standards with exemplary family life that existed prior to European and missionary contacts. Rev. Father Michael Moran reporting from Kumbo after touring the entire Bamenda Region in 1923 stated emphatically that the people had nothing to learn from Europe about family life; while, administrative officers presiding over cases in Native Courts, testified that theft and lying were literally unknown[6].

---

[6] These stories resonated from Nso to Kom, Bum, Wum, Mamfe and Kumba. Regardless

By the late 50s individual members of Parliament and Government without exception were also strong leaders and ardent Christians in the Catholic, Presbyterian and Baptist Churches, where some of them were zealous pastors. This impact originated from the fact that Voluntary Agencies (the Missions) preponderantly controlled education at the primary, secondary and teacher training levels, where Religious Knowledge and Moral Education were emphasised and imparted by ordinance, as much in Government and Native Authority (NA) schools as in Mission institutions. The same procedure applied to health and social services that were largely controlled by these Christian missionary denominations known as "Voluntary Agencies". To the extent that these agencies expressly existed and functioned strictly in accordance with British Colonial Government policy in its colonies together with their Mandated and later Trust Territories, the results can therefore be regarded as Anglo-Saxon oriented.

A cursory examination of the apparent geographical disparities that exist between the North and South-West Regions ultimately turns out to reveal that these are in fact, complementary and indeed are a spectacular natural heritage for the mutual benefit of the inhabitants of both Regions and for Cameroon as a nation. Intimate interactions at the individual, family, cultural, linguistic, economic, social, political and spiritual levels, after over a century of co-existence established much more than a fragile, political, inorganic unity. Rather what has evolved over time has been a vibrant spiritual union of hearts and minds bonding the people, which cannot so easily be severed by rabble rousing.

It is an acknowledged notion that the integral unity of the whole, generally depends on the solidity and harmony of its constituent parts beginning with the family, through the village and clan up to the division and region. The processes of devolution taking place in many old nations of the world including our very own colonial masters; France and Britain after centuries of highly centralised existence testify to this fact. National

---

of the pressure, the people generally insisted on firsthand knowledge and the truth. These can be found in the accounts of Messrs W E Hunt, Edward G Hawkesworth, Cantle among others, and later on, those of Collumpton and Malcolm Milne and John Percival in the late 1950s to early 1961. See Anthony Ndi, *Mill Hill Missionaries and the State in Southern Cameroons, 1922-72; also Southern West Cameroon revisited, 1950-1972*, Vol 1.

integration "erected" on the foundation of fraternity, peace, justice and shared common values become solid blocks for building a nation that can endure. In Southern Cameroons there was a general awareness and deliberate attempts made to suppress and eliminate the vices of ethnicism, sectionalism, tribalism, bribery and corruption both in private and public life. This was deliberately undertaken as a conscious political option by successive Administrations and by the various Christian denominations operating in the Territory. Unity was understood to mean not "unity in uniformity" but "unity in diversity" respecting differences such as exist in a salad bowl; a concept that was implemented right down to primary school syllabuses Southern Cameroons. There was freedom of choice and action at all levels.

Although both Britain and Germany, former colonial masters made appreciable material and political contributions to the evolution of Southern Cameroons as a distinct political entity, Britain through its Nigerian "black" colonial overlords was overtly responsible for much of the economic and administrative underdevelopment and backwardness of the Territory. In the ultimate analysis Britain stifled its political evolution towards independence. On the other hand, while Christianity played a primordial role in the rise of the "Golden Age" in Southern Cameroons, the imposition of the autocratic One-Party system and lay state mentality after re-unification under President Ahidjo deliberately and systematically muffled and extinguished it.

### Living Lessons of History: Global

An important point about History is its value as a predictive tool for inculcating national integration. It is a universally acknowledged fact that has been consciously and judiciously used in the education syllabuses of great nations to good effect. Our bicultural, bilingual and multi-ethnic diversity offers a rich background and provides an excellent source and reason for the institution of a similar approach in the Cameroon educational system. Properly handled, History could instil mutual understanding, tolerance and respect for each other's cultural heritage as well as dedication to duty, transparency and assiduity in public and private affairs, the foundations of which already existed in the federal constitution. As a source of wisdom and means of nation building, History comes next only to the Bible.

However, unlike the Bible or the Koran, History is neutral and stands neither for nor against, it is simply a record of the facts as they happened. Consequently, it is amoral. It does not forgive, and those who fail to learn the lessons of History inevitably pay a high price for their transgressions. World History is littered with the graves of countless leaders and individuals such as: Adolf Hitler, Benito Mussolini, Slobadan Milosevic, Dada Idi Amin, Jean Bedel Bokassa, Marcias Nguema, Samuel Doe; Mobutu *Sesse Seko Kuku Ngenda Waza Banga* (the Invincible Warrior or 'the cock who leaves no chick untouched') of Zaire and Sani Abacha, who flouted and neglected the lessons and wisdom of History. We are inescapably bound to, and are an indelible part of our past – playing the ostrich, and not to know what happened before we were born, simply because we were not there, is to remain forever a child.

One decade down memory lane, on the African scene, Ivory Coast (Côte d'Ivoire) finally stabilised; while next door the deadly 'Ebola epidemic', a well-known but yet incurable disease crept in and wrought great havoc claiming some five thousand lives in the neighbouring states of Liberia, Guinea Conakry, and Sierra Leone. It is only recently that it has been brought under control. In Libya, General Muammar Gadhafi was ultimately flushed out but unfortunately chaos has brought in ISIS shattering fragile unity that once prevailed in that country; Tunisia, the root of the "Arab Spring" as well as Egypt are gradually regaining normalcy; Southern Sudan reverted to serious civil strife with incredible bloodletting and the situation there is still fluid much like the *al Shabab* Moslem terrorist insurgency in neighbouring Somalia. Neighbouring Central African Republic is gradually recovering from the *Seleka* coalition of rebel Moslem groups locked up in battle against the Anti-*Balaka,* a Christian group in a stubborn and distressing civil war.

In Nigeria on the other hand, there was another fierce, veiled Moslem Jihadist insurgency called, '*Boko Haram*'("Western Education is Bad"), an incredibly pointless brutal, terrorist, gang that within a few years overran several North Eastern Nigerian States frequently foraging into Cameroon burning, maiming, raping, abducting and viciously murdering thousands of innocent citizens. It is currently being quelled by a combination of

Chadian, Niger, and Malian and Cameroonian troops after Nigeria had proven itself helpless at their hands. However, this inglorious story was more than balanced by the fact that for the first time in its fifty-four years as an independent country, the mighty Nigerian nation, the biggest and easily the richest on the African continent organised elections in March 2015 that were universally acknowledged as: free, fair, transparent and credible, with the incumbent, President Goodluck Jonathan peacefully and gracefully conceding victory to his opponent Retired General Mohammadu Buhari. With a popularly elected government now in power there can be little doubt that the *Boko Haram* insurgency would sooner rather than later become a spent force and a matter of history.

Elsewhere, the *Arab Spring* has continued to fester and degenerate in: Syria, Yemen and much worse in Iraq, which is in the throes of the *Islamic State of Iraq* (ISIS or ISIL), an extremist, brutal, Jihadist Islamic movement out to re-establish an Islamic Caliphate. They have proved most intractable but nevertheless are on the wane. In Europe, the Ukraine suffered a relapse with the balkanisation of its Eastern flank and the Crimea tearing off with the covert support of Russia. Meanwhile, the number of migrants from the areas of conflict and unrest in Northern Africa, Somalia, Eritrea and the Middle East struggling to get across the Mediterranean Sea into Europe drown in hundreds on a daily basis. This is becoming an intractable problem for the Europeans powers.

Put on a scale, the decade has witnessed little positive change in terms of world peace and stability, while internally in Cameroon, after the Green Tree Agreement, which resolved the Bakassi Peninsula Boundary Conflict between Nigeria and Cameroon, the latter has remained fairly peaceful and stable but for the refugee influx and defence problems accruing from the *Boko Haram* insurgency in Nigeria and the Central African Republic civil war draining resources that otherwise should have gone into development, investment and social services in the country. This further demonstrates just how much the world has become a global village especially now that it is taking a combination of: Nigerian, Chadian, *Nigerien* and Cameroonian forces to face the *Boko Haram* insurgency in the region.

## Triumph for The Rule of Law: Kofi Anan

I endorse the historic and matchless advice inscribed in gold given by Kofi Anan, the iconic UN Secretary General, under whose auspices the Green Tree Agreement was struck. Nothing in recent Cameroon history approximates this blue print. The Green Tree Agreement was the formal treaty which resolved the century old bloody, *Cameroon-Nigeria* border imbroglio over the oil and natural gas rich Bakassi peninsula. It transferred authority over Bakassi Peninsula from Nigeria to Cameroon, a historic process aptly described as: the "Triumph for the rule of law" by the Secretary-General of the UN, Kofi Anan. The dispute with roots running as far back as to 1913, 1981, 1994, and 1996 resulted in armed clashes between Nigeria and Cameroon. The dispute was referred to the *International Court of Justice* and on 10 October 2002, the ICJ ruled in favour of Cameroon. This was the first ever, of its kind on the African continent. On departing from Cameroon in 2000 and after deep reflection, Kofi Anan the Secretary-General of the UN, who resolved this intractable problem, in his wisdom, cautioned:

> *I leave Cameroon with the impression that there is only one Cameroon, multilingual and multi-ethnic. I encourage dialogue of these stakeholders. In every country, there are problems of marginalization. The way it has to be solved is by dialogue and not by walking away.*[7]

The hope is that the ruling elite in Cameroon hearken to these words of wisdom and strive to implement them in accordance with the spirit, in which they were delivered. It had called for dialogue and reason rather than intimidation and obstinacy; an approach similar to that which led to the Green Tree Agreement, such that we do not have to endure hurts, wait for another century and have to go to the *International Court of Justice* at the Hague.

---

[7] Former UN Secretary General, Kofi Annan, on the Anglophone Problem in 2000.

PREFACE TO THE NEW EDITION

# Footprints on the Sands of Time

As well, there are innumerable statesmen, nationalists, heroes, heroines and African leaders, who lived edified lives and have left brilliant footprints worth emulation. Among these are: Kwame Nkrumah of Ghana, Leopold Sedar Senghor of Senegal, Julius Nyerere of Tanzania, Jomo Kenyatta of Kenya and living monuments like Nelson Mandela and Frederik Willem de Klerk of South Africa and Kenneth Kaunda of Zambia. Here at home there are several nationalists, heroes and role models who laid down their lives for the Cameroon Motherland. These include amongst others; Martin Paul Samba, Rudolph Douala Manga Bell, Reuben Um Nyobé, Félix Roland Moumié, together with countless missionaries, catechists and pastors and traditional rulers who sacrificed their lives fighting battles against: ignorance, disease, poverty, superstition and instilling unity through fraternal love. To be able to move forward with confidence both at the individual, collective and national level, we need to be conscious of this fact and the determination to leave our own footprints in whatever small ways determined to leave our portion of the country better than we met it. Indeed this was part of the essence in the "Truth and Reconciliation Commission" which was initiated in South Africa and is presently being replicated in many other countries.

For the purpose of inculcating national consciousness, basic knowledge of our History should not be the preserve of a few; but even that of children who can remember to celebrate their birthdays and above all; citizens with the civic responsibility to vote and pay taxes deserve to know something about why and how they do these things and consequently about their Motherland. This knowledge forms the basis for informed loyalty, patriotism and nationalism. If we do not know where we are coming from, we cannot for certain say where we are going to, and even worse, define our own identity. We are likely to repeat errors of the past, if we do not know and avoid them and, although we cannot change the past we can use its knowledge to shape and improve the future.

Civic knowledge therefore is every citizen's right and should be handled formally in schools as well as informally by the mass media for the public at large using anecdotes, didactic material, moral lessons and whatever else works to extol and showcase our historic and ancestral icons, role models, heroes and heroines. It is perhaps the best and cheapest way to fight bribery, corruption and election rigging and in the ultimate analysis, cutting down on expenditure invested on defence, the forces of law and order and the penitentiary services, following the simple principle that it is better to "prepare and prevent, than to repair and repent".

Finally, it should be known that every being, everything that exists or happens in time and space is an intrinsic part of, and has its history. Whether we know it or not, whether we love it or hate it, we live in and are part of the current of history. To ignore this it would be acting like the foolish cock, which imagines that if it does not crow, the day will not break. We can either be active "makers" of history leaving indelible "positive" or "negative" footprints on the sands of time; its "victims," or simply passive, anonymous elements, but we cannot exist outside history. Not to know what happened before we were born is to remain forever a child. History is about "being" and that is why theologians logically maintain that God, the Creator of the universe is the indisputable Author of all History.

## A Great Debt of Gratitude

I could not handle the requests for a reproduction of the book, an updated version or a practically new version because my hands were full, until the recent insistence by Prof. Jude Fokwang, Department of Sociology, Regis University, Denver, USA, that there is certainly a felt need for a second edition of the book to be published internationally and made available on the internet especially for the Cameroon Diaspora. Other than the fact that he is exclusively responsible for the onerous task of arranging for the publication, he has done extensive analytical editing bringing out several pertinent observations that have helped to edify the contents of the work. To this extent, he literally qualifies as a co-author. Indeed this publication is the response to his request, which hopefully may tackle some of the vital issues, throw further light and ignite positive curiosity on where further information could be sought to meet outstanding questions. If on the other hand, the issues raised stimulate constructive debate seeking solutions to some of the problems that bedevil our beloved motherland, then some of the objectives of this publication would have been achieved. For the same reason, I am greatly obliged to Dr. Michael Lang of the

## PREFACE TO THE NEW EDITION

History Department of the University of Bamenda for proofreading the manuscript and making crucial suggestions that have helped to shape and strengthen its contents.

The lapse of ten years since the publication of the first edition of this book has witnessed a colossal erosion of some of the outstanding personalities who immensely contributed to that publication. The illustrious contributors, who have passed away include: Mr. John Mofor Ndi, who as a top administrator in Southern Cameroons, graciously shared with me his rich experiences as well as rare archival material and Professor Richard Gray, who was much more than a supervisor and mentor. He literally moulded me into whatever I have become academically, his memory remains overwhelming. Mrs. Elizabeth Chilver, a great actress and a monument on Southern Cameroons research in the social sciences, gave me every imaginable assistance and encouragement till she lost her sight and finally passed away recently. Toeing the line, have been Dr. Omer W Yembe, literally an elder brother, role model and mentor and recently Mr. Nicholas Ade Ngwa, a retired Principal Civil Administrator and an iconic personality, who played a pivotal role on the socio-political and administrative podium of Southern Cameroons. He made significant contributions to the appendix as well as wrote the foreword to the first edition of this book. Whenever, I needed an objective clarification or a crucial document of the time, I turned to him for clarification. His recent passing away has been a monumental loss to this nation. At the personal level, I miss these gigantic individuals immensely and for Cameroon as a nation, each of them leaves a yawning gap hard to bridge. We owe it to posterity to exploit and project as far as possible, whatever visions they bequeathed for use as solid blocks for positive nation building.

Anthony Ndi,
Foncha Street, Nkwen
13 June 2015

## Chapter One

# PHILOSOPHICAL AND HISTORICAL CONCEPTS OF THE "GOLDEN AGE"

In an endeavour to find an appropriate definition and illustration for the title of this book: "*The Golden Age*", recourse is sought to the **Renaissance**, the spectacular historical period in Italy (spreading to Europe) between 1400 and 1600, characterised by exceptional and unbeatable: painting, sculpture, architecture, allied arts and science. These were associated with the iconic names of: Galileo and promoters of the humanist culture: Dante, Giovanni Boccacio and Francesco Petrarch together with Leonardo Vinci and Michelangelo.[1] Thus, it was an exceptional and distinct epoch when juxtaposed against the period that preceded it and the one that followed it and, unanimously came to be acknowledged as the "Renaissance" (or "Rebirth") in Italian, European and indeed, world history. Consequently, since the renaissance was an epoch of unique and exceptional achievements it also came to be recognised as its *Golden Age*.

Therefore, in classical terms, the notion of a "*Golden Age*" in the history of any State or Nation is relative, contextual and generally referred to in retrospect, when such an epoch is contrasted with the periods before and after it. This loosely tallies with the *Cambridge Advanced Learners, Dictionary*, which defines a "Golden Age" simply as: "A period of time, occasionally imaginary, when everyone was happy or when a particular art or business was very successful."[2] The *Encarta Dictionary* like the *Merriam*

---

[1] *Microsoft ® Encarta ® 2009. © 1993-2008 Microsoft Corporation.* All rights reserved.

[2] *Cambridge Advanced Learners, Dictionary* 3$^{rd}$ Edition

*Webster Dictionary* identifies it practically, as a: "Period of excellence; of great prosperity or achievement especially in the Arts." In classical mythology, it is seen as the earliest period in history, a sort of utopian: "Garden of Eden," when human beings lived without labour or sorrow. This was followed in contrast by the Silver and Bronze Ages, the Age of Heroes, and an Iron Age of labour and strife. The term is also applied to great periods of literature in national cultures; for instance, to the late Republican and Augustan ages in Rome (from the 6th century bc to the 1st century ad), and the 17th century in France and *Spain*.[3]

Finally, *Encyclopaedia Britannica* elaborately identifies and confines the "Golden Age" in Latin literature, to the period, from 70 BC to AD 18, during which the Latin language was brought to perfection as a literary medium and many Latin classical masterpieces were composed. It is further subdivided into two major sections, the *Ciceronian* period dominated by Marcus Tullius Cicero, and the Augustan Age. In Spanish history, the Golden Age began with the partial political unification of Spain about 1500; when its literature was characterized by patriotic and religious fervour, heightened realism and a new interest in earlier epics and ballads, together with the somewhat less-pronounced influences of humanism and *Neo-Platonism*.[4]

Furthermore, *Encyclopaedia Britannica* categorizes the "Golden Age" within the context of the "Ages of Man", in classical legend and poetry, the earliest of which was the Golden Age. This was an age of innocence and happiness, when strife and injustice were unknown; the period when Cronus (the Roman counterpart of Saturn) ruled the world. No agriculture was necessary, since the earth produced on its own an abundance

---

[3] ibid., *Microsoft*

[4] In late medieval and early Renaissance, literary forms as the chivalric and pastoral novels underwent their final flowering. They were replaced by the picaresque novel, which usually described the comic adventures of low-born rogues and which was exemplified by Miguel de Cervantes Savedra's monumental novel Don Quixote a satirical treatment of anachronistic chivalric ideals, combined pastoral, picaresque, and romantic elements in its narrative and remains the single most important literary work produced during the Golden Age. Spanish poetry during the period was initially marked by the adoption of Italian metres and verse Spanish poetry eventually picaresque. (*q.v.*; 43 BC–AD 18), it was a period of mature literary achievements by such writers as Virgil, Horace, and Livy.

of everything people needed, and the climate was unvaryingly mild. In contrast, after the *Golden Age*, came the Silver Age, less happy than the earlier period, when people were obliged to labour for their livelihoods and build homes to protect themselves from the elements. In the succeeding Ages of Bronze and Iron, crime, violence, slaughter and warfare spread throughout the world.[5] In this instance it was therefore an idealistic, hardly attainable utopian age but a vision to hope for.

\* \* \*

## The Golden Age in Southern Cameroons

There are therefore basically, three standard versions of a "Golden Age"; the first of which in Greek and Roman legends refers to a mythical period, when perfect innocence, peace and happiness reigned. The second concept confines it to the era of classical writers in Roman literature (27 BC-14 AD), while the third notion simply describes a Golden Age as the most flourishing epoch in a nation's history.[6] Of these, it can be observed that the first model emphasises the idealistic virtues of innocence, peace and happiness, which, though highly desirable are relative and unattainable in the real world. The second notion is even more circumscribed, as it is limited to ancient history. It is therefore the third definition that is applicable to the Southern Cameroons context, the rise and fall of which is examined in this book. On the whole, it contained in its own limited way, many of the ideals listed above.

The example of such an exceptional experience in the history of Southern Cameroons is equally remarkable in that the early "prime actors" on the political stage, literally without exception were exclusively Christian

---

[5] In his "Works and Days", the Greek poet Hesiod listed five ages, inserting an Age of Heroes between the Bronze and Iron Ages. Hesiod's Age of Heroes consisted of those who took part in the Theban and Trojan wars

[6] *The New Webster's Comprehensive Dictionary*, Deluxe Encyclopaedic *Edition*, Trident Press International, 1998, see also; "Golden Age. "Encyclopaedia Britannica, *Encyclopaedia Britannica, Ultimate Reference Suite*. Chicago: Encyclopaedia Britannica, 2011.

or products of Christian Missionary establishments[7]. Their collective perceptions of life and life styles impeccably stamped this Christocentric influence on the: socio-cultural, moral, economic and, above all, on the political outlook of the various post - colonial national governments of the period. Those who lived the experience vividly recall the extraordinary manner in which the state was run in the decade spanning from 1954 to 1965 in particular and roughly up to 1970 with nostalgia. The broad features of that era included: Freedom of speech, the press and religion[8]; social security, harmony, peace and justice; a budding multi-party democracy characterised by relatively free, fair, transparent, credible and regular elections with peaceful handover of power. Among the highly cherished colonial legacies inherited from Great Britain were; a functional Westminster-type parliamentary system pivoted on a House of Assembly, House of Chiefs (or Senate) with an executive and judiciary with strict observation of the principle of the separation of powers, checks and balances, among the legislatures, the executive and the judiciary. These institutions ensured a largely corruption free civil service and police force with a promising self-sufficient agro-industrial based economy. With these the future was full of hope, bright and inspiring.

To buttress these institutions and ensure transparency in public affairs, a solid system of "Audit" established by Article 44 of the Southern Cameroons Constitution provided for a Director of Audit, a constituted personality appointed by the Prime Minister but who could only be removed by a 2/3 majority of Parliament. He controlled all the services of Government and Corporations and laid the Audit Report every year on the table of the House, where it was submitted to the Subcommittee

---

[7] All the original 13 and subsequent Southern Cameroonian MPs to the Regional and Federal Houses of Assembly at Enugu and Lagos, and even the Traditional Rulers; Chief Joanes Manga Williams and Fon Vincent S Galega 1I were Christians. In fact, there were three Rev. Pastors among the MPs! Even when the number of MPs was raised to 34 in 1961, the status quo remained the same.

[8] U.S. President Franklin D. Roosevelt in the State of the Union message he delivered to Congress on Jan. 6, 1941 stated these freedoms to be the freedom of speech and expression, the freedom of every person to worship God in his own way, the freedom from want, and the freedom from fear.

of Parliament, the President of which was the Leader of the Opposition. By this principle, the Leader of the Opposition was directly integrated into the administrative machinery and was constitutionally, a watch-dog against any malpractices by the government in power. To ensure that the Director of Audit was not obstructed in any way in the discharge of his duties, his position was made incompatible with any other post, his salary was not debated in Parliament, but paid from the Consolidated Allocation Fund, while all records and stores were open to him or those authorised by him."[9] This kept the Government, its parastatals and corporations perpetually in check and curbed corruption.

In sequel, there was an independent Judiciary, (originally) a multinational civil service, an intrepid, robust press, and a promising agro-industrial based economy. With a population approaching the one million mark in 1961, the citizens, an enlightened, modest and realistic people were aware of their circumstances, contented, happy with prospects for a brilliant future. Therefore, when placed in proper perspective, these descriptions fairly qualify this period to be categorised as a distinct epoch in the brief history of Southern Cameroons. This stands out perceptibly, when juxtaposed with the preceding period of stagnant British Colonial Rule (1922-1954) that preceded it, and the oppressive, autocratic, and *assimilationist* era that was gradually but abrasively introduced in September 1966 with the creation of the One Party System, the "Cameroon National Union" (CNU), actually the oracle of President Ahmadou Ahidjo. This all pervasive weapon was finally used to put an end to the existence of the Federal Republic of Cameroon, meaning the dismantling of the Federated States of East and West Cameroon and their legislatures including the House of Chiefs in 1972. As well it marked the end of the 'Golden Age'.

In outline, as a political era, the commencement of the Golden Age in British Southern Cameroons became apparent from the late 1940s to

---

[9] See, *Federation of Nigeria, Report of the Director of Audit on the Accounts of the Government of the Southern Cameroons for the Year ended 31st March, 1959*, Government Press, Buea, 1960; West Cameroon, *Report of the Director of Audit on the Accounts of the Government of West Cameroon for the year ended 30th June, 1965*, Government Printer, Buea -1967 and West Cameroon *Report of the Director of Audit on the Accounts of the Government of West Cameroon for the Year ended 30th June, 1970*, Government Press, Buea:

the mid-1950s, facilitated by constitutional, socioeconomic and political changes originating in Nigeria of which the UN Trust Territory of British Southern Cameroons was administered as an integral part. This colonial period also coincided with greatly enhanced post-war missionary activity not only with evangelisation but equally with educational and social welfare services further heightened by local decentralisation and the introduction of democratic reforms which led to the representation of British Southern Cameroons in Legislative Assemblies in Enugu and Lagos in Nigeria. The apogee was struck in the decade spanning 1954-1965, characterised by its attainment of a *Quasi Federal status*, which provided for internal Self Government for the Territory in 1954, followed by the highly profiled United Nations organised Plebiscite of 11 February 1961. This was followed by "Independence" and "Reunification" with the Republic of Cameroon on 1st October 1961[10].

Outstanding political developments of this crucial period included: the hotly contested elections of February 1959 after which power changed hands most peacefully from the ruling KNC/KPP alliance of Endeley and Mbile to the Opposition KNDP of Foncha; the historic 11 February 1961 plebiscite; the inconclusive but revealing Buea Tripartite Conference of 14-17 June, 1961; the Bamenda All Party Conference, 26-28 June and above all, the *Foumban Constitutional Conference*, 17-21 July 1961 followed by the Yaoundé Tripartite Conference in early August that year. This latter translated and enacted the resolutions of the Foumban Constitutional Conference into legal form. It was the Foumban Constitutional Conference which established the Federal Republic of Cameroon comprising the *co-equal*, bilingual and bicultural States of East and West Cameroon, comprising the former Republic of Cameroun and Southern Cameroons. On the whole, in Southern Cameroons, this was a period of boundless hope, confidence and justified pride marked by a blossoming

---

[10] There are those who argue that Southern Cameroons never really became independent, as there were no instruments of independence such as a national flag, an anthem or a motto. It simply assumed those of the Republic of Cameroon. Still others maintain that there was no true "reunification" as the greater Kamerun of 1884-1915 was left out. Yet others hold that the process of independence was supposed to be presided over by the UN, which never took place, hence there was no legality to sanction the process.

multiparty democratic system expressed through political mutations, coalitions, regular and frequent elections, peaceful changes of government, defections, carpet crossings, vigorous political campaigns and uninhibited parliamentary debates[11] and, above all the peaceful handover of power from the ruling party to the opposition. There was robust debate at all levels, but throughout its existence, there was no violence, bloodshed or loss even of a single life. Thus, it was essentially spectacular and unique.

However, Southern Cameroons suffered a disastrous decline beginning with the dissolution of the multiparty system in 1966, reaching its lowest point with the abolition of the federal constitution generated at Foumban and the Federal Republic of Cameroon itself in 1972. After that the President was "granted" or in fact, practically arrogated to himself, powers to rule for twelve months by decree, without reference, even pretentiously to parliament. This was the climate characterised by a stifled freedom of speech within which the Federal Republic of Cameroon was dismantled in 1972. The actual process itself lasted barely two weeks from 6 May, when President Ahidjo made the announcement landing at the airport after a visit to France and 20th May 1972, when the famous referendum daubed the "*Peaceful Revolution*" was strangely organised in the thick of the rainy season. The facts surrounding this event have remained mysterious and inexplicable to ordinary Southern Cameroonian thinking especially as the climate was one in which no one could raise a finger to question or oppose the President.

Nevertheless Mr. Nerius Namaso Mbile, a journalist and member of the defunct West Cameroon parliament, and consequently a prominent contemporary and prime political actor in reflection cautiously recorded his feelings of that devastating event in his autobiography. To this effect he dared to lament: "*On 20th May 1972 President Ahidjo set aside the Constitution of the Federal Republic of Cameroon*", and the "*Federated States, their Governments and their legislative assemblies ceased to exist in favour of a unitary system ... so ended our Golden Days of the West Cameroon House of Assembly at Buea*". Mbile, leader of one of the earliest political parties in

---

[11] For example, voter turnout during the Plebiscite in 1961 was 90%; between 1951 and 1961 there were six popular elections including the plebiscite.

Southern Cameroons, the Kamerun People's Party (KPP) and co-founder of the Cameroon People's National Congress (CPNC) further designed a graphic epitaph for the tombstone of this most nostalgic era. It appropriately, poetically reads: "*House of Assembly, Buea, Born, October 26th 1954, Died 30th May 1972*". This marked the darkest day in Southern Cameroons Westminster democratic practice for which they had fought for decades. Within context, Mbile sadly continued with an upwelling of nostalgia and regret. Using Muna, Ahidjo had finally succeeded to abolish the:

> Federated states, their governments and their legislative assemblies ceased to exist, in favour of a unitary system …. Mr. ST Muna who was doubling as Prime Minister of West Cameroon and Vice President Of The Republic served as Campaign Manager for the North West Province in the referendum asking the republic to adopt the Unitary System… We the members of the onetime Regional Assembly in Buea packed home our bags… ***so ended our golden days of the west Cameroon house of assembly at Buea.***[12]

These remarkably grave, metaphors cautiously employed by NN Mbile, a seasoned journalist to describe this calamity, fairly well encapsulate the pent up emotions of the mass of Southern Cameroonians about its "*Golden Age*"[13] and the vandalization of an institution which symbolised that state and embodied its lofty hopes and expectations as expressed by the pioneer Commissioner of Southern Cameroons, Brigadier EJ Gibbons, when he launched the Southern Cameroons House of Assembly on that momentous day, 26 October 1954. What further renders the entire event inadmissible and heartrending is the fact that President Ahmadou Ahidjo later boasted that he had bastardised the "so called (Westminster type) parliamentary system." This was tantamount to destroying the soul of a people, the one institution that incarnated their supreme hopes and expectations and for which they had spent their whole political existence

---

[12] Mbile NN, Cameroon *Political Story; Memories Of An Authentic Eye Witness* Presbyterian Printing Press, Limbe, 1999, pp.246-247

[13] Ibid Mbile, p.247

fighting to accomplish.

Much earlier in 1958 during the Victoria Centenary Celebrations, in the volume; Introducing the Southern Cameroons, authored by the Government of Southern Cameroons itself led by Dr. Emmanuel Mbela Liffaffe Endeley, it had been proudly declared: "*The Government is based on the healthy political party system which is common to all British Overseas Territories and is formed from the party or parties commanding a majority in the House of Assembly*".[14] The economy, he maintained was vibrant and promising. Thus the grandiose dream of Southern Cameroonians nursed for twenty-five years including the Golden Age veritably became "Paradise Lost".

## Prime Political Actors: Christian Formation

Early Southern Cameroonian leaders and founders of political parties and pressure groups such as: Peter M Kale, Dr. Emmanuel Mbela Liffaffe Endeley, Robert Jabea B Kum Dibongué, Nerius Namaso Mbile, John Ngu Foncha, Augustine Ngom Jua, Solomon Tandeng Muna and subsequent waves of parliamentarians, who even included Rev. Pastors such as: Jeremiah Chi Kangsen, Jeremiah Ando Seh and David Y Nyanganji together with dozens of seasoned school masters, products of their time and circumstances, all without exception came in from distinct Christian backgrounds and were practising Christians. Since they were directly and actively involved in the business of statecraft and nation building, their spiritual, moral and socio-cultural upbringing impinged directly and radically on government policies. This constituted the Southern Cameroons signature and identity card by which its citizens were identified at home and abroad. The proverb that "A fruit does not fall too far away from the parent tree", is exemplified by the life styles of this breed of Cameroonian leaders, who for the most part lived very austere lives, bereft of conspicuous consumption and excessive accumulation of wealth.

On the other hand, twice in consecutive years, 1988 and 1989 at the

---

[14] See Government of the Southern Cameroons, *Introducing the Southern Cameroons*, Federal Information Service, Lagos, p.26; NN Mbile, *Cameroon Political Story; Memories of an Eye-Witness*, Presbyterian Printing Press Limbe, 1999, pp.247-7.

national level, Cameroon topped the list of the most corrupt countries worldwide, and yet again this year, (2015) the Minister of Communication vehemently protested against the announcement by Transparent International that Cameroon had come second to the top as the most corrupt country in the world. No one of course, can gainsay the fact that the maximum security jails in Yaoundé and Douala accommodate the equivalent of the rank and file of our entire cabinet together with the cream of the Managing Directors of parastatals caught in the web of the massive embezzlement of public funds. Yet for well over forty years following a decree of 1976, the government of Cameroon declared that a pass in religious studies at the GCE Ordinary and Advanced Levels will not be reckoned among the passes required for obtaining employment in government service or for pursing further studies even for confessional schools.[15] Even after government had been arm twisted into accepting Religious Studies in 1995 and 1997 for the GCE O and A Levels, government stance has remained steadfast against its recognition and equality to all the other subjects. On the other hand, by the Anglo-Saxon system in former Southern / West Cameroon religious teaching was compulsory in all institutions, public and confessional.

The ministers and parliamentarians were also for that matter generally forward-looking statesmen and politicians with a strong sense of mission, passion for moral rectitude and commitment to their Southern Cameroons Fatherland. Like their West African and Nigerian contemporaries: Dr. Kwame Nkrumah of Ghana, Professor Leopold Sedar Senghor of Senegal, Ahmed Sekou Touré of Guinea; Dr. Nnamdi Azikiwe, Chief Obafemi Awolowo and Sir Mallam Abubakar Tafawa Balewa, (Nigerians), zealous patriots– these were men of character, vision, timbre and conviction to whom ideological principles and national interests took precedence over narrow ethnic, sectional practice of nepotism. It is therefore not surprising that this generation of politicians in Southern Cameroons were modest and passed away without amassing any conspicuous wealth.

---

[15] See Decree No. 76/385 of September 1976. See also, *Cameroon Panorama* no. 691 of January 2016 for: "An Open Letter to the Prime Minister, Head of Government of the Republic of Cameroon on the Place of Religious Certificates".

PHILOSOPHICAL AND HISTORICAL CONCEPTS OF THE "GOLDEN AGE"

## *Prime Political Actors*

*Fig 1. Mr. P M Kale; Fig 2. Dr. E M L Endeley; Fig 3. Mr. J N Foncha; Fig 4. Mr. N N Mbile; Fig 5. Mr. A N Jua; Fig 6. Mr. S T Muna*

These socio-political and economic nemeses which swept through the African continent were later intrusions, when greedy, grabbing politicians, opportunists, adventurers and power hungry soldiers dabbled into the political arena. The world-view of the former was broad, altruistic, patriotic, nationalist and Pan-Africanist. This ideological frame of mind was a major reason why in the context of the bipolarity of the Cold War era, the Southern Cameroons delegations sent to the United Nations (UN) to sort out the political options for the impending plebiscite in 1961 were finally, easily persuaded to drop the third alternative of independence, which provided for the Territory Standing alone, on its own by the Afro-Asian bloc of nations. These generally stood for larger, viable units and strong states capable of withstanding further balkanisation of Africa, fearing absorption either by Capitalist West or Communist East. The vision and mission was one of viable African states, capable of standing their ground as true Africans.

*Fig 7. Malcolm Milne, Acting Commissioner*

## Malcolm Milne: Acting Commissioner of Southern Cameroons

A great deal could be said for the quality and calibre of the civil service and political leadership, which ran the affairs of Southern Cameroons during its Golden Age. However, because of brevity, just one pertinent example is cited here, namely; Malcolm Milne, the Acting Commissioner of Southern Cameroons, who together with Mr. Johnson O Field OBE, the Commissioner ran the affairs of the Territory during the crucial years running up to the plebiscite, 1958-1961. In fact, Malcolm Milne's observations are significant for other reasons; including the fact that he had the experience of having served variously in Aden, the Gold Coast and Nigeria prior to coming to Southern Cameroons. He was therefore well placed to make pertinent observations in "comparative" terms that were objective, critical and precise, as dictated by circumstances. His views therefore should be taken seriously.

A typical Colonial Administrator of his time, Malcolm Milne set out to execute British colonial policy to the letter in Southern Cameroons with total dedication. This was based on directives dictated from the seat of government in Whitehall, London which to him were unquestionable and regarded as imperial dogma. For Southern Cameroons, these were centred on having its existing integration with Nigeria formally consolidated following an impending plebiscite scheduled for February 1961. However, the situation was extremely complicated and quite early in the contest; the top administrators on the spot including Malcolm Milne and his boss Johnson O Field, the Commissioner together with CE King, the British Ambassador to Cameroon in Yaoundé, took sides in favour of the CPNC, the party which stood for integration with Nigeria. Towards this objective, they left nothing to chance even with the readiness to bribe and cajole MPs to cross the carpet in favour of the opposition.[16]

As a result, while discretely backing Dr. EML Endeley and the CPNC who pursued this policy, Malcolm Milne literally "reviled" Dr. JN Foncha, leader of the KNDP, which campaigned for reunification with Republic of Cameroon as an individual for that reason. The point is that throughout

---

[16] See Appendix 11 on Mrs. Josepha Mua, special representative for women.

this period, JO Field and Malcolm Milne in their administration hardly had a positive remark or kind word to make about Foncha, the KNDP, which he led and his administration in their reports to the Colonial Office. In fact, they were generally prejudiced to the extreme. This is precisely what makes his final comments after he had just presided over the lowering of the Union Jack at Tiko International Airport and handing over power to President Ahmadou Ahidjo on 1st. October 1961 so memorable. His observations about Foncha and his administration here are of special significance because they came at the end of his service in the Territory after nearly fifty years of deep reflection and maturity, in his biography, while on retirement.[17]

Within context, after an inspection tour of the Local Councils in Bamenda Province in1960, Malcolm Milne was full of praise and admiration for what he saw and paid glowing tribute and homage to; the intelligence and tact of the people, who would while knowing the solution to a problem, carefully design the final decision and leave it for the Divisional Officer to make the ultimate pronouncement himself. On reflection, writing fifty years later, he was passionate and noted: *"I felt vaguely then, and know for certain now, that working with these men had greatly enriched my time in the civil service. There was something very special about that corps; their service was their watch word."*[18] Even more pertinently, referring to the Foncha Government, which officially he disliked and castigated because they backed secession from Nigeria, he came clean and paid glowing tribute, noting with nostalgia how: *"Then I was dealing with individual ministers, with cabinet committees or in the case of Southern Cameroons with a small Government. Almost without exception they were people of high intelligence, who knew exactly what they wanted."*[19]

This is of special significance, as here he was literally describing his

---

[17] Malcolm Milne's autobiography, *No Telephone to Heaven- From Apex to Nadir- Colonial Service in Nigeria, Aden, The Cameroons and The Gold Coast, 1961.* Meon Hill Press, 1999.

[18] Malcolm Milne, *No Telephone to Heaven- From Apex To Nadir- Colonial Service In Nigeria, Aden, The Cameroons and The Gold Coast*, 1961, Meon Hill Press1999, London, p.254.

[19] Ibid. Malcom Milne p.409.

opponents, who comprised Foncha as an individual and his entire cabinet for whom, while in office, he did not have a single positive or kind word. Of all outstanding tributes that could be paid to the Foncha administration, Malcolm Milne's compliments are a class apart, especially as he further regrets the harm done by the British colonial administration to the "nice, loyal little people of Southern Cameroons". They had frustrated their desires and attempts towards extending the UN Trusteeship until they could achieve independence before engaging on negotiations for reunification with Republic of Cameroon. Finally, the British blocked Southern Cameroonian objectives towards attaining full sovereignty by brutally excluding the famous; "Third Option" for independence from the plebiscite options on 11 February 1961. Finally, these facts played heavily on Malcolm Milne's conscience and he became most remorseful in pleading on his own behalf and that of the British Government. As a final point, he recommended that the British Government should make good the harm they had done to these people or, they would rue it someday.[20] This admission was a heavy indictment that continues to weigh on the British government in simple logic, law, equity and moral justice till today especially after the Kenyan Mau Mau reparations last year (2014).

## Political Consciousness in Southern Cameroons

Until the Eastern Nigeria Regional Crisis of 1953, there were no Southern Cameroonian political parties with truly nationwide appeal projecting independence as a goal. In fact, typical of most African colonies, nationalism in Southern Cameroons was a by-product of the Second World War, when African (Cameroonian) veterans returned home having fought with the Allied Powers and defeated Germany, another colonial power, in fact the original colonial master of Kamerun. In many cases, these courageous black soldiers stood their ground, where their white counterparts trembled. Above all, it was Africans who saved France from the claws of German occupation and restored the country to General Charles de

---

[20] Ibid. see also, Anthony Ndi, *Southern West Cameroon Revisited*, 1950-1972, Vol One, *Unveiling Inescapable Traps*, Paul's Press, Bamenda 2013, pp.301-308.

Gaulle. Of particular significant, it was at Douala, the economic capital of Cameroon, that he first landed and made his passionate, historic appeal for African support in return for political freedom. Thus the European myth had totally been debunked. All put together, the African veterans began questioning the right of European over-lordship of Africa.

At the international level, promises had been made by the European powers that in return for their support during World War II, they would be granted a measure of autonomy. This really was the substance of the Brazzaville Conference in February 1944 at which France made concessions and promises, which raised African expectations. Reporting some time later it was noted how:

> *The French are attempting to carry out the principles of the Brazzaville Conference (January 30-February 8, 1944), and turn their 'Empire' into a Community of equals. France's complete freedom from race or color prejudice is a very favorable element in this difficult endeavor.* The late Governor-General Eboué, the moving spirit of the Brazzaville Conference, was a pure-blooded Negro. His widow was elected to the National Constituent Assembly.[21] (My emphasis)

The fact that after having achieved their goal of pushing out the Germans from Paris, the French began dragging their feet and were reluctant to implement the resolutions of the Brazzaville Conference only worsened matters and drove the Francophones to take other, generally violent options, which were detested as Marxist. This largely explains the rise of Trade Unions and nationalist movements with radical options such as the *Rassemblement Democratique Africaine* (RDA)in French Africa as a whole and the *Union des Populations Du Cameroun* (UPC) in French Cameroun.

The other very pungent move was the Atlantic Charter which led to the creation of the United Nations to replace the moribund League of Nations. It was a joint declaration by the United States and Britain, issued during World War II, expressing certain common principles in their national policies to be followed in the post-war period made on

---

[21] Microsoft ® Encarta ® 2009. © 1993-2008 Microsoft Corporation.

August 14, 1941, by President Franklin D Roosevelt and Prime Minister, Sir Winston Churchill after a series of conferences aboard a warship in the North Atlantic Ocean off the coast of Newfoundland. In it: "The two leaders declared that the US and Britain sought no territorial, or any other, aggrandizement from the war. They proclaimed the right of all peoples to choose their own form of government and not to have boundary changes imposed on them".[22] These awakened, emboldened and empowered nationalist movements throughout the world but more especially in Asia and Africa, who made their influence felt at the UN.

However in most British colonies, this change was mostly evolutionary, constitutional and non-violent. There was much that the British did that was wrong but these grievances were generally anticipated, defused through discussions and met constitutionally. British misrule in Southern Cameroons concerned with lack of economic development –which was mostly benign, by way of omission, and hardly noticeable to the average Cameroonian. The direct aggressors were Nigerians, particularly the Ibos, whom they confronted at every twist and turn but hardly ever the "invisible" British colonial masters, who in any case lived secluded lives in Government Residential Areas (GRA).

---

[22] Ibid

*Fig 8. Kwame Nkrumah, being presented a carved elephant tusk by Mr. JN Foncha, newly elected PM of Southern Cameroons, February 1959*

## The 1953 Eastern Nigeria Regional Crisis

Consequently, it required bold, possibly outrageous issues that could easily galvanise popular passion in the absence of real or imaginary atrocities associated with British colonial policies, which fortunately or unfortunately did not exist, to jolt national consciousness among the "gentle, peaceful people" of Southern Cameroons. Thus, eventually, it was the outlandish episode: the Eastern Regional Crisis in Enugu, Nigeria, which was tactfully manoeuvred by Endeley to unleash passionate national resentment in Southern Cameroons. In Nigeria, they had bonded themselves together as "Benevolent Neutrals" openly declaring: "We are Southern Cameroonians. We are not Nigerians". This was an identity battle cry for secession from Nigeria and a burning desire for a "return" to an autonomous Southern Cameroons homeland. Endeley captured the mood of the entire nation, when he returned home to Southern Cameroons, criss-crossing the country with his bloc of "Benevolent Neutrals" physically displaying boulders purported to have been shot at them by Ibos in Enugu.

*Fig 9. Dr Nnamdi Azikiwe*

This did the trick as it was more realistic and dramatic from the live experience of the populace conversant with arrogant Ibo character in the North and South West Regions of Cameroon. It quickly captured the passion and imagination of the "masses" who were shocked and gave unqualified support to Endeley's Kamerun National Congress (KNC) especially from 1953-1957. However, Mbile and Kale, who continued to identify with Nigeria, formed the Kamerun People's Party (KPP), which was regarded as a sell out and, an appendage of Dr. Nnamdi Azikiwe's NCNC. They were booed and, predictably, drew very feeble support and lost massively to Endeley's KNC in the 1954 election. The national mood in the country was decisively for a genuine Southern Cameroons Fatherland and nothing less could suffice. Interestingly, this spirit was tenacious until the plebiscite in 1961. In the meantime, Endeley's KNC continued to enjoy massive support from 1954 until 1957, when he himself changed his mind and began preaching in favour of "association with Nigeria". It equally explains why the KNDP of Foncha, gained and maintained central ground until it was torpedoed by Ahidjo in 1966 with the introduction of the one party system, the Cameroon National Union (CNU). In other words the Southern Cameroons ethos remained politically indomitable from 1940 till 1966.

## A Flourishing Pacifist, Democratic Westminster Parliamentary Culture

Already by post- Second World War (1945) up to 1954 Southern Cameroonians had begun strongly to identify themselves as a geographical, economic, social, cultural, spiritual and political entity militating within the proto-nationalist organizations of the time, such as; GJ Mbene's Cameroon Welfare Union (CWU) formed at Victoria in 1939, as a forum for raising issues in protest against British neglect of Southern Cameroons and, its continued administration as an integral part of Nigeria without representation. At about the same time in Lagos, Mr. Paul M Kale with Dr. EML Endeley and others raised the banner of the Cameroon Youth League (CYL) on the pattern of the Nigerian Youth League seeking representation, secession from Nigeria and a separate regional status for Southern Cameroons. It was from associations like these that the next set of proto-nationalist organizations such as the Cameroon National Federation (CNF) of Endeley, a transformation of the CYL, which advocated separation from Nigeria and eventual unification with French Cameroon and, the Kamerun United National Congress (KUNC) of Robert Jabea Kum Dibongue and Nerius Namaso Mbile, which pursued a similar policy. Dibongue working together with Endeley's CNF, next formed the Kamerun National Congress, the first nationwide political party aimed at secession from Nigeria and eventual reunification with French Cameroon at the Mamfe All Party Conference in 1953. The Kamerun People's Party of Kale and Mbile equally launched there at Mamfe opted for integration with Nigeria.

*Fig 10. Prime Minister, JN Foncha and Fon Galega II of Bali, chat with Brigadier EJ Gibbons OBE, first Commissioner of Southern Cameroons.*

All of these were organized just before the *Quasi Federal status* was achieved the following year precisely in October 1954. In fact, the first mile stone in Southern Cameroons political history was reached, when after all the constitutional arrangements, the thirteen elected members met in their own national parliament, the *Southern Cameroons House of Assembly on 26 October 1954 with Dr. EML Endeley as Leader of Government Business*. It was granted Self Government or Home Rule under the status of a Quasi Federal Territory. The full significance to this event was given by the first Southern Cameroons Commissioner, **Brigadier EJ Gibbons, OBE**, who acting as Governor and in place of the Her Majesty the Queen, delivered the inaugural address to the "brand" new Southern Cameroons House of Assembly. This key note address carried a triple significance as it was solemn, historic and, in fact, prophetic.[23] In propounding his vision and mission for the new parliament, he instinctively set the agenda that was to be adhered to ever afterwards during its brief existence, by that institution in Southern Cameroons:

---

[23] Wache Francis, "Parliamentary Eloquence: The First Assembly of West Cameroon Democracy", *Cameroon Life*, Vol II, No 3, 1992

> The manner in which we hold this, the inaugural meeting of our new Southern Cameroons Government, place freedom, responsibility and service far above empty show and material advantage. Honourable members, we must be steadfast in this spirit in the years to come. We must never allow vanity or greed to divert us from the pursuit of our true objective, which is the freedom and welfare of the common man and woman who dig in the beloved soil in this our territory. The lesson of history has been that if any people persist steadfastly in this line of conduct, however poor and small it may be, however humble have been its origins, in the end it will succeed and there will be added to it prosperity and honour and the respect of the world[24].

This memorable and heavily loaded address, with every word weighted and put in place was either used as a syllabus or a template by the pioneer and subsequent Members of the Southern Cameroons House of Assembly. This apparently was the tradition and the same calibre of parliamentarians and governments comprising such intellectuals and exemplary statesmen who never misplaced their steps as confirmed by Malcolm Milne, the Acting Commisioner of the country nearly fifty years later, precisely in 1998, when he published his biography[25]. Here, the tributes paid to this category of people and others were not isolated cases as several officials and visitors said as much.

The Public Service distinguished itself and the country as a whole became an ideal nation, hence the title of this book. This was precisely because; Southern Cameroons inherited and pursued the Westminster Parliamentary Democracy, literally to the letter. Although the 1954 budding Southern Cameroons House of Assembly took off with one political party, Endeley's Kamerun National Congress (KNC) by 1955, there had arisen three viable political parties in the Assembly: the KNC, KNDP and KPP and actually by 1959, the five-year-old opposition KNDP had

---

[24] See Nfor, N Nfor, *The Southern Cameroons: The Truth of The Matter*, Bamenda 2003, pp. 58-62. Indeed, this timeless quotation deserves to be cast in gold and posted at the entrance into the erstwhile Southern Cameroons house of assembly.

[25] See Malcolm Milne, *No Telephone To Heaven*.

taken over power from the KNC/KPP alliance in elections that were universally acclaimed as free, fair, transparent and democratic followed by a peaceful handover of power. After independence and reunification with Republic of Cameroon, this fledgling democracy began suffering suffocation with the creation of the One Party System in 1966, which introduced dictatorial rule and finally it was simply extinguished in 1972.

After its abolition, President Ahmadou Ahidjo was exuberant and boasted: "*I have progressively transformed this country from a disorderly and irresponsible parliamentary system into a presidential one. I know that leaves some people disgruntled but it had to be done.*"[26] Yet, in his own words when laying the foundation for the reunification of Southern Cameroons and the Republic of Cameroon at the famous Foumban Constitutional Conference and emphatically repeated in 1968, the President had unequivocally maintained:

> Our constitution makes provision for a president and vice president elected by universal suffrage on the same list and who must each come from a different federated state; it makes provision for an assembly elected likewise by universal suffrage. *At the level of the Federated States we have kept the classic parliamentary regime, where the executive is responsible to parliament and where, as a corollary, the assembly can be dissolved by the head of state on his own or the advice of the Prime Minister.*[27] (My emphasis)

This became the style of government after the suppression of the Federal Republic of Cameroon in 1972. Generally, with this approach of double talk, it is difficult to quote the president with any certainty, since he held it as a special privilege to change his mind over any issue regardless of its gravity as in this case, it referred to not only changing his own words, but violating the very constitution of which he had sworn to be custodian and guarantor.

---

[26] *Afrique Biblio Club (Abc) Paris*, 1980.42.

[27] See Ahmadou Ahidjo, *Contribution To National Construction*, Presence Africaine, Paris, 1968. pp.26-27

*Fig 11. Left, Mr. Ndeh Ntumazah; Right, Mr. A W Mukong. Founder and co-founder of the One Kamerun (OK) Party in Southern Cameroons in 1957*

After the attainment of the Quasi Federal status, the next burning issue of national interest in Southern Cameroons was "reunification" with French Cameroon, the flames of which had been ignited by Robert Jabea Kum Dibongué and the French Cameroon Welfare Union (FCWU) in 1948. It was this goal that tore Foncha and Jua away from the KNC and led to the formation of the Kamerun National Democratic Party (KNDP) in 1955 since Endeley had reneged on reunification. As independence and reunification approached with anticipated political upheavals, it was time for further mutations, coalitions, carpet crossing and the creation of yet more political parties. This led to the KNC/KPP Alliance in 1959; the formation by Kale of the Kamerun United Congress (KUP) and finally, the merger of the KNC/KPP Alliance into the Cameroon People's National Congress (CPNC) in 1960. Messrs Ndeh Ntumazah and Albert W Mukong, who were hell bent on immediate and unconditional reunification with French Cameroon founded the One Kamerun (OK) party inspired by Um Nyobé's (UPC) ideological conviction that; "Everyone will recognise, speaking in Christian terms, that God created only one single Cameroon."[28] The Cameroon United Congress (CUC) of Solomon Tandeng Muna and Emmanuel Tabe Egbe created after their expulsion from the KNDP was the precursor, indeed a subterfuge by Ahidjo for hastening the process towards the One Party system, the Cameroon National Union (CNU) in September 1966.

It is remarkable that up to this point all the early political actors: Southern Cameroons MPs, Ministers and Members of Government including Members of the House of Chiefs without exception, were staunch Christians some of whom were Church Ministers. This Christian stamp impacted indelibly on the formulation of the policies that laid the foundation for a unique Southern Cameroons. For the same reason, the various political parties professed an unblemished, pacifist culture drawing on spiritual and ethical values which advocated non-violence and respect for human life. This was profound and explains why throughout the political history of the Territory, even during its most turbulent period there was never any resort to violence or much worse, loss of life. Contesting political parties during elections were known to travel in the same campaign convoys and would use a common land-rover roof or soap box to "attack" each other's political platform and thereafter sit down to share jokes, common meals and drinks.[29]

The same spirit prevailed in the Southern Cameroons House of Assembly, where after hot debates on the floor, MPs retired to the Senior Service Club for mutual coffee breaks or to the Parliamentary Flats where they resided during parliamentary sessions to share common rooms, facilities, discussions and meals. The prevailing adage was that of; "The force of argument and not the argument of force". One spectacular occasion was when Foncha defeated Endeley at the General Election in February

---

[28] Willard R Johnson, *The Cameroon Federation, Political Integration in, a Fragmentary Society*, Princeton University Press, New Jersey, 1970. p.138. For the unique geographical features of Southern Cameroons, see The Government of Southern Cameroons, *Introducing the Southern Cameroons*, Federal Information Service, Lagos, 1958, pp.8-10. and for "Victoria as the melting pot of Southern Cameroons" see, Victoria Centenary Committee, Victoria, Southern Cameroons, 1858-1958, BM Book Depot, Victoria 1958, p.93.

[29] Mbile. Eyewitness p.170

1959. At the handing over, the spouses and their husbands were caught on camera embracing and hugging each other. At all times and in all places, this was unique. The 11 February plebiscite was superbly well organized to the point of unanimous satisfaction. This impression came freely from the UN plebiscite Commissioner himself, Dr. Djalal Abdoh, an Iranian. In his report to the UN General Assembly he noted:

> One of the outstanding aspects of the plebiscite in the southern Cameroons was the remarkable calm which prevailed during all its phases, despite the density of the political campaigns during the last weeks during the last weeks preceding the polling. It is with great satisfaction that I pay tribute to the people of southern Cameroons for the respect they showed for law and order.[30]

*Fig 12. Dr. Djalal Abdoh, UN Plebiscite Commissioner for Southern Cameroons is the gentleman on the left with his left hand on his mouth. He is conferring with colleagues over the counting process.*

On their return from the UN after the plebiscite disagreements, Foncha and Endeley agreed on a truce calling for peace and harmony to

---

[30] See the UN Commissioner's Report to the UN General Assembly, 1961, Addendum to Agenda, item 13 para112. p.1.

prevail throughout the territory. And, indeed there was reported "total agreement at the Bamenda All Party Conference" in late June 1961 and with the same spirit the Southern Cameroons delegates proceeded to the Foumban Constitutional Conference the following July. At that conference, the two leading protagonists of the powerful Southern Cameroon delegation seems to have sung from the same song sheet. At the close of the deliberations all is said to have concluded in perfect harmony as had been the case at the Bamenda All Party Conference. The pacifist, harmonious, Christian stamp inherent in the Southern Cameroons political ethos was abundantly demonstrated on the floor of the Foumban constitutional conference by EML Endeley, the opposition leader who, in his opening speech astonishingly addressed President Ahidjo, the UPC Terrorists and the delegates in unequivocal terms:

> If I, as opposition leader, and my colleagues can reconcile with Foncha, I cannot see why those who are the opposition and gone wild in the bush cannot reconcile with your government. I have had great reason to feel that Mr. Foncha is an enemy to me and I would not work together with him, as the terrorists have felt against president Ahidjo. We have come to set an example that by working together, we can make a better country. If by this example which I have set with my colleagues we cannot produce a peaceful Cameroon, then we will be a laughing stock to the country.[31]

This is explicit enough and speaks volumes of what had happened and what was possible for Southern Cameroons all being equal. Perhaps what little remains to add is that in proceeding to the Foumban Conference both the Government and the Opposition subscribed an equal number of delegates as they had done at the Bamenda All Party Conference and travelled as a unit to Foumban either by air from Tiko International Airport or by land from Bamenda. In fact, the CPNC leaders made more interventions than the KNDP during the Foumban discussions as amply borne by the records.

Again, but for the destabilizing agents factored in by Ahidjo, and

---

[31] *Southern Cameroons Press Release* No. 1468.

obstacles raised during the coalition between these parties, under the administration of AN Jua in 1965 - 1968, the prospects were bright for a unique One Party coalition state constructed democratically. But, unfortunately, the process was foiled by Ahidjo who saw it as an obstacle to his brand of One Party rule especially as he was poised to launch the CNU as his mouth piece and could not brood any contrary opinion. Already by this time, he had literally banished resistance and placed all the opposition leaders in Republic of Cameroon behind bars. Consequently, he had come to Foumban with only a handful of twelve delegates exclusively members of his UC party, while on the other hand, Foncha and Endeley turned up with a large delegation of twenty-five Southern Cameroonians comprising a cross section of all the political parties, traditional rulers, civil society and the administration!

## Complementary Geographical, Political, Economic and Historical Factors

Southern Cameroons (North and Southwest Provinces) has been described variously as "The Switzerland of Africa", "The land flowing with milk and honey," The tourist destination of choice or "Africa in miniature". Certainly these perceptions held by tourists, administrators, pastors and economists fairly reflect the realities of the country. The depth of its attractions and riches do not result from the similarities of its features but rather from the composite diversity of its human and natural resources. By nature, culture and history, the country is roughly bisected into two geographically distinct regions; a hot relatively low-lying coastal, tropical forested south, endowed with rich marine, fauna, plant variety and volcanic soils, bounded by a picturesque northern tropical savannah grassland region with rolling hills and a cool climate, excellent for grain culture and animal husbandry. Both North and South are complementary holding interminable natural appeals for visitors and investors alike.

In addition, broadly, the people of the Coastal and Forest Regions are of Bantoid origin with acephalous cultures, while the more thickly populated northern Grassland inhabitants, who mostly claim Tikar, Widekum and Chamba roots, are semi-Bantu, and are ruled by semi-divine monarchs in Chiefdoms or "Fondoms". Historically and politically, the Country has had a rich chequered past. Western commerce, Christian activity and colonial experience originated in the southern Forest Zone decades before penetrating into the Bamenda Grasslands, which was originally affected by the devastating Chamba and Fulani slave raids of Modibo Adama, a flag bearer of the Jihad from Sokoto of Othman dan Fodio, who went as far south as Banyo and Foumban. This southward Moslem advance was arrested by German colonisation in July 1884 consequently; this bipolarity has shaped the political divisions of the North and South West Regions since precolonial times.

In fact, although German Kamerun was administered as an integral unit, the North and South West Regions of grave necessity "naturally" emerged as a socioeconomic and cultural entity set apart in the early 1890s. This arose from the German plantation labour policy, which over the centuries has spontaneously further come to bond these Regions, together. With the vast plantations at the coast operated by the Woermann, Jantzen and Thormalen commercial companies, there arose an interminable demand for plantation labour. This was facilitated after Zintgraff's tour of the grasslands stretching as far as to Kentu and Yola during which he discovered that robust manpower abounded around the Bamenda Plateau. The labour recruitment agencies soon brought about an involuntary connection of the planters, tribal states and rulers, workers and the German administration but in the main, the process ultimately laid a solid link connecting the grasslands through the forest to the coast. Actually, between 1901 and 1909, there was a thorough labour assessment and manpower allocation in all the over thirty-one pacified villages under Bali suzerainty to as far as Bafut, whose Fon was sent on exile until the labour quota with which the Fondom was charged could be met in full. Yet, Bafut was not an exception, as the same policy was inflicted on the Moghamo villages and Ngyembu. These early stages of labour recruitment were intense, ruthless and barbaric in the Bamenda Military District close to the Fondom of Bali Nyonga, the main labour supplier and contractor with its vassal states which were within easy patrolling distance. Labour recruitment took the following forms:

> A small supply of adventurous volunteers to Westafrikanische Pflangzungsgesellschaft Victoria and to government service, a large flow of

penal labour rounded up in punitive expeditions or extracted from defeated villages, and another provided by chiefs either under contract to licensed recruiters or to stave off their visits and those of military patrols.[32]

The fact is that the greater number of these recruits who went to the plantations at the coast, sometimes up to 75% never returned. There were numerous labour recruitment scandals. In the year, 1913-1914 alone 11.000 men were recruited through normal channels, 2.000 of whom were destined for work in the plantations and on the railways. The *Stationsleiter* (Station Master) complained that: "The flower of Bali youth had been sacrificed to plantation interests."[33] Being a high state official himself, this statement amounted to a serious indictment on German Colonial labour policy. Though German Kamerun was administered as a single unit, the socioeconomic, cultural and possibly, political configuration of what was to become British Southern Cameroons comprising the grasslands, forest and coast was already apparent and took a blurred shape through closely yoking the human resources of the northern grasslands (Bamenda) to the plantation resources of the coastal south (Victoria) with Mamfe, Bangwa and Kumba as transit routes. Very likely, this informal pragmatic socioeconomic and geographical arrangement is what suggested itself to the negotiators for the partition, who included: Frederick Lord Lugard the Governor General of Nigerian, Major General Charles Dobell, who was appointed Commissioner of British Cameroons and General Joseph Aymerich, who became Commissioner of French Cameroon. This agreement was finally confirmed at the Versailles Treaty in 1919, which sanctioned the division of former German Kamerun between France and Britain as Mandated Territories of the League of Nations.

Thus, like the two sides of a coin, the evolution and blending of the geographical regions of the North and South West Regions towards a freely and spontaneously knitted and integrated: economic, social, cultural,

---

[32] Elizabeth Chilver, *Native Administration in the West Central Cameroons 1902-1954*, nd. p.95

[33] ibid, p. 97.

spiritual and, finally a political entity drawing on its diverse human and natural resources began intensively during the German colonial era. The Germans, who had acquired vast plantations at the coast, sought full-bodied manpower from the Bamenda highlands to work on them after expensive and colossal failure with foreign labour recruited variously from Sierra Leone, Liberia, the Gold Coast, Togoland, Nigeria and the Congo. The bonding of these regions was further accentuated during the British Mandate and Trusteeship periods owing to their relatively benign and liberal policies. These policies yielded great expectations as they encouraged elaborate missionary activity, which in turn greatly united the peoples and permeated their cultures.

It deserves to be emphasised that even though the British Colonial Administration did not itself create any serious socioeconomic impact in the country among other palpable and not so visible contributions their tolerant policy which permitted the main line religious denominations of the time; the Basel, Baptist and Catholic missions to operate freely in the Territory, on the whole laid the solid groundwork for the climate that nurtured the rise and blossoming of the Golden Age in Southern Cameroons. Through their provision of sound educational, health and social welfare services they consciously invariably laid the foundation for nationalism and national unity in the territory. All of this was work in progress and no one can lay claim to a perfect State of Southern Cameroons, but what is obvious is that it was way ahead of similar states with a brilliant and promising performance record. Above all, it indicated what could be achieved even with limited human, natural and material resources when managed by honest, dedicated, resourceful, and a people –minded leadership with a liberal and democratic spirit. Given that in history everything is relative, to a considerable extent, this was the calibre of leadership Southern Cameroons was endowed with.

## Chapter Two

# LEGACIES: COLONIAL, CHRISTIAN AND INDIGENOUS

### British Heritage: Integrity and Self-Reliance

The British colonial policy hinged on the glorified theories of a "Sacred Trust" and the "Dual Mandate" both of which declared paramountcy of African interests in their colonies has been challenged as mere pious talk by critics in some quarters. However, juxtaposed within the present day Cameroon context, it was by far a more advanced, functional and fruitful version of the much paraded version of "Devolution" being canvassed in this country. The pragmatic British implementation of this theory through "Indirect Rule"(IR) or "Native Administration" (NA) as the best means of ruling the indigenous people effectively, and at the lowest cost, ultimately yielded intrinsic dividends in sustainable self-reliance, self-actualisation and self-rule among Southern Cameroonians. First experimented in India, Uganda, Northern Nigeria and later tried out in various parts of Nigeria, the system was based on "Native Authority." It involved the administration of the indigenous people through their own traditional or better still, "natural" rulers and institutions after extensive intelligence, assessment and reassessment reports conducted by administrative officers (AOs). It resulted from systematic sociological, geographical, anthropological and historical investigations.

In Southern Cameroons, which comprised two broad categories of Native Authorities among the semi- Bantu polities of the Bamenda Grasslands and the Bantoid ethnic groups of the Forest and Coastal South, Indirect Rule or Native Administration through (Native Authorities) was officially introduced in the territory in 1922. But the vital studies for its actual implementation were only completed by the late 1920s. The highly centralised Grassland polities were ruled by powerful, monarchical, semi-divine heads of tribal states, "Fons" claiming Tikar, Widekum or Chamba origins, while the more acephalous, decentralised clans and ethnic groups of the Forest and Coastal South were organised around "Chiefs" and Lineage Heads. It was therefore these leaders; Chiefs, Fons and Lineage Heads who were appointed "Native Authorities" and invested with powers to rule their own subjects according to their own traditions and customs closely shadowed by British AOs. Thus at best, the Anglo-Saxon attributes with which the inhabitants of the North and South West Regions came to be identified were inculcated not by deliberate commission as the French did in the case of "assimilation" and direct administration in East Cameroon but rather by "default" through delegation by the British colonial authorities, who relegated power and authority extensively to the Missionary bodies acting as Voluntary Agencies and furthermore, realistically to the traditional rulers acting as Native Authorities under the policy of Indirect Rule.

*Figure 13. Southern Cameroons Police on Parade*

This closely followed political memoranda issued in 1906 by lord Lugard its author. It roughly indicated the attitude to be adopted towards Native Rulers, some of whom had never enjoyed such power and authority before, so as to uphold their "prestige" and influence. The Government was to treat them, as:

> .... an integral part of the machinery of administration. That there are not two sets of Rulers - the British and the Native working either separately or in co-operation, but a single government in which the Native Chiefs have clearly defined duties, and an acknowledged status, equally with British officials. These duties should never conflict, and should overlap as little as possible. They should be complementary to each other, and the chief himself must understand that he has no right to his place and power, unless he renders his proper services to the State.[34]

Accordingly, the Governor General of the Federation of Nigeria issued Ordinances which categorised them and determined the extent of the powers of each NA. They dispensed justice in harmony with native laws and customs in Native Courts (NCs), while NA police and messengers handled law and order, peace and security. The judiciary was organised in such a way that the Customary Court system was allowed to coexist with the British Courts. The jurisdiction of the Customary Courts was limited to applying customary law.[35]

The NAs also assessed and collected their own taxes, ran their own Native Treasuries, budgeted and appropriated funds for various services.

---

[34] I F Nicolson, *The Administration of Nigeria*, 1900-1960, Oxford, The Clarendon Press 1969 p. 144; Lord Lugard, *The Dual Mandate in British Tropical Africa*, Frank Cass & Co. Ltd., London 1965, pp. 96-97, 194 passim. This has exhaustively been treated in Chapters 2 and 3. It was the source of serious perennial conflicts between the Catholic Church and the British Colonial and Native Administrations until the early 30s. For more on the efficiency of the NAs, see *Introducing the Southern Cameroons*, pp. 26-27. For pictures and brief introductions, see E W Ardener, *Historical Notes on the Scheduled Monuments of West Cameroon*, Government Printer, Buea, 1965.

[35] The High Court in turn "observed and enforced native laws and customs not repugnant to natural justice, equity, and good conscience, nor incompatible with any law in force". Native laws and customs were applicable "where the parties involved were natives as well as between natives and non-natives, where injustice would be done to either party by a strict adherence to the rules of English Law". The Southern Cameroons High Court Law of 1955 Sect. 27 spelt out other technical legal limitations to their application, Notes by Barrister Luke K Sendze.

With time they increasingly became autonomous and efficient administrative units within which the locals practised self-government: running their own educational and health institutions with fairly effective veterinary and inoculation programmes. Sanitary Inspectors ensured hygiene and sanitation at all levels in the villages and suburbs. Other NA organs undertook the construction and maintenance of roads, culverts, bridges, rest houses and infrastructure as well as forest conservation and agricultural demonstration farms among other responsibilities. Further introduction of Community Development and assistance from organisations such as the Swiss Association for Technical Assistance (SATA) enabled the principle of self-reliance to become even more deeply entrenched in Southern Cameroonians. In fact, long afterwards the central Government tended to depend on NAs to function effectively. It is interesting that their health programmes taking serious care of drainage, hygiene and general cleanliness greatly controlled malaria, cholera etc. in places like Victoria, Buea, Tiko and Muyuka.

*Fig 14. Left, HRH Fon Galega II of Bali Nyonga, Right, Chief J Manga Williams of Victoria. They Represented Southern Cameroons as Native Authorities (NA) in Nigerian Legislatures.*

With the introduction of representative local governments and the elective principle, Christians and products of the Mission Schools gradually assumed key positions in the NA Councils. In 1947, Paramount Chief Joanes Manga Williams of Victoria and Fon Vincent S Galega II of Bali became the first NAs selected to represent Southern Cameroons in the Eastern Regional Assembly at Enugu. Interestingly, though supposedly "Natural Rulers" both men were Christians and educated mission products, aspects which best qualified them for selection from among scores of their colleagues. This emphasises the prevalence of Christian influence in the administrative system.

The NA system continued to evolve and by the 1950s Councils coalesced into Federations and Confederations combining and sharing their human and natural resources with the positive consequences of detribalisation, national consciousness, national unity and the much sought after national integration. They also subscribed members to parliament where they made their views heard. Thus during the Eastern Regional Crisis in 1953, Rev. Jeremiah C Kangsen, the Hon Member of Parliament for Wum NA in the Eastern Regional House of Assembly wrote back to his Constituency, the Federated Local Clan Councils of Kom, Wum, Bum, Beba-Befang and Essimbi firmly and clearly underlining their identity as a political component in Southern Cameroons, whom he proudly represented in the Eastern Regional House of Assembly in Nigeria. In this he confidently maintained:

> The Eastern House of Assembly has been dissolved because some irresponsible people in the NCNC have planned to obstruct the peaceful working of the Eastern Government, which is your Government. *They went so far as to prevent this year's Government budget and thereby preventing social services from getting to you. In fact, you have by their action this year lost a big sum of money for your intended hospital.*[36]

Generally, with very limited resources the NAs learnt to run their

---

[36] For details, see Victor Julius Ngoh, *Constitutional Developments*, pp.95–105; Mbile, *Cameroon Political Story*, pp. 47-76. In comparative terms, the present talk about devolution is sheer child's play.

shoestring budgets with stringency, maximum efficiency and as far as possible with or with or without government assistance. The typical self-reliant, independent and outspoken attitude of Southern Cameroonians partly arose through this experience. This, coupled with the pacifist influence of the mission products rendered British Administration in the territory relatively mild, peaceful, liberal and benevolent, consequently attracting large numbers of French Cameroonian immigrants. To many of them, the French colonial policy of assimilation with its corollaries the *indigenat*, "*corvee*", the worrisome laissez- passer and later, the terror of the UPC guerrilla war was oppressive and offered a bleak and an unpredictable future. With a population exceeding 17,000 mostly around the plantation towns of Kumba and Victoria Divisions in the 1950s, it was these Francophone immigrants who formed the FCWU, which sowed the seeds of reunification that was later to shape the political destiny of Southern Cameroons.[37] Their greatest desire was to find solace and shelter under the comparatively more peaceful and liberal colonial policy exercised in Southern Cameroons. Their ultimate desire was to have this system extended to French Cameroons as well.

What clearly emerged with the implementation of the policy of IR was the fact that there was little interference by the Colonial Administration with the traditional way of life of the people, while the British stayed aloof and could hardly be identified with any negative acts of commission or omission in Southern Cameroons since the masses continued to deal with their own rulers as of old. Throughout the entire colonial period no serious incidents of opposition to British administration was recorded in the Territory. In fact, conflicts mostly arose between the AOs who were protective of the NAs on the one hand, and the Missionaries, especially the Roman Catholic priests and their zealous followers on the other. They were opposed to the insatiable demands and forceful manner in which these polygamous Chiefs acquired wives for their harems and also because they suppressed their Christian subjects.

---

[37] 11 By 1960, 25,000 East Cameroonians had sought refuge in Southern Cameroons; Plebiscite figures quoted in "*Kamerun Times*", February 11, 1963. See also Johnson, pp.91-5.

## British AOs as Defenders of African Traditions

The handful of British Administrators in the Country individually and mutually were by and large highly disciplined, upright and discreet people, who tried to live courteously with little intermingling or interference with the "natives", thereby setting high moral and ethical standards.[38] Consequently their indirect influence on the masses by virtue of their small numbers and aloofness was minimal. What subsequently emerged generally speaking, as an "Anglo-Saxon" culture in "British" Southern Cameroons was anything but "British". In reality it was to a large extent the work of the missionaries to whom the British Colonial Administration "surrendered" all aspects of character formation and education formally and informally in the Territory.

A cursory statistical scrutiny of the disposition of expatriates in Southern Cameroons by 1960 is explicit and reveals that the British were by far a minority in their own territory. The total number of British administrators, civil servants and their families together with other expatriates in the private sector resident in Southern Cameroons at the best of times totalled far less than 100, in fact, 88-100; while the Mill Fathers alone numbered over 60 excluding the scores of Rev. Sisters and Lay Mission Workers. The Basel and Baptist Missionaries and their families on the other hand, combined with their foreign lay helpers involved in evangelisation numbered several scores more. To these could be added the close to 300 German planters, whose influence, however was mainly limited to the plantations and only up to the outbreak of the Second World War in 1939. Thus simply by their sheer numbers, the impact of the American and European missionary expatriates collectively through the products of their numerous institutions was overwhelming noting that Christians at independence besides monopolising the control of the political and socioeconomic structures accounted for over 50% of the total population of Southern Cameroonians.

Officially and practically, British colonial policy stood indisputably in

---

[38] It is little surprise therefore, that unlike the Germans before them, there were hardly any mulattos resulting from British interaction with local women.

defence of the traditional rulers. Unlike France which pursued the colonial policy of direct administration and assimilation, the British never at any time intended to, or attempted to impose the British way of life on their colonial subjects. Rather, by their very policy of "Indirect Rule" and its corollary the "Dual Mandate," the African personality, his traditions, way of life and customs had to be distinctly retained, safeguarded and upheld as far as they did not contradict the norms of Common Law and decency.[39] Interestingly attempts by "natives" to copy European behaviour were regarded by some of these officials with ridicule and scorn since the Africans were supposed to maintain their primeval "Africanness."[40] It was cardinal administrative policy to defend the traditional rulers who administered their subjects under the policy of Native Administration as Native Authorities without relent and pretty often to ridiculous degrees against any radical forces of change. Generally, these were promoted by the Christian missionaries and their adherents.

Of the three Christian Denominations operating in the Territory, the Roman Catholic Mission, through their priests, catechists and zealous followers were singled out as the greatest defaulters. In particular, Catholic doctrine condemned polygamy, especially the brand practised by the Fons, District Heads and Notables, who at the same time officially acted as the Native Authorities and therefore constituted the very bedrock of Indirect Rule and British Administration in the Territory.

Some of the Fons like those of Kumbo and Kom ran harems in excess of one hundred royal 'wives' in the Bamenda Grasslands and Mamfe, with flash points in the Mission Villages at Shisong, Njinikom and Baseng, where runaway chiefs' wives found sanctuary. The Catholic Church protested against the practice and manner, whereby young women were rounded up and forced to become Fons or chiefs' wives. They openly and

---

[39] The October 1931 Concordat was basically an attempt to disentangle the mounting conflicts arising from a doctrinaire implementation of I.R. by the AOs and the excess zeal with which some Catholic missionaries and Christians with disregard for some traditions.

[40] See Oake, *No Place For A White Woman*. See also; Ndi, Anthony ed. *A Concise Centenary History of The Catholic Church: Archdiocese Of Bamenda, 1913 -2013:* Archdiocesan Information Services3014. pp. 76-78.

blatantly defended those of the women who sought their protection on the basis of both religious and human rights in the Native Courts and furthermore admitted and protected them in the famous *Christian Villages* at Shisong, Njinikom and Baseng. But the traditional rulers firmly backed by the British Colonial Administrative Officers regarded this as interference with their traditional laws and customs, which made the control of their villagers difficult.[41]

These conflicts kept mounting up to the extent that by 1930 the traditional rulers and British administrators could not bear the interference any longer. Disrespect for the Fons and protecting their runaway wives in Christian Villages was only one of the infractions with which the Catholic priests and their zealous adherents were charged; they were also known to flog their Christians for offences connected with sexual misconduct as well as other misdemeanours. Mr. EJ Arnett, the Resident to whom Indirect Rule had literally become: "A divine revelation, a sort of natural law", this had simply become intolerable and he proposed the expulsion of these missionaries from Southern Cameroons if they were not ready to respect the Traditional Rulers, the NAs and traditions of the people under the system of IR.[42]

The situation got so serious that the Governor General had to come in person to resolve it at a high level meeting called at Buea in October 1931. The situation was important enough to warrant the retrenchment of two Catholic missionaries while Mgr. Peter Rogan made a written commitment to better control his priests against infraction of traditional administration. On the balance, the AOs on behalf of the NAs undertook to deliver equal justice to Christians and animists alike in Native Courts, and conflict situations as well as freedom to Christians in the villages and much more. This was because some traditional rulers had taken to meting out open injustice to Christians both at home and in the courts, while, the bias attitude of the AOs towards some priests was abhorred. Even

---

[41] Ndi, Anthony ed. *A Concise Centenary History of the Catholic Church: Archdiocese Of Bamenda, 1913 -2013:* Archdiocesan Information Services3014.*chapter 3.*

[42] Ndi, *Mill Hill Missionaries in Southern West Cameroon, 1922-1972*: Paulines Publications, Africa 2005, pp.88-93.

more importantly, the Governor gave the Bishop the right to approach him directly without going through the administrative bottle necks in the event of any serious complaints raised by Christians against mistreatment at the hands of the Fons and AOs. In fact, it turned out to be a typical *Bill of Rights* for Christians of all denominations for around this time; it had become obvious that most of the NAs were exceeding their powers, while the products of the missionary institutions especially the Roman Catholic Mission were becoming significant and influential in Native Administration affairs.

*Fig 15. Hon SN Tamfu & the Fon of Tabenken about to fire den guns at a traditional celebration*

This was the precise indication of the contradictions that were inherent and emerging from the blind implementation of the policy of Native Administration. Without a return to the drawing board, with this reform there could hardly ever have been any meaningful changes or progress. In a way therefore, the radical socioeconomic, cultural and political development that took place in British Southern Cameroons was largely in spite of, rather than because of the British policy of Indirect Rule, whose contributions only mildly and indirectly affected the attitudes and character of the people. So, for the British to be attributed a role they never set out to play or an objective which was never on their colonial agenda is definitely misleading.

In fact, after a 300 mile trek of the territory, the Lieutenant Governor, Sir Walter Buchanan Smith made a most revealing observation at the 24th session of the Permanent Mandates Commission meeting in 1932. In this remarkable statement he admitted that the Northern Nigerian model of Native Administration had been followed rather slavishly as:

> *There was little room, in the current system for the Christian and educated members of the community. The new trend towards decentralisation might seem chaotic but it would, he believed, give more scope to schooled men in the management of local affairs. Even school boys, he suggested, might take a share of the work in smaller councils and conciliar authorities' proposed.* This was a far cry from the early 'twenties, when scribes and literate hangers-on were schooled out of meetings in an effort to increase chiefly prestige and self confidence.[43] (My emphasis)

In actual fact, this was revolutionary and was an open admission that change had finally come and Mission products were ready to shoulder and gradually began to take over some of the affairs of Native Administration. Furthermore, the Lieutenant Governor openly commended the efforts of Bishop Peter Rogan in particular and the work of the Missions in general as agents of development.

---

[43] Elizabeth Chilver, *Native Administration in The West Central Cameroons, 1902-1954*, p.118.

*Fig 16. The Governor General of Nigeria, H E, Sir James Robertson unveils Victoria Centenary Monument in 1958*

## Evolution of a Christo-centric Southern Cameroonian Culture

To many young minds the description of life in Southern Cameroons would sound like fantasy. In practical terms, the so-called Anglo-Saxon culture, actually a "Southern Cameroonian Anglophone culture" was pervasive; apparent in the offices, schools, hospitals, plantations, churches on the highways, at formal and informal social occasions practised by individuals in the discharge of their services both in private and public affairs. Initially, "Francophone Cameroonians" especially, mistook it for naivety; but in reality it was a "culture" identified with diligence, civility, broad-mindedness, moral probity, forthrightness, duty consciousness and above all, the assertive, fearless ability to stand up for one's rights and convictions in the face of all adversity. As a "culture of truth", generally, in Nigeria, declarations made in court by Southern Cameroonians were admitted without reservation.⁴⁴ On the surface, this culture was so omnipresent that it became fashionable to be Christian, while even non-Christians assumed Christian habits and above all, took Christian names without the formal Christian initiation of Baptism. This was most prevalent in the plantation towns and villages, where workers who belonged to none of the Christian denominations simply took Christian names as a matter of convenience and even pride by which they came to be generally known and addressed. However, substantial numbers of them after this finally, fully undertook the required catechetical course and became formally baptised as adult Christians.

It was something of an unwritten ethical code of conduct and became the identity card, the hallmark of the typical "Anglophone" West Cameroonians⁴⁵, who until the late seventies could hardly be mistaken in the manner in which they dressed, spoke and bore themselves; in short, in their total public comportment.⁴⁶ The most notable hallmark of this "assumed" British heritage remains the famous accord between Mgr. Peter Rogan and the Lieutenant Governor General of Nigeria, Sir Donald Cameron in October 1931. He had come specifically at the request of the Resident, Mr. Arnett to put an end to the reports of the mounting clashes caused by the Catholic priests, catechists and their zealous followers, who stifled the functioning of the NA system in several areas in the Territory. After the agreement, the Lt. Governor made an undertaking on behalf of the rank and file of the British Colonial Administration to ensure equal rights, freedom and justice for all Southern Cameroonian citizens, regardless of whether they were animist or Christian and, by which the latter were encouraged to assert their civil liberties.⁴⁷While this single

---

⁴⁴ Subject of panel discussions with Messrs Foleng, Bijingsi, Ngiewi Asunkwan and Kari with Written Notes from Mr. Cyril Ebu.

⁴⁵ Several e.g. Trusteeship Council AR 1974-566, para 566, BA 1947/2 for joint administration of Cameroons and Nigeria; also, Examination of 1947 AR by Trusteeship Council 4th session 27/1/49, BA 1947/4

⁴⁶ Fonlon, *A simple Story Simply Told or The Rise of Dr. Pavel Verkovsky, First Archbishop of Bamenda*, CEDER, Yaoundé, 1983, p. 10.

⁴⁷ See Anthony Ndi, *Mill Hill Missionaries In Southern West Cameroon, 1922-72*, pp.77-93

operation was only one of the factors making for peace and harmony to prevail in the areas of conflict, it is worth remarking that from then until independence, no further breaches on the magnitude of what had been recurrent earlier were recorded thus indicating that the parties concerned largely adhered to the terms of the accord even if these were never openly published and circulated. Justice, freedom of expression and religion had become an accepted way of life for the average Southern Cameroonian, so to speak, by the 1960s.

## Post-Primary Products of Secondary and Teacher Training

The influence of the United Nations Trusteeship Council (UNTC) operating under the auspices of the UN Visiting Missions on the other hand, helped to perfect this culture further since the people were repeatedly encouraged to air their grievances through them to the UN - General Assembly without any fear of vindictiveness by the British colonial administrators.[48] But the real groundwork was laid by the missionaries from the various pulpits in churches, market places and through the convents, health clinics and the various women's associations. The greatest impact however came through the rising number of primary and secondary schools and above all, the teacher training colleges touching the lives of thousands in these institutions and scores of thousands more throughout the country simply as Christian converts.

The role of the well-groomed, Primary School Teacher in general and that of the Headmaster, popularly known as "HM" in particular, as agents inculcating an English-type of education is well established. Such a teacher would invariably have received the rigorous physical, moral, intellectual and social formation either initially at Kake, then at Kumba and later, at one of the highly rated Teacher Training Centres wholly run by the missionaries of the Roman Catholic, Basel or Baptist denominations. He was the role model, leader and trusted adviser to the Fon, Chief or Council of Elders in the village. He and his staff set the standards for moral rectitude,

---

[48] There were several of these props e.g. Trusteeship Council AR 1974 para 566, BA/1947/2 for joint examination of Cameroons and Nigeria; also, Examination of 1947 AR by Trusteeship Council 4th Session 27/1/49, BA Ba 1947/4.

integrity, social order and decorum. As the country evolved politically, they were popularly elected as local representatives into the NA Councils and eventually as MPs to Parliament. On the whole, the HM was the point of reference and an epitome of the Missionary-Manager, Supervisor and Visiting Teacher in Voluntary Agency schools in many ways; as well as of the Education Officer and Divisional Officer.[49] The reality that by 1970, West Cameroon had struck its goal of "100% trained teachers" five years ahead of the target date set by the Organisation of African Unity and UNESCO indicates the extent to which the State of West Cameroon was self-sufficient in teachers providing quality primary education.

Here it should be noted that of the over 500 primary schools in the Country in 1960, Government possessed only five, one for each Division with the NAs running a handful of the others, while 99% belonged to the Voluntary Agencies or: the Roman Catholic Mission (RCM), Basel Mission (BM) and Cameroon Baptist Mission (CBM). However, Government regulated education in content, structure, enrolment and teachers' salaries through grants-in-aid. To meet the goals of rapid educational expansion and education for all, the Foncha Government introduced "Education Rating" and later "Lump Sum:" which every adult male tax payer with or without children of school going age had to pay with their poll tax. This afforded a six-year programme of free primary education for all children from Infants One to Standard Four. Government provided building grants and paid equitable salaries to all teachers in Assisted Mission Schools, Government and Native Authority (NA) schools. This fact equally explains why schoolmasters, mostly from the "Missions" accounted for over 75% of the MPs in the Southern Cameroons House of Assembly and, as well provided the Foncha Administration a ready pool from which they drew badly needed Administrative Officers and civil servants especially following the sudden, massive pull out of expatriate and Nigerian civil servants as the country approached independence and reunification[50]

A summary of the work ethics of the time is well articulated by

---

[49] Fonlon, *A Simple Story Simply Told*.

[50] Emmanuel A Aka, *The British Southern Cameroons* 1922-1951; *A Study in Colonialism and Underdevelopment*, Nkemnji Global Tech, Platteville, Madison, 2002, p.251.

Professor Bernard Fonlon,[51] which makes this era in the history of Southern Cameroons expressly vintage and nostalgic. Reflecting on his stint as a "Pupil Teacher" in the early forties at Shisong, Kumbo, then only a Standard Four Roman Catholic Mission School with Headmasters and teachers of the statures of Messrs. Frederick Mubang Tanyi, William Patrick Lebaga and Vincent Domatob, Fonlon recalls his own attitude to duty: "at a period and in an environment where conscientiousness, devotion to duty and earnestness in its execution were regarded as rather in the nature of things."[52] He adds that if it had entered his head to choose a watchword in those days it would have consisted of the single word expression: "Thorough." Yet, the BM and CBM contemporaneously ran comparable schools with much the same high level of competence in stations like Victoria, Soppo, Buea, Bombe, Nyasoso, Bali, Mankon, Bafut, Mbengwi, Wum, Belo, Kumbo, Ndu, and Mbem, spread throughout the Country.

A similar scenario obtained in the Southern Cameroons police force, a wholly secular institution, which though deficient in numbers was heavily supplemented by the NA police and messengers. Prospective police recruits had to meet strict physical, mental and high moral standards. They received their rigorous training at Ikeja, Lagos and later at Mutengene, Cameroon under the Grenadier Guards. Friends to civilians, they went about armed only with batons and it was an awful offence attempting to corrupt a police officer. Orderliness in the force went beyond the police officers; it was exercised right down to their homes and households. Dr. Elias M Nwana, whose uncle was a "cops," vividly recalls how: "To be a police child was to be disciplined, to be clean, to be neat, to take orders and obey them without complaint, to have your parent's house inspected for cleanliness every Saturday by the Provost. That is how we lived in the barracks."[53] Probity was exercised in all aspects of private and public life. For example, in the Treasury Department at Buea in 1964:

---

[51] He was the first holder of a doctorate degree in East and West Cameroon.

[52] Fonlon, *A simple Story*, 1983, p. 10.

[53] EM Nwana, Tracing My Roots through the Njuh Vaatkuna and Mfum Wadinga Family Lines, Adelphi Graphics Ltd London, 2004, p.10.

Mr. John Foleng as a young accountant promptly called in the police to arrest a pensioner who out of gratitude for the fact that he had promptly calculated and paid his retirement benefits was about offering him a five thousand franc "dash" [tip] in appreciation. This in the ethics of the time was unacceptable and considered outright bribery and corruption punishable by law.[54]

Yet, Mr. Foleng was not alone in this category; he was typical of a prevailing culture, which cut across the civil service, the private sector and above all was typical in Christian establishments.

*Fig 17. Mr. John IE Foleng, a highly qualified young accountant. He worked in the Treasury Department, Bueu.*

Complementing these views at a purely official and supervisory level, the feeling was the same; Mr. Cullompton a Senior British Administrative

---

[54] Group discussion with Messrs. John Foleng, John Bijingsi and Dr. Elias Nwana.

Officer who served in the Nigerian and Cameroon civil service from 1928 to 1956 and frequently deputised for the Commissioner of Southern Cameroons, in comparative terms and from long experience confidently remarked that for his career, he was; "faithfully looked after by Cameroonians who were very loyal and for whom he gained real affection." Referring to his carriers (from Bamenda), who were "splendid in physique" and in whose hands his life was depended for over a fortnight; "They never put a foot wrong, yet could have done anything to make life awkward for me." He equally maintained that; "The Cameroon women were more prosperous and happier than those in Sierra Leone and Ghana."[55] This was in reality a microcosm of the general attitude and approach to duty in what could be considered with hindsight, the "Golden Age" of Southern (West) Cameroon. Cullompton's observations tally extensively with those of Malcolm Milne although they served in the territory at different periods.

The moral stamp on civic responsibility rising from missionary influence was unmistakable and the prospects for a Southern Cameroons State built on such a foundation barring the subsequent political vicissitudes were certainly boundless. Rev. Father Ben Stukart, a critical and keen observer, who always referred to Cameroonians as "my people," confirmed this view and, as publisher of the Catholic Information Bulletin (CIB) encapsulated it in an editorial in 1964 when he evoked:

> The people in West Cameroons are wonderfully kind.' This remark has been made by all foreign visitors who have travelled in the country. It would perhaps be too preposterous to attribute this national characteristic entirely to the influence of the church on people. No doubt, the Cameroon people are kind by their very nature. But, again, it would be no exaggeration to say that the Catholic Missionaries have left an indelible mark on the Cameroon people among whom they have worked. Isn't it the spirit of simplicity and of hard, devoted labour, that spirit of easy approach and joviality, which is the characteristic of our missionaries?[56]

---

[55] Cullompton, "Talk to the Probus Club," 1982, "*The Early Days Memories in the Cameroons*" p.5; see also, W F Newington, *West Coast Memories*, London, 1993, p. 51.

[56] *CIB No. 24*, March 1964, the Editorial

While he confidently spoke as a Catholic priest, the Basel and Baptist Missionaries could not have said anything less for their own achievements. On the other hand, Rev. Fr. Arthur McCormack, one of the early principals of St. Joseph's College, Sasse, visiting West Cameroon after sixteen years absence as an international expert in population matters was marvelled at the rapid progress that had been made in the fields of education, health and the economy. After his visit, the priest wrote back in admiration of what he had seen, noting:

> I would have liked statesmen of developing countries which have racial or nationalistic troubles to have seen how in friendship and partnership, peoples of different nations and races are working together for the development of the Cameroons - the same friendliness and courtesy, the same welcome to the stranger were in evidence, the same fine people of a beautiful country with leaders more concerned with the progress of their country than personal position or power.[57]

This is not to suggest in any way that Southern (West) Cameroon was a perfect Garden of Eden but the fact that these salubrious observations came from people of diverse backgrounds: administrators, pastors, tourists, casual visitors and numerous others is significant. All the same, these few examples taken from among many unmistakably depict the true profile of the people and the country.

For one thing, the length and breadth of the Territory entirely situated within the tropical rain forest and lush savannah with an active volcanic range of mountains stretching from the Atlantic Ocean in the South to the cool Bamenda Highlands in the north is endowed with some of the richest variety of soils, climates and vegetation producing an assortment of food and cash crops. This accounts for the thousands of hectares of land along the Coast that were sequestered by the German commercial interests for their vast plantations. It equally explains the relative absence of starvation and the existence of a comparatively robust and virile population especially in the northern portions. This is why it was regarded as a land

---

[57] Ibid, also *Introducing the Southern Cameroons*, pp.18-21,

flowing with milk and honey, which missionary influence complemented with Christian morality and spirituality. Writing about "This beautiful and fertile coastline and its people of Victoria and the nearby countryside" in 1958, Dr. Endeley pointed out that:

> In recent years the area around Victoria has developed to be the commercial centre of the young and rapidly developing territory of the Southern Cameroons. Its ports of Tiko and Bota buzz daily with ships off-loading cargo for the country's economic and social development and carrying away the rich and ever-growing natural resources from the adjoining plantations and forests in the form of bananas, rubber, cocoa, palm produce and timber.[58]

Beginning faintly in the late 1930s and gradually taking shape by the early 1940s, the Southern Cameroons nucleus had acquired a form that kept growing from strength to strength nurtured by several interlocking factors of its geography, economy, culture and the political climate. The advent of German and British colonial administrations provided the socioeconomic, geographical and political frame work within which traditional and Christian missionary cultures blended and flourished between 1940 and 1966 to give the people a unique cultural identity beginning from the colonial to the national administrations. The people and their leaders were repeatedly described as: peace loving, hard-working, loyal, honest, committed and intelligent abundantly endowed by nature with an abundance of human and natural resources.

## Southern Cameroons Culture: British Foundations

This account of the contributors to the speciously celebrated "Anglo-Saxon Culture" merely, as far as possible attempts to evaluate the precious inputs made by each of the major contracting parties: the Colonial State, the Foreign Missions and the indigenous traditions and customs of the people to this unique character with which the Territory has subsequently

---

[58] *Victoria Centenary* p. vi

come to be identified. In the first place, due tribute must be paid to the British Colonial Administration in British Southern Cameroons for providing the overall security, administrative structures, the geographical framework and political freedom within which the indigenous inhabitants were able to develop the sense of a common history, of belonging and of a common identity. Again, they deserve to be credited with implanting in the people through their policy of Indirect Rule, principles of personal dignity, integrity, self-reliance, self-actualisation and self-confidence. In comparative terms, the British colonial administration did much to instil freedom and a democratic way of life intended to satisfy the legitimate aspirations of its citizens: social, cultural, economic and political on the overall to reduce poverty, illiteracy and rampant disease. But outside this there is little else for which the British require special commendation because even then they had the capacity to do better especially economically, which they abjectly failed to do.

Mr. Johnson O Field, the last British Commissioner of Southern Cameroons in his farewell address at Bota Wharf in 1961, admitted the accusation that Britain had not done enough for the economic development of the Territory but also stated that they were leaving Southern Cameroonians with a legacy of self-reliance and a democratic way of life. On the same wave length, referring to the Foumban Constitutional Conference, at which the discussions towards a Federal Constitution for the re-unified states of British Southern Cameroons and the Republic of Cameroun were underway in 1961, the editor of the Cameroons Times, a leading Southern Cameroons journal captured this sentiment when he succinctly commented in its editorial:

> We are bringing into this union a great inheritance of viz: Democracy, the English have not given us fine roads and fine buildings but they have given something far more valuable: a democratic way of thinking and a fine educational system. With this inheritance we need not be afraid to meet our brethren across the border for we are not coming empty handed.[59]

---

[59] "*The Cameroon Times*" nd. (1961), the leading newspaper at the time

This inheritance of a democratic way of life and fine education became inestimable assets that assisted Southern Cameroonians enormously in communal development and self-sufficiency in the absence of any demonstrable economic, infrastructural and material investments bequeathed by the British Colonial Master as contrasted with the substantial French contributions and investments in East Cameroon through the policy of assimilation, which until 1958 continued to regard French colonies as Overseas Provinces of France.

It is commonly acknowledged throughout the North and South-West Provinces of the Republic of Cameroon by those who lived the Southern Cameroons experience, especially during the period between the Second World War and Reunification and, even up to the era of the Federal Republic in the state of "West Cameroon"; that they were indeed a distinct and unique people not merely identified by reason of political boundaries and a peculiar administrative system, but far more concretely by reason of their specific character with their own history, visions, common aspirations and fears; in short, with an indelible cultural identity.

This had been the overriding factor when they decided to vote overwhelming during the plebiscite against integration with the Federal Republic of Nigeria, but instead chose to become an autonomous coequal-state with East Cameroon within the Federal Republic of Cameroon. Southern Cameroonians did this as an entity, which was well aware of its distinct moral fibre as a "people". This distinction was made even more emphatic by their East Cameroon, Francophone "Brothers," who described this "character" or "culture", as being typically "Anglo-Saxon[60]. This appellation arose in actual fact, from the perception of the typical Southern Cameroonian, whom their Francophone compatriots brought up under the French colonial policy of Direct Administration and assimilation thought the British in Southern Cameroons had used the same approach in administering that sector of the Country.

However much, it may be conceded that the British made valuable contributions to the evolution of the State of Southern (and later, West)

---

[60] This was the positive usage and connotation but pejoratively they are also called: *"Anglofools"* or "Les Anglos" identified with naivety, insatiability and complainants of marginalisation by the majority Francophones (East Cameroonians).

Cameroon; nothing could be further away from the truth as far as it concerns their specific contributions to their cultural identity as a distinct people. By the Way, these English-speaking Southern (West) Cameroonians had a distinctive outlook and way of life that went further than the mere fact that the educated ones among them spoke the English Language or a version of it. So, therefore," language" could not even be the qualifying factor. Instead this "greater culture" touched all Southern Cameroonians, literate and illiterate, urban and rural, cutting across all social, religious, ethnic and sub-cultural boundaries. It was to be experienced in the offices, on the highway, in the plantations, privately and openly in the people's general attitude to life.

## German Colonial Impact

Compared to the Germans for whom a sizable proportion of Cameroonians still held considerable fond memories twenty-five years later, the incumbent British Administration (1916-61) had made an impalpable economic impact in the Country even by the 1950s. The cultural impressions of the Germans who prior to the British had administered the Territory from 1884-1915 was reflected to varying degrees in the life of Southern Cameroonians. On the whole, nostalgia for German rule was demonstrated especially along the coastal towns of Victoria, Buea and Tiko and throughout the plantations. Of the 264.000 acres of "enemy" plantation land advertised by the British Government in 1924, the Germans alone bought back 207.000 acres. By 1939 there were 285 Germans most of whom were members of the Nazi Party compared to 86 British nationals in a Territory that was supposedly, officially British.[61] With such inferior numbers British culture could not be expected to dominate in the territory. Even more importantly, it was difficult to distinguish what was British from what was considered good and worthy, which was essentially

---

[61] Ndi, "The Second World War in Southern Cameroons and its Impact on Mission State Relations, 1939-50" in Africa and The Second World War, David Killingray and Richard Rathbone eds, MacMillan Press Ltd, 1986, pp. 204-232. See also Simon J Epale, Plantations and Development in Western Cameroon, 1885-1975: A Study in Agrarian Capitalism, Vantage Press, New York, 1985. p. 114-115.

the substance of missionary culture and other inputs.

Subsequently, the Germans overwhelmingly dominated the cocoa, banana and rubber plantations employing well over 25.000 workers and, as well controlled all import and export business in "British Southern Cameroons". This was very unlike the French Mandated Territory of East Cameroon, where all ex-enemy, German plantations had wholly been bought over by Frenchmen explicitly to obliterate any lingering notions or influence of the erstwhile German colonial masters in the Territory. In other words, the backbone of the economy and the totality of the proletariat were in the hands of the Germans in Southern Cameroons unlike in French Cameroon where it was entirely in the hands of the French. This was further facilitated by the notion that the French colonial policy of assimilation saw French Cameroon as an extension of France or France Overseas, where French citizens were admitted as permanent settlers. Even on the spiritual plane, all foreign nationals of the Basel Mission were either pure Germans or Swiss-Germans, as were all Baptist Missionaries, while a significant number of Catholic Missionaries were also of German or Italian nationality. Ironically, therefore, the British became an indistinct and a far from effective minority in their own Mandated Territory. Mr. Godwin, an Administrative Officer of seventeen years standing put it better reporting from Bamenda Division a little earlier. Fully aware of the circumstances and implications of this delicate situation, the administrator seriously cautioned:

> Owing to the present unsettled times in which we live and with regard to the very uncertain hold we exercise upon the conduct of the native affairs in the Cameroons – due principally to inadequate political staff – the present juncture would be a most inopportune moment to introduce any influence which would in any way be calculated to minimise or depreciate our efforts.[62]

Like many of the administrators, who interacted directly with the masses at the grassroots, they were candid and tended to report precisely

---

[62] NAB Sd/1917/5 No. E/171 /1917 of 8/9/17

what they observed was amiss. It was obvious to him that the British Government was being haunted by their own policy of socio-political and economic neglect of British Southern Cameroons. He was concerned about the impression the 'natives' conceived of the British and, in a way was advising the administrative hierarchy on the policy to be pursued following the end of the First World War especially in Bamenda, where some four hundred 'native' ex-German soldiers who besides having fought for them had been interned with the German soldiers in the concentration camps at Fernando. After discharge they were craving for the return of the Germans to the Cameroons. He was uncomfortable and pointed out how:

> In this portion of the Cameroons we have an overwhelming native population, and as, in many of our ventures in Empire Making- with natives - we do a great deal on 'bluff'. I can assure that 'bluff' was never worn more threadbare than it is in this Division at present. I cannot compromise and save my face indefinitely and that is one of the reasons why it is not advisable for any missionaries to commence their activities here at present[63].

*Fig 18. Bismarck Fountain, Buea*

---

[63] NAB Ibid. See also, Anthony Ndi, "Mill Hill Missionaries and the State in Southern Cameroons, 1922-1972", School of Oriental And African Studies, (SOAS) university of London, 1983, unpublished PhD thesis.

In between the Wars Britain had continued to play, what amounted to no more than a minimal caretaker role and never failed in any way or form at any time to demonstrate the awareness of its tenuous hold on the Mandated Territory of Southern Cameroons. It failed positively to create any serious economic, social, cultural or political influence on the Territory or on its inhabitants. With the outbreak of the Second World War in 1939, scores of Cameroonian veterans of the First World War embarrassingly offered to serve on the side of the Axis Powers in the German Army. Even worse, all along the coastal towns, people freely toasted to Adolf Hitler, the "Fuhrer" and at social gatherings, sang the German National Anthem and openly celebrated the early German victories of the War in Europe. British neglect was paying off in the most negative manner.

The Chief Secretary analysing this gloomy situation doubted the chances of the British Administration gaining any cooperation from the natives were the Germans to enter Southern Cameroons. Britain was barely reaping what it had sowed all along in the Territory after two decades of benign neglect.

> In fact, the apathy only heightened with the progress of the War. Although in its chequered history Cameroon went through only thirty years of German rule and some forty of Anglo-Nigerian administration, the British Mandate period was also overwhelmingly dominated by German influence, though without legal title. Consequently, German influence sank deeper into the people; for it was these memories that were conjured and became beacons for re-unification at independence in 1961.[64]

This explains the nostalgic "K" factor in the spelling of "Kamerun" after the German appellation. All the early Southern Cameroonian political parties adopted the German "k" for Kamerun. These included the: KUNC, KNC, KPP, KNDP and OK. Similarly worth mentioning is the fact that the KNC and the KPP later, on changing their platforms in 1959 from reunification with French Cameroon to integration with Nigeria equally

---

[64] Ibid. Killingray and Rathbone.

reverted to Cameroons with a "C" discarding the "K" in their appellations. The coalition understandably then became the CPNC.[65]

Were the issue of imparting the so-called "Anglo-Saxon culture to have been determined simply by the length of time Britain administered a given colony, then it should have been most apparent in Eastern Nigeria with which Southern Cameroons was jointly ruled as an integral part and which by the way was a Region of the Federation of Nigeria, Britain's original dependency from 1884-1960. Interestingly, this was not exactly the case because of its policy of Indirect Rule, which stressed the paramountcy of African interests.

Actually, throughout the Federation of Nigeria, Southern Cameroonian citizens were noted for their honesty, reliability and diligence. This is testified by the fact that wherever they found employment, whether in the public or private sectors, Cameroonians were invariably entrusted with posts of responsibility and generally rose to the top. A quick glance at the personalities who were taken over from Nigeria at reunification in the civil service, army, the police force and education amply illustrates this point. For that matter, even recruits absconding from the Nigerian army in 1939-40, told the plain truth maintaining that they did not understand why they had to fight in the war. It was in order to raise this flagging loyalty of Southern Cameroonians to the Union Jack, that it was hurriedly arranged for the Governor General of Nigeria to make a special visit to the Territory in 1943-44, within the Second World War; as, while Cameroonian recruits were deserting at Calabar, those at home displayed generalised apathy for the war cause.[66]

---

[65] E.g. during the Eastern Regional Crisis in 1953, Southern Cameroonian members both in the Regional and Federal Houses of Representatives in Nigeria declared "Benevolent Neutrality" in Nigerian politics. See Mbile, *Eyewitness*, pp 44-76. It should be noted also that all political parties in Southern Cameroons; KUNC, KNC, KPP, KNDP and OK adopted the "K" factor in their names referring to their unique German roots, see Edwin Ardener, "The Kamerun Idea" in *Dream of Unity*; also Ardener, "The Kameroon Idea", *West Africa*, September 13, 1958.

[66] Rathbone and Killingray, *The Second World War*.

*Fig 19. Woermann, who together with Jantzen and Thormalen opened enormous agricultural estates in German Kamerun, precursors of the present day vast CDC plantations*

## Perennial Colonial Legacies: British and German

The German contributions to the Southern Cameroons culture cannot be minimised by any reckoning. Enduring German influence in the Territory is easily demonstrated, by the fact that with the approach of the Second World War, there was universal panic among the rank and file of the British Administrators. This was because there was a general clamour among the workers in the plantations directed by local Nazi leadership for the expulsion of the "ineffective" British from Southern Cameroons and the immediate return of the Germans, who had been "unjustly expelled" after the First World War. By default, Southern Cameroons, a British Mandated Territory was by virtue of its history and economy so tightly held in the German grip that as war approached in 1939, the news was "on the lips of every boy in the higher classes of the primary school" aided and facilitated by the older generation of Cameroonians, who yearned for the German era. The heavy Nazi presence on the plantations enhanced the propaganda machinery raising high hopes that Southern Cameroons would soon return to the German Reich, clearly depicted in nationalist poems such as:

Our plea and aspirations lie
To see our rights fulfilled,
That soon the German flag may fly
On Kamerun's old German soil[67]

What clearly emerges from this brief analysis therefore is the reality that the State of West Cameroon, as part of the Federal Republic of Cameroon, which metamorphosed from British Southern Cameroons, inherited this peerless Character largely from a complex combination of moral Christian teaching and traditional indigenous mores. The most that could be attributed to the British and even the German colonial masters in this connection, is that they provided the Territory with the English Language, and its structural, political, judicial and administrative framework, while the missions collectively and the indigenous customs and traditions of Southern Cameroons overwhelmingly, were responsible for its socio-cultural and ethical essence and content.

Consequently, whereas, a solid "Southern Cameroons Culture" did indeed emerge in the Country, the; "Anglo-Saxon" theory is exaggerated and, for the most part a figment of imagination and a glorified myth. At best it was an essentially Francophone perception and description of a truly and authentically Southern (West) Cameroon culture. Its continuous popular usage among West Cameroonians basically carries a socio-political connotation, where the emphasis on culture is shifted to the fact that the British handed down the English Language (in this context eulogised as the 'Queen's Own Language') and the framework described above, which were essentially veneer, external structural trappings compared to the core substance and essence supplied by ethical Christian teaching collectively with the intrinsic traditions and morals of the indigenous people. And for that matter, Southern Cameroonians who speak English articulate a distinct "Cameroonian" version of that language, just as the Nigerians, Ghanaians, South Africans, North Americans, Australians and other foreign English speakers do. Of course they are not for that reason

---

[67] Simon Joseph Epale, *Plantations and Development in West Cameroon*, 1885-197:1, A Study in Agrarian Capitalism, Vantage Press, Chicago, 1985 pp 114-115; Victor Le Vine, pp 124-5.

necessarily referred to as Anglo-Saxons!

It must also be remembered that the British Mill Hill elements in the Cameroons Mission were exceedingly few, while the predominantly Dutch members of the Society had no sympathy whatsoever for the retrogressive British colonial policy of Native Administration, the main reason why there were such sharp clashes between the priests and the British Administrators, who frequently referred to them as "strangers".[68] Between the BM and CBM, up to 1939 practically all the missionaries were either purely German or "German-aligned" nationals which is why they were so adversely affected by the internment of "enemy aliens" after 1940 with the outbreak of the Second World War. In other words, they were almost to the person, "aliens". In terms of numbers, British missionaries were on the whole few, and what the missionaries collectively imparted on the people were Christian ethics. Consequently, it did not matter very much to the majority of the missionaries whether Southern Cameroons remained integrated with Nigeria, joined French Cameroon or stood on its own after the plebiscite and at independence. Their basic mission was to serve the "People of God", instil Christian ethics and morals regardless of their status and nationality.

## Emergence of a Unique Southern Cameroons Culture

The formation of a genuine Christian culture in Southern Cameroons did not come easy. This was because in the first place, in the context of the time, i.e. post World War I, after the defeat and expulsion of the Germans, only new Christian missionary organizations without any German connections were allowed to enter the Territory now under British mandate. These were not easy to find. When finally admitted they had to formally established firm Christian structures that could propagate such a culture. Unfortunately, the war had totally destroyed whatever ground work had been laid by various missionary organizations under German colonial rule.

---

[68] Mr. Cantle, the D.O in Bamenda pointedly regarded the priests at Njinikom: Stokman (Dutch) and Schmid (German) as foreigners not well disposed to British administration procedures. See, Cantle to Resident 9/5/30 sd/1929/2. The Resident and SSP shared this view. See also Lynch to Chiefsec 11/7/30 sd/1929/2.

In fact, during the period 1915- (1920)1922, there were absolutely no European missionaries in British Southern Cameroons. The French Sacred Heart Fathers who briefly operated in Bamenda Division from 1920-1923 were neither welcomed by the powerful traditional rulers especially in Nso and Kom in Bamenda, nor by the British Administration who as an alternative applied for a British Catholic Missionary organization to replace the German Sacred Heart and Pallotine Missionaries. The same situation applied to the German Protestant missionaries, who had to be replaced by English speaking ones.

After lengthy administrative and diplomatic negotiations involving White Hall, Mill Hill and the Holy See, it finally resulted in the arrival of the Mill Hill Missionaries in the country in March 1922. They were closely followed by the Cameroon Baptist Missionaries in 1924 and the Basel Missionaries in 1925. These were therefore the three mainline missionary organizations that operated in the Territory up to and beyond independence and reunification. Given that the British Colonial Administration fully conscious of their limitations literally surrendered all educational and socio-cultural services in the hands of these religious organizations, it is little wonder that Christian influence came to permeate the totality of Southern Cameroonian life. Thus, they set up their pastoral structures to cover up the entire territory, the North and South West Regions, which by 1960 had reached every nook and cranny of the territory which even up to independence Government influence had not touched.[69]

However, during the early decades of the introduction of Indirect Rule, better known as Native Administration (NA) exercised through Native Authorities (NA) up to 1930, relations between the Traditional Establishment and the Roman Catholic Mission authorities were characterized by mounting hostility. In practical terms, this ranked the Rev. Fathers, Catechists and their zealous followers against the Fons and notables, who as NAs reigned supreme especially in the Bamenda Grasslands and Mamfe staunchly backed by the British Administration since these Fons acted as Native Authorities.

There were flash points in the "Mission Villages" (Catholic Mission

---

[69] See, John Percival

settlements) at Shisong in Kumbo, Njinikom in Kom and Baseng, under Mamfe. These conflicts arose largely from the fact that the Catholic Church emphasized monogamy and strongly opposed the brand of polygamy practised by the Fons and most of all, the manner in which they recruited girls for their vast harems sometimes running to over a hundred as was the case in Kom. Since the Fons acted as NAs, they received the unflinching support of administrators like Mr. EJ Arnett, the Resident to whom IR, had become an inviolable doctrine "a divine revelation, a sort of natural law."[70] These disagreements intensified to the extent that by 1930, the British colonial administration threatened expelling the Mill Hill Missionaries if they persisted in undermining the authority of the Fons who were the NAs. However, by 31 October 1931, the tremendous work the missionaries were carrying out and the defects in the NA system were becoming apparent and an agreement was reached with these realities in mind.

In fact, between 1930 and 1940, beginning with the suicide of Chief Ntoko Epie, the District Head of Bakossi in prison at Kumba in August 1932, while facing embezzlement charges of tax money, the bulk of the Fons and District Heads throughout the country were indicted and either served short terms of imprisonment or were disciplined for one fault or the other. Until then, Chief Ntoko Epie had been brandished by the administration as an exemplary Native Authority. After this rude shock, it turned out that most of the NAs had been exceeding their powers and there were practically no chiefs and DHs, Grassland or Forest, who under the circumstances could fully satisfy the conflicting demands of their traditions and the prescriptions of the NA Ordinance and remain faithful to both. At about the same time, the Roman Catholic Mission was vindicated and emerged as a most viable partner in development on whom the Colonial Government increasingly leaned.[71] Through their control of education, which was the greatest catalyst in development the

---

[70] NAB Resident to SSP 14/3/31 BA Sd/1931/5

[71] Ndi, "Mill Hill Missionaries and the State in Southern Cameroons, 1922-1972," A Thesis Submitted in Partial Fulfilment for the Doctor of Philosophy of the University of London, 1983. Pp. 199-200.

main line Missions acting as Voluntary Agencies came to literally control the socioeconomic and, eventually the political life of the country as well, in every sense. Rightly, as Francis Cardinal Arinze put it in the context of the time:

> The school was a major means not just of evangelization – in the sense of the baptized, but of what we now call development, all round development. We can say that the school at least in Nigeria, but also in many other parts of Africa, is the most powerful instrument of integral human development[72].

And, indeed, Missionary "Christian" culture in Southern Cameroons went even much further, it was all pervasive. Alone, by 1940 there were some thirty Roman Catholic Mission (RCM) Stations each staffed with at least two expatriate priests. Structurally, each of these comprised a complex of: a permanent church building, presbytery, a primary school with staff quarters, a convent, a health centre (dispensary and maternity home), frequently with an orphanage attached. Practically, wherever, there was a Mission Station whether Basel or Cameroon Baptist Mission (CBM) with a resident missionary, these structures were replicated. There spontaneously sprang up around them subsidiary settlements of people who supplied vital services as: cooks, stewards, artisans, drivers, mechanics, bricklayers, carpenters, mechanics and electricians with a whole range of unskilled labourers: carriers, sawyers and stone diggers. To various degrees in addition to the Christians and products of the schools, these categories of workers were usually zealous agents of Mission culture. Given that unlike government headquarters, which were situated along the main roads, these Mission institutions were established in remote areas, where they could better meet the spiritual and material needs of the masses. Their multiplier effect could therefore well be imagined.

In addition, the Christian conduct and influence emanating from the categories of the 'nuclear' occupants of the Mission compounds on the surrounding communities was considerable and infectious. Other than

---

[72] *The universe*, Sunday march 14, 2004. P.14

those named above, these individuals usually included the headmaster, teachers, catechists and their families; the priests, Rev. Sisters, Rev. Pastors and their families, nurses, technicians and domestic servants. These besides the school children constituted an impressive combination. "Elite" of sorts, they formally and informally became role models especially as they lived close to and shared in the lives of the community; their joys and sorrows, successes and failures, hopes and fears; the ingredients of love which also bred patriotism. Gradually with increasing interaction they unmasked the myth of the white man and instilled the sense of the equality of all races as preached from the scriptures.

A typical example to cite is that of Rev. and Mrs. Gilbert Schneider, Baptist missionaries. From 1947 till the mid-1950s, they opened and operated a Baptist Mission Dispensary at Warwar in Mambila, on the northern border between Southern Cameroons and Nigeria; some four days trek from the end of the motor road and over five hundred miles from Victoria at the coast. The point is that, here, these missionaries freely intermingled with the local people and brought up their children in their midst without undue discrimination.[73]

However, this was only one of a dozen of such missionary families, who reached out to Southern Cameroons peasant families in very simple and practical ways. These descriptions only cover the period up to the acquisition of the Quasi Federal status in Southern Cameroons in October 1954, after which there was explosive development especially in the field of post primary, teacher, technical and secondary education which further empowered the people in all other areas of development. Government reliance on the Missions was colossal; to imagine that out of over six hundred primary schools, Government and Native Authority Schools accounted for less than a handful, where even the staff comprised of Mission products with routine morning prayers and moral instruction in these institutions.

Consequently, Christian spiritual contributions to the evolution of patriotism, nationalism and national identity resulted in the first place from

---

[73] Ndi, *Mill Hill Missionaries in Southern West Cameroon*, 1922-72 Prime Partners In Nation Building, Paulines, 2005. P.97

the core Christian message itself of fraternal love and Christ's appeal that all may be one. That is to say that patriotism and nationalism in Southern Cameroons had a powerful spiritual content. To quote an extreme example of a nationalist, who is generally classified as a Communist; Reuben Um Nyobe, founder of the UPC, who preached immediate reunification and independence of the Trust Territories of British Southern Cameroons and French Cameroon. As a prelude to his ideology, he postulated that: "God Himself knows that Cameroon is one." However, the Christian missionaries in a bland manner propagated unity through their network of catechumenates, congregations, churches, mission fields, parishes and dioceses within acknowledged hierarchies.

Still, at the spiritual level, practically, all the denominations demonstrated their belief in this philosophy when they spontaneously, routinely offered prayers for peace, unity, harmony and prosperity for the pastoral and political leadership of the country and more practically during ecumenical services. Then of course, through their educational institutions, which catered for several thousand children at the primary school level and a few thousands in the expanding secondary school institutions, their hospitals, dispensaries, maternity homes, leprosaria, convents and other institutions, which were attended by all and sundry from all parts of the country. There was a fusion of diverse ethnic groups, thus breaking tribal, geographical and sectional barriers.

With the progress of time and the rush to opening post primary institutions direct lessons in civics, history and geography further enlightened the children and in later years progressed through various alumni. It is remarkable that Southern Cameroons enjoyed free primary and adult education by 1960 and that by 1970 it had achieved the 100% trained teacher target prescribed by UNESCO, one of the few African countries to hit that mark when contrasted with the fact that at reunification, Republic of Cameroon was still struggling to set up a credible teacher training system and ended up absorbing the mass of trained Southern Cameroons teachers by offering them more attractive conditions and higher salaries. This resulted in destabilisation among the voluntary agencies from which considerably large numbers of teachers were withdrawn.

## Religious and Moral Education

One of the least disputable means by which tender consciences and character were moulded resulting in the so-called Anglo Saxon outlook among the people of British Southern Cameroons was through Religious and Moral Education. The colonial system of education received from the British had a very strong socio-cultural and moral background and content. Thus Religion was taught in all educational institutions whether public or confessional, jealously guarded and inscribed into all educational codes, ordinances and practices. In GTTC, Kumba as in all Government and NA schools morning devotions at the beginning of each school day were mandatory. And for that matter, practically all the students at GTTC Kumba, which trained quality teachers for the whole country, were Christians and subsequently, since Government could not cope with the heavy intake of students, permission was granted to the Missions to open several denominational Teacher Training Colleges in the late 1940s.

Placed in its proper historical perspective, the primordial position of Moral Instruction in Education was prescribed in the first "Education Code of Nigeria: Colony and Southern Provinces Number 15 of 1926", which of course included Southern Cameroons. By it there was a graded course of Religious Instruction approved by each proprietor of the Voluntary Agency Schools, while in the NA and Government Schools the course was imparted by any qualified religious teacher or by a missionary of the denomination with the most prominent influence in the area. The 1944 Education Act made it obligatory on all schools within the State system to begin every school assembly with a period of religious worship.

For this reason, Religious Instruction was necessary and indeed, a prerequisite for all Government Assisted Schools. These conditions were repeated verbatim in the "Education Ordinance of Nigeria No. 39 of 1948" and again in that of 1952, which regulated education in the Southern Cameroons until 8 July 1976. [74] Consequently, Religious Knowledge

---

[74] British Educational Policy for Africa derived much from Lord Lugard's Dual Mandate - to make the Africans economically viable and an economic asset to the world and prepare them for eventual self-government. In 1925 the British Government came out with a White Paper on Educational Policy in Tropical Africa, which encouraged

was a requirement in all Teachers' professional examinations, the West African School Certificate and later on in the GCE and all other external Anglophone examinations.

*Fig 20. Left, Dr E M L Endeley and Bp. Peter Rogan; Right, St Francis' Teacher's Training College, Kumba.*

Significantly, immediately after the inauguration of the Southern Cameroons House of Assembly "Sessional Paper No. 9 of 1955" formally placed before the nascent Southern Cameroons House declared abundantly: "Government appreciates the fundamental influence of sound religious training in the formation of character and it is our intention therefore to see that Religious Instruction takes its rightful place in the curriculum of all schools". After independence, in response to the UNESCO Mission Report of 1962, with great foresight the West Cameroon Government came out with another document entitled, "West Cameroon Educational Policy Investment" in which again, it made its mind perfectly clear, reiterating still more forcefully the 1955 policy on Education and

---

Voluntary Agencies emphasising Religious Education and collaboration with Government. See R J Mason, British Education in Africa, OUP, London, 1959, pp.37-64.

its impact on the formation of sound character.[75] For this purpose the teaching of Religion (not only Christianity) was made compulsory in all West Cameroon Government educational institutions. With a sense of foreboding, as lately as 1971, barely a year before the abrogation of the Federation, it further cautioned that unlike in East Cameroon, all Federal Government institutions in West Cameroon were obliged to include Religious Instruction in their curricula.

## Impact of Re-Unification on Education Policy

Most incredibly, the first shock occurred when Government Bilingual Grammar School, (BGS), the first ever, was opened at Man O' War Bay (in 1963) and later transferred to Molyko, Buea. Indeed not only was it the first Government Secondary School in the State of West Cameroon, it was a "Federal Government" institution enjoying a special status with privileges not available to any Mission Secondary School. On being approached by the Pastors of the Presbyterian Church in West Cameroon and the Cameroon Baptist Convention as well as a Catholic priest on the vital issue of teaching Religious Knowledge in that School, the French expatriate principal was blunt, in fact, arrogant in his rejection and told them point blank that BGS, Buea was an absolutely different category and tradition from every other College in West Cameroon.

Though new and strange to the State of West Cameroon, this policy already obtained in the Francophone State of East Cameroon after the French tradition. In fact, it took the intervention of the Minister of National Education for the principal to cave in to the demand of the clergymen. But even then, that was only a special concession made for a specific school and for a particular period, while the Federal Government policy remained unchanged. In later years BGS, Molyko reverted to its original policy by erasing Religious Knowledge or Moral Instruction from its timetable pure and simple.

---

[75] R J Mason, Ibid.

*Fig 21. Top, St. Joseph's College Sasse, Buea opened in 1939, and the first secondary school in Southern Cameroons. It provided manpower for the civil service; bottom, Man O'War Bay, Victoria, where Bilingual Grammar School, Buea, the first Government Secondary School was originally opened in 1963*

However, the final blow came with Decree No. 76/385 of 3 September 1976, concerning the administration and pedagogic organisation of Private Education, Article 39 of which stipulated that a pass in Religious Knowledge at the GCE was not to be reckoned among the qualifications for employment. Even more puzzling, this Decree was supposed to apply even to teachers in Catholic, Protestant and private schools as well. The debilitating effects of the rivalry among the various religious

*Fig 22a. Dr E M L Endeley & wife congratulate Mr. J N Foncha after CPNC defeat by KNDP and replacement by Foncha as Premier*

*Fig 22b. Left, J O Field, Commissioner of Southern Cameroons and right, HE Sir James Robertson, Governor General of Nigeria*

*Fig 22c. Top, Prime Minister, A N Jua acquiring land for CCAST at Bambili, Bamenda; bottom, President Ahmadou Ahidjo being received in Buea, West Cameroon.*

denominations in West Cameroon are fairly well established. However, it was precisely in this area where they had experienced the worst divisions among themselves that at this hour of the greatest threat, the Protestants and Catholics found strength in solidarity and common action.

In February 1977, the Moderator of the Presbyterian Church in West Cameroon, Rev. Jeremiah C Kangsen, the Executive Secretary of the Cameroon Baptist Convention, Rev. Pastor Samuel Ngum, Mgr. Pius Suh Awa, Bishop of Buea Diocese and Mgr. Paul Verdzekov Bishop of Bamenda Diocese; leaders of the Christian Denominations in the North West and South West Provinces of Cameroon, again unanimously addressed a compelling memorandum on this burning issue to the Minister of National Education, but he remained unmoved. This adamance further got inscribed into the civil service code which proscribes the recognition of the academic value of GCE passes in Religious Studies as qualifications for employment in the civil service or for higher studies in Cameroon.

The consequences of this prohibition have been held largely accountable for the steady erosion of the ethical values that constitute the highly cherished Southern Cameroonian version of the "Anglo-Saxon culture" and the rapid onset of moral degeneracy, corruption and the near complete absence of professional consciousness especially in the Public Service. Not surprisingly for two consecutive years in the late 90s, precisely in 1988 and 1989, Cameroon as a nation was rated the most corrupt country in the world. Just as a reminder to make the point that Cameroonians have learnt no real lessons since then, yet again, last year, (2015) the Minister of Communication took to the mass media loudly denouncing another indictment by Transparency International, that Cameroon had been ranked the second most corrupt nation in the world. This might have been intended for external consumption. However, internally, Cameroonians have repeatedly listened to the Head of State vigorously denounce the existence of rampant corruption in the various corps of the civil service, the police and forces of law and order, and even the Judiciary. Of course, proof of this is the existence of the large number of high ranking government ministers and directors of parastatals behind bars in the maximum security prisons in Yaoundé and Douala. Given that finally, GCE Ordinary and Advanced Level were finally admitted and standardized by the Cameroon GCE Board, the next logical step is to accord these very important subjects, the badly needed official recognition that equates them to all the other academic subjects with the anticipation that they could eventually be made compulsory conscious that their intrinsic value pervades the human person and society as a whole, with the state reaping enormous socio-political, economic and moral dividends.

## Chapter Three

# THE SOUTHERN CAMEROONS: CHARACTER

### Integration with Nigeria: Ramifications

Britain informally administered Southern Cameroons as an integral part of its Nigerian colony right from the aborted Condominium in 1916 through the Treaty of Versailles till when it had the process confirmed by the newly created League of Nations in 1922. Thereafter, it was administered as a British Mandate of the League of Nations an integral part of Southern Nigeria from 1922-1946, and later as a British Trust Territory of the United Nations after its creation, from 1946-1961. In either case, the joint administration was a mixed blessing to the people of Southern Cameroons. At one level; Nigeria was the land of reference; which possessed all that was good and desirable, the Golden Fleece in matters of education and development. The same attraction applied to matters of the economy; commerce and industry. The best Southern Cameroonian brains and talents found challenging opportunities at educational institutions in Enugu, Calabar, Lagos, Ibadan and elsewhere in Nigeria. But the stark reality was that only a minute few of those qualified benefitted from these facilities because the Territory was indirectly and remotely governed through Nigeria during all the British Mandated and Trusteeship periods from 1916-1961.

During the League period, up to 1946, the Territory was managed all the way from Lagos. However, with the creation of the Federation of Nigeria comprising three Regions: the Yoruba West, with its capital at Ibadan; the Hausa-Fulani North with its capital at Kaduna and the Ibo East with its capital at Enugu, Southern Cameroons directly came under the purview of Enugu, which was the Regional capital. This was considered decentralisation, which logically should have brought Southern Cameroons closer to the Regional Headquarters administered by a Lieutenant Governor responsible to the Governor General in Lagos. However, in practical terms, the Ibos, who dominated the Eastern Region, took over total control of Southern Cameroons with the collusion of Britain since it served their interest. Structurally and practically therefore, Southern Cameroons was administered as a "colony of a Region" of their Nigerian Colony, pejorative as it sounds.

## The Ibo Vector

Right from the beginning with the failed attempt at the joint administration of German Kamerun by France and Britain in March 1916, through the Peace Treaty of Paris to the Treaty of Versailles in 1919 and, up to the League of Nations, France never budged from its determination to administer its share of the Trust Territory as an integral unit and separate "colony" like all its other colonies. Britain on the other hand, despite all protests, first at the League of Nations and later at the United Nations, insisted to have its section, which it further divided into two, administered as integral parts of its Nigerian colony. Thus British Northern Cameroons was governed as an integral part of Northern Nigeria while British Southern Cameroons was administered first as part of the Southern Provinces of Nigeria until 1946, when it was integrated with and administered as part of the Eastern Region of Nigeria. All protests by the Cameroon Youth League that since it was a UN Trust Territory it deserved to be managed separately fell on deaf ears as Britain was determined that the mutilated sections should eventually at independence become permanent parcels of its Nigerian colony. British insistence on administering it in combination with Nigeria was based on the frivolous excuse that it was too tiny and slender to be a colony on its own, yet along the same West African coast they had the Gambia, which was even tinnier. Their experts went ahead to postulate without justification that Southern Cameroons represented a considerable charge on Nigeria.[76]

---

[76] Nfi Joseph, Nigerians on *Mission In The British Southern Cameroons*, Baron Printing

Thus in addition to Britain as colonial master Southern Cameroons was burdened yet with another layer of even more exploitative *black imperialist, colonial masters*. Initially, these included: the Hausa, Yoruba, Ibibios, Efiks and Ijaws but above all the Ibos, each of which left their impressions in the territory and even worse, helped to under - develop it contradicting the pious British claim that they were on a civilizing and educating mission in the Territory, further maintaining that; separation from Nigeria would deprive the people (British Southern Cameroons) of the invaluable opportunities of political education and advancement which they would derive from their integration with a large and highly developed area[77]. Mr. Solomon T Muna, a veteran politician who had served as a Minister in the NCNC Government in Eastern Nigeria, from that experience, observed that the black imperialism of Nigeria was far worse than white imperialism.[78]

Consequently, the nicknames by which Southern Cameroons was called such as: "The colony of a colony"; "The colony of the region of a colony", pejorative as these sounded were appropriate. Ultimately, they were not sufficiently descriptive as Southern Cameroons came to be an Ibo back-yard, a ready farm which they exploited with impunity. Positively famous as an enterprising and hardworking people, they permeated all the nooks and crannies of the public and private sectors and at all social levels in the Territory. On the down side, Ibo clannishness, brutality and exploitation in the territory are well documented. Wherever they were established, they violated all traditional taboo and sacred norms and institutions. In the Bamenda Grasslands, they seduced even the wives of Fons and in the South West Region they were accused of inconceivable crimes ranging from rape, murder, to land grabbing, extortion and treasonable plots to overthrow the government.

Actually, owing to the numerous and incalculable crimes with which the Ibos were associated especially among the Bakweri people, the Bakweri

---

House, Cow Street, Bamenda , 2014,p.45

[77] Nfi Joseph, Nigerians on *Mission In The British Southern Cameroons*, Baron Printing House, Cow Street, Bamenda , 2014,p. 26

[78] See Ndi, *Mill Hill Missionaries*.P.217

Native Authorities were led to issue a series of laws restricting their activities throughout Victoria Division where they were forbidden to acquire landed property, houses, sell or let farmland. Bakweri women were forbidden to sell food to or communicate with Ibo men. Where land had mistakenly been sold to Ibos the Council offered to compensate and recover such property. The same restrictions were applicable in Kumba and Mamfe, where additionally, the Ibos were accused of cannibalism, feasting on indigenous women who got married to them. There was no known offence that the Ibos were not guilty of. Thus the proverb emerged that the "Ibos were a people given to excesses who never did anything until they had truly over done it."

Mr. Richard Kumengisa, a renowned retired English Literature teacher and literary critic of international repute, humorously uses an episode to demonstrate how this happened in Nso, one of the most powerful and respected traditional Fondoms in the Bamenda Grasslands. He sets this out theatrically as a typical incident in Kimbo Market in Kumbo and puts it in its historical perspective:

> *Our part of the country suffered a double colonisation up to 1961. As a UN Trust Territory; Britain, ruled it as a part of Eastern Nigeria. The British was the milder part of our twin colonisations. The subtle and more terrible was the colonisation within that colonisation.* It was from the people of Eastern Nigeria. They were mostly the Ibos and the Efiks resident in Bamenda and most of Southern Cameroons. Thus independence for us was not because of political liberation from the white man but also because of freedom from the Ibos. So, the black colonialists did as they liked most of the time. They could do and do, what they wanted they took.[79] (My emphasis)

In those days, Ibos were notorious for economic exploitation. They regarded Southern Cameroonians as primitive, backward, second class citizens, good for little else but exploitation and bullying. Being the black unruly colonialists they were, they were a painful burden to bear especially

---

[79] See Richard Kumengisa, *Mati Wun* (Leave Me Alone): Mankon, Bamenda 2005.

as the British colonial masters were mild, benevolent and hardly visible. Richard continues expressly:

> The worst part of our chastisement was in the market, where the Ibos had given themselves a monopoly for the sale of cloth and a number of imported goods with inelastic demand. Our people were relegated to wood charcoal and locally produced food. Asking the price of anything from an Ibo man in the market was tantamount to buying it. Woe betides the Southern Cameroonian if he dared refuse to buy a thing after asking the price. The sounds of the tambourines would fill the market place - a sign for rallying the Ibos. An unequal fight would ensue and, as the Ibos had a heinous *espirit de corps*, a good number of them would together beat up the would-be buyer to within an inch of death.[80]

The outrageous, domineering and high-handed behaviour of the Ibos was such that even before independence, they were expelled from some major Fondoms in Bamenda notably; Kimbo and Bali, where they had initially settled in significant numbers, but had become intolerable as well as in Victoria, Kumba and Mamfe in the South West Region. That is to say, this happened throughout Southern Cameroons at the same time. Just to further make the point that Ibo notoriety in Southern Cameroons was ubiquitous, Joseph Nfi in: *Celebrating Reunification and The Eleventh Province*, quoting a socio-political analyst Mr. Pius Soh begins by capturing the sentiments of the people at the time, noting that:

---

[80] Ibid. In the anecdote, the peak was reached in Kumbo market when Wikikai, a naïve villager had come to buy a piece of cloth for his wife's outing. In one of the sheds, he identified a particular colour and was about bidding the price, when Okafor, the Ibo trader hastily folded and thrust it at him. Wikikai was puzzled and as he struggled to find out what the matter was, Okafor landed two deafening blows on his cheeks. Tempers were quickly aroused and the Ibo traders playing tambourines rallied round to cheer up Okafor, an expert boxer who was raining deadly blows on the dumbfounded villager to their pleasure. Stunned, all Wikikai did was to shield himself using his left arm but finally with his back to the wall; he turned round and landed Okafor a deadly blow which sent Okafor reeling and crashing to the grounded. It took water and fanning to revive him by which time the villagers had carried Wikikai the champion home on shoulders in glory to his wife, though without the cloth. The significance of the episode is that it silenced the Ibos in Kumbo and they were subsequently sent out of the Fondom.

First and foremost, the people were not happy with the Igbo domination of the administration and trade. They were rich and had become very arrogant and sadistic. They were guilty of vices such as profiteering, rape, adulteration of palm wine and drugs, land expropriation, fraud, theft etc. They committed a number of oppressive acts in Abakpa Market in Bamenda and in the other towns of Southern Cameroons.[81]

Every facet of the history of Nigerians in Southern Cameroons tends to sound incredible and puzzling precisely because the British pursued an ambiguous and conflicting policy in the Territory. It had been with massive Nigerian assistance during World War I, that the British recaptured most of German Kamerun including: Douala, Yabassi, Bafia, Banyo and, with French collaboration defeated the Germans in Yaoundé and Efulen. In effect, the British crushed the Germans in most of the Territory but inexplicably at the Treaty of Versailles in 1919 effortlessly delivered 80% of the spoils to the French taking only: "That part of German Kamerun that was of interest to reshape Nigeria", giving it better boundaries.

Evidently, the British had fought the war with massive Nigerian support and largely in Nigerian interest. The Versailles Treaty was therefore appropriate payback time to compensate and appease Nigerian rulers such as: the Emirs of Bornu, Yola and Muri who had lent them assistance; to reconstitute their Emirates that had been dislocated and mutilated by the earlier Anglo-German boundaries and considered as extensions of Nigeria. British disregard for their Mandated and later Trust Territories of British Northern and Southern Cameroons was innate. For example, Lord Lugard writing back to his wife in March 1916 just around the time of the failed Condominium expressed his reluctance with the territory he was taking over on behalf of his government. He noted candidly: "The little bit I have taken over will give me as much work as a much larger area."[82] This aversion became the trade mark of British colonial administrative policy in Southern Cameroons from that date in 1916 till it was

---

[81] Joseph L Nfi, Dr. *Celebrating Reunification and the Eleventh Province in Cameroon*, university of buea, 2013, pp 79-80. He quotes, Soh, *Dr. John NGU Foncha; the Cameroon Statesman*, Bamenda, CSSR, 1999, p.44.

[82] Margery Perham, *Lugard: the Years of Authority* (London1960) p.545, quoted in: Elizabeth Chilver, *Native Administration in the West Central Cameroons* 1902-1954, p. 90.

finally dumped into the laps of a reluctant foster administrator, President Ahmadou Ahidjo in October 1961.

British Northern Cameroons was also deliberately disconnected from Southern Cameroons because the British had an ulterior motive to have the segmented sections fully integrated into portions of their Nigerian colony at independence. So, while being firmly attached to Nigerian Provinces by road, sea, river and air communications to toughen those bonds they were geographically, economically and politically severed from their Southern Cameroons kith and kin. In fact, the British regarded it as a natural, historical, cultural and economic part of Northern Nigeria maintaining that integration with Nigeria would provide invaluable opportunities of political education; and ambiguously that: "It was not and would not become an integral part of Nigeria." Paradoxically, this was precisely what they tactically manoeuvred British Northern Cameroons to become: "*Sardauna's Province*" subsequent to the 1961 Plebiscite.[83]

In the case of British Southern Cameroons every square mile of the land was carefully mapped out to serve strategic Nigerian socioeconomic and political interests around; the Cross River and Rio Del Rey Basins with Calabar and Efik traders in mind. The Mungo River on the other hand was accepted as a boundary because it provided access to the sea for plantation produce, while the Bamenda Grasslands served as an economic source of kola nuts and ivory for the Nigerian Hausa markets. Dschang plateau including Bangwa, Mbo and Mundane were acquired essentially to fence off the Anglo-French boundary, to prevent the flow of Grassland trade towards Nkongsamba, as well as prevent smuggling with French Cameroon. Without any proof, it was assumed and repeatedly emphasized that Southern Cameroons would represent a heavy charge on the Nigerian budget. This was the stigma which they later got *Sir Sydney Phillipson* to confirm in the famous Phillipson Report. It was later tactically presented at the United Nations to ward off the Third Option of independence for Southern Cameroons in the plebiscite of February 1961 on the unfounded argument that it was perpetually indigent.

---

[83] See, *Post Watch: Political Punch No.* 003.2005 by Elie Smith; Citizens of the former Northern Cameroons join southern Cameroonians to celebrate United Nations Day October, 24, 2005.

Thus as it turned out Nigerians, especially the Ibos with British collusion set out with a contradictory mission: to civilize, annex, colonize and *Nigerianise* Southern Cameroons but what they ended up doing was under-developing the territory and alienating themselves from the people. The brutality, spitefulness and overbearing attitude of the Ibos acting like conquerors contributed more than any political party could have done to cause revulsion against integration with Nigeria during the plebiscite in Southern Cameroons. The Ibo "black imperialists" shielded within the enclosure of their "private backyard", out of the glare of international attention and consequently without accountability to anybody, operated with impunity in Southern Cameroons. As a result, the massive vote for reunification was a resounding veto against Ibo domination.

## Deliberate Scheme to Under-Develop the Territory

This resulted from the fact that, being overpopulated and for the most part unemployed at home, the Ibos particularly and other Nigerian ethnic groups simply migrated across the border and inundated Southern Cameroons in various capacities as: transporters, civil servants, traders, craftsmen, teachers and labourers. Statistically by 1960, Nigerians accounted for 30% of the plantation work force and 25% of the civil service while in the major towns of Kumba, Mamfe, Tiko and Bamenda they controlled over 90% of the private economic and commercial sectors. In the coastal towns of Victoria, Tiko and especially in Buea, they settled on 'native' land and as a result, aggravated the volatile Bakweri land problem[84]. Even worse, Southern Cameroons was regarded as the dumping ground for less qualified and less educated Nigerians especially those who did not have the basic Standard Six certificate. Nfi gives the example of a certain Victor Odewole, who was appointed as Divisional Officer for Mamfe, but who the Resident, Mr. EJ Arnett discovered was 'hopeless', lacking any sense of method and order' not even qualified to be a third class clerk and recommended his retrenchment. This mediocrity was prevalent in the schools and institutions headed by these Nigerians and yet these were

---

[84] See Mbile, *Eyewitness*, p. 66; Ndi, *Mill Hill Missionaries'* pp 216-18.

those who complained about the backwardness of Southern Cameroons and demanded for special allowances for being posted there. In fact, civil servants sent to Southern Cameroons, regarded it as punishment, but at the same time held tenaciously to such positions, while the artisans amassed massive wealth scooped from the territory.

In these capacities, they infiltrated and dominated the entire Territory. Nigerian heads of service, who occupied nearly all the positions in the country, were reluctant to employ Cameroonians and easily found fault with those already engaged who often were causelessly dismissed and replaced with fellow Nigerians. Roads were constructed specifically to link up Southern Cameroons with Eastern Nigeria, while Tiko and Victoria Sea Ports together with Mamfe River Port were directly linked up to Calabar and Port Harcourt. Cameroon Schools were flooded with poorly qualified Nigerian teachers, while obstacles were placed against the opening of secondary schools, teacher training and technical institutions in the public and private sectors in the territory.

Consequently, these facilities became possible only after the acquisition of the Quasi Federal status in 1954. In fact, one of the first acts of the Southern Cameroons House of Assembly was the authorisation granted to Bishop Peter Rogan to open Queen of the Holy Rosary College, Okoyong, Mamfe, which had been blocked at Lagos with the excuse that there were numerous empty places in Nigerian girls' colleges and so there was no need to open another one in the Cameroons. This was despite the forceful arguments raised by the Bishop on the difficulties Southern Cameroonian girls faced in Nigeria. After this there was an urgent rush by the various religious denominations, exclusively missionaries of: the Roman Catholic Mission, Basel Mission and Cameroon Baptist Mission to establish secondary schools and teacher training colleges.

The fact that all within ten years of gaining the Quasi Federal status by Southern Cameroons over a dozen of these post primary institutions, excluding scores of primary schools were opened, still without meeting the expanding demand for admission by qualified candidates manifestly demonstrates how much integration with Nigeria had retarded development in Southern Cameroons. Among these new institutions were: Saker Baptist College, Victoria for girls; Sacred Heart College, Mankon for boys; Our Lady of Lourdes, Secondary School, Mankon for girls;

St. Bede's College, Njinikom, mixed; St. Augustine's College, Kumbo, mixed; Joseph Merrick Baptist College, Ndu; Presbyterian Secondary School, Besong Abang, Mamfe; Presbyterian Secondary School, Kumba together with Bilingual Grammar School, Molyko, Buea and Cameroon College of Arts Science and Technology, Bambili all within ten years of Southern Cameroons acquiring a Quasi Federal status away from the Nigerian stranglehold; 1954-1964. Prior to these there were only: St. Joseph's College, Sasse opened in 1939 in the face of stiff opposition by the Lagos Government; Cameroon Protestant College, Bali opened in 1949; St. Peter's College, Bambui opened in 1948, TTC, Batibo opened in 1949, Baptist Teacher's Training College, Great Soppo, Buea and Regina Pacis College, Bonjongo.

The two lone government institutions existing in the Territory prior to 1954 were; the Normal School (1925) later converted to TTC Kake opened in 1931, which was pretty restricted, at best it handled less than thirty students in all. It was the highest educational establishment in Southern Cameroons before SJC Sasse. The other institution was Government Technical College, (GTC) Ombe, opened in 1950. These examples of post primary institutions, which were never able to handle the large number of qualified candidates craving for education, clearly illustrates how educationally, integration with Nigeria had hampered educational progress in the Territory. Given that overall development hinged on the level of education available in the country, this demonstrates how Nigerians with British connivance deliberately "under-developed" Southern Cameroons since without or with low educational facilities only Nigerians filled up whatever opportunities were available leaving the mass of Cameroonians in the cold.

Yet it was continuously drummed down the throats of Southern Cameroonians that Nigeria was their saviour and that financially the country thrived on Nigerian largesse. The brain washing to this effect was encapsulated in the statement first made by Sir Allan Lennox-Boyd, the British Colonial Secretary at the 1957 London Constitutional Conference, stressing that: "Many of the best friends of the Cameroons do not foresee a destiny more likely to promote her prosperity and happiness than continued association with Nigeria." It became a singsong that was repeated at most official circles and, especially was the take-home message delivered by

## THE SOUTHERN CAMEROONS: CHARACTER

Malcolm Milne, the Acting Commissioner of Southern Cameroons at the Plebiscite Conference called at Mamfe on 10-11 August 1959, to decide on the crucial questions to be asked during the impending plebiscite to determine the fate of the territory. Regardless of whatever else happened afterwards, this emphasis together with Sir Sydney Philippson's Report already sealed the fate against independence for Southern Cameroons[85].

Ibo notoriety led them to be generally regarded throughout the country as: addicted dog-eaters, cannibals, rapists and murderers, while their effrontery in the market place was well-known. They were bold enough or even foolhardy to have raised a tribal Ibo flag in Tiko in 1949. These traits seem to have been imbedded in their ancestry. Dr. Nnamdi Azikiwe, one of the best known Nigerian nationalists, a great orator and charismatic Ibo leader and founder of the NCNC addressing the first Ibo State Conference, had remarked with characteristic arrogance: "It would appear that the God of Africa has created the Ibo nation to lead the children of Africa from the bondage of ages ... the Ibo nation cannot shirk its responsibility from its manifest destiny".[86]

Finally, leading other Nigerian compatriots in the Southern Cameroons civil service they organised what would have been a most deadly strike to paralyze the Foncha Administration. Fortuitously one of the tracts for this purpose was inadvertently served to a Cameroonian office cleaner, who immediately took it to the authorities. An emergency cabinet meeting was organised that night and by morning all the Nigerian civil servants were served with termination letters and locked out of their offices, which were taken over by their Southern Cameroonian substitutes. Thus the Foncha Government was saved from a major catastrophe.[87]

Of course, the Nigerians were unstoppable as, barely six days to the plebiscite; precisely on Sunday 5 February 1961, a last ditch attempt was

---

[85] Anthony Ndi, *Southern Cameroons Revisited, 1950-1972: Unveiling Inescapable Traps*, Vol. One, Paul's Press, Bamenda, 2013, P106. Also published by Langaa Research & Publishing CIG, Mankon, Bamenda, 1914

[86] See *West African Pilot* (Lagos) 8 July1949, quoted in Ngoh, *Constitutional Development in Southern Cameroons*.

[87] *See* Pius Soh, *Dr. John Ngu Foncha the Great Statesman*, p,170

made on the life of Dr. John Ngu Foncha, the PM to derail his trolley as he travelled from Mudeka to Tiko on a meet the people's tour. The PM escaped without injury although some members of his entourage and family members sustained serious though nonlife threatening injuries. The culprits were arraigned.[88] Time and luck once again eluded the plotters and their compatriots as finally victory in the plebiscite was tremendously and emphatically delivered to the KNDP, who stood for reunification with Dr. John Ngu Foncha as Prime Minister. Put otherwise, it was a resounding veto against Ibo hegemonic and insensitive arrogance in Southern Cameroons.

In the ultimate analysis, by all these actions the Nigerians, especially the Ibos had shot themselves squarely in the foot by over antagonising the people. As one adage holds it, the Ibos never did anything until it was overdone. The very first thing the Foncha Government tackled on taking office in 1959 was to inaugurate the Southern Cameroons Public Service Commission with the appointment of Mr. Jack A Kisob as the officer in charge with a five-member assiduous team. Their supreme directive was the *Cameroonisation* of the Southern Cameroons Civil Service, an objective that was achieved with resounding success and acclaimed throughout the region."[89] What the Ibos inadvertently did in the ultimate analysis was converting the "Ibo factor "into a "vector", which hardened the hearts of Southern Cameroonians against integration with Nigeria when it came to choosing between an independent Federation of Nigeria and the independent Republic of Cameroun. In fact, when the occasion came, there was not much of a choice between the two and even though the Republic of Cameroun was engaged in fierce fratricidal terrorist warfare the vote for reunification was a *fait accompli*, directly a veto against Ibo hegemony.

### Nigerianisation: Impact on Plebiscite Options

The issue of the reunification of British Southern and French

---

[88] Discussions with Madam Anna Atang Foncha and some family members, April 1914. Mathias Foncha, his son, one of those seriously hurt in the accident was also present.

[89] *West African Pilot* (Lagos) 8 July 1949

Cameroon originally and largely a "French Cameroon" immigrant worry championed by the French Cameroon Welfare Union (FCWU) gradually shifted from the periphery to the very heart of Southern Cameroons politics by the 1950s. It provided content for the proto-nationalist groups such as: the CYL, CNF and KUNC prior to the rise of broadly nationalist parties such as the KNC and the KPP and finally was responsible for the mortal split between the KNC and the KNDP in 1955 which ultimately careered the country into the referendum in 1961. In fact, this process was the most volatile and the period, has remained the most momentous in Southern (West) Cameroon history.

After the protracted, frustrating and inconclusive plebiscite conferences held variously at Mamfe, Bamenda, London and New York, three broad spectra of opinion emerged among the political parties, traditional rulers, civil society, students unions and other pressure groups. These comprised the KNC/KPP Alliance, which clearly settled for Southern Cameroons attaining independence either by integration with independent Nigeria, or by reunification with independent French Cameroon. On the other hand, the KNDP opted for an extended period under British Trusteeship followed by exploratory negotiations for reunification with French Cameroon, while the One Kamerun, (OK) party which shared this platform additionally wanted immediate and unconditional reunification. The Kamerun United Party, (KUP) a direct product of the Mamfe Plebiscite Conference demanded unqualified independence for Southern Cameroons pure and simple.

However, by late 1960, under mounting pressure from the Cameroon public and with much cooler heads, there was a convergence of views towards annulling the impending plebiscite in favour of independence for Southern Cameroons as a separate political entity. The two major opposing political parties, the KNDP and the CPNC (or KNC/KPP Alliance) tended to accept this suggestion. This was the message conveyed by the agglomeration of delegates to the London Conference comprising: Messrs JN Foncha, ST Muna, AN Jua and WNO Effiom, Fon Galega II and Chief SB Oben for the KNDP, and Dr. EML Endeley, Messrs PN Motomby-Woleta, SE Ncha and Rev. JC Kangsen for the CPNC. Mr. PM Kale went as leader of the KUP, while Mr. J O Field, Commissioner of Southern Cameroons and Sir Iain MaCleod, Secretary of State for the

Colonies joined at the Round Table Conference in London in November 1960. Noteworthy at this conference was the statement of commitment made by the UK Colonial Secretary that:

> A vote for attaining independence by joining the Republic (of Cameroun) would mean that, by an early date to be decided by the United Nations after consultation with the Government of the Southern Cameroons, the Cameroun Republic and United Kingdom, as the Administering Authority, the Southern Cameroons and the Cameroun Republic would unite in a Federal United Cameroon Republic. The arrangements would be worked out after the plebiscite by a conference consisting of representative delegations *of equal status* from the Republic and Southern Cameroons. ...The United Nations and the United Kingdom would also be associated with this conference.[90](sic)

However without any obvious explanation at the time, the London Talks ended up in thin smoke, although for many politicians Foncha was held to blame for their collapse. Still worse, the safety clause introduced by Sir Iain Macleod was never implemented.[91]

## "Third Option" Saga: Covet British Agenda

British attitude towards Southern Cameroons right from the "Condominium" in 1916, when German Kamerun was provisionally partitioned between them (Britain and France, Allied Powers in the First World War) altogether, British attitude towards Southern Cameroons, its own Trust Territory until independence in 1961 remained patently ambiguous and even contemptuous. Despite the superior contributions they had made towards the expulsion of the Germans, the British readily and unconvincingly conceded 80% of the territory they had strenuously acquired to France during the territorial negotiations from 1916-1922 on the excuse

---

[90] Nfor N Nfor, The *Southern Cameroons: The Truth of the Matter*. Bamenda, 2003.p.55.

[91] *Cameroon Champion*, Vol. 1 No.3 of 5/11/60 announced date for London Talks and reported that there was a growing school of thought for independence for S. Cameroons.

that they lacked the administrative staff for anything larger.

The British were more interested in "tidying up their colonial frontiers with Nigeria," and Lord Lugard bitterly complained that the western strip they had acquired though small in size was going to be as worrisome to govern as a much bigger area. Thus, *ab initio*, Southern Cameroons was inconsequential in the territorial equation and basically subjected to:"The imperatives of compensatory diplomacy... sufficient to improve Nigeria's strategic position as well as enable Britain to bargain for all former German colonies in Southern Africa".[92] Put on record as far back as 1916, the British seemed to have abided by this policy to the letter until the closing days of 1961, when they handed over the Territory for fostering to Republic of Cameroon under President Ahmadou Ahidjo at independence.

## *The Endeley (KNC) Government, 1954*

*Fig 23. Dr. E M L Endeley: Leader of Government Business*

Brigadier E J Gibbons: Commissioner of the Cameroons and

---

[92] Colonial Office [CO] to Governor General of Nigeria, March 1, 1916 in Lovett Z Elango, *The Anglo-French Condominium in Cameroon*, 1914-1916, *History of a Misunderstanding*, Navi Group Publications, Limbe, 1987, pp. 62-73.

President of the Southern Cameroons
House of Assembly and of the Executive
Council.

| | |
|---|---|
| Mr. J. Murray: | Financial and Development Secretary |
| Mr. C A Burton: | Legal Secretary |
| Mr. J Brayne-Baker: | Official Member |
| Mr. S T Muna: | Unofficial Member, interested in Work & Transport |
| Mr. F N Ajebe-Sone: | Unofficial Member, interested in Education |
| Mr. S A George: | Unofficial Member |
| Mr. V T Lainjo: | Unofficial Member |
| Rev. J C Kangsen: | Unofficial Member |
| Mr. L Roberts: | Clerk to the Council |

\* The Unofficial Members were MPs appointed from the Majority Party (KNC) in the House of Assembly to sit in the cabinet, while Official Members were civil servants (expatriates), who also sat in the House of Assembly and served to explain Government Policies.

In this regard, additionally, the Colonial Office instructed the Governor General of Nigeria to inform General Dobell, the Commander of the British forces in Kamerun that:

> Owing to considerations of general policy affecting our relations with the French... in the conquest of the Cameroons...His Majesty's Government have felt obliged to accede to the desire of the French Government that with the exception of the portions mentioned below the whole of the Cameroons should be administered by the French during the remainder of the war.[93]

Of course, all these temporary agreements were subsequently confirmed at the Treaty of Versailles and the League of Nations in 1922. At best, Southern Cameroons had been used merely as a bargaining chip to

---

[93] Ibid, p72. See also, Ndi, "The Second World War in Southern Cameroons and its Impact on Mission-State Relations" in, *Africa and the Second World War*, Killingray and Rathbone, eds. pp. 204-232.

tidy up colonial frontiers with Nigeria. In the meantime, the Nigerian Government supposedly undertook all financial responsibilities on behalf of the territory.

After that, against all protests at the League of Nations for Britain to administer the Mandated Territory of southern Cameroons as a separate unit from 1922-1945 and again during the UN 'Trusteeship period from 1946 until independence on 31 October 1961, Britain administered the territory first as an integral part of Southern Nigeria, and then as an integral part of Eastern Nigeria. Yet, Britain had signed the Trusteeship Agreement with the UN on 13 November 1946, Article 3 of which clearly stipulated:

> The administering authority undertakes to administer the Territory in such a manner as to achieve the basic objectives of the international trusteeship system laid down in Article 76 of the United Nations Charter. *The administering authority further undertakes to collaborate fully with the general assembly of the United Nations and the Trusteeship Council in the discharge of their functions*[94].

Britain deliberately defied all the decisions of the UN to which it was signatory in the interest of its Nigerian colony at the expense of The Trust Territory of Southern Cameroons. Consequently, at the UNTC, examining the facts taken from the official documents submitted by Britain itself, the Soviet Union Delegate indicated the extremely low-level of development the Territory had achieved after forty years of British rule. He referred to the fact that:

> Industry in Cameroons was non-existent and agriculture still very backward. There were no railways and the inadequacy of the road network made certain areas inaccessible during the rainy season. The situation in the educational and medical fields, particularly in the Northern Cameroons, was far from being satisfactory. The indigenous inhabitants had obviously come to the conclusion that they must take matters into their

---

[94] See UN Trusteeship Agreement of 13 Nov. 1946

own hands, recognizing that only independence provided the conditions in which former colonies and Trust Territories could develop their full potentialities.[95]

The entire British colonial period was one of striking benign economic and administrative neglect with the Territory consistently being regarded as an economic liability, whose budgets grudgingly always had to be subsidised from the generosity of the Government of Eastern Nigeria. This unfounded "assumption" totally ignored the reality that since the affairs of the Territory were inextricably managed together with those of Eastern Nigeria, stringent accounts, especially of sources of income were hardly kept. With hindsight, this might simply have been a trick to impress the fact that Southern Cameroons was insolvent and could never survive on its own resources as an independent sovereign state, and therefore, could only achieve independence either by leaning on Nigeria or the Republic of Cameroon.[96]

And, when eventually Southern Cameroons had the opportunity, after having begun to enjoy some measure of Self-Government in 1954, full self-government in 1958, and was headed for full sovereign status in 1961, Britain once more placed serious impediments on its way. Amazingly, not long after reunification and independence, the South-West Province singly, increasingly became a significant breadwinner for the entire Federal Republic of Cameroon. British policy of underdevelopment in the country was so apparent that when appealing for funding for his numerous development projects for Buea Diocese in the mid-1960s, Bishop Jules Peeters accurately referred to West Cameroon as "a healthy, bouncing, orphan baby" with boundless investment opportunities, but which unfortunately received assistance neither from Britain, France nor the United Nations[97].

---

[95] The Cameroons Under United Kingdom Administration: Report by Her Majesty's Government in the United Kingdom of Great Britain and Northern Ireland to the General Assembly of the United Nations for the Year 1959, London, 1960. p104

[96] *Cameroon Times*, Vol. 5 No. 93, Wednesday, August 1965.

[97] See, Bishop Peeter's Invitation to Father General In July 1969, in Anthony *Ndi*,

## THE SOUTHERN CAMEROONS: CHARACTER

So far, all of this was speculative and circumstantial until the declassified British secret files on the Trust Territory of Southern Cameroons under British Administration came to hand in 1998. With their release, it became irrefutable that Britain indeed had deliberately used its power and influence to prevent the "Third Question" or "any idea of prolonged period of continued trusteeship or separate existence of the Southern Cameroons being raised at the United Nations," and promised to be tough with Foncha because it was thought that firm, action then would save Britain a great deal of trouble later.

### *The First Endeley (KNC) Ministerial Government*

*Fig 24. The Southern Cameroons Executive Council, 1958*

Dr. E M L Endeley:     Premier and Minister of Local Government
Rev. Jeremiah Ando Seh:     Minister of State
Mr. F N Ajebe-Sone:     Minister of Natural Resources
Mr. Vincent T Lainjo:     Minister of Social Services
Mr. N N Mbile:     Minister of Works and Transport
Mr. J O Field:     Commissioner of the Cameroons, President

---

*Mill Hill Missionaries In Southern West Cameroon, P.167.*

|  |  |
|---|---|
|  | of the Executive Council |
| Mr. A D H Patterson: | Financial Secretary |
| Mr. J S Dudding: | Deputy Commissioner |
| Mr. B J Walker: | Legal Secretary |

The overriding British apprehension was that any such independence or temporary sovereignty granted to Southern Cameroons would likely influence Northern Cameroons not to join Northern Nigeria. Behind it all was the idea to compensate the powerful Emir of Sokoto for assisting Britain in the war against the Germans in Kamerun. The British Government next, proceeded to coax the Afro-Asian bloc, the Secretary General and all those involved in the negotiations to ensure that the Third Option did not pass at the General Assembly of the UN. While outwardly displaying fervent support for the Foncha Government, the British Administration secretly and outrageously argued that:

> Instead of trying to please everyone and failing might it not be worthwhile trying to please one side, viz: Nigeria? If we try to appear impartial both Nigeria and Afro-Asian bloc will believe that our real aim is to keep Southern Cameroons as a colony and military base. *By coming down firmly on the "third question", we will keep Nigeria as a friend and blunt the teeth of our enemies*[98]. (My emphasis)

Of course, it is obvious whom the British regarded as their "enemies", and it is no longer disputed that the Southern Cameroons delegation to the Foumban Constitutional Talks was tactfully and deliberately denied technical and legal expertise backing, both by Britain and the UN Trusteeship authorities. Much worse, the British Government bluntly declared that relative to Northern Cameroons, which they intended should join Nigeria, Southern Cameroons and its inhabitants on the other hand, was

---

[98] See Appendix 1 Declassified British Secret Papers: the British Government restrained Foncha from putting up the Third Option. He therefore proposed a slow process; See, J N Foncha, "Startling Revelations from British Declassified Documents on Southern Cameroons" in Letter to the Secretary of State for Foreign and Commonwealth Office, London, 30/09/98 para. 8. Also, Written notes from Mr. Cyril Ebu.

"undoubtedly expendable". Most of all, it was precisely at this point that the British openly and loudly declared that they were withdrawing their defence forces from the Territory on 30 September 1961`or at independence, without any substitute arrangement. The whole idea being to pull the rug from under Foncha's feet to facilitate the collapse of his government as he prepared for the Bamenda All Party Conference followed by the much anticipated Foumban Constitutional Conference. Nothing could be worse and all the parties protested in vain.

*Fig 25. The Foncha (KNDP) Government, 1959*

| | |
|---|---|
| Hon J N Foncha: | Premier |
| Mr. A N Jua: | Minister of Social Services |
| Mr. S N Nji: | Parliamentary Secretary, Minister of Commerce and Industry |
| Mr. E T Egbe: | Speaker of the House of Assembly |
| Mr. M N Ndoke: | Minister of State |
| Mr. S T Muna: | Minister of Finance |
| Mr. P M Kemcha: | Minister of Natural Resources |
| Mr W N O Effiom: | Minister of Works and Transport |
| Mr. J M Bokwe: | Minister of Cooperatives and Community Development |
| Mr. J H Nganje: | Parliamentary Secretary, Ministry of Local Government |

Mr. M M Monono: Parliamentary Secretary, Ministry of Works and Transport
Mr. J O Field: Commissioner of the Cameroons, President of Executive Council
Mr. A D H Patterson: Financial Secretary
B G Smith: Attorney General

The British were ready to stop at nothing in frustrating Foncha and those seeking a form of independence or prolonged tutelage under the United Nations Trusteeship Council to the point of scheming to have the lady MP (Mrs. Josepha Mua, the Women's Special Representative) decamp from the KNDP to the CPNC in order to topple the Foncha regime and hand over power to Endeley, who stood for integration with Nigeria[99]. It is equally explicit that the ambiguity initially expressed by Lord Lugard in 1916 was subsequently entrenched into a policy of benign neglect for "British Southern Cameroons". During the Lancaster House Conference, Foncha was plainly told by the Secretary of State for Colonies, Mr. Allan Lennox-Boyd, that the future of Southern Cameroons best lay with Nigeria and that the keys of the Bank of England would not be handed over to him if he persisted with seceding from Nigeria. British disregard for the Territory therefore arose in the main from economic considerations. This was further illuminated in the secret correspondence, which maintained that:

> Independence for the Southern Cameroons would face us with considerable problems. They would expect financial support from us to the tune of perhaps one million pounds a year and also that we should leave our troops in the country to defend them. If we meet these requests, it would be expensive for us financially and militarily and we should be accused of 'neo-colonialism'. If we missed the requests Ghana, Guinea or the Russians would no doubt be only too pleased to help. In short, this is not a course we should at all encourage Foncha to adopt... We should

---

[99] Ibid. Appendix 1

not encourage Foncha to go the United Nations at all.[100]

As a result, Britain manoeuvred Northern Cameroons into voting for integration with Nigeria, while at the same time scheming to deprive Southern Cameroons of the inalienable option of the "Third Question" at the impending Plebiscite. By this it would have attained full sovereignty given that other smaller and equally poor or even poorer nations including: The Gambia, Gabon, Sao Tome, Equatorial Guinea and Togoland were accorded that right. Britain was thus favourably disposed to kill two birds with one stone thereby gaining the eternal gratitude both of France and of Nigeria to the detriment of Southern Cameroons.

Consequently, during the 11 February 1961 Plebiscite, Southern Cameroonians went to the polls more like lambs being led to the slaughter slab, confined to two unpalatable choices. The sagacious Fon Achirimbi II of Bafut described this episode lucidly as one in which the choice was between two undesirable alternatives, integration with Nigeria, which he depicted as the "Deep Sea" and reunification with French Cameroon, which he equated with "Fire," since the Trust Territory under the imposed terms could only attain independence by integrating with Nigeria or reunifying with the Republic of Cameroon. However, the factors that established a distinct Southern Cameroons character and culture had become firmly established by 1961.

Still demonstrating the degree of political consciousness and freedom of choice that was prevalent in Southern Cameroons prior to the Plebiscite of 11 February 1961, one anecdote quickly comes to mind. It is about *Maa Agatha*, the vintage mother of Professor Bernard Nsokika Fonlon, who during the plebiscite boldly and deliberately voted for integration with Nigeria, in total contradiction of all that her highly erudite son as a top militant and leader in the KNDP, preached and practised. Coming home after the poll, he asked his mother, where she had cast her

---

[100] Ibid; Mrs Josepha Mua had to be rushed from the maternity, where she had just had a baby to participate in a crucial debate, where the KNDP was faced with certain defeat if she didn't participate, given that KNDP and CPNC were stalemated at 13:13 after Hon. J M Boja crossed the carpet from KNDP to CPNC. Discussions with Mr. Nick A Ngwa, March 2005.

vote, and to his surprise she calmly replied, "In the black box of course, Endeleys". On further trying to find out who, "had fooled" her to do that sort of thing. She then politely reminded him of a certain kinsperson, *Pa Jacob Lingong*, who of course, Professor Fonlon knew, lived in Republic of Cameroun, but not what had happened to him. His mother then revealed that: "They cut him up limb by limb and sliced him to pieces. Now tell me, how you could expect me to join a people who do that kind of thing?"[101] Conscience bound, she could not therefore vote for the future of Southern Cameroonian offspring to be bound up with such brutes. It was the turn of the learned professor to be stunned and speechless, faced with the shrewdness of his unlettered mother. She had exercised her vote judiciously against Human Rights Abuse in Republic of Cameroun, without all the ideological, political and ethnic considerations her son and all the other politicians loaded the exercise with. In other words, the old sagacious lady showed her son a "red card" with sound reasons.

## "The Third Option": Other Pertinent Insights

Further insights on the issue of the "Third Option" in the plebiscite came from Mr. John Percival, a critically minded Englishman and one of the 25 Plebiscite Officers engaged by the UN in Southern Cameroons. He was deployed in Bum (Wum Division), hundreds of kilometres away from Buea. He was therefore well placed to sample the feelings and opinions of the populace in such a far flung off area and make objective observations about issues surrounding the plebiscite. His first remark about the people as a whole was that they were well informed socio-politically and economically, probably from contacts with UN Visiting Missions, which encouraged freedom of expression through petitions and complaints. These coupled with the numerous elections the country had undergone prior to the plebiscite, which at all times involved vigorous campaigns by competing political parties with contrasting platforms kept the citizens

---

[101] See unpublished article by Rev. Prof. Joseph Tangka, "Grannies Verdict on Southern Cameroons."" He quotes from Prof. Fonlon's Confessions in, *To Every Son of Nso*.

well informed. Of course, put together all these only supplemented the work of the Missions which by then had penetrated all nooks and crannies of the territory in their job of holistic evangelisation. So, by the time of the plebiscite Percival thought, the people he met were fairly mature and knew exactly what they wanted but unfortunately were not given the opportunity or the means to articulate it.

## *Benign British Neglect*

Although engaged by the UN, Percival, after seriously examining the arguments on the ground, came to the conclusion that the plebiscite was: a wholly and totally expensive, time wasting and, an unnecessary and unjustified exercise. This arose from the fact that most of the people he met continued to plead for the period of Trusteeship to be prolonged for a little longer so that they could be better prepared to make informed decisions about their future. Because the British had done little for economic development in the territory, it looked more like they were escaping their legitimate responsibility as Trustees required by Article 72(b) of the UN Trusteeship Agreement. With regards to the degree of "benign neglect" with which the British Colonial Administration was repeatedly charged, Percival was shocked that: "People who lived only a morning's walk from the DO, had spent the best part of a lifetime under British rule without setting eyes on a white man. And now that they were setting eyes on one it was closing days before independence."[102] There could be no better indictment against British colonial administration in Southern Cameroons than this.

It was obvious to him that the plebiscite was: "A cynical public exercise designed to demonstrate to the world at large that the people of Southern Cameroons were being given freedom of choice, whereas the only choice they wanted was denied them". Like Mr. K. Lees, his compatriot, colleague and counterpart, the Plebiscite Officer for Bamenda, both men were all the time confronted with the same type of questions in the field by the people: who were perplexed with the attitude of the British and the UN

---

[102] John Percival, *The Southern Cameroons Plebiscite, Choice Or Betrayal*: Langaa Research And Publishing CIC, Mankon, Bamenda. Pp.77-78

with the omission of the Third Option of independence in the plebiscite. They could not understand why Southern Cameroons could not stand alone. "Why should a poor man sell his independence to join with bigger and richer men?" Thus to Percival living the reality of the moment in time and circumstance: It was quickly made clear to him:

> That they wanted no part of it and that they saw the whole thing as a sham, a cosmetic exercise in democracy. The only decision they were allowed to make was whether to throw in their lot with Nigeria or with French Cameroon, and they wanted neither of them. All the other decisions had been taken thousands of miles away by officials who thought they knew better than the people themselves.[103]

*Fig 26. Fon Achirimbi II of Bafut with Gerald Durrell*

Many of the people wanted the white man to stay at least for the time being and were angry to think that the British were going to abandon them forcing them to choose between the Nigerians whom they considered 'cannibals' and the 'Frenchy people', whom they considered as robbers.'

---

[103] Ibid.

The real choice of independence was denied them.[104] These observations are not different from those of Fon Achirimbi of Bafut and therefore buttress the fact that the Fon's views reflected the feelings of the other Fons and the people whom they ruled.

## Southern Cameroons: High Ethical Standards and Values

Over and above Christian teaching were the remarkable traits inherent in most of the traditions and customs of Cameroonians themselves, which both the missionaries and the colonial administrators generally acknowledged and openly admired. Thus it would be remembered that writing from Kumbo Mission in 1923, a "Parish" which then literally embraced the entire Bamenda Division, Father Michael Moran commended the extraordinary moral and cultural values of the people in the spheres of family life, respect and honesty, which he considered superior to those existing anywhere in Europe. He further specified that crimes and misdemeanours such as; "stealing and telling lies were unknown."[105] Again, at another level and a little later, farther to the South, in the Tropical Rain Forest Region, during the spectacular trials of Catholic priests and catechists at Kumba in 1930, the DOs were marvelled by the degree of veracity and accuracy demonstrated by the Christian complainants and witnesses, who insisted on telling the truth. They would on no account accept anything they were not sure of first hand.

Much later, aspects of this distinctive West Cameroonian culture, which had become generally apparent, equally attracted the attention of the Superior General of the Mill Hill Missionaries, Father Noël Hanrahan, who, visiting in 1972, as preparations were underway for the inauguration of a Regional Major Seminary for West Cameroon, thought it would make an enormous enrichment to the Universal Church, under the auspices of inculturation as a "mirror of the spirit, talent and style of the people,"

---

[104] Ibid.

[105] Reports on Moran "royally received" in Campling to Superior General 14/6/23 MA Cams. 1921, Box 2.

which should be reflected in the formation of the young priests there.[106] Mr. John Percival, a Plebiscite Officer who was posted to Bum in Wum Division from about July 1960 to March 1961 shares a similar experience from a very distant part of Southern Cameroons. He notes how:

> In those days in Southern Cameroons theft was almost unknown. I left the house unlocked, even though it was stuffed with things that might have seemed highly desirable to the most of the population. There were violent incidents ... but anyone who overstepped the mark was likely to be hauled in front of the local court by his neighbours. Nobody starved, nobody was alone or uncared for.[107]

Of course, these were the cultural traits inherent in the people, on which Christian values had been embedded and which became the moral and ethical basis and outlook of the so-called "Anglo-Saxon Culture" in later years. Given that Percival was reporting from Bum in Wum on the borders with Nigeria and several hundred miles from the capital at Buea is of immense significance of the universality of the culture and for that matter, British Administrative officials had not even frequented this part of the Territory.

Furthermore, the British administrators throughout the colonial period were extremely limited in numbers. The extensive, road-less, mountainous Bamenda Division for example, in the 1950s was administered by only four DOs, who toured the area either on foot or on horseback. Worse still, always aloof, they operated from their Government Residential Areas (CRAs), where they literally barricaded themselves, sufficiently distanced from the "Native Quarters" and even for purposes of leisure when they would more easily have been disposed to mixing up with the locals; they continued to be cocooned in Senior Service (SS) Clubs, microcosms of apartheid. Areas of social contact were rare or simply non-existent. These

---

[106] Inculturation is used in the context of Ecumenism. See Austin Flannery, ed., *Vatican Council 11, The Conciliar and Post Conciliar Documents*, Dominican Publications, Dublin, 1988, pp.41-45. This involves the incorporation of certain cultural traits into the liturgy.

[107] John Percival, *The 1961 Cameroon Plebiscite, Choice or Betrayal*, Langaa Research And Publishing CIG, Mankon, Bamenda, 2008 P xiv.

British officials were therefore at best a source of curiosity whenever they ventured out on tour than people who were expected to influence the masses with their Anglo-Saxon mores.[108] In fact, IR and its elaboration in euphemistic terminologies and titles, such as the "paramountcy of African interests "or the "Dual Mandate" only further prescribed separate development for Africans and Europeans or more appropriately, the development of Africans in European interests. It was an expansion of these policies that fertilised the grandiose theories behind the evolution of apartheid in South Africa and the "Unilateral Declaration of Independence" (UDI) by Ian Smith in Southern Rhodesia.

*Fig 27. The Southern Cameroons National Assembly in Session*

Hence, to term what emerged at the end of the Germano-British colonial administration in Southern Cameroons exclusively as an "Anglo-Saxon" culture, an idea that in itself would certainly have turned any typical Englishman blue, is a total misnomer and contradiction of terms. Rather, as we have seen, it was an overwhelmingly mission-generated culture zealously defended by the missionaries, catechists, pastors and their fervent Christian followers; the bedrock of which was native to the Territory. The British contribution to this notion though high-sounding,

---

[108] Mary Elizabeth Oake, *No place for a White Woman*, Neill and Co.' Ltd, Edinburgh, nd.; also W.F Newington, "West Coast Memories", 1993, an unpublished autobiography.

comparatively comprised little more than the intangible coating of administrative and political structure, which for that matter they shared in good measure with the Germans and, within which, bonded by a common colonial past, the Southern Cameroons state structures developed.

## Components of a Unique Southern Cameroons Culture

The formation of a genuine Christian culture in Southern Cameroons did not come easy. This was because in the first place, in the context of the time, i.e. post World War 1, after the defeat and expulsion of the Germans, only new Christian missionary organizations without any German connections were to be allowed to enter the Territory now under British Mandate. These were not easy to find. When finally admitted they had to formally established firm Christian structures that could propagate such a culture. Unfortunately the war had totally destroyed whatever ground work had been laid by various missionary organizations under German colonial rule. In fact, during the period 1915- (1920) - 1922, there were absolutely no European missionaries in British Southern Cameroons. The French Sacred Heart Fathers who briefly operated in Bamenda from 1920-1923 were neither welcomed by the powerful traditional rulers in Bamenda nor by the British Administration who as an alternative applied for a British Catholic Missionary organization to replace them.

After lengthy administrative and diplomatic negotiations involving White Hall, Mill Hill and the Holy See, this finally resulted in the arrival of the Mill Hill Missionaries in the country in March 1922. They were closely followed by the Cameroon Baptist Missionaries in 1924 and the Basel Missionaries in 1925. These were therefore the three mainline missionary organizations that operated in the Territory up to and beyond independence and reunification. Given that the British Colonial Administration fully conscious of their limitations literally surrendered all educational and socio-cultural development in the hands of these religious organizations, it is little wonder that Christian influence came to permeate the totality of Southern Cameroonian life. Thus, they set up their pastoral structures to cover up the entire territory, the North and South West Regions, which by 1960 had reached every nook and cranny of the territory and which even up to independence the Government influence had not touched.

However, during the early decades of the introduction of Indirect Rule, better known as Native Administration (NA) exercised through Native Authorities (NA) up to 1930, relations between the Traditional Establishment and the Roman Catholic Mission authorities were characterized by mounting hostility. In practical terms, this ranked the Rev. Fathers, Catechists and their zealous followers against the Fons and notables, who as NAs reigned supreme especially in the Bamenda Grasslands and Mamfe staunchly backed by the British Administration since these Fons acted as Native Authorities. There were flash points in the "Mission Villages" (Catholic Mission settlements) at Shisong in Kumbo, Njinikom in Kom and Baseng, under Mamfe.

These conflicts arose largely from the fact that the Catholic Church emphasized monogamy and strongly opposed the brand of polygamy practised by the Fons and above all, the manner in which they recruited girls for their vast harems sometimes running to over a hundred as in Kom. Since the Fons acted as NAs, they received the unflinching support of administrators like Mr. EJ Arnett, the Resident to whom IR, had become an inviolable doctrine "a divine revelation, a sort of natural law".[109] These disagreements intensified to the extent that by 1930, the British colonial administration threatened expelling the Mill Hill Missionaries if they persisted in undermining the authority of the Fons who were the NAs. However, by 31 October 1931, the tremendous work the missionaries were carrying out and the defects in the NA system were becoming apparent and an agreement was reached with these realities in mind.

In fact, between 1930 and 1940, beginning with the suicide of Chief Ntoko Epie, the District Head of Bakossi in prison at Kumba in August 1932, while facing embezzlement charges of tax money, the bulk of the Fons and District Heads throughout the country either served short terms of imprisonment or were disciplined for one fault or the other. Until then, Chief Ntoko Epie had been brandished by the administration as an exemplary Native Authority. After this rude shock, it turned out that most of the NAs had been exceeding their powers and there were practically no

---

[109] NAB Resident to SSP 14/3/31 BA Sd/1931/5

chiefs and DHs, grassland or forest, who under the circumstances could fully satisfy the conflicting demands of their traditions and the prescriptions of the NA, and remain faithful to both. At about the same time, the Roman Catholic Mission was gradually being vindicated and emerged as a most viable partner in development on whom the Colonial Government increasingly leaned.[110] Through their control of education, which was the greatest catalyst in development the main line Missions acting as Voluntary Agencies came to literally control the socioeconomic and, eventually political life of the country in every sense. Rightly as Francis Cardinal Arinze put it in the context of the time:

> The school was a major means not just of evangelization – in the sense of the baptized, but of what we now call development, all round development. We can say that the school at least in Nigeria, but also in many other parts of Africa, is the most powerful instrument of integral human development[111].

And, indeed, Mission culture in Southern Cameroons went even much further, it was all pervasive. Alone, by 1940 there were some thirty Roman Catholic Mission (RCM) Stations each staffed with at least two expatriate missionary priests. Structurally, each of these comprised a complex of: a permanent church building, presbytery, a primary school with staff quarters, a convent, a health centre (dispensary and maternity home), frequently with an orphanage attached. Practically, wherever, there was a Mission Station whether Basel or Cameroon Baptist Mission (CBM) with a resident missionary, these structures were replicated. There spontaneously sprang up around them subsidiary settlements of people who supplied vital services as: cooks, stewards, artisans, drivers, mechanics, bricklayers, carpenters, mechanics and electricians with a whole range of unskilled labourers: carriers, sawyers and stone diggers. To various

---

[110] Ndi, "Mill Hill Missionaries and the State in Southern Cameroons, 1922-1972," A Thesis Submitted in Partial Fulfilment for the Doctor of Philosophy of the University of London, 1983. Pp. 199-200.

[111] *The Universe*, Sunday March 14, 2004. P.14

degrees in addition to the Christians and products of the schools, these categories of workers were usually ardent agents of Mission culture. Given that unlike government headquarters, which were situated along the main roads, these Mission institutions were established in remote areas, where they could better meet the spiritual and material needs of the masses. Their multiplier effect could therefore well be imagined.

In addition, the Christian conduct and influence emanating from the categories of the 'nuclear' occupants of the Mission compounds on the surrounding communities was considerable. Other than those named above, these individuals usually included the headmaster, teachers, catechists and their families; the priests, Rev. Sisters, Rev. Pastors and their families, nurses, technicians and domestic servants. These, besides the school pupils constituted an impressive combination. Elite of sorts, they formally and informally became role models especially as they lived close to and shared in the lives of the community; their joys and sorrows, successes and failures, hopes and fears; the ingredients of love which also bred patriotism. Gradually with increasing interaction they unmasked the myth of the white man and instilled the sense of the equality of all races as preached from the scriptures.

As indicated above, Rev. and Mrs. Gilbert Schneider, dedicated American Baptist missionaries from 1947 till the mid-1950s operated a Baptist Mission Dispensary at Warwar in Mambila, on the northern border between Southern Cameroons and Nigeria. The point is that, here, these missionaries freely intermingled with the local people and brought up their children in their midst without undue discrimination.[112] However, this was only one of a dozen of such missionary families, who reached out to remote Southern Cameroons peasant families in very simple and practical ways. These descriptions only cover the period up to the acquisition of the Quasi Federal status in Southern Cameroons in October 1954, after which there was explosive development especially in the field of post-primary teacher, technical and secondary education, which further empowered the people in all other areas of work and development.

---

[112] Ndi, *Mill Hill Missionaries in Southern West Cameroon,* 1922-72 Prime Partners In Nation Building, Paulines, 2005. P.97

Government reliance on the Missions was colossal; to imagine that out of over six hundred primary schools in 1960, Government and Native Authority Schools accounted for less than a handful, where even the staff comprised of Mission products with routine morning prayers and moral instruction in these institutions.

Consequently, Mission contributions to the evolution of patriotism, nationalism and national identity resulted in the first place from the core Christian message itself of fraternal love and Christ's appeal that all may be one. That is to say they had a strong spiritual content. To quote an extreme example of a nationalist, who is generally classified as a Communist; Um Nyobe, founder of the UPC, who preached immediate reunification and independence of the Trust Territories of British Southern Cameroons and French Cameroon. As a prelude to his ideology, he postulated that: "God Himself knows that Cameroon is one." However, the Christian missionaries in a mild manner propagated unity through their network of catechumenates, congregations, churches, mission fields, parishes and dioceses within acknowledged hierarchies, throughout the entire territory touching all the nooks and crannies.

At the spiritual level, practically, all the denominations demonstrated their belief in this philosophy when they spontaneously routinely offered prayers for peace, unity, harmony and prosperity for the pastoral and political leadership of the country. Then of course, through their educational institutions, which catered for several thousand children at the primary school level and a few thousands in the expanding secondary school institutions, their hospitals, dispensaries, maternity homes, leprosaria, convents and other institutions, which were attended by all and sundry from all parts of the country there was a fusion of different ethnic groups, thus breaking tribal, geographical, social and other barriers. With the progress of time and the rush to opening post primary institutions direct lessons in civics, history and geography further enlightened the children and in later years progressed through various alumni associations. It is remarkable that Southern Cameroons enjoyed free primary and adult education by 1960 and that by 1970 it had achieved the 100% trained teacher target prescribed by UNESCO, one of the few African countries to hit that mark when contrasted with the fact that at reunification, Republic of Cameroon was still struggling to set up a credible teacher training system and ended up absorbing the mass of trained Southern Cameroons teachers by offering higher salaries.

## Proto-Nationalism

The Christian Missions were not only catalysts of development; they spearheaded political thought and action as well. Herbert Kane, a prominent missiologist explicitly maintains that the contributions of the Christian church to reform and development in Africa have been great and that without the groundwork laid by them especially in education, "not a single country in black Africa would be independent today" and that no one knows this better than the African himself.[113] Narrowing down this analysis to Nigeria of which Southern Cameroons was for forty years an integral part, Professor Ayandele another prominent missiologist, adds that, ironically, it was these Christian missionaries, who heralded British rule in Nigeria and, who when the time was ripe, also began the process of its termination, with the Church acting as the cradle of nationalism. He goes further to state that:

> There was hardly any strand of nationalist movement between 1922 and 1960… the origins of which cannot be traced to missionary activity. The first generation of educated Nigerians was pre-eminently equipped for a nationalist task by their learning. Unrestricted access to the bible, with its notions of equitability, justice and non-racialism, provided the early converts with a valid weapon, which they were not reluctant to employ against the missionaries, who brushed their ideas aside.[114]

---

[113] Herbert Kane, *Understanding Christian Missions*, Baker Book House, Michigan, 1976, pp. 221-224.

[114] EA Ayandele, The *Missionary Impact On Modern Nigeria 1842 -1914*, Longmans Green and co Ltd. London 1966

By post-Second World War up to 1954 Southern Cameroonians had begun identifying themselves as a geographical, economic, social, cultural, spiritual and political entity within the proto-nationalist organizations like GJ Mbene's Cameroon Welfare Union formed at Victoria in 1939, as a forum for raising issues in protest against British neglect of Southern Cameroons by having it administered as an integral part of Nigeria without representation. At about the same time in Lagos, Mr. Paul M Kale with Dr. EML Endeley, JN Foncha and others raised the banner of the Cameroon Youth League on the pattern of the Nigerian Youth League seeking representation, secession from Nigeria and regional status. It was from associations like these that the next set of proto-nationalist organizations like the Cameroon National Federation of Endeley, a transformation of the CYL, which advocated separation from Nigeria and eventual unification with French Cameroon.

The Kamerun United National Congress (KUNC) of Robert Jabea K Dibongue and Nerius N Mbile, which pursued a similar policy both of which eventually combined with Endeley, formed the Kamerun National Congress, (KNC)[115] the first nationwide political party still aimed at secession from Nigeria. The Kamerun People's Party equally formed at in 1953 at the Mamfe All Party Conference stood for integration with Nigeria. All of these were organized just before the Quasi Federal status was achieved the following year, precisely in October 1954. After the attainment of the Quasi Federal Status, Southern Cameroons continued to contribute six members to the Federal House of Representatives in Nigeria, one from each Division, one of whom was appointed Federal Minister in Nigeria. This explains how it was that Chief Victor E Mukete became Minister without Portfolio and later Federal Minister of Research and Information from 1955 -1959 in the Federal Republic of Nigeria.[116]

However, what is significant is that all the political actors who emerged without exception were staunch Christians among whom were a handful

---

[115] There were numerous personality clashes among: Endeley, Kale, Mbile And Dibongue in quest for leadership so much so that although Mbile And Dibongue were at the helm of the KUNC Mbile had opted out and it was endeley and Dibongue who merged the CNH and KUNC to form the KNC while Mbile and Kale formed the KPP.

[116] For details see, *My Odyssey: The Story Of Cameroon Reunification*

of Church Ministers. The various political parties all professed solid pacifist culture drawing on spiritual and ethical values which advocated non-violence and respect for human life. This was profound and explains why throughout the political history of the territory, even during its most turbulent period there was never any resort to violence. Contesting political parties were known to travel in the same campaign convoys and would use a common land-rover roof or soap box to attack each other's political platform and thereafter sit down to share jokes, common meals and drinks[117].

The same spirit prevailed in the Southern Cameroons House of Assembly, where after hot debates on the floor MPs retired to the Senior Service Club for mutual coffee breaks or to the parliamentary flats where they resided during parliamentary sessions to share common rooms, facilities, exchange views and meals. The prevailing adage was that of; "the force of argument and not the argument of force". One distinguished occasion was when Foncha defeated Endeley at the general election in February 1959: at the handing over, the spouses and their husbands were caught on camera embracing each other. At all times and in all places, this was unique.

On their return from the UN after the plebiscite disagreements, Foncha and Endeley undertook a truce and called for peace and harmony to prevail. And, indeed there was reported 'total agreement at the Bamenda All Party Conference" in late June 1961 and with the same spirit proceeded to the Foumban Constitutional Conference the following July, where again the two men leading the powerful delegation seem to have sung from the same song sheet. At the close of the deliberations all is said to have concluded in perfect harmony. However, the pacifist, non-violent, harmonious, Christian stamp inherent in Southern Cameroons political ethos was abundantly demonstrated on the floor of the Foumban constitutional conference by EML Endeley in his opening speech when he directly addressed President Ahidjo, the UPC Terrorists and the delegates noting unequivocally:

---

[117] Mbile. Eyewitness p.170

*Fig 27a. Top, voters line up for Plebiscite vote; Bottom, Premier J N Foncha at a Press Conference after Plebisicite*

*Fig 27b. Top, Bamenda All Party Conference 26-28 June 1961. Note Fon Galega II of Bali, Prominent among others; Middle Foncha, PM with Jua, Muna and Kemcha to his left; Note the presence of three British colonial officials in attendance including the Attorney General (It is repeatedly alleged that the British were not consulted or invited to the Bamenda all party conference nor to the Foumban Conference but they were present at both)*

*Fig 27c. Top: some Southern Cameroons delegates to the Foumban Conference flew in by air from Tiko International Airport. Here at the Koutaba Military Airport, left to right are: ST Muna, PM Kemcha, Dr. EML Endeley and JN Foncha. Bottom: Delegates at the Foumban Conference in front of the sultan's palace: the three central figures are: President Ahmadou Ahidjo, JN Foncha and Sultan Njimoulouh.*

# THE SOUTHERN CAMEROONS: CHARACTER

*Fig 27d. Top: Note, President Ahidjo in white, flanked by Charles Assale and Moussa Yaya on his right. Bottom: Inside the Conference Hall, Note Endeley and Foncha with microphones in front of them, flanked by Muna and Kemcha on the right with Jua and the Attorney General to the left*

*Fig 27e. Top: cross section of audience at the Foumban Conference; Middle: Prime Minister, JN Foncha decorated by Sultan Njimoulouh as Prime Minister, Charles Assale looks on Bottom: in the Conference Hall, sitting right to left are: the Attorney General, Jua, Foncha and Muna.*

*Fig 27f. Top left, Malcolm Milne, Deputy Commissioner of Southern Cameroons receives President Ahmadou Ahidjo at Tiko International Airport as he comes to preside over the independence day celebrations. Note Joseph Lafon in the background. Top right, Ahmadou Ahidjo presides over the independence celebrations in Buea. Bottom left, Independence Day celebration at Buea Mountain Hotel: The British Ambassador to Cameroon, C E King reads the Queen's speech. Bottom right; Governor General of Nigeria, Sir James Robertson, left, received by JO Field and JN Foncha*

*Fig 27g. Left, Endeley and wife; Top Right and bottom, Foncha and Ahidjo dance at the Independence celebration, Mountain Hotel Buea.*

If I, as opposition leader, and my colleagues can reconcile with Foncha, I cannot see why those who are the opposition and gone wild in the bush cannot reconcile with your government. I have had great reason to feel that Mr. Foncha is an enemy to me and I would not work together with him, as the terrorists have felt against president Ahidjo. We have come to set an example that by working together, we can make a better country. If by this example which I have set with my colleagues we cannot produce a peaceful Cameroon, then we will be a laughing stock to the country.[118] (My emphasis)

This is explicit enough and speaks volumes of what had happened and what was possible for Southern Cameroons all being equal. Perhaps what little remains to add is that in proceeding to the Foumban Conference both the Government and the Opposition subscribed an equal number of delegates as they had done at the Bamenda All Party Conference and that they travelled as a unit to Foumban by air from Tiko or by land from Bamenda. In fact, the CPNC leaders made more interventions than the KNDP during the discussions as borne by the records. Again, but for the destabilizing agents factored in by Ahidjo, and obstacles raised during the coalition between these parties, under AN Jua in 1965, the prospects were bright for a unique One Party State constructed democratically.

However, the process was foiled by Ahidjo who saw it as an obstacle to his brand of One Party rule especially as he was poised to launch the CNU as his mouth piece and could not brood any contrary opinion to his. In short, the CNU soon became his oracle; one that recognised only his voice and no other. Already by this time, he had literally banished resistance to his rule and placed all the opposition leaders in Republic of Cameroon behind bars and had come to Foumban with only a handful of twelve delegates exclusively members of his UC party, while on the other hand, Foncha and Endeley turned up as a team with a delegation of twenty-five Southern Cameroonians comprising a cross section of all the political parties, traditional rulers, civil society and the administration! What is more, they turned up at the Foumban Conference speaking with one voice as can be found in the verbatim reports of that conference just as they had done at the Bamenda All Party Conference prior to proceeding to Foumban, a month earlier. All the press reports, official and private confirmed the fact that the Foumban Constitutional Conference concluded in perfect harmony receiving standing ovations from the audience.[119] The problems with reunification and the premature demise of the

---

[118] *Southern Cameroons, Press Release* No. 1468.

[119] Southern Cameroons Government, *Press Release no. 468 of July 24th 1961.* "Foumban Conference ends in complete agreement on major issues"

FRC definitely cannot be found in the procedures and recommendations reached at Foumban.

## Chapter Four

# THE EMERGENCE OF A GENUINE DEMOCRATIC CULTURE

## National Integration: Building Socio-Religious and Political Bridges

Southern Cameroons naturally bisected into the North and South West Regions quite easily lent itself to the introduction of the British colonial policy of "Indirect Rule." Practically this was translated into "Native Administration" and executed through Native Authorities, Native Courts and Native Treasuries which with further evolution were combined into federations. In fact, the system can be said to have carried out administrative business at the local level with excellent results. On the other hand, the various Mission denominations viz: the Roman Catholic Mission, the Basel Mission and the Cameroon Baptist Mission generally adopted subtle, fraternal approaches towards blending the scores of disparate ethnic entities that constituted Southern Cameroons into a genuinely amalgamated community. However, this did not come easy as colonial rule borne out of rivalry introduced Christianity injected with the germ of division.

As a result the fierce inter-denominational rivalry inherited with colonial rule from foreign missionaries reached a climax by the 1940s and gradually began dissipating by the late 1950s, it being realised that religious squabbling obstructed development, rendered cordial relations among neighbouring villages and even between members of the same family holding different religious convictions hostile, unpleasant and ultimately unchristian. Fortunately with educational advancement, nationalism and movement towards independence by the mid to late sixties, there was a rapid onset of mutual understanding, tolerance and cooperation among the various Christian denominations emphasising the real essence of Christianity centred on fraternal love. This entailed increased coming together formally and informally, for joyous and sorrowful occasions, ecumenical services, prayers for Christian unity and joint fund-raising activities for church projects.

Above all there was the introduction of the Focolare Movement initiated by Chiara Lubich, a deeply religious and pious Italian lady from the adverse experiences of the First World War. This world-wide ecumenical organisation with its headquarters in Fontem, has branches in Bamenda, Buea and Douala, preaches and practises living the "Word of Life" towards the objective that "all may be one". Periodically they organise the "Mariapolis" an ecumenical jamboree bringing together Christians and even Moslems of all denominations in fraternal love, towards living the moment. On the whole, the trend has been one in which the various main line Christian denominations, which have thoroughly penetrated both the North and South West Regions to their extremities organised from outstations at the grassroots, through churches, congregations, parishes up to dioceses, presbyteries and fields. Individually and collectively, they establish a marvellous net-work of communications for holistic evangelisation using their reputable educational, health, social welfare services and institutions to reach out to the masses. It is therefore significant that some of the early politicians were pastors and in fact, that all the political leaders were practising Christians.

However, for the Christian denominations, the Catholic Church as a matter of policy ensured that admissions into their pioneer institutions in Southern Cameroons such as: St. Joseph's College, Sasse; Queen of the Holy Rosary College, Okoyong; St. Francis', Training College, Fiango, Kumba; St. Peter's College, Bambui; St. Paul's College, Bonjongo and Regina Pacis College Mutengene had stipulated quotas for admission from each of the political Divisions in the Country as well as from the Protestant Denominations. This was mandatory.

To different degrees the BM and the CBM pursued similar policies in institutions like Cameroon Protestant College, Bali; Saker Baptist College, Victoria and Joseph Merrick Baptist College, Ndu. In fact, this was colonial government policy as well and so each institution was a microcosm of the entire territory. Consequently, up to the present moment this is replicated in the alumni entrenched throughout the territory. All of this was besides the manner in which these religious bodies were organised demographically, structurally and the way in which they deployed their personnel throughout the Country, which evidently, positively made for national integration and maintained a North-South West balance. National integration resulting from these institutions has remained on the increase. Increasingly, there are numerous levels and occasions for interdenominational interaction especially among the mainline Christian denominations; the Catholic, Presbyterian and Baptist over ordinations, baptisms, raising of funds for various development projects, weddings, Lenten and Easter celebrations and countless others. There are literally, statutory ecumenical celebrations such as the annual week of Christian unity, which bring together all denominations in common prayer.[120]

*Fig 28. Mungo Bridge christened "Reunification Bridge"*

On the other hand, the strenuous efforts of the main political actors towards bridging the gaps and forging an organic political integration

---

[120] Generally this takes place from 18th -25th January every year.

between the peoples of the Forest Zone and those of the Bamenda Grasslands are well documented. These efforts were clearly demonstrated in the nature, formation pattern and composition of the various political parties and governments that surfaced in the heydays of multiparty democracy in Southern (West) Cameroons. During the first elections held in the Territory in 1954, Endeley's Kamerun National Congress (KNC) was the only party, and it carried with it all the thirteen MPs, assigned to the Southern Cameroons in the Eastern Region of Nigeria House of Assembly.

Conventionally and rationally, seven of these were selected from the Bamenda Grasslands and six from the Forest and coastal south. Endeley's leadership position was wholly unchallenged. In the 1953 election to the Eastern House of Assembly, the KNC won twelve of the thirteen seats, seven of which came from the Grasslands, five from the Forest Zone, and one Independent MP, Hon SE Ncha from Mamfe Division. Following the granting of the Quasi Federal status to Southern Cameroons in 1954, Endeley as Leader of Government Business formed the first Government, which significantly included Messrs. Solomon T Muna, Vincent T Lainjo and Rev. Jeremiah C Kangsen from the Bamenda Grasslands with only Messrs. Samson A George and FN Ajebe-Sone from the Forest Zone. However, in 1957, after the first truly multiparty election keenly fought by Mbile's Kamerun Peoples' Party (KPP), formed in1953 and Foncha's, Kamerun National Democratic Party (KNDP) formed in 1955; the KNC won six seats, the KNDP, five and the KPP, two of the thirteen parliamentary seats. Again the Government which Endeley formed in 1958 was balanced and comprised; Rev. Jeremiah Ando Seh and Vincent T Lainjo from Bamenda and NN Mbile and FN Ajebe Sone from the Forest zone.

## A Magnificent, Peaceful Hand-Over of Power: 1959

The 1959 elections to the Southern Cameroons House of Assembly were still more fiercely and keenly fought with the KNDP winning fourteen seats in the enlarged Assembly of twenty-six places, while the KNC/KPP Alliance won twelve. After the defection of Hon. JM Boja, a Wum Member of Parliament from the KNDP to the KNC/KPP Alliance, Parliament was stalemated at 13:13, although the KNDP formed the Government with Mr. Foncha as Premier. Again, the Foncha Government in terms of balancing the North-South divide, like Endeley's before him was enlightening as he even went further to topple the balance in favour of the South West Region. In his cabinet of ten members, seven positions including that of Speaker went to the Forest Zone while only four went to the Northern Grasslanders. Another democratic dimension of the 1959 elections is that although they were organised by Premier Endeley (KNC), they were marginally won by Mr. Foncha, the KNDP Opposition leader; followed by a peaceful, harmonious and dignified handover of power.

In like manner, on 31 March 2015, Nigeria made political history when General Mohammadu Buhari, Leader of the Opposition All Progressive Congress Party (APC) floored President Goodluck Jonathan the sitting President in a presidential election by a wide margin of over 2.5 million votes to take over that highly coveted, powerful office. Nigeria, the largest, richest and most dominant African nation currently has been facing serious challenges including: widespread corruption, crushing poverty and above all, the Boko Haram insurgency. This event was considered such a unique experience in Nigerian political history that its leaders and the country at large were inundated with congratulatory and good will messages from top world leaders: American, British, French, German and Russian because this was the first time ever in over half a century of independence that the country was achieving this stunning democratic victory. All predictions both from within and outside had painted doom and gloom from the sad experience of fifty-four years of independence when the country had seen nothing but bloody take-overs, coup d'états, military overthrows, assassinations, chaos and worse of all, one of the most bloody and fratricidal civil wars in African history.[121]

Thus placed in context, it would easily be recalled that for fifty-six years, 1922-1961 Britain officially stubbornly administered Southern Cameroons as an integral part of its Nigerian Colony against all counsel at both the League of Nations and the United Nations that it being a Trust Territory, it deserved to be administered separately so as to receive closer attention. As independence approached, Britain and Nigeria did everything to frustrate Southern Cameroons attaining independence as a separate

---

[121] The Biafran War raged ferociously with devastating effects from 1966-1970.

state and imposed premature reunification with Republic of Cameroon on its citizens at the Plebiscite of 11 February 1961. British Northern Cameroons, which, unfortunately fell prey to the Anglo-Nigerian ploys and became *Sardauna's Province* and later, Gongola State suffered massive socio-cultural, economic and political marginalisation and neglect. Because of this backwardness, it easily fell prey to the agents of Islamic Fundamentalism and became the hot bed of '*Boko Haram*' ("Western Education is bad").

In comparison Southern Cameroons, which had survived these British and Nigerian intrigues after disentangling itself from the Eastern Region Crises in 1953, worked out its own salvation and soon distinguished itself, as the most democratic, most peaceful, literally corruption free state with a blossoming middle sized, self-sufficient economy. As a consequence, its citizens were relatively happy, progressive and understandably optimistic everything being equal.[122] Remarkably, the democratic handover of power which marked the apogee of its 'Golden Age', happened some fifty-four years ago, precisely in February 1959, when its political leadership demonstrated an even more magnanimous and glorious handover of power which in the Southern Cameroons instance was taken as absolutely normal attracting no undue local or international attention. This practically demonstrates how far ahead of Nigeria Southern Cameroons was in matters of democratic culture.

However, in a proper context and in comparison, the outstanding point is that the acclamation accorded the Nigerian leaders, especially President Goodluck Jonathan, the incumbent for the gracious and magnanimous manner in which he conceded power and congratulated his victorious opponent, General Mohammadu Buhari,[123] was happening fifty-six years after the Southern Cameroons experience, its size notwithstanding. Of equal importance is the fact that it had gone through a similar but more glorious, memorable and fantastic experience as the occasion went beyond

---

[122] The Southern Cameroons *Golden Age* was prematurely terminated by the suppressive Ahidjo Regime.

[123] This has been headline news in mass media; eg. *The Post Weekender*, no. 01616 of Friday April 03, 2015, p.1.

## THE EMERGENCE OF A GENUINE DEMOCRATIC CULTURE

a mere phone call. As described earlier, this, happened after Dr. EML Endeley, the incumbent Prime Minister, did not simply call to congratulate his victorious opponent, Dr. John N Foncha to concede victory, but together with his spouse went over to physically shake hands and embrace each other in public and in the full glare of cameras, which documented that event for posterity.

This of course, took place at the apogee of the Golden Age of Southern Cameroons but was regarded as in the ordinary course of things and nothing extraordinary. What had happened was a sequence in the normal political life in the Southern Cameroons State; peaceful, self-sufficient corruption -free and enjoying all the internationally prescribed freedoms. It is this startling contrast going down memory lane nearly sixty years ago, that vividly marks out the Golden Age of Southern Cameroons as what it became after disentangling itself from Nigerian politics and was poised for greater achievements had the life of that State not been prematurely blighted in 1972.

*Fig 29. Mr J N Foncha, Vice-President of the Federal Republic of Cameroon and Mr. A N Jua, PM of West Cameroon inspect Guard of Honour*

## Political Landscape 1951-72: Contextual Analysis

Quite a number of facts can be deduced from the analysis of the political landscape in Southern Cameroons broadly, from 1951-72. In the first place, membership of the major political parties generally cut across ethnic, regional and religious divides. In fact, until 1955, all political leadership in the Country unquestionably originated from the coastal South with: Kale and the CYL Endeley and the CFN, KNC and CPNC; Dibongue and the FCWU, KUNC and KNC, KPP and KUC while Mbile led the KPP. Endeley's leadership position was largely unchallenged and undisputed and if anything, it was Mbile and Kale his "kinsmen" who first questioned his integrity, authority and reliability, and formed the first political parties to challenge him.

Again, in all the governments he formed and led, Endeley leaned on northern grassland support, while Foncha and Jua relied preponderantly on politicians from the Forest Region in their administrations. In fact, in the governments he formed in 1954 and 1958, Endeley leaned heavily on grassland politicians, while Foncha and did the same thing with bias in favour of the forest and coastal political leadership. As regards debates in parliament and campaigns in the field, it is reported that the KNC and KNDP politicians occasionally travelled in the same convoys, "attacked" each other's platforms, mounted on the same landrover roof or soap box to deliver their addresses and, after that shared common food and drinks.

The same attitude obtained during Parliamentary debates, when Government and Opposition MPs would bitterly assail each other on the floor but retire to friendly chats in the coffee room during breaks in the Buea Mountain Club and elsewhere. Even one like Mbile, who was very vocal and frequently uncharitable in criticising his political opponents, admits of the 1957 election that: *"Though the election campaigns sounded bitter and acrimonious there was always some element of humour, laughter and song that accompanied the meetings."*[124] He further makes the pertinent remark that:

---

[124] Mbile, p. 96. He was a sharp critic of the Grassland hegemony of Foncha and Muna but also thought Endeley, with whom he frequently disagreed and agreed, was certainly an insolent weakling "not worth two pence when it comes to facing consequences squarely, and your inglorious capitulation during the 1953 constitution crises gives the

*"It is to our credit that even in the years of bitter politics, there was not a single case of extreme action like murder, violent assault or people 'jumping into the bush"* (i.e. terrorism). He continues: "We fought the plebiscite and we bowed to the will of the majority of our people right or wrong".[125] Unlike the *'maquisards'* in French Cameroon, now rehabilitated and generally recognised as nationalists, "freedom fighters and liberators who fought and sacrificed their lives for the freedom that Cameroon now enjoys", there were no such political martyrs in Southern Cameroons.

Dr. EML Endeley, OBE easily the best-known Southern Cameroonian political leader tended to be mercurial. At one level, he was the epitome of all that could be desired in leadership, statesmanship, physical build, intelligence, simplicity and self-abnegation, but he could also vacillate, as over the issue of reunification, or become vindictive and tactlessly arrogant, as when he advocated the partitioning of the country during the 1961 plebiscite declaring that, he would not accept, "to jump into a precipice with the tribes of Bamenda, Wum, Nkambe and Mamfe because they have more tribesmen to cast blind votes".[126] Ironically, not only did the CPNC lose massively in the plebiscite; he personally lost by 75% in his own Victoria constituency, while Nkambe voted 66% in his favour for integration with Nigeria! Generally throughout the political life of Southern (West) Cameroon, Victoria from which Endeley came remained a KNDP stronghold, while Nkambe certainly and Kumba (after the creation of the KNC/KPP alliance) frequently, tended to be loyal to the KNC. Yet Nkambe was in the extreme north of the Bamenda Grasslands, while Victoria was at the heel of the Coastal, Forest Region. Mr. Emmanuel Aka converts this analysis into simple statistical form and maintains that:

---

world a vivid memory of how much you can be relied upon to face unpleasant results of a stand.'" See Ngoh, Constitutional Developments pp. 151-152.

[125] Ibid., Mbile, *Eye Witness* p. 332.

[126] Endeley described voters in Mamfe and Bamenda as primitive naked, ignorant tribesmen and boasted that even if they didn't vote for him, trees and stones would elect him. Also, Aka, *The British Southern Cameroons*, p. 195. On resigning from the KNC in 1958, Mr. Joseph N Lafon among many things accused Endeley of insensitivity, arrogance, tribalism and vindictiveness. See, *The Cameroon Voice*, Vol.1, No. 111, Dec. 1958, p7. The paper was published in University College, Ibadan.

In fact, unlike Nigeria and French Cameroon, the main political parties in Southern Cameroons were national rather than tribal and regional until after independence. In the 1957 elections, for example, the KNC got only 38% of the votes in Victoria; 42%in Kumba; 39% in Mamfe and 51% in the Grassfields region, while the rest of the votes were given to the KNDP. Indeed many of Endeley's staunch supporters were from the Grassfields Region and many of Foncha's strong supporters were from the coastal districts.[127]

It has also been repeatedly stressed that the democratic process in Southern Cameroons was reasonably well developed and that elections were comparatively free, fair and transparent especially during the peak of its Golden Age, 1955 -1965. This fact is encapsulated in the glowing tribute paid at the highest level to the people of Southern Cameroons by the Iranian UN plebiscite Commissioner himself, Dr. Djalal Abdoh in his Report to the UN General Assembly in which he expressly noted that:

> *One of the outstanding aspects of the plebiscite in the Southern Cameroons was the remarkable calm, which prevailed during all its phases, despite the density of the political campaign during the last weeks preceding the polling.* It is with great satisfaction that I pay tribute to the people of Southern Cameroons for the respect they showed for law and order.[128] (My emphasis)

It is in the irony of things; that barely five years after reunification, the budding democratic State of West Cameroon was plunged into a single party dictatorship and thirty years later, the Republic of Cameroon into which it had become integrated was groaning under the phenomenon of the "Introduction of multiparty democracy".

---

[127] Ibid. Aka, For those who argue that the Victoria KNDP vote was influenced by the large 'grassland' settler element in that region, there is no equivalent explanation to offer in the case of Nkambe.

[128] The UN Plebiscite Commissioner's Report to the General Assembly, 1961, Addendum to agenda, item 13 para 112 p.1.

## Emergence of a Unique Public Service

On becoming Leader of Government Business and later, Premier of Southern Cameroons, Endeley recruited Nigerians, notably, the Yoruba of the Western Region into the civil service and the Judiciary until competent Southern Cameroonians could be trained to replace them. With the bitter experience of the Eastern Regional crisis, the Ibos for the time were purposely left out. The Southern Cameroons Public Service with an advisory Public Service Commission was instituted in February 1960. However, in 1958:

> Out of a total of 7.184 persons employed in the government service, 5.161 were Cameroonians, 1.877 were other Africans and 146 were non-Africans. Of this total, 4.328 were employed by the Department of Public Works. The number of Native Authority staff was estimated at 1810.[129]

Those engaged in the PWD were mostly labourers leaving less than 200 Cameroonians in the various strata of administration. This was a serious handicap. To make matters worse, as independence and reunification approached there were massive resignations of expatriate civil servants, some of which overtly were intended to embarrass and cause the collapse of the Foncha Administration. Above all, there was an exodus of Nigerians in the private sector, especially Ibos, the peak of which was a near fatal assassination attempt on Premier Foncha's life by three Ibibio men. They plotted and indeed undertook to derail his trolley as he travelled from Mudeka to Tiko on Sunday, 5 February 1961, leaving several members of his entourage and family seriously wounded and hospitalised.[130]

In the mean time, the Foncha Government through the, "Cameroonisation Office" engaged experienced, long serving Grade II Teachers into the

---

[129] UK Report 1959, p101.

[130] Mr. Foncha came out without a scratch but his son, Matthias Foncha and Private Sect, were badly injured. The police arrested the suspected assassins, Kamerun *Times*, 20 Jan. 1961. Story confirmed by Mrs Anna Foncha and Mr. Matthias Foncha himself.

civil service. For professionals, West Indian nationals were recruited into the judiciary and as secretaries, while Cameroonians were sought and sent for specialised training.[131] The government established the southern Cameroons Recruitment Committee in May 1959 with precise instructions to eliminate foreign domination in the civil service. The Cameroonisation policy was extended to the private sector, which led to a new breed of Cameroonian functionaries; bureaucrats and technocrats.

The Foncha Government applied this policy systematically and methodically; recuperating Cameroonians, who were working elsewhere and integrating them into the public service, while yet recruiting others afresh. Southern Cameroonians with expertise of any form were engaged and even the untrained and unskilled got jobs as cleaners and watchmen. The idea was first to be a Southern Cameroonian and then to train and excel on the job. However, to meet the manpower needs for the long run there was a massive education crusade. Grants in aid were given to the various Religious Denominations, while Government, the CDC and foreign scholarships were granted to Cameroonians studying in Nigeria, Ghana, and Tanzania as well as in Britain, Germany and the US. This system was so effective and productive that by the time of the merger of the civil service of West and East Cameroon to form a federal civil service, West Cameroon with only 20% of the population provided many more graduate civil servants than their East Cameroon counterpart.

The competence of the Southern-West Cameroon civil service remains inestimable, proverbial and nostalgic to those who experienced it. Operating without computers but equipped with highly motivated, assiduous and diligent personnel, a civil servant employed on 29th of the month was sure to be paid his due salary at month end just as those who retired had their pension benefits paid on the spot or spread over a period of months. Retirement was an occasion to look forward to after a job well done marked by celebrations festooned with medal awards, gifts, tributes and eulogies formally and officially by family, friends and colleagues.

---

[131] Group discussions with Messrs Foleng, Ebu etc. Mr. Jack Kisob was in charge of the Cameroonisation Office.

## THE EMERGENCE OF A GENUINE DEMOCRATIC CULTURE

## Harmony, Honesty, Political Consciousness

The warmest recognition of this class of workers (civil servants) came from Malcolm Milne, the Deputy Commissioner of Southern Cameroons, one best placed to have assessed them. Initially, for political reasons, he was also very critical of the Foncha Administration. However, towards the end of his service in Southern Cameroons and looking back in comparative terms with his time in Aden, Ghana and Nigeria, he rated the low to middle grade civil servants in Southern Cameroons as of exceptional quality. To him their watch words were honesty, loyalty, hard work and, above all, "service." And, of the top grade politicians with whom he worked from 1958-1961, which comprised a small government; in his estimate were: "Almost without exception people of high intelligence who knew exactly what to do"[132].

John Percival, another critical Englishman serving as one of the Commissioners of the United Nations Organised Plebiscite in Southern Cameroons in 1961, from far flung Bum Village in Wum Division over three hundred miles from Buea made a most pertinent remark of the advanced state of political alertness and moral probity of the people there. He noted that the people in general were very mature, knowledgeable, highly evolved ethically and politically. Wherever he went, the people wanted to have nothing doing with the Nigerians, whom they pejoratively considered 'cannibals' and the 'Frenchy people' whom they regarded as 'robbers', what they desired was 'independence' pure and simple, which the British Government and the United Nations suppressed. Of the extraordinary moral probity of the people, he notes:

In those days in Southern Cameroons theft was almost unknown. I left the house unlocked, eleven though it was stuffed with things that might have seemed highly desirable to most of the population. There were violent incidents …. but anyone who overstepped the mark was likely to be hauled in front of the local court by his neighbours. Nobody starved.

---

[132] See, Malcolm Milne, *No Telephone to Heaven*, p. 254; John Percival, the 1961 plebiscite; *choice or betrayal*, Langaa Research and Publishing CIG, Mankon, Bamenda 2008, p. xiv; Anthony Ndi, *Southern West Cameroon Revisited, 1950 -1972*, Paul's Press, Bamenda, 2013, p. 127.

Nobody was alone or uncared for.¹³³

Nor was John Percival's an isolated experience about the political outlook and moral values of the people. His colleague, Mr. K Lees, the Plebiscite Officer for Bamenda, another Englishman like himself, had similar experiences about the people in his own area of operation over one hundred miles away. He was frequently confronted in the field by the people who were puzzled by the attitudes of the British Government and the UN over the omission of the Third Option of independence for the impending plebiscite. In Lees' words: "One question was always asked: "Why have we not had a third choice? Why can we not stand alone? Why should a poor man sell his independence to join with bigger and richer men?"¹³⁴ This is to say it was a sort of universal desire manifested throughout the Territory and, finally it turned out that 'reunification' with the Republic of Cameroon was massively endorsed during the plebiscite simple because it was the only manageable alternative to independence. Even more so reunification was previewed by the KNDP as the final stage in the process after independence must have been achieved.

Despite the accusations, recriminations and threats to partition the Country that had characterised the campaigns leading up to the plebiscite, the spirit of peace and reconciliation continued to prevail. Accordingly, Premier JN Foncha and Dr. EML Endeley, Leader of the Opposition met at Buea on 11 November 1961, after the endorsement of the Plebiscite results by the 15th Session of the UN General Assembly, signed a truce and called on all citizens and organs of public opinion to refrain from all acts of provocation which would make unity difficult. The document further called on all political parties and interested bodies to make detailed studies of proposals with a view to evolving a draft constitution that would be generally acceptable to all the people.

This was one of those virtues that distinguished Southern Cameroonian politicians, the ability to forgive, forget and to move on - a typical Christian tenet. The same genial attitude was demonstrated at the handing-over ceremony after Foncha defeated Endeley in the 1959 elections,

---

[133] Ibid., Percival

[134] Ibid.

## THE EMERGENCE OF A GENUINE DEMOCRATIC CULTURE

which were acclaimed as free, fair, transparent and peaceful. The prevailing atmosphere on that occasion was one of genuine conviviality as the leaders and their spouses shook hands in public. This culture continued to evolve and mature with highlights demonstrated during the Bamenda All Party Conference, which brought together all the political parties, traditional rulers, the Native Authorities, the Administration, political pressure and student groups just as had been the case at the Mamfe All Party Plebiscite Conference in 1959. It was the same team that proceeded to Foumban the first historic meeting between the two former Trust Territories of Britain and France.

The point is that they came out with a consensus, unanimously endorsing a common platform for the Foumban Constitutional Conference and finally at Foumban itself they continued to speak with one voice. To immortalise this, Dr. Endeley declared in the face of the mortal divisions between Ahidjo's UC and the opposition parties, whose leaders were behind bars and made to pay heavy fines after which they were proscribed. The UPC leaders including those who had declared for peace were not spared, while as Endeley pointed out; he as the opposition leader and his colleagues had reconciled with Foncha. He could therefore not understand why Ahidjo and his opposition gone wild in the bush could not reconcile.[135] To further drive home the point of their unanimity between foncha and himself as well as their parties even more emphatically he further noted:

> We have come to set an example. I have come to set an example that by working together, we can make a better country. If by this example which I have set with my colleagues we cannot produce a peaceful Cameroon, then we will be a laughing stock to the country.[136]

Southern Cameroon politicians were generally knowledgeable, self confident and indeed proud individuals. Looking back at what took place at Foumban when the delegates were suddenly served copies of the highly

---

[135] *Press Release No. 1468*

[136] Ibid

centralised Republic of Cameroon constitution to critically examine and prepare for debate with their francophone counterparts. They took three and half instead of the five days allocated to them by President Ahidjo even though the document had to be translated into English from French. This gave them the opportunity to further demonstrate their political maturity, the distinction of their Anglo-Saxon heritage and expertise in the art of constitutional craft; in fact, superiority over their Francophone counterparts in such matters. Nerius Mbile confidently and proudly put it out graphically nearly forty years later thus:

> Indeed against the background of having attended four conferences, three in London and one in Nigeria, several of us in the west Cameroon contingent felt confident to be more than a match for our francophone counterparts for none of them could claim the expertise of more than four months ... and lobbying in the corridors and committee rooms of Lancaster House, London and Lagos. In men like Endeley, Foncha, Muna, Jua and my humble self, to name only these feeling was that in wrestlers on hearing the drums and music of their popular sport ...[137](sic)

In fact, for the famous Foumban Constitutional Conference both the KNDP ruling party and the CPNC opposition contributed an equal number of delegates with the entire Southern Cameroons contingent totalling 25 to Ahidjo's paltry 12, as he turned up without any of his own opposition party delegates, the leaders of which were all behind bars on spurious political charges. Difficult to relate at the time, this was the onset of the institution of his one party concept because after their release from jail, the parties were simply smothered.

However, what clearly emerges is that during this period Southern Cameroons had extensively evolved a mature political culture and was exceptionally directed by a leadership comprising: simple, visionary, austere, honest and peace loving and realistic people, almost without exception; vintage products of their epoch. As already largely demonstrated it was

---

[137] NN Mbile, *Cameroon Political Story; Memories of An Eyewitness* (Presbyterian printing press, Limbe, 1999) p.165.

distinguished not only by good governance, peaceful handover of power but the people living within their means enjoyed free primary and adult education, further crowned by ideal, efficient civil and judicial services practically corruption free. Again, the strong moral and ethical stamp was essentially christo-centric in substance. Credit here goes to the British Colonial Government which vehemently emphasised the teaching of religious and moral education in all schools state and confessional.

## The Fourth Estate: Viable Role within the Law

A fundamental British colonial heritage in Southern Cameroons was the freedom of expression, which was particularly exercised through the mass media, or the Fourth Estate. In fact, this played a vital sensitising, educating and, especially moralising role in the lives of the people. Over and above the limited radio coverage from Lagos, Enugu and later on at Buea, there were formal and improvised newspapers such as Mgr. Rogan's Sasse Letter, the Catholic Information Bulletin, the Sunday Letters published by the various parishes, the CBC's Baptist Voice and the PCC, which even then owned a printing press (Presbook) at Victoria.

*Figure 30. SDO, Nick Ade Ngwa receives Federal Minister and his entourage from Yaoundé in Victoria, Fako Division*

There were also as indicated, the lone State-owned radio station that initially operated from Buea and the Government Gazette, while political parties possessed and operated their own newspapers. The KNC/KPP alliance and later CPNC ran the Cameroon Chronicle and the Cameroon Champion; the KNDP leaned towards the Cameroon Times, while others like Cameroon Outlook, Cameroon Star and Cameroon Telegraph were freelance and private papers. In between these, several other journals, periodicals and press releases mushroomed in accordance with the socio-political tempo. Much like the liberal political system, both the radio and newspapers, whether public or private were unencumbered, virile and vocal. For example there were popular radio programmes such as "Where are we?" interestingly run on the State radio which were highly critical of the society at large and of government functionaries in particular. Attempts to suppress it failed due to public clamour for its freedom.

As an individual Mr. Patrick Tataw Obenson was an example of a born journalist actually, a second batch Cambridge Certificate graduate of Sasse College, he adopted the pen-name of "Ako-aya", literally translated as "Let them take and cook". He singled himself out as a superbly talented valiant, satirist, who in the 1960s and 1970s as the One-Party system was being introduced, actually a dictatorial, police state with massive suppression of press freedom; he constituted "a one-man opposition, the best watchdog of the period". More pertinently, Angwafor his biographer maintains that Tataw was one person who was:

> As fearless as he was courageous, it is not surprising that Ako-Aya was not liked by every member in our society. And of course, this group was made up of people who had been exposed for perpetrating one vice or the other - bribery, corruption, tribalism, alcoholism, prostitution, abortion, adultery and cheating.[138]

He was very popular with the masses and his satirical column "Ako-aya' published in Cameroon Outlook was voraciously read; although his sharp pen spared no one, not even close friends and relatives or even himself.

---

[138] EN Ngwafor, *Ako-Aya (An Anthology)*, Institute of Third World Art & Literature, London, 1989, p.92. Ngwafor, Ibid.

Tataw literally wept over the decline of Victoria, the town founded by Alfred Saker in 1858, and the birthplace of British Southern Cameroons, a decade before its name was quietly and rather causelessly and inexplicably replaced with "Limbe".

As Professor Ephraim Ngwafor further points out: "Tataw Obenson spearheaded a moral crusade... bent on achieving social, political, cultural and economic reforms" seeing in himself a prophet who came to sensitise the conscience of every superior officer with his popular advice, "Thou shall not oppress the poor."[139] The moral lessons learnt at Sasse were bearing fruit and proving the fact that one man can make a difference. Newspaper editors and columnists were generally courageous and largely incorruptible; they were frequently taken to court, detained and imprisoned but the press remained unmuzzled, subject only to the law until after 1966. And for that matter, both individuals and Governments took each other to court, expected and had justice delivered.

Therefore, it did not create any undue sensation when Mr. Jerome Gwellem, editor of a newspaper faced Mr. Augustine Ngom Jua, the Prime Minister in open court or that Tataw Obenson was escorted from prison, where he was serving a term for libel to bury his mother. In this connection in its short existence Southern (West) Cameroon also experienced a good number of Commissions of Inquiry instituted against suspected officials of both the public and private sectors, the recommendations of which were fairly well executed. These included the commissions that probed into affairs surrounding the Department of Lands And Surveys, POWERCAM and another which focused on Mr. Nerius Namaso Mbile, Secretary of State for Education in the Muna Government 1968-1972.

He was alleged to have used his office to gain admission for two ladies into the Government Teacher Training College, (GTTC) Kumba. Even more embarrassingly, he was on mission abroad in Germany and Great Britain, when the Commission was instituted and while pending the results of the Commission, he was sacked from his ministerial position before he could even report on his trip, which actually had been a study tour. The Tanjong Mixed Commission worked intensely for nine days and

---

[139] Ngwafor, Ibid.

produced a solid report and recommendations which were implemented with immediate effect. To imagine that a whole minister could be relieved of his functions with immediacy for the 'mere' admission of two ladies despite his strong defence is unimaginable in modern Cameroon, where these are daily occurrences affecting scores and hundreds of students for which hardly any one is seriously called to account. In his case, Hon. NN Mbile referring to the attitude of the PM against him, took great exception noting:

> If such authority were sought to investigate ... His Excellency in considering the request, would naturally have borne in mind the competence of a committee of civil servants pure and simple to inquire into the discharge of a secretary of state of his constitutional duties without the courtesy of the Secretary o State being invited to say a single word in defence of himself and his actions, and even when (he) was not in the country.[140]

This was justice for all across the board that knew no bounds and indicates precisely how strict the system was. The simple assertion was that as such a well placed personality, he was not supposed to be associated with such a mean act. But this fledgling democracy grounded on transparency, law and order was not allowed to blossom but muffled after reunification by President Ahidjo and his regime.

---

[140] See, NN Mbile, *Cameroon Political Story: Memories Of An Eye-Witness, Presbyterian Printing Press, Limbe, 1999 p.245*. The commission was headed by Mr. E Tanjong and included Messrs JT Nchamukong and JN Tamen, the ladies at the root of the investigation were: Miss Awoh Susan Mary and Miss Fontem Grace, who had not fully qualified but were granted admission into GTTC, Kumba, allegedly with indirect pressure from the Secretary of State for primary education, Mr. NN Mbile. Together with the minister, the girls were dismissed. The story was confirmed in every detail in an interview with Hon. PC Fonso, who was the principal of GTTC, Kumba, and the person, who wrote the report exposing the minister on 21 April 2016.

*Fig 31 President Ahmadou Ahidjo being received in Buea, West Cameroon*

## Plantation Labour and National Unity

In the context of National Integration and the wisdom that knowledge liberates, and disperses narrow mindedness, ignorance, prejudice and superstition on which demagogy breeds; historical research should be encouraged to educate the masses on the issues raised above. The developments of the 1990s culminated in serious polarization characterized by heightened sectionalism, tribalism and exclusivist practices with crevices emerging between Francophones and Anglophones, as well as between North Westerners and South Westerners. New pejorative and incisive terminology such as: "Sons of the Soil", "Come no go" and "Settlers" came into parlance with sporadic outbursts of violence, which the press noted was reminiscent of Rwanda.

Examined in the context of the high concentration of immigrant and settler populations in towns such as: Limbe, Tiko, Muyuka, Kumba, Buea and their environs, it is immediately obvious that these migrants were attracted there by the rich, fertile, volcanic soils, accessibility by land and sea and the concentration of large plantations and agro-industrial conglomerates. What perhaps is not so obvious is the historical background to the bulk of these settlers, which dates back to the German colonial economic policy. This was focused on stark economic exploitation without any pretext or apology and led to the sequestration of vast expanses of ancestral Bakweri lands that were in turn leased to large-scale planters: the Woermann Company, the Jantzen and Thormalen Companies.

*Fig 32. Left, Zintgraff; Right HRH Fon Galega I of Bali. They undertook a blood pact, literally, drank each other's blood in a palm wine concoction as a sign of intimate friendship.*

Initially, they imported labour from as far away as Liberia, Sierra Leone, Togoland, the Gold Coast (Ghana) and the Congo but these foreign migrant workers were soon found to be too expensive and cumbersome to maintain. The need therefore arose for the search of an urgent supply of cheap local labour. Zintgraff's explorations of the Bamenda Grasslands and the blood pact, which he undertook with Fon Galega I of Bali Nyonga, was intended to harness the influence of this powerful ruler in the Kamerun hinterland for the sole interest of German imperial economic policy. Subsequently, the authority of the Fon was further enhanced and his paramountcy stretched and established over thirty-one neighbouring villages, some of which were forcibly relocated for the supreme purpose of paying taxes and supplying ready labour to the plantations at the Coast. In fact, to ensure that the subject villages remained pacified and loyal to Bali-Nyonga suzerainty, the Germans trained, equipped and maintained a militia for the Fon. These troops were freely used for conducting local wars and labour raids in the vassal villages.

The method of recruiting labourers for the plantation was crude, indiscriminate, reckless and brutal, as the young men were seized often at gunpoint. They then had to trek the three-hundred-mile journey to the coast, where they faced the hot, humid, inclement weather and tropical diseases, especially malaria against which many had no immunity. Mortality rates were extremely high, frequently hitting 10%. In 1904 alone, Fonyonga II is reckoned to have supplied 1700 able-bodied men to the plantations constituting nearly 50% of the entire Bali "Empire" given that by a census of 1912, it had less than 4000 able bodied men left. Paradoxically, Adametz, the Station Manager himself, reviewing this cruel practice and the drain of the Bali population observed with peculiar frankness: "The flower of the Bali Nation lies on the Cameroon Mountain"[141]

The number of labourers "press-ganged" by the Bali troops and dispatched to the German plantations up to 1915, when they were defeated in World War 1, many of whom perished, must have been stupendous. To regard the descendants of people who laid down their lives for the economic sustenance of this country with such levity as happened in the1990s does nothing to help national integration. Cameroonians should be helped to know better. By the same token and for the same reasons, studies deserve to be conducted about how the Ewondos, Bassas, Bamilekes and Ibos are found in such appreciable concentrations in some towns and suburbs of the North West and South West Provinces. It may require upgrading our primary and secondary school history and geography syllabuses as well as special programmes by the mass media.

---

[141] Report by Bamenda Stationscef, Adametz, 13 May 1913 quoted in Ndifontah B Nyamndi, *The Chamba of Cameroon, A Political History*, Editions CAPE, Paris, 1988 p. 113. For historic pictures and descriptions of some of these people and monuments, see Ardener, Historical Notes.

## The Economy: Tidy, Portable Affordable and Promising

Since Cameroon is presently headed for devolution, some fundamental historical knowledge becomes important. Such knowledge would be the basis of the way forward - aware of our strengths and weaknesses because although we cannot change our past, we can use its knowledge in the present to shape our future. In fact, in this case, there are some valuable lessons that emerge from what existed in Southern Cameroons. Other than the exemplary political institutions there were socioeconomic ones e.g.: The West Cameroon Development Agency ran services such as the Santa coffee estate where not only superbly finished, canned Arabica coffee was produced but vegetables and cold stores with fresh meat were supplied especially to: Kumba, Mamfe, Buea and Victoria together with the Yoke river besides supplying cheap and regular hydro-electricity through POWERCAM, also harnessed the Sawmill for processing and sawing timber; the Marketing Board with Headquarters at Victoria had processing plants for cocoa and coffee in Kumba and handled the import and export of these cash crops; a thriving (national bank) Cameroon Bank (CAMBANK) with headquarters at Kumba had branches in all the Divisional Headquarters.

Southern Cameroons, the Switzerland of West Africa was a veritable tourist destination of choice. These facilities were amply provided by the "Cameroon Hotels" a chain of hotels providing services especially at Victoria which had extensive tourist potential, but as well as in Buea (Buea Mountain Hotel), Mamfe and Bamenda (Ring Way); There was the Tingo Experimental Rice Farm run by the Chinese; Wum Area Development Authority (WADA) in Wum handled animal husbandry especially using cattle ploughing techniques together with superb woodwork. However, as well, there were corporations like: Elders and Ffyes, PAMOL and CDC, while there was SONAC in Bamenda and Kumba. Several Private international enterprises operated: John Holt, Emen Textiles, Britind Industries, especially in Victoria for retreading tyres and making solid umbrellas some of which functioned perfectly as recently as 2013 but on the whole, every Division had an enterprise planted within its precincts. But for the CDC and PAMOL, practically the rest of the service industries and parstatals were either physically transferred to Douala or simply mismanaged by the new occupants and vapourised soon after the abolition of the FRC in 1972[142]. The picture painted here is that of a small self contained State, which lived within its means and whose citizens were satisfied and happy. There were no excesses, surpluses or unnecessary waste and shortages; just enough to bring about contentment, hence the title Golden Age, one to cherish and keep in memory of what was achieved and is still possible if there is a will. A quick point to make is that all of these enterprises did not envisage the existence of huge reserves of oil in the Bakassi Peninsula, which only happened in 1969.

## National Integration: Spiritual Ethos

Finally, it should be realized that the main Christian Denominations; the Catholic Church with its Metropolitan See at Bamenda, the Presbyterian Church in Cameroon (PCC) with its Synod headquarters at Buea and the Cameroon Baptist Convention (CBC) with its headquarters in Nkwen, Bamenda have played a tremendous role in fostering national integration and national unity, especially since overcoming the hostilities engendered by interdenominational rivalry up to the late 1950s.Beginning with the biblical fiat that "all may be one "and applying the law of fraternal love, the activities of the churches have always been tempered by the holistic concern for the human person; body, mind and spirit for the individuals and community at large.

Above all, with, their numerous educational institutions; primary and secondary schools, teacher training colleges; health centres, clinics and hospitals are located where they are most needed in remote and rural areas hardly reached by Government services. These establishments strive to serve the entire North and South West Provinces equitably. The Cameroon Baptist Convention divided into the Northern and Southern Zones (representing the North and South West Provinces) as indicated with the

---

[142] Stories abound especially in Victoria (Limbe) of residents simply being brutally ushered out of parastatal offices and houses by new Francophone occupants, who had purchased them brandishing certificates of ownership. The tale is also told of a Francophone principal who carted away from GTC, Ombe in broad daylight with impunity, rare machines inherited from British technicians to private businesses in Douala.

Convention's Capital at Bamenda has Soppo as its sub-headquarters for the Southern Zone. It is further decentralized into Churches or Congregations, Associations and Fields; while an elected President, General Secretary and Directors of Boards head the Convention. The Presbyterian Church in Cameroon as well is highly egalitarian, and is organized through Churches, Parishes and Presbyteries of which there are twenty-two under the General Synod. An elected Moderator, Synod Clerk and Financial Secretary oversee the entire structure at the apex.

On the other hand, the Catholic Church in the North and South West Provinces as part of the National Episcopal Conference of Cameroon [NECC] is organized under the Bamenda Provincial Ecclesiastical Province (BAPEC). It comprises four Dioceses: Bamenda Archdiocese, Buea, Kumbo and Mamfe, (1999) each of which is headed by a Bishop, with Bamenda Archdiocese as the Metropolitan See with an Archbishop. Each Diocese is further subdivided into Zones or Deaneries, Parishes and then, Mission Stations and Outstations.

Statistically, Bamenda Diocese for example, created in 1970 with 129.784 Catholics by 1975 had risen in population to 153.252 Catholic Christians with 150.287 Presbyterian and 32.938 Baptist Christians. However, thirty years later on the occasion of celebrating the "Centenary of its evangelisation" (1913 2013) even after the excision of Kumbo Diocese, in 1982 the newly created Bamenda Archdiocese alone, had literally exploded in growth at all levels with the numbers bouncing up to 410.000 Christians distributed over forty parishes. This is a far cry from the 1.741 Christians it took off with in Njinikom Parish in 1927 of which Bamenda was an outstation till 1935. While the statistics for the PCC, CBC and the numerous new Christian or evangelical movements are not immediately available they would be no less impressive as there is exponential Christian population growth out of a total population of 1.457.053 for the North West Region.[143] Church attendance on Sundays and other Christian activities and celebrations are appreciable. There is substantial economic development but, the extent to which this growth has impacted on the morality of the people is not so obvious especially

---

[143] Centenary history, pp. 22&24.

with the rampant crime wave. This of course is affected by several other factors including the shattered economy, unemployment, easy communication and mobility especially of criminal elements in the urban areas. In relative terms, the Moslem population has grown massively since its timid introduction in the 1930s with mosques visible in most towns. Their socioeconomic and political impact on life in the erstwhile North and South West Provinces is also significant.

Furthermore, Church appointments in all the Denominations whether lay or clerical as far as possible were and continue to be centred on competence, qualification, experience, availability and generally respect national and regional balance without sacrificing efficiency and merit. Through their numerous Christian activities, meetings, ordinations, inductions, rallies, pilgrimages, various competitions, retreats conferences and conventions, these churches reach out meaningfully to their faithful in the remotest corners throughout the North and South West Regions, and increasingly across the Mungo[144] with East Mungo Congregations, Presbyteries and Parishes, in the new spirit of ecumenism, dialogue and inculturation. Some Catholic organisations such as the Catholic Women's Association have fully gone national and international, penetrating all Catholic dioceses in Cameroon but mostly retaining their Anglophone character. To various degrees, the Christian Women's Fellowship of the PCC as well as those of the Cameroon Baptist Convention have made similar inroads but always with a strong Anglophone touch. The mainline Churches in former West Cameroon therefore offer the most credible and practical approach to nation building, subtly creating national integration, national unity and national consciousness using Christian tenets founded on fraternal love. Not only are these Churches growing in numbers, there is much to show for the profundity of their faith by performance and sheer Christian witness. While this works for the general good of the nation, the net impact effusing from the North and South West Regions through spiritual overflow is viable and fairly palpable.

---

[144] The River Mungo naturally divides former east Cameroon from Southern Cameroons and is commonly used without imputing any political motives.

## Chapter Five

# DECLINE OF THE FRC: INTERNAL AND EXTERNAL FACTORS

## Ahidjo's Agenda for Dismantling Southern (West) Cameroon

President Ahmadou Ahidjo, an astute, unassuming, charismatic personality rose to power in French Cameroon as leader of the "Young Moslems", the main political party of the Moslem dominated northern Cameroon. He then used it as a springboard for launching the *Union Camerounaise*, a much more encompassing political union which further united Moslem north with a national outlook. With northern Cameroon solidly behind him, Ahidjo could then face the more shattered Christian south. This was particularly because in 1960 with the UPC rebellion and the imposition of a State of Emergency, Ahidjo was most unpopular in the South of the Country. The Southern Christian political parties led by Soppo Priso and Bebey Eyidi bonded themselves into the "*Forces Vive de l'Opposition*" were so powerful that Ahidjo won by just a single vote in the Assembly. Consequently, he developed a dread for Christians as a whole and for Catholics in particular. This apart, he was at best a reluctant, late convert to the concept of "Cameroon reunification" with (British Southern and Northern Cameroons), out of which however, he hoped to make political capital by using the large Moslem population of (British) Northern Cameroons to counterbalance the turbulent Christian population in both (British) Southern Cameroons and the southern region of former French Cameroon.

But the decision of (British) Northern Cameroons, the northern component of "British Cameroons" in its second plebiscite of February 1961 to integrate with Northern Nigeria instead, struck a mortal blow to

Ahidjo's ambitions. Subsequently, he developed serious doubts as to the wisdom of proceeding with reunification talks with Foncha on Southern Cameroons, which had a Christian population exceeding 840,000 without the anticipated Moslem counterweight from British Northern Cameroons. He despatched a powerful delegation to the UN led by his Minister of Foreign Affairs Mr. Charles Okala, where he harangued the General Assembly at length. Failing there another team was sent to The Hague where they fought aggressively to have the plebiscite results of Northern Cameroons annulled but again to no avail. To drive home the depth of his disenchantment and wrath, Ahidjo declared 1 June 1961, a "Day of National Mourning" with flags flown at half-mast for the loss of British Northern Cameroons.[145] As a result, he and his advisers devised strategies for neutralising this complex hydra-headed geopolitical problem with religious, ethnic, cultural and demographic implications posed by the reality of reunification with Southern Cameroons alone without Northern Cameroons.

These frantic moves resulted from the fact that the political prospects for Ahidjo in 1961 were particularly bleak and precarious. His majority in the National Assembly was slim and he was haunted by mounting fears of being toppled by a looming coalition of Anglophone Christians and their Southern counterparts in French Cameroon. There were also ominous prospects of the Bamenda Grasslanders combining forces with their Bamileke kith and kin, the second homeland of the UPC insurrection with which he was currently grappling. The threat that Foncha who was broadly popular with all these groups would overshadow him to become the first President of a reunited Cameroon became a real nightmare.

## Onset of the "Grand Unified Party"

There can be little doubt that put together these threats helped in no small way to create the paranoid character he became and especially his cynical attitude to Southern Cameroons. Outwardly, unassuming,

---

[145] JF Bayart "The Neutralisation of Anglophone Cameroon" in Richard Joseph, *Gaullist Africa: Cameroon Under Ahmadu Ahidjo*, p.84. See also *Daily Times*, Monday February 1959 and *Kamerun Times*, Wednesday 31/5/61.

paternalistic, composed, respectful and affable, he was an astute and manipulative politician, who could not brook any opposition or rivalry and was determined to defuse this state of affairs. He started unfolding his hidden agenda by floating the idea of a "Grand Unified Party " or simply the Grand National Party in 1961, a lofty proposal garbed in attractive robes. It was to be an all-inclusive party in which everybody would find space for their views. This gradually attracted the dissipated opposition party leaders in Southern Cameroons but it was objectionable to the KNDP leadership, who had just swept through the plebiscite and the parliamentary elections in 1961 with a crushing majority in parliament where they won 29 of the 34 seats in the enlarged Southern Cameroons House of Assembly. Even more intimidating, the KNDP won all the ten seats in Federal Assembly in the elections of 1963.

The KNDP as a party was therefore posed for celebrating an unfettered period of democratic parliamentary government, the vision first set for Southern Cameroons by its first Commissioner, Brigadier EJ Gibbons, when launching the first parliament on 26 August 1954. There was no reason to contemplate grouping parties to form a single party state although there was consideration for forming a democratic one party state through getting the opposition CPNC to decamp or cross the carpet and freely join the KNDP.[146] On the other hand, while the CPNC opposition dreaded being crushed out of existence, Ahidjo's fears and suspicions about Foncha and the possibility of uniting with Bamilekes and Christians increased. This background is essential for understanding the nocturnal meetings between Ahidjo, Endeley and Mbile and finally the support for Muna to undermine the KNDP.

Thus it was after these repeated defeats at the polls that Endeley and Mbile, left in the cold and whose initial efforts for coalition with the KNDP were scoffed, fell prey to Ahidjo's bait. They seized the opportunity and opened up secret negotiations with Ahidjo during his maiden visit to Buea in 1960. In an open letter to the KNDP, Endeley called for discussions towards a merger of all parties into one national party. His clarion

---

[146] Actually this came to pass in 1965 in the Jua government but Ahidjo was most upset and asked them to disband as it was against the interest of national unity

call was taken up by the Cameroon Chronicle, the CPNC mouthpiece, which in its editorial issued an ultimatum for the KNDP to dissolve and join Ahidjo's UC before January 1962. It went further and requested President Ahidjo to step in and redeem West Cameroon from the vices of tribalism, nepotism in the civil service, political warfare and rivalry, which were bedevilling the KNDP under the Foncha Administration.[147] The KNDP viewed this as the onset of the one party syndrome of dictatorship and the idea was rejected outright at the party's 1962 congress.

Nevertheless, Endeley and Mbile persisted in private talks with Ahidjo, with Endeley affirming his commitment to the idea of a single party, maintaining that "no one need be considered redundant"; he and his CPNC party were "ready to go into union with any other friendly and truly national group or groups, for the purpose of speeding up national reconstruction and economic development of our Country". To Endeley's mind, "The national party ... will abolish once and for all the bane of mushroom parties which bedevil our political life" and bring peace, prosperity and progress to our people. Accordingly, in February 1963, Hon. Samuel Ngeh Tamfu, a fervent CPNC stalwart tabled a motion before parliament calling for the realisation of a single party through "the absorption of all existing political parties in one single one" to the embarrassment of the KNDP which under the prevailing political climate emphasising national unity they could not reject outright.

However, they amended the motion and accepted it in principle; but the KNDP was essentially playing for time, which unfortunately was not on their side. In making this appeal, Endeley was convinced that:

> We can operate a one party system, which would certainly guarantee that everybody has the right to express opinions within the party. This would make the best use of the talents we have in the country, and we could evolve a system of agreement without engendering animosity.[148]

Of course, such a party could remain only at the level of theory with

---

[147] Willard Johnson, *The Cameroon Federation*, p.265.

[148] Johnson p.262. Also, *Cameroon Times*, Monday, 28 April 1962.

pious hope which in practice could not be implemented. However, finally, this was what Ahidjo promised but abjectly failed to deliver, because in any case, he only meant it to be a political campaign slogan. Thus Dr. EML Endeley, *Officer of the British Empire* (OBE), who more than anyone else had laboured tirelessly to usher in democratic ideals to Southern Cameroons, finally offered Ahidjo all the facilities and excuses he needed to immolate multi-party democracy in West Cameroon for rather inauspicious reasons.

As a consequence, the CPNC and its leadership, generally staunch advocates of democracy and multipartism, paradoxically, turned round to advocate the introduction of a one party system. For this reason, Hon. SN Ajebe Sone eloquently made the point in a parliamentary debate on 14 February 1963 claiming that West Cameroon was filled with depression, confusion and general discontent. The survival of the CPNC after its devastating defeat in the 1961 elections in which the KNDP won 29 of the 34 seats in the enlarged Southern Cameroons House of Assembly and even much worse its failure to win even a single seat in the Federal Assembly, raised the fear that: "The KNDP was doing everything to erase the CPNC almost to the man and wipe it out as a political party. The CPNC therefore felt that only a single party could end this sorry state of affairs."[149]

Endeley's persistent struggle for a single party state was because he saw it as the only opportunity for The CPNC to come out of political wilderness. It was apparent that the KNDP was bent on dominating the West Cameroon political stage, replicating what the UC had done in East Cameroon; establishing a single party regime on their own terms before embarking on the rugged road towards a national party with the UC. The KNDP strategy was to neutralise the CPNC as a political factor in West Cameroon politics.[150] Even then the CPNC as a party remained fractured to the extent that JO Field after an assessment of the political situation concluded that: "Dr. Endeley seems to be a spent force and there is no

---

[149] West Cameroon Press Release no.2221 of 14 February 1963

[150] Mbu Etangondop, 'Federalism In A One Party State" *in*, Cameroon From A Federal To A Unitary State, *Ngoh Victor Julius ed. Presprint, 2004*

love lost between him and Mr. Mbile, who are both working against each other. The party is in danger of falling to pieces."[151] This shattered and weakened the West Cameroon political landscape, precisely the chaotic situation which President Ahidjo needed to create his grand unified party, but in a milder manner than what he did to those who dared to oppose him in East Cameroon. There, the parties were proscribed and their leaders thrown in jail.

However, not surprisingly, as soon as President Ahidjo took over, Endeley's lofty ideals of a national, all-embracing, one party, democratic system were flung to the winds; for example, first he ruled for six months without parliament after unification in 1961and then more extensively for twelve months in 1972, when he declared the 'Peaceful Revolution'. Here JF Bayart, Richard Joseph, Willard Johnson and Emmanuel Aka, analysts of the Cameroon political scene are wholly agreed that Ahidjo was thoroughly hypocritical and insincere and that his: "Emphasis on national unity and national integration was a disguise to assimilate English-speaking Cameroonians and destroy their Anglo-Saxon cultural heritage."[152] They were vintage prophets as in time; all of this has come to pass as perfectly as predicted. By a press law issued in April 1966 as the CNU was being launched, all newspaper publications had to be censored by the administration and by this: "the rump of the newspapers was reduced to absurd praise singers, propagandists and apologists for the system".[153] This atmosphere prevailed and intensified throughout Ahidjo's autocratic rule.

Interestingly, it was at the peak of its glory in 1965 with the appointment of AN Jua as PM that the germ for the demolition of the aspiring State of West Cameroon was disseminated. This began with the introduction of the One Party system (CNU) which like malignant cancer rapidly ate through the political tissue of the State manifesting itself in the "List System", the "One Party state syndrome", autocratic rule and finally, the abolition of the State of West Cameroon itself. Under the One Party dictatorial system, the wish of the President automatically became

---

[151] CO554/2249 XC 3406: Report by JO Field to the Colonial Office

[152] Richard Joseph, p.82, Aka p.258 and Johnson, p.265.

[153] Ibid, Richard Joseph.

law without equivocation. Or, as Bayart better puts it, using the example of the famous 20 May 1972 Referendum; it was not necessary for the President to order the manipulation of the voting in any election, it was generally understood and an acknowledged fact that:

> Administrative authorities, party officials, and the police make it their business to understand from his declarations the results needed and then achieve them by whatever means necessary. The abrupt and arbitrary announcement by the Head of State on 2 May, 1972 that within three weeks a referendum would be held on the question of abolishing a Federal State that had been laboriously constructed, meant in effect, that within three weeks a Unitary State would be established with an overwhelming "YES."[154]

In examining the implications of these political manoeuvres and truly radical changes for the people of Southern Cameroons, it deserves to be remembered that whether as a Quasi Federated State within the Federal Republic of Nigeria, or simply as the North and South West Provinces in the Republic of Cameroon, its inhabitants as a distinct minority with a common colonial experience, history, demographic disposition, culture and visions, always fought to preserve their cultural identity in the face of all the vicissitudes. For this reason, its representatives declaring themselves "Benevolent Neutrals" had bolted out of Nigeria during the Eastern Regional Crisis in 1953 then voted massively and decisively in the 1961 Plebiscite for Reunification with their "Brothers" in Republique du Cameroun. This quest for identity had been the subject of the deliberations at the Foumban Constitutional Conference and the substance of the Federal Constitution that was produced. Although the new Federal Republic of Cameroon was supposed to be a co-equal, bilingual and bi- cultural state, apparently everything weighed in favour of the French-speaking majority downsizing the West Cameroon Anglophone component to second class, citizens, neglected, marginalized to the brink of total subjugation

---

[154] Richard A Joseph, *Radical Nationalism in Cameroon – Social Origins of UPC Rebellion*, Oxford at the Claredon Press, 1977, p.181. ff. Also Bayart, p.84, ff. See Cameroon Times Vol. 6 No. 40, Sat. 9 April 1966, CPNC condemns List system.

and assimilation[155].

## Externally Provoked Rebellion to Topple KNDP

Remotely orchestrated by Ahidjo in his intrigues with ST Muna and finally playing into his hands, was the fission within the KNDP. As Foncha prepared to take up his post as Vice-President of the Federal Republic of Cameroon in 1965, a fierce power tussle ensued between Jua and Muna over succession to the leadership of the KNDP and as Prime Minister of the State of West Cameroon. Again, this spectacle superbly suited Ahidjo, who since 1961 had become all powerful, acting in the triple capacity of:

> Head of State, head of government and head of the political party controlling the government and therefore enjoyed the powers of hydra-headed dictators known in history. The parliament was reduced to a rubber stamp; the judiciary was also under his control; he could appoint, promote, and dismiss its personnel. In effect, the constitution had no provision for the division or separation of powers.[156]

The situation was additionally worsened by Foncha's indecision as he supported one, and then the other of the candidates. However, when he finally settled on Jua, he incurred the full wrath of the Muna camp, who regarded him as the devil incarnate and the rift within the party became fatal. Foncha thus became isolated by both sides, while his resultant transfer to the Headquarters at Yaoundé as Vice-President further estranged him from his power base, the masses in West Cameroon. Although President Ahidjo favoured Muna, he, for the time being in 1965, bowed to popular opinion and appointed Jua as PM. The rupture within the KNDP degenerated still further leading to the expulsion from the party of the nine

---

[155] See, Memo to The Head of State by the Cameroon Anglophone Movement, Douala, 5 December 1991.

[156] Aka, p. 258. It literally became a doormat, see Nyo'Wakai, *The Law in My Time*.

renegades together with Muna, who led them by Foncha. Bayart again put it expressively:

> The President favoured the humbling of Foncha and participated in the process by encouraging the divisions among west Cameroonians. By advising KNDP moderation (unlike his own policy in the east)... he prevented the KNDP from gaining absolute control in the West[157]

*Fig 33. Like Mr. A N Jua and Mr. S T Muna, both Nzoh and Egbe were candidates for elections to key posts in the KNDP party at the 9th Convention, which sparked serious discords and dissent within the Party*

There can be no doubt as to the fact of Ahidjo's competence as an astute and often brutal master juggler. This came out clearly in the manner in which he drove a wedge between Jua and Muna, with the major objective being the dismantling of the KNDP and finally cutting the ground under Foncha, whose success at the polls was getting excessive and a threat to Ahidjo's own position. Actually in the melee, Ahidjo became the arbitrator in a struggle which he had skilfully instituted. This turned out to be his

---

[157] Bayart, "The Neutralization Of Anglophone Cameroon" in Richard Joseph, *Gaullist Africa*, p.86.

master stroke for concluding the demolition of the Federation, which he had never liked. Thus:

> He then played skilfully on the confrontation between Muna and Jua. Letting the former know he was the favoured one, yet accepting the latter as Western Prime Minister, all the while permitting the temporarily eclipsed aspirant continued federal resources. Muna was thereby kept in reserve for the opportune moment when Ahidjo would pull the rug from under Jua.[158]

Some political analysts have interpreted this as a "colossal blunder" by Foncha as the KNDP by this action lost some of its best brains and afterwards, Jua asserted his independence and began dealing directly with Ahidjo without any further reference to him. Nevertheless, Foncha explained that after attaining its original objective of reunification, the KNDP was next set on reconciliation and nation building but the expelled traitors were self-seeking opportunists. Even worse, after resounding defeats by Jua both at the 9th KNDP Convention and again in Parliament, Muna had refused to accept the results insisting that "only the President of the Federal Republic" had the right to appoint the PM. Foncha maintained that he could not under the circumstances and by the Party's own constitution tolerate such insubordination.[159] Ahidjo astute as always, sized the situation and exploited it thoroughly to bring about the extinction of the KNDP and the exits of Foncha and Jua from active political life. At the time, it was not as clear as it became later, that Ahidjo and Muna had been secretly working together to torpedo the KNDP as

---

[158] ibid.

[159] Foncha is blamed by many for being too soft and for "moralising politics". He preached peace at the cost of vital political issues. After dismissal in 1970 he was literally imprisoned in his own compound, restricted in movement and hemmed in by police and gendarmes, who checked every single person that visited him. Yet he continued to support the Government "in the name of peace". *Cameroon Times*, Vol. 5 No.107 Sat. 13 Nov. 1965. Also *Cameroon Times* Vol. 6, No. 29 Sat. March 12, 1966, captioned "Jua Hits Foncha". At the 9th KNDP Convention in Bamenda in 1963, Muna won 73 votes to Jua's 175, Egbe 95 to Nzoh's 159 and in the West Cameroon Parliamentary Meeting of 9 May 1965 Muna got 09 votes- to Jua's 23.

part of Ahidjo's ultimate design to dismantle the FRC. It now became clear why ST Muna had insisted all along after suffering repeated defeats at the KNDP conventions and in Parliament in his contest with AN Jua for party and Government leadership, that only the "Federal" president could appoint the Prime Minister of West Cameroon. Ahidjo had been seeking for an opportunity to destabilise the Southern Cameroons political structure especially to undermine Foncha's political base since 1962 and interestingly in those early days Foncha unsuspectingly used Muna as the herald and go-between himself and Ahidjo.

However, the defectors without delay formed the Cameroon United Congress (CUC), which was very much the West Cameroon version of Ahidjo's Union Camerounaise (UC). It was part of Ahidjo's grand scheme to discipline diehard federalists such as Jua and Foncha, while rewarding unionists and centralists through patronage in political appointments as he did with Muna and his cohorts. Strangely enough, Muna at the Foumban Constitutional Conference in 1961 had gone further than the mere "federation" agreed at conference advocating for a looser union. In fact, by implication, he advocated for a "confederation" and resolutely maintained that:

> Unification between Southern Cameroons and the Republic of Cameroun might take the form of a loose federation with the aim of preserving the individuality of the Southern Cameroons state [and] the union should be a union from which both sides draw strength.[160]

But ironically beginning in 1968, he, Muna became the very tool in Ahidjo's hands for the creation of a highly centralised Unitary State through the demolition of the West Cameroon House of Assembly, House of Chiefs, the Federal constitution and finally, even the identity of the West Cameroon State, which he had passionately advocated should be upheld.

In subsequent developments, after the defections of Messrs EE Ngone, FN Ajebe-Sone and SN Tamfu from the CPNC to the KNDP, only Endeley and Mbile, the rump of the party remained. In the end, they

---

[160] Aka, p. 246

too were absorbed into the Jua "national" or better still "KNDP-CPNC Coalition" Government in 1966. Actually, to all intents and purposes this was a matter of expedience given that the CUC had become the pseudo-official opposition and the KNDP badly needed the support of the CPNC to survive. This move earlier made by Endeley and Mbile in 1961 had been rebuffed by the KNDP. This time Mbile was appointed Secretary of State for Public Works, while; Endeley took up the newly coined post of Leader of the House of Assembly thus accomplishing the goal he had set out for himself and the CPNC since 1960. It was also the ultimate progression in achieving the contrasting objectives towards which he and Ahidjo had been working. In another sense it was timely because the Southern (West) Cameroons political scene had become by Willard Johnson's estimate:

> Increasingly parochial in orientation and localised in support, and the party system progressively fragmented until it finally crumbled into a heap of factions, each of which was included in a single national party organised at the initiative of President Ahidjo and the Union Camerounaise.[161]

Systematically, President Ahidjo torpedoed the entire West Cameroon political set-up. He retained Muna and Egbe, the CUC renegades who were Federal Ministers in his government and thus neutralised the Jua victory and undermined Foncha's authority.[162] He continued to court the favour of both camps, who to maintain their political positions vied for allegiance and loyalty to him the author and dispenser of all power and patronage. Ahidjo disregarded the fact that West Cameroon pursued the Westminster parliamentary system of Government in which all ministers first of all had to be elected Members of Parliament from their various

---

[161] Johnson, p. 285. He made it look like the CNU was created through the volition of the various parties, whereas they were literally forced to join the UC of Ahmadou Ahidjo

[162] Now with hindsight, it is obvious that the parties were coaxed and did not submit willingly to the union. It was a smokescreen created by ahidjo to install Muna and his surrogates in power since they became the main beneficiaries of top positions in the new party (CNU).

constituencies with only the majority party being invited to form the Government. In short, all ministers were MPs in the first place, and were responsible to their constituencies. These principles totally contradicted the objectives of the one party system and Ahidjo spared no effort to demolish it root, stem and branches.

## The Ahidjo "Imperial" Presidential Style

On the other hand, in the Presidential system, which Ahidjo introduced, ministers were appointed on the basis of their loyalty to his Grand Unified Party and ultimately to his person. Henceforth they were selected not because they were the choice of their constituents through popular elections and majority in Parliament, but solely because of their devotion bordering on "subservience" to the person of the President since the process did not even require ratification by Parliament. This was a major blow the West Cameroon democratic system suffered and from which it never recovered. The nadir was reached in 1968, when President Ahidjo put aside Hon AN Jua, the elected MP and PM and appointed Muna, who was neither an MP nor had been elected by the members of the West Cameroon House of Assembly to preside over it as their new PM.

What actually transpired was ominous, as Ahidjo had personally assured Jua on the evening before that he would certainly be retained as PM of West Cameroon. However, on the morning of 11 January 1968 the President despatched a sealed note to the Speaker of the National Assembly appointing Muna as PM, while he took off for Yaoundé leaving the MPs stunned in total disbelief. This was under the circumstances an aberration because Muna was by all counts an outsider imposed on an elected Parliament, an indication that worse was to follow.[163] Thereafter, Muna himself abandoned the Westminster Parliamentary system and began appointing Ministers and top officials in his government who were not elected members of Parliament. This new approach undermined the essence of popular elections and introduced confusion as there was a mixture of two incompatible procedures, one based on responsibility to

---

[163] Mbile, pp. 20-9; Johnson, p. 276.

the electorate and the other purely on loyalty to the person of the PM or the President. Above all, it intensified and perfected the sycophancy so well initiated by Ahidjo.

## The Final Act

The final act began with President Ahmadou Ahidjo expressing his total displeasure at the coalition that had taken place between the KNDP and CPNC as well as the National Government formed by Jua in 1965, which most analysts considered the high point of democratic and popular administration since it was all inclusive. However, to President Ahidjo these moves had been taken not in the best national interest but for selfish reasons and against his call for a national party. Yet again, the UC support for the CUC was made abundantly clear in a row that erupted between the UC and the KNDP in the Federal Assembly. Hon. Nzoh Ekhah-Nghaky, Secretary General of the KNDP lucidly argued that since the original "Unity Group" had solely been one between the KNDP and the UC, the CUC renegades deserved to be expelled from the Federal Assembly, as in the circumstances they had no legitimate base. The response from Hon Moussa Yaya was straightforward uncompromising and ultimate. Clarifying issues once and for all, the UC Secretary General propounded without equivocation:

> There can be no question of expelling Hons. Muna and Egbe from the Unity Group...Their expulsion from the KNDP Sub-Group does not expel them from the Unity Group. If the KNDP does not like their existence in the Unity Group, the KNDP can resign. We want to tell our friends of the KNDP not to push us to a precipice where we will have either to fall over or to react violently. [164]

This was brutal and uncompromising no dabbling with ideas of democracy and reference to past agreements. The message was clear and the writing on the wall bold enough for even the blind to feel. The KNDP

---

[164] *Cameroon Star* Vol. 1 no 9 Monday 30 May 1966.

and the CUC hurriedly tried to mend fences but President Ahidjo had made up his mind and promised in a secret meeting with CUC members to right the wrongs in West Cameroon. This did not take long to happen since righting the wrongs meant the demolition of the KNDP and demotion of its leadership.

*Fig 34 From Left to right Hon. Ajebe-Sone, PM Augustine N Jua, SDO Ngwa and DO Mbuyonga during the PM's Official Visit to Muyuka*

Unfolding this scheme, Ahidjo without delay summoned all the leaders of the West Cameroon political parties together with the two Prime Ministers of the States of East and West Cameroon, and issued an ultimatum by which they were instantly required to dissolve in favour of a single party. Not surprisingly, the CUC was the first party to comply, with Endeley astonishingly further lavishing glowing tribute to President Ahidjo, who:

> With his usual generosity, candour, and love of fair play, has come one step towards us warring West Cameroonians and volunteered to dissolve his large and well established Party, the UC, so that we may meet him

half way and together build the CNU on a stable basis of equality with no advantage to privilege to any one big or small."[165]

With the MPs still in a state of astonishment, Mbile sarcastically quipped in Parliament: "Before now, we knew who was who. Today, child, mother, father, are all in one party. One is in no position to know his or her opponent." And strangely, as it soon turned out, Endeley's pious dreams were too far removed from Ahidjo's own concept of a *"Grand Unified Party"*, which literally was his mouthpiece.

### *The Jua (KNDP-CPNC Coalition) Government, 1965*

| | |
|---|---|
| Mr. A N Jua: | Prime Minister |
| Mr. P M Kemcha: | Minister of Finance |
| Dr. E M L Endeley: | Leader of the House of Assembly |
| Mr. Patrick Mua: | Secretary of State for Interior |
| Mr. S T Tamfu: | Secretary of State for Economics and Planning |
| Mr. S E Ncha: | Secretary of State, Prime Minister's Office |
| Mr. J H Nganje: | Secretary of State Cooperatives and Community Development |
| *Mr. F N Ajebe-Sone:* | Secretary of State for Agriculture |
| *Mr. J N Nsame:* | Secretary of State for Forest and Veterinary Services. |
| *Mr. S N G Yor:* | Parliamentary Secretary Ministry of Agriculture. |
| *P M Kale:* | Speaker of the House of Assembly |
| *Mr. N N Mbile:* | Secretary of State Works and Transport |
| *Mr. J N Lafon:* | Secretary of State for Local Government |
| *Mr. L M Ndamukong:* | Secretary of State, Education and Social Welfare |
| *Mr. M M Monono:* | Parliamentary Secretary, Ministry of Works and Transport |
| *Mr. A W Daiga:* | Parliamentary Secretary, Ministry of Local Government |
| *Mr. B P Ayuk:* | Acting Clerk |
| *Mr. F Patcha:* | Sergeant at Arms |

---

[165] Johnson, p.285.

Devastated by these developments, the already precarious KNDP position was further aggravated. On the thirty-member committee set up for the formation of the new party, (CNU) it was accorded barely four places and worse still, the Drafting Committee, ironically was chaired by Mr. Emmanuel T Egbe, a former renegade KNDP member of the CUC with Mr. Samuel M L Endeley representing the CPNC, while only Dr. Bernard Fonlon and Mr. Nzoh Ekhah-Ngahky sat in for the KNDP. With the preponderance of the UC on the Draft Committee, the rest of the satellite political parties were simply absorbed into Ahidjo's party, which changed little except in name. In other words, the UC in essence metamorphosed into the Cameroon National Union (CNU).

The Executive of the emerging political party comprised: President Ahmadou Ahidjo himself as "President" with Mr. John N Foncha and Dr. Pierre Tschoungui, PM of East Cameroon, as VPs. Thus far, President Ahidjo had manipulated himself into the supreme and unassailable position of head of the party and head of Government. He alone dispensed political patronage, which he effectively used to entice support for himself as well as penalize his opponents. Since there was no scope for opposition or dissent of any kind, ambitious Southern Cameroonian politicians and opportunists rivalled one another in displaying their loyalty to the "President of the Republic" to the point of incredible sycophancy and subservience.

## The Creation of Federal Inspectorates

Further duplicating, complicating and confusing the administrative structures, the FRC was mutilated into six Federal Inspectorates. The State of West Cameroon, which had its own Government with a Prime Minister, House of Assembly and House of Chiefs, constituted one of these Regions, while East Cameroon comprised the other five. Mr. Jean Claude Ngoh, the Federal Inspector of West Cameroon wielded conspicuous and inexplicable power and authority which rivalled and almost overshadowed that of the elected Prime Minister of the State of West Cameroon disregarding the "*equal status*" clause inscribed in the Federal constitution between the States of East and West Cameroon. Frequently, during the mid-1960s the State of West Cameroon was referred to as "The Federal Inspectorate of Western Cameroon". However, when the Federal Inspector proceeded to flying the National Flag on his car, this episode sparked off an open fracas between them, as Hon. AN Jua, the PM refused to be further sidelined.[166]

*Fig 35. New Secretaries of State in the Jua Coalition Government (Messrs. Nsame, Tamfu and Mbile).*

However, the appointment of the Federal Inspector of West Cameroon immediately drew sharp, prophetic criticisms from the West Cameroon press. The Kamerun Times in its editorial of 7 April 1962, considered the move unrealistic and too precipitated. It questioned the basis for the appointment of a person who was: "a complete, stranger to the administrative system of West Cameroon, having been born, bred and educated in East Cameroon and therefore versed only in methods of administration

---

[166] See, Ministry of Information and Tourism, Federal Inspectorate of Western Cameroon – Federal Republic of Cameroon, Edition Paul Bory, Monaco, 1967.

different from those in the region in which he is the administrative head." East and West Cameroon the paper pointed out had two different systems of administration, one patterned after the French and the other after the English. With competent West Cameroonians who could fill that position, "the appointment made a mockery of the principle of Federation and was reminiscent of the colonial era when appointments were made without consultation."[167] In practice, the Federal Inspector handled and coordinated all federal services and could investigate both state and federal officials. Apparently, unofficially at his service was Mr. Dibongue, who seemed to have specialised in writing negative reports about Foncha and Jua. The decree of its creation literally placed the Federal Administrator above the elected PM to the extent that the West Cameroon Government addressed a memo to the President of the FRC that the Federal Inspector wielded more powers than the Vice President of the FRC, which was considered a negation of democratic practice.[168]

Yet more astonishing and ominous for the citizens of West Cameroon was the introduction of the "Gendarmerie", a wholly strange law enforcement body, who unlike the West Cameroon police carried arms and came directly under the charge of the Federal Inspector. The sadistic approach to the maintenance of law and order by this new element struck terror in the people and vociferous complaints about their rampant flogging, raping and even shooting resounded throughout the Country, from Victoria through Mamfe to Nkambe without apparent redress. They were a law to themselves and did not recognise even their own counterparts, the police from whose hands they frequently wrested suspects for instant justice.[169] Thus gendarme brutality provided the West Cameroon public

---

[167] *Kamerun Times*, Monday, 7 April 1962.

[168] NAB, Top Secret no. 323/CFI/CAB/ PR, Representation to HE, President of the FRC. also, Ngoh, *The Untold Story Of Cameroon Reunification*, 1955-1961: Presprint Plc, 2011, pp.90-91

[169] See *Cameroon Times*, No 171, Victoria, Monday 29 Nov. 1962; Editorial "It's unfair"; *Cameroon Times*, Victoria, Monday 26 Novi 1962; Victor J Ngoh, "The Origin of the Marginalisation of Former Southern Cameroonians (Anglophones), 1961-1966: A Historical Analysis" nd., an address at Buea University. For graphic details see Richard Joseph, pp. 93-99, Truth about Cameroon" and, p.107ff 'Agents and Instruments of the

with a foretaste of the proper meaning of reunification.

## Phobia for Catholics: The Ndongmo Affair

In his bid for political control of Cameroon, President Ahmadou Ahidjo brooked no real or imaginary threat to his power and authority. Initially it was the dread for Christians as a whole, but soon it turned into a rabid fear of the Catholic Church, which had a sizeable population in the Country especially after reunification. A classic example of this phobia was demonstrated in the "Ndongmo Affair."[170]

Mgr. Albert Ndongmo, the popular, charismatic and articulate Bishop of Nkongsamba Diocese, consecrated in August 1964 was arrested at Douala Airport on Thursday 27 August 1970, just as he was returning from Rome, where he had gone for consultation with the Holy See. This unprecedented event stunned the nation at large and sent shock waves among the Catholic community in particular, as it coincided with the creation of Bamenda Diocese and the appointment of Very Rev. Fr. Paul Mbiybe Verdzekov as its pioneer indigenous Bishop. This was news of momentous significance for the people of West Cameroon, but unfortunately at this moment of superlative joy the Church was saddled with the prospects of the Ndongmo Affair, which cast a dark shadow on the subsequent celebrations marking the consecration of the Prelate.

Over at Yaoundé, the national capital on the other hand, the Minister of Justice, Mr. Felix Sabal Lecco,[171] a Catholic himself gave a press conference in which journalists were made to listen to an alleged tape recording of a confrontation between Mgr. Albert Ndongmo and a number of the most dreaded and most wanted *Union des Populations du Cameroun* (UPC) terrorist leaders in the Country by the Government: Messrs. Ernest

---

Police State'; Also Willard Johnson, pp.202-3.

[170] See Appendix II, notes by Barrister Luke K Sendze who held briefs on behalf of the Cameroon Bishops' Council, Mgrs. Jules Peeters and Paul Verdzekov at the trial. It was a wholly trumped up affair.

[171] Mgr. Ndongmo maintains that Sabal Lecco was Prefect of Nkongsamba, see *Jeune Afrique Economie*, No.148 *Mensuel* Octobre 1991 pp121-122.

Ouandie, Celestine Takala and Gabriel Tabe, also known as *Ouambo "Le Courant."* The Minister issued a statement to the effect that justice would take its course and that the Cameroon Government would not link up the Catholic Church with the Ndongmo Affair. Sadly, this declaration was not borne out by subsequent developments.

*Fig 36. Mgr. Ndongmo standing left of Pope Paul VI at the Vatican, Rome*

It would be recalled that at the peak of terrorism in French Cameroon in the mid-1950s, the UPC had vented its frustration and anger on the Catholic Church for supposedly supporting the French Colonial Establishment in the Territory through the assassination, abduction, decapitation and maiming of Priests, Rev. Sisters, Rev. Brothers, Catechists and church workers, with untold damage to Church property. It was therefore a cruel twist of irony that fifteen years later, the same Catholic Church had become the object of persecution by the Establishment itself accusing it of collusion with the same terrorist group.[172]

The vilification of Mgr. Albert Ndongmo resulted basically from the fact that the President was convinced that there was a conspiracy within

---

[172] Richard A. Joseph, *Radical Nationalism in Cameroon - Social Origins of UPC Rebellion*, Oxford .at the Clarendon Press, 1977, pp. 177- 8, 258-61, 294-5. It is a comprehensive study of the party and the rebellion.

the Catholic hierarchy to overthrow him and install either a Catholic or other Christian leader as President. Even though the Minister of Justice declared that the Government did not intend to link the Catholic Church with the Ndongmo Affair, there were virulent attacks on the Church in party line talks, radio and political meetings, with orchestrated demonstrations in several parts of the Country, while in Buea and Bamenda mock coffins of Ndongmo were paraded in the main streets by party stalwarts. Anti-Catholic riots were organised in several towns in Northern Cameroon, the Moslem region from which the President originated. Within the same period, Brother Justin Keandie, the Marist Missionary principal of Sacred Heart College, Mankon, Bamenda was summarily expatriated on specious allegations of subversion. This was a common charge and those who came under it never had a chance to free themselves. The overall mood of the people in West Cameroon tended to be one of sullen resignation, fear and distrust of the Government.

## The Ndongmo Treason Trial: Lessons

The Ndongmo Treason Trial is typical of the Ahidjo political style. The attacks and counter attacks by the government forces during the UPC terrorist insurrection (1955-1970) had led to enormous loss of life and incalculable devastation to property with ever increasing ferocity and insecurity without let off. What transpired was that, President Ahmadou Ahidjo had personally requested Mgr. Ndongmo in whose Diocese the rebel leadership was entrenched to use his negotiating skills so that peace could return to the country through dialogue between the rebels and the State. To this effect, the then Prefect of Nkongsamba, Mr. Felix Sabal Lecco had issued Mgr. Ndongmo the necessary papers (Laissez-Passer) and fuel to enable him carry out this all too important assignment.

However, no sooner had the rebel leaders been brought out of the jungles than they were arrested, as well as Mgr. Ndongmo as he returned from Rome. They were charged with High Treason and tried in a military tribunal in Yaoundé, which maintained a hotline with the Presidency. Paradoxically, they were prosecuted by those who should have been protecting and defending them if not Ndongmo in particular, given that he had been issued the necessary official papers by the prefect.¹⁷³ Paradoxically, it was, it was the self same Felix Sabal Lecco, the former Prefect of Nkongsamba, who had become Minister of Justice in the Ahidjo Government in Yaoundé, who now was testifying against Ndongmo and the terrorists. Only two exceptionally courageous Cameroonian lawyers, Messrs Fon Gorji Dinka and Luke K Sendze held brief for Mgr Ndongmo at the request of Bishops Jules Peeters of Buea Diocese and Paul Verdzekov of Bamenda Diocese respectively, while the French lawyers invited for the defence, on the other hand were repatriated on arrival at the Air Port.

The defence lawyers pointed out that Mgr. Ndongmo had already been sentenced to death even before the trial began as there were mass demonstrations with mock coffins of him throughout the country. And indeed, Mgr. Ndongmo and his associates were duly found guilty and sentenced to execution by firing squads. This sentence for Ndongmo was later commuted to life imprisonment and after five years, to a presidential reprieve followed by exile to Canada.[174] At each stage, the President made as much political capital as possible out of the episode.

It became obvious even to the international community that President Ahmadou Ahidjo had developed a phobia of an imminent assassination by Mgr. Ndongmo, while his Government increased its suppression of the people and found excuses in mounting smear campaigns and witch-hunting against Catholics. "The Times" newspaper of London came out with a subtle but highly significant editorial in the morning of 8 January 1971 entitled, "A call for Mercy in Cameroon."[175] It was certainly international pressure and newspaper captions such as this as well as the Pope's appeal for clemency that won a break in the persecution of Catholics and a reprieve instead of an execution for Mgr. Ndongmo as was the case with Ernest Ouandié with whom he had been arrested and charged. He faced

---

[173] Paradoxically, it was the self-same Felix Sabal Lecco, the former Prefect of Nkongsamba who had now become Minister of Justice.

[174] For details See *Jeune Afrique Economie*, pp.117-134.

[175] See CP News page 1970 p. 9, also CP No. 125, May '72 p. 8ff; CP No. 504, Oct 1999, pp 24-25; CP No 138, June 1973, p.20.Barrister Luke Sendze, a prominent Bamenda based lawyer was sent to the defence of Mgr. Ndongmo by Bamenda Diocese. Written notes by Mr. Cyril Ebu.

a firing squad publicly at Douala.

There was a portentous feeling among the people that the State of West Cameroon had lost its identity and was rapidly being assimilated and ruled by a truly dictatorial regime complete with a spy network, secret and public torture of innocent citizens.[176] Anglophones were systematically being sidelined and replaced with Francophones resulting in a sense of fear and insecurity, disillusionment and helplessness among the masses. As one who had undertaken a careful study of the Cameroon Federation; placing these problems in a global African context, Willard Johnson seriously cautioned:

> Every African Society is now confronted with a severe problem of cultural and political integration. Cameroon is not alone. Indeed it is a microcosm of almost all of new Africa precisely in this respect. Like all leaders of new states, those of Cameroon must find ways to control if not eliminate ethnic rivalry, regionalism, religious competition, status and even class conflict... Cameroon stands apart, however, in as much as, to the myriad other internal discontinuities just mentioned, it adds one between British and French colonial legacies."[177]

In fact, this was a fairly accurate analysis of how the seeds of fragmentation were sown by the Government itself in West Cameroon. In perspective, the anti-climax began progressively with the President acting as if he was executing a preset, well-planned biennial schema.

---

[176] The most celebrated example which went right up to the International Court of Justice at The Hague among scores is that of Mr. Albert Mukong, a human rights activist. See, Albert Mukong, *Prisoner Without a Crime*, Editions Nubia, London, 1990. As for protests against marginalisation, assimilation and even "reunification" there are numerous publications e.g. Nfor N Susungi, *The Crisis of Unity and Democracy in Cameroon*, 1991; Albert Mukong, ed, The Case for Southern Cameroons, CAMFECO, Enugu, 1990; Rev. Njah Peter Toh, *The Anglophone Problem*, Bamenda, 2001 and, "A Tribute to Late Hon. ST Muna" by the Southern Cameroons People's Conference, Ambassador Henry Fossung, 28/1/2002, Bamenda, p. 20.

[177] Johnson, p. 286. *Cameroon Star* Vol I No.9 Monday 30 May 1966, also "KNDP laid to rest" *Cameroon Star* Vol I No 30 Monday, 10 August 1966.

## Meteoric Rise of Solomon Tandeng Muna

On 11 January 1968, President Ahidjo felt sufficiently safe and secure to depose Jua and appoint Muna as PM of West Cameroon. The former was a hot headed democrat and diehard federalist, while the latter was a centralist and opportunist, ready to bid his commands.[178] In quick succession, two years later in 1970, Foncha the other staunch federalist and co-architect of Cameroon reunification was inexplicably sacked and, yet again replaced by Muna, who was reinstated into the combined powerful positions of Prime Minister of West Cameroon and Vice President of the Federal Republic of Cameroon, in defiance of the constitutional amendment by which Foncha had been forced to relinquish his other post as PM on becoming Vice-President of the FRC in 1965. These positions earlier declared incompatible were simply brushed aside by Presidential fiat. Paradoxically, it had been the self same President Ahidjo, who by a constitutional amendment had declared the holding of both positions; PM of West Cameroon and VP of the FRC inadmissible for Foncha, who now installed Muna to handle both powerful positions by decree. The President was all powerful and could make and unmake at will. As Justice Nyo' Wakai, an insider actor aptly saw it, the Cameroon constitution in the hands of President Ahidjo and his colleagues had become nothing better than a door mat.

With uncommon audacity, in a bold front-page commentary after the dismissal of Jua and the appointment of Muna in 1968, the Cameroon Times courageously, though still guardedly commented sardonically, quoting Voltaire:

> Such is the way of human beings. Today, they acclaim you for a hero and tomorrow they are jubilant spectators when the hangman's noose closes round your neck. This is apt when it suits the occasion but in this

---

[178] Externally, to the public, The Jua administration was accused of financial and political scandals involving the Cameroon Bank; but already in 1967, the die was cast when two prominent members of the Jua cabinet; PM Kemcha and FN Ajebe Sone were excluded from the CNU list which included all the Muna supporters. see, House of Assembly Official Debates, Official Report (Government Press,1968) P.6

instance, there is no similarity. West Cameroonians required progressive change. Public opinion virtually demanded it. Anyone who was blind or deaf to this was living in a fools' paradise... Perhaps the biggest lesson the new helmsmen should learn is to avoid what killed the goose.[179]

The true import of this commentary lies in the fact that it was written at a point in time when censorship had literally set in. Meanwhile, immediately after his dismissal, Foncha was politically quarantined "like a trapped rat in a cage" and practically placed under house arrest. He was treated like a common criminal and guarded twenty-four hours a day by gendarmes, who monitored the movement of every visitor who entered his modest compound at Nkwen in Bamenda.[180]

## Ready Tool Kit for Demolition of the FRC

With Muna firmly in his grip, the tool kit for the demolition of the FRC was all set and its accomplishment was only a matter of time, which was in short supply. Thus president Ahmadou Ahidjo was set to administer a coup de grace to the Federal Republic, which came within another two-year span after the Muna appointment with the stage-managed Referendum the proffered options of which were as pointless as the choice between *"Oui"* and *"Yes"*, and the predictable results approved the President's wish by 99.99%.[181] The UN organised Plebiscite at reunification in 1961 had been entirely a Southern Cameroons affair, but that of 1972 inexplicably was arranged to include the State of East Cameroon with an overwhelming population but with no obvious stakes. This feat was appropriately daubed the "Peaceful Revolution," following which the Federal Republic of Cameroon was declared "bogus" and dissolved in favour of the "United Republic of Cameroon".

The Federated States of East and West Cameroon were abolished

---

[179] Cameroon times, Wednesday 28 February 1968.

[180] Pius B Soh, *Dr. John Ngu Foncha, The Cameroonian Statesman*, Centre for Social Sciences, Bamenda, 1999. P.196

[181] Richard Joseph, pp.80-8, Mbile, pp.246-7.

together with the Houses of Assembly and the West Cameroon House of Chiefs, which were now considered duplicative, too expensive and unnecessary. However, on careful examination it becomes obvious that the States especially, West Cameroon were intended to collapse since they were deprived of most sources of income and burdened with those which involved heavy expenditure. This bore heavily on West Cameroon, which had suffered neglect and underdevelopment under Anglo-Nigerian administration. By making the states liabilities and parasites to the Federal Government the way was covertly being paved for the abolition of the FRC on the grounds of insolvency. Paradoxically, the final blow for the liquidation of the FRC was ushered in by the discovery of huge reserves of oil and gas in the *Bakassi Peninsula* which automatically raised West Cameroon from penury to the *el Dorado* of Cameroon. Logically, therefore West Cameroon should have become self-sufficient but constitutionally, the Federal Government had tactfully been accorded all the heavy sources of revenue. This was carefully done:

> Including foreign aid, leaving the governments of the federated states with very little financial autonomy, the federal government made the governments of the federated states financially dependent. This severely curtailed their powers. Indeed, by claiming for itself nearly all the most important functions of state business, the federal government ensured the redundancy of the governments of the federated states.[182]

Despite the accusations that the FRC was costly and had bogus administrative structures, a couple of years later, the budget of the new highly acclaimed "Unicameral Parliament" more than doubled that of the combined dissolved State Assembles together with the House of Chiefs. The President of the United Republic of Cameroon, Head of State and President of the Cameroon National Union was granted or, more appropriately "arrogated" to himself, plenary powers to rule single-handedly by decree without pretence or reference to Parliament for twelve months.

What resulted from these carefully organized manoeuvres was a totally

---

[182] http://lucy.ukc.ac.uk/Chilver/Paideuma/paideuma-Indirec-2.html

shattered political landscape in West Cameroon. In a bid for survival, the erstwhile political leadership took to stigmatizing, mudslinging and back-stabbing one another. With such discordant voices ringing from Endeley, through Foncha and Jua to Muna, there were hardly any individuals left to express the genuine feelings of their compatriots openly as these "leaders" tended to compete more in singing tunes that best addressed the wishes of "*Grand Camarade*", the author of all political, social and economic patronage. However, it deserves to be added that the political atmosphere was over ridden with suppression occasioning widespread fear.

It therefore took courageous journalists and tactful satirists of the calibre of "Ako-Aya" to air the mounting fears of the voiceless masses. For example, on the occasion of the 10th anniversary celebrations of Reunification (1961-1972), Tataw Obenson grieved over the moral decadence that had gripped the once beloved Southern Cameroons and tersely noted:

> Industries have sprung up, salaries have increased.... like myself you can tell me the changes you have undergone these ten years. Ten years ago, I only drank one bottle of Star Beer a week; today I can knock down ten especiale [183] a day. Ten years ago, I did not know what they call girl friend, today, I have started a scholarship scheme and they are going to Britain one a year.[184]

Finally, engulfed in a climate of heavy suppression complete with secret police networks, torture chambers, underground prisons and a muzzled press, the last nail was driven into the coffin of the "Golden Age of Southern Cameroon". This deepened the feelings of distrust, disillusionment, resentment and revulsion among the people and provided fertile ground on which revisionist and nationalist dissident movements sprouted.

The point of insincerity has frequently been missed when analysing the dynamics of the 1961 Foumban Constitutional Conference and

---

[183] "Special" was a very popular beer produced by Brasseries du Cameroun around that time.

[184] In this connection Mr. Peter Ndembo Motomby-Woleta bought the "*Chronicle*" newspaper from Nigeria for the KPP. It later served the KNC/KPP Alliance.

subsequent adverse developments in the political life of West Cameroon supposedly consequential from it. Instead of focusing on the "bad faith", the absence of political will and insincerity repeatedly displayed by Francophone administrations in the light of the subsequent abrogation of solidly reached agreements that were jointly brokered, including even the Constitution, the fundamental law of the land, unnecessary issue is taken for example, with the composition and venial flaws of the Southern Cameroons delegation to the Foumban talks.[185] A lot of this is done without reference to the relevant documents. For example, complaining about the composition of delegates to that conference, it turns out that Southern Cameroons despatched twice as many delegates i.e. twenty-five to twelve from Republic of Cameroon, all from Ahidjo's UC, while those from West Cameroon comprised both the ruling KNDP, the Opposition CPNC, the OK, Chiefs and the administration.

*Fig 37. Hon S T Muna seated second from left.*

## *The Muna (Mixed) Government 1968*
Mr. S T Muna:          Prime Minister
Mr. H N Elangwe:    Deputy Prime Minister and Minister of Finance
Mr. B T Sakah:         Minister of Local Government

---

[185] Discussion with Dr. JN Foncha, April 1999. He strongly believed that there was much bad faith with our "brothers" because they do not keep to their word.

Mr. M N Luma: Secretary of State Prime Minister's Office
Mr. J C Kangkolo: Secretary of State Natural Resources
Mr. N N Mbile: Secretary of State Lands and Surveys
Mr. B T B Foretia: Secretary of State, Public Service
Mr. J C Wanzie: Secretary of State for Primary Education
Mr. S N Tamfu: Secretary of State, Prime Minister's Office
Mr. Moutchia: Secretary of State Public Service

At the conference, President Ahmadou Ahidjo had received a standing ovation when he declared in his keynote address:

> You know that even before the Referendum and since then during our talks with Mr. Foncha, we chose a federal framework... It was because linguistic, administrative and economic differences do not permit us to envisage seriously and reasonably a State of the unitary and centralised type. It was because a confederal system on the other hand, being too loose, would not favour the close coming together and the intimate connection, which we desire. A federal structure therefore, would be the only one, which suits our particular situation.[186]

Further, referring to the profound fraternal and conciliatory attributes of the discussions, he postulated that:

> The value of a constitution is not measured by the length of its articles, but its well thought out and reasonable application by men animated by the same patriotic spirit and by the same desire to build a national community, in the bosom of which all strive to work for the common good, prosperity and peace, and putting aside all partisan ideas.[187]

And, in conclusion, Foncha, the leader of the Southern Cameroons delegation to the Foumban Conference emphatically proclaimed: "The recommendations we made stem out of the brotherly feeling we have

---

[186] Foncha to the Minister of External Relations, Paris, France, 30/12/98. Para. 6.

[187] Soh p. 156

towards the Republic of Cameroun. We feel that we are building our house, and not building a house for anybody, and any suggestion we make to strengthen that house you may be sure stems from our very best interest." In his turn, Endeley expressed his "great pleasure" in associating himself with his colleague the Premier of Southern Cameroons, prophetically maintaining that:

> We were here with an open heart to work as a team. We have succeeded in working as a team in looking through the proposals, which were placed by your government before the Southern Cameroons delegates.... Much of the desire of the people of Southern Cameroons to unite with their brothers will depend on the attitude of the people of the Republic of Cameroun and the manner in which they treat those proposals.[188]

It is therefore obvious that, the Foumban Talks ended up on a near "perfect" harmonious note and the collapse of the Federal Republic of Cameroon can hardly be limited to its shortcomings. Above all, its Article 47/1 plainly stipulated the inviolability of the Federal Constitution stating that: "Any proposal for the revision of the present constitution which impairs the unity and integrity of the Federation shall be inadmissible;" and furthermore, that; "Proposals for revision shall be adopted by simple majority vote of the Members of the Federal Assembly provided that such majority includes a majority of the representatives in the Federal Assembly of each of the Federated States." Nothing could be more explicit.

But, as it suited his whims and caprices, President Ahmadou Ahidjo as Head of State and chairman of the CNU party had these provisions brushed aside in 1972 in favour of a Unitary State. This fate would have befallen the constitution had it been "cast in iron" so to speak, or; signed, sealed and delivered by the best of constitutional jurists, whether in Whitehall in London or in the Champs Elysees in Paris. There is no perfect constitution; what ultimately matters, generally, is the "spirit" and not the "letter" of any accord.

Regardless of its limitations, in subsequent years the recurrent cry

---

[188] Ibid 153

has been for a return to the 1961 Federal Constitution or a version of it. On deep reflection, two decades later, following the inconclusive Tripartite Talks held in Yaoundé in December 1991, Dr. John N Foncha in a Memorandum to the Cameroon people continued to stress that:

> The unity of any country depends on the happiness and prosperity of its people and not simply on having one parliament with its uncertain system of government. It depends more on the ways the people try to handle their affairs within their Federated States in the ways they judge to be the best, and the freedom to do so especially as they can introduce new and better ways of carrying on the affairs of their Federated States... The system lends itself to keen competition by emulation among the Federated States, leading to rapid progress in the whole Federal State.[189]

*Fig 38. The Ahidjo Government, 1975; Front row from left to right: Messrs Ayissi Mvodo, Sadou Daoudou, Paul Biya, Ahmadou Ahidjo, Samuel Eboa, Enock Kwayeb and Emmanuel T Egbe.*

He regretted the fact that Government participants at the Tripartite

---

[189] See "A Memorandum on the Return to Federalism in Cameroon", presented by Dr. JN Foncha, to all Patriotic Cameroonians, Nkwen, Bamenda 20 Dec. 1991.

Conference showed deep distrust and suspicion for any form of federalism for fear of secession even from one like him, who all along had displayed abiding loyalty to the State and faith in national unity. Dr. Foncha, a thoroughgoing pacifist, cautioned that the proper unity of a nation is that of hearts and souls, love and respect of one another for the peace and prosperity of all. In fact, he maintained all along that at no moment did he ever regret the option he had taken for reunification and that given another chance, he would do the same thing because he believed it was the best thing for Southern Cameroons and the entire Cameroon state. His first option had been secession from Nigeria followed by extended UN Trusteeship, independence and negotiated reunification between an independent Southern Cameroons and an independent Republic of Cameroon but this was torpedoed at the UN. He had no apologies to make for reunification because it was the right and logical way, the only difference being that finally it was precipitated. The problem with reunification was not in the fact but the manner in which it was executed by the leadership, which violated the accord and shattered the federal terms which had been agreed as the indispensable foundation for the union. It was therefore illogical to regard him as a secessionist although all that had been happening was tantamount to pushing the Anglophones out of the union they had massively brought about.

## Chapter Six

# VIOLATING THE "INVIOLABLE FEDERAL CONSTITUTION"

### Ahidjo: Enigmatic Character

President Ahmadou Ahidjo, who ruled Cameroon from 1960-1982, was at best something of a 'Benevolent Despot', but on the whole was an unmitigated dictator and is difficult to define or categorise, a view shared by his official biographers. However, they affirm that his iron clad rule was necessary for building a modern nation. For sure, he was mercurial; with a great capacity for double speak tendencies and the freedom to change his mind at will on major issues without explanation or apology to anybody. These policies are best illustrated by the manner in which he administered Southern-West Cameroon from 1961-1972.

On the nature of the Federation, *Article 47(1) of the Federal Constitution* resulting from the Foumban Constitutional Conference was explicit, clear, simple and categorical: "*No bill to amend the constitution may be introduced if it tends to impair the unity and integrity of the federation*". It is pertinent that President Ahidjo was the Chairman both of the Foumban Constitutional Conference and the Yaoundé Tripartite Conference, which tidied up and formulated the resolutions of the Foumban Conference into the fundamental Law of the Land. *He appended his signature to validate both documents and above all solemnly swore to be the guarantor and protector of the Federal Constitution.*

On the theme of "Reunification" between the two States; British Southern Cameroons and French Cameroon, Ahidjo had been vocal and consistent during his maiden visit to Southern Cameroons of July,14-17 1960 both in his spontaneous and prepared addresses, first on arrival at

Tiko International Airport and subsequently at Buea and Victoria. Later on at the UN that year, when requested to come clean on his stand with regard to reunification, he remained steadfast and unequivocal reiterating that reunification was to be on the basis of "equality". Formally, at Buea, he had declared, and it was officially reported in the Press Release that:

> Unification was a natural cry and debt bequeathed to us by our parents. He repeated that his government's desire was reunification and not annexation and that reunification would be on a federal basis. In a final declaration before he took off, he declared. I am not going into the French Union[190].

Next, addressing the UN General Assembly that same year on this topic, he manifestly declared without any ambiguity or equivocation:

> I would not like firmness and clarity of our stand to be interpreted as a desire for integration on my part, which would sound the death knell to the hopes of our brothers under British administration. In other words, if our brothers of the British zone wish to unite with an independent Cameroon, we are ready to discuss the matter with them but we will discuss it on a footing of equality.[191]

Given that the venue where this speech was delivered was the UN in the glare of the international community, the entire quotation but, especially the second sentence emphasising the phrase, "on a footing of equality" is of special significance in circumstances where the President kept vacillating. Next, on the floor at the Foumban Constitutional Conference the following year, in his key note address, President Ahidjo as a corollary to his previous addresses at Tiko, Buea, Victoria and the UN continued to affirm:

---

[190] See Southern Cameroons, Press *Release* no.911 of 19 July 1960.

[191] *Recueilles Des Discours Presidentiel, 1958-68* (Paris, *les Nouvelles Editions*, 1979) pp. 8-9.

We approach all these questions with total goodwill, with neither regret nor bitterness. The majority has already taken their stand and there is no other clear thing to do today than to respect the will of the people by building for them a future framework that they have fixed. ... You know that even before the referendum and since then during our talks with Mr. Foncha, we chose a federal framework. It was so because linguistic, administrative and economic differences do not permit us to envisage seriously and reasonably a state of the unitary and centralised type ...[192]

These three block quotations come from eloquent speeches that were solemnly delivered by President Ahmadou Ahidjo on some important occasions on the topical issue of the Reunification of the two Trust Territories of British Southern Cameroons and French Cameroon (before its independence in January 1961). These are chosen from among many and clearly demonstrate the mindset of President Ahidjo on different occasions.

## Ahidjo: Consistently Inconsistent

What is noteworthy here, is his consistency in affirming the key issues of: equality between the two states, the choice of "federalism" from among other options as the most appropriate mode for the two states coming together; the total exclusion of obnoxious ideas such as; "annexation", "integration" or "assimilation of the smaller by the bigger state" i.e., Southern Cameroons by East Cameroon; the respect for existing administrative and other differences between them; the importance of dialogue, fraternity and above all, respect for the will of the people as the expressed through the plebiscite of 11 February 1961. Another very momentous insertion made on the floor of the Foumban Constitutional Conference arose from the Anglophone delegates who were uncomfortable with the phrase "one and indivisible" with regard to the nature of the amalgamation of the two states which they found "repugnant". There and then, Ahidjo asked for it to be expunged or deleted immediately, pure and simple.

On the other hand, still of supreme importance, President Ahidjo's

---

[192] National Archives, Buea (NAB), *Press Release*, No. 1467.

opinions were thoughtfully taken care of and finally encapsulated in Article 47 (1) of the Federal Constitution, which he as Chairman of the Conference and Head of State, solemnly signed and swore to defend. It simply and clearly stated as indicated above, that: "No bill to amend the constitution may be introduced if it tend to impair the unity and integrity of the federation."[193] Thus it was inconceivable for him as the custodian and defender of the same federal constitution to become its ultimate violator.

Ben Bella, nationalist, former President of Algeria and hero of that country's struggle for independence, was also a contemporary of President Ahmadou Ahidjo and together they attended conferences especially the OAU and exchanged pertinent ideas. Interviewed by Marthe Moumie in 2006, Ben Bella had a few striking observations to make about his colleague. He noted:

> *I had many heated discussions with former President Ahmadou Ahidjo, who, with the support of France, severely repressed UPC militants' revolts. To me, he was nothing but a bloody dictator.* During OAU meetings, we used to have very harsh arguments. I remember during the first OAU meeting, President Ahidjo vented his anger on Egyptian President Nasser and all those who were opposed to colonialism.[194] (My emphasis)

So, incredibly, Ahmadou Ahidjo was not in favour of independence for French Cameroun. This clearly emerged in correspondence he had with Andre Marie Mbida, the Prime Minister, whom he succeeded. In his letter to Mbida on 15 May 1957, Ahidjo made his views on this issue mighty clear with reference to a speech he had made, noting:

> You talked of: political opinion, of independence of autonomy, of the issue of integration into the African union. You also talked of the status of our nation, Cameroon. Allow me, sir, to tell you and the whole Assembly that this is not the right way to tackle the matter. The day the status

---

[193] See the Federal Republic of Cameroon Constitution in the appendix.

[194] The interview is contained in Marthe Moumié's book entitled: *Victims Du Colonialism Francais*, Editions Duboris, 2006. See, *The Post*, no. 01631 of Monday June 01 2015.

of our nation was voted, some people complained, telling us that our country's fate needed to be decided, once and for all. Those people were curious to know on which grounds we chose not to declare ourselves in favour of independence. You said Cameroon was marching towards independence[195].

Next, he came out even more forcefully on the topic, stating clearly:

Let me, on behalf of the Cameroonian union, bring some precisions. Independence means sovereignty. We strongly believe that no Cameroonian is against our country getting its sovereignty. And if we are against immediate independence of our country, permit me to say; Dear Prime Minister, neither France nor you - if you obtain the nomination from the Legislative Assembly tomorrow, talk less of the Legislative Assembly itself, have the right to decide on the future of our nation.[196]

Thus Ahidjo's stand on the capital question of autonomy for French Cameroon was lucid; he and his party wanted none of it, nor was he in favour of reunification. He stood for perpetrated colonial rule. It is ironical that he was nominated Prime Minister and became not only the President of independent French Cameroon but of a reunified Cameroon as well, albeit a reluctant one. He was simply abiding by the will of his colonial masters, without a declared personal conviction over the issues at stake. There can be little doubt as to the ramifications of this paradoxical situation.

*It is befitting that Ahidjo's biographers deliberately characterize him variously as: A man, who was unemotional, one who regarded any show of emotions in public as a sign of weakness; one who hated public debate; hardly smiled in public; a man who was studiously patient; determined, hard-hearted; unpredictable and an individual who liked to be considered something of a mystic.*[197]

---

[195] Ibid.

[196] *The Post*, no. 01631 of Monday 01 June 2015.

[197] See; Richard Joseph ed, Gaullist *Africa* chapters 3 and 4; ABC, *The History of Cameroon, Ahidjo* and Political Bureau of the Cameroon National Union, Paul Bory

By no means exhaustive, these descriptions from three sources fairly well depict the enigmatic personality of President Ahmadou Adhijo, of uncertain paternity, which might have had something to do with the fact that he was brought up solely by his very caring mother, who was determined to see him succeed in life. In the ultimate analysis, he was so many diverse personalities, a legion, put together in one. But for these sources, it is easy to accuse any honest description of President Ahmadou Adhijo as exaggerated or bias. Consequently, whatever is put out here keeps as close to the sources as possible with ample objective illustrations.

For example; after the emphatic declarations made above on the indissolubility of the federation; barely a year after the Foumban Constitutional Conference, at the subsequent UC Congress holding at Ebolowa from 4-6 July 1962; President Ahidjo declared to the delegates:

> It was unthinkable to tamper with the republican form of regime; it was the republic which had to transform itself into a federation, taking into account the return to it of a part of its territory, a part possessing certain special characteristics. The question therefore was not one of the birth of a new republic with federal form. Bowing to this logic, we decided, therefore, to amend the constitution of 21$^{st}$ February 1960, since language and cultural differences needed to be given legal consideration[198].

All the earlier proclamations he had made at Tiko, Buea, Victoria, the UN and Foumban portions of which are quoted above were thrown to the winds. In fact, soon after this he referred to "reunification" not as a consequence of the supreme will of the people of Southern Cameroons in the plebiscite, which he had maintained had to be respected, but this time, as an *"imposition on us by the UN"*. Thus it becomes impossible to keep track of the President's line of thought in interpreting his speeches (some of which lasted hours!).

Apparently, when Third World power hungry leaders start expressing themselves in lengthy, often meaningless outburst challenging and

---

Publishers, Monaco, 1968.

[198] See; Ebolowa UC Congress of 4-6 July 1962

attempting to reinterpret, correct and domesticate ageless philosophies and concepts like 'democracy', it usually marks the onset of justification for the introduction of tyrannous, autocratic and dictatorial rule concentrating power in their hands. Contextualised, it is much like trying to reinvent the wheel and, on the balance calls into question the academic, intellectual and mental credentials that backup such audacious pronouncements. Most if not all of President Ahidjo's serious declarations were made initially at UC congresses and later on at the CNU ones. This was what precisely happened at the UC Building at Yaoundé in September 1963. With an outburst of simulated impassioned fury against the concept of "democracy". As if provoked by an invisible foe, the President bellowed in a fit of rage:

> For heaven's sake, let us adapt this democracy to our own realities, which are not the same as those of other countries. We have extolled the single and unified party in order to achieve indispensable national unity. In order to achieve it ... certain ones had to resort to dictatorship. The monarchy which existed there was, in my estimation worse than the single party. The citizens because they were against the policy of the king or emperor, paid for their opposition with their lives and were decapitated. Thank God we have not come to that[199].

Here comparison is being made of 18th century Europe and 21st century independent Cameroon in Africa, after, countless wars and revolutions had taken place to bring about liberalism, socialism democratic change and even independence to his own country. In practical terms, if indeed he knew the substance of his speech, he was comparing 18th century despotic rule in Europe to 21st century 'advanced' democracy in Cameroon, coming two centuries later – most dissimilar circumstances! Of course, this was a display of abject ignorance of the facts of history.

To demonstrate the lessons he had learnt from this rich European history; on record we know what he had done to the opposition leaders in East Cameroon, all of whom were thrown behind bars and their parties smothered. Worse even happened to the UPC leadership together with

---

[199] Willard Johnson, p.197

their rank and file, dozens of whom were publicly executed as a deterrent; some even after they had been discharged and acquitted in civilian courts. Trials of political activists were transferred to makeshift military tribunals, where they were invariably found guilty by semi illiterate soldiers acting as judges.[200] However, this time at the inauguration of the UC Building in Yaoundé, it was a signal that President Ahidjo was preparing the ground to carry out some truly atrocious policies.

In effect, the demise of the *Golden Age* became discernible in September 1966 with the imposition of the "One Party" system through the introduction of the Cameroon National Union, (CNU), which practically was a mere christening or amplification of Ahidjo's own *Union Camerounaise* (UC), the catalyst and core as it merely absorbed all the other political parties but itself basically remained unchanged. He had begun by eliminating all opposition to his personalised rule in East Cameroon and succeeded in cowing, splitting and incorporating all the parties in West Cameroon into his UC. The next significant step in this process of annihilating the State of West Cameroon came with the deposition of AN Jua, the popular, democratically elected Prime Minister, who was the leader of the KNDP majority in the West Cameroon Parliament in 1968.

Ahidjo replaced AN Jua with ST Muna, his minion, who was neither an elected Member of the West Cameroon House of Assembly nor leader of the largest party in the House of Assembly. This was the highly cherished democratic practice in the comportment of the Westminster Parliamentary system of Government inherited from the British Colonial Masters, universally acclaimed as the Mother of Parliaments. Of this, Dr. Endeley the Prime Minster in 1958 during celebrations marking the Centenary of the Founding of Victoria had been justifiably proud, regarding it as one of the most cherished legacies inherited from the "British Government and prevalent throughout the British Commonwealth of Nations". Muna's imposition set the entire system into disarray as after that he himself did not recognise or respect the rules of the game and began appointing people regardless of their status into his cabinet. Two years later in 1970, Ahidjo, who had arrogated all powers to himself using

---

[200] See, Luke Sendze, Appendix II

the CNU, causelessly sacked Dr. JN Foncha with ignominy from the post of Vice President of the FRC. In violation of the constitution, he again had Muna raised to fill in that position in addition to single-handedly running the State of West Cameroon at his master's behest.

## Folly and Deceit Entrenched As National Policy

Any lingering doubts as to the odious role President Ahidjo played in the demolition of the FRC, which it was claimed he had been instrumental in constructing were systematically and finally dispersed when he himself boasted of his dark deeds, which he regarded as bravado. In fact, it is demonstrable that all the stages of the demolition process had actually been carefully planned and meticulously executed with President Ahmadou Ahidjo in the pilot's seat. It clearly emerges from a critical analysis of his speeches and actions that he had never in the least believed in the concepts of: federation, democracy or sharing power with anybody. However, it marks the height of folly and contradiction that he could outwardly have been appearing to build what he covertly was tearing down to shreds at the same time. A nation constructed on the foundation of folly and deceit cannot hope to withstand the stresses of socioeconomic, cultural and political development which demand transparency and probity in public affairs for enduring progress.

This policy was tactfully engraved at the *Union Camerounaise* (UC) reform congress, which held at Maroua in September 1960, where President Ahidjo announced the creation of a "Great National Partie Unifié" (Grand National Party). With several tendencies elbowing each other within the party, hovering between the total elimination of the opposition parties and their implantation or absorption into the UC, Ahidjo's suggestion finally prevailed. In fact, it was the most liberal compared to the radical conservative views raised by hardliners within the party like Moussa Yaya and Samuel Kame, who thought such liberalism would be counterproductive in putting down the UPC rebellion, while Charles Assale steered a middle course towards a mass, grassroots party. For East Cameroon, the immediate target was the opposition parties, which, it was decided had either to be absorbed within the UC or to be annihilated out right.

Already by mid 1961, the parties and group of parties led by Victor Kamga and Pierre Kamdem Ninyim had moved over to join the UC.[201] However, it did not save Ninyim from execution or Kamga from being deposed as Minister of Finance and finally being thrown in jail. The same fate befell Charles Okala, Minister of Foreign Affairs who headed the *Parti Socialiste Camerounais* (PSC). He rejected Charles Assale's example of surrendering to absorption within the UC towards the formation of an illusory *Partie Unifié*, a guise for the single party, describing it as democratic suicide. Of course, Okala and all the other opposition leaders: Dr. Bebey Eyidi, Mayi Matip and Mbida, who collectively turned down his offer to join the UC, and circulated a manifesto against it appealing to ethnic and religious sentiments, got a brutal response from the Ahidjo Regime. The four including Okala were arrested on the basis of a Decree of 12 March 1962, tried, convicted, imprisoned for three years each and heavily fined.[202] Next, Ahidjo's gaze was focused, even more intensely on the politicians of West Cameroon with whom he was then conducting negotiations on the delicate question of reunification. As he further elaborated at a press conference in November 1961, it was to be:

> A *Great National Partie Unifié* in which Cameroonians would enter freely after becoming convinced [about its desirability] and a party in which will prevail democracy, freedom of expression and where several tendencies would coexist, it being understood of course that the minority would uphold the opinions reached by the majority.[203]

The emphasis on democracy, freedom of expression and admission of several tendencies is significant. Its target was the acquisition of power for the goal of national unity. Unlike the UPC, whose platform was adopted,

---

[201] Of course, this did not save Kamdem Ninyim from execution in 1963 on charges of complicity in a murder case while, Victor Kamga was dropped off as Foreign Minister and subsequently imprisoned.

[202] See *Gaullist Africa*. p.65

[203] Richard Joseph ed. *Gaullist Africa: Cameroon Under Ahmadou Ahidjo*, fourth dimension publishers 1976, p.61.

but whose leadership was decapitated and its attempts at coalition spurned, there was no clear mission, vision, ideology or principles governing the party. Apparently, it was just a pragmatic ruse to win support and gain power. This precisely was what happened under the indefatigable leadership of Moussa Yaya, as Secretary General, when between January 1959 and July 1960 at the UC Congress at Ngaoundére, membership had grown exponentially jumping from 15.000 to 30.000, all within seven months.[204] In addition to being a grassroots movement, it promised individuals and groups, whatever they desired; reliance on the French hierarchy, clerical liberalism (with Mgr. Jean Zoa Catholics and other Christians in view), and support to traditional rulers. Islam as a religion and Moslem attire, were a given though not openly declared. It was therefore an all-inclusive party or rather a 'movement' as it meant everything to everybody.

## Grand Partie Unifié (The Grand Unified National Party)

On crossing over to West Cameroon, which was his main target, Ahidjo canvassed support for his '*Grand Partie Unifie*'(Grand Unified National Party), promising that it was to be a free, open, grassroots egalitarian movement within which everybody would have a say, meaning that it was going to be thoroughly liberal and democratic. In fact, this was the main reason why it appealed to the Anglophone politicians who even up to the Foumban Constitutional Conference saw him as a 'God send' leader. The UC political platform agreed with the democratic principles inherent within the Westminster Parliamentary system prevalent in West Cameroon. This is likely what would have attracted people like Dr. Endeley to anticipate the single or One Party system given the promises, declarations and assurances made by Ahidjo and his cohorts like Moussa Yaya that in it every one would find a place and have a voice.

## The Fonlon "KNDP Memorandum of Protest to Ahidjo"

It will be recalled that after reunification, the two ruling parties of

---

[204] Ibid, pp.52-63.

the Republic of Cameroun, the *Union Camerounaise* (UC) of President Ahmadou Ahidjo and of West Cameroon, the Kamerun National Democratic Party (KNDP) of Dr. John Ngu Foncha went into a coalition in 1962 with the agreement that either party would run the affairs of their separate states, without any interference from the other and that both would subscribe to administration at the centre (Federation). With Ahidjo as President and Foncha as Vice President, it was assumed that the pair worked harmoniously together and that the parties at the federal level equally worked in close collaboration. Consequently, it was a rude shock when on 1 August 1964 Dr. Bernard Fonlon came out with the lengthy, pithy "KNDP Memorandum of Protest to Ahmadou Ahidjo" after three years of apparent collaboration declaring that in all that time practically nothing had worked between the coalition partners. The incisive document noted with utter dissatisfaction the exclusion of the KNDP from all the decision making processes and called for inclusion henceforth. It suggested joint machinery for this purpose, called for a revision of the constitution and a council of ministers that would discuss all government projects before submission to the Head of State. These suggestions were to be implemented before the end of the transitional period due in 1966.

In Fonlon's words: "We of the KNDP know the fervour and the determined will that animated the struggle of our people for reunification, and the high hopes that fired this struggle. We have also come to see what this enterprise means to Africa. He regretted that there was disillusionment, discontent and frustration sinking and spreading such as could wring and crush the human spirit, adding: "There is nothing so calculated to wring and crush the human spirit as to know what should be done and yet to have to stand by impotent and see the opposite taking place. This desperation can become explosive." The KNDP demanded a genuine part in the making of this country. There was nothing extraordinary in the demand as, "Wherever there is a coalition government negotiations on ministerial portfolios is an absolute prerequisite", which unfortunately had not taken place for all the three years; he wondered who was responsible. To Fonlon, the constitution was the soul of the state:

> The shape we want to give to our country is that of a unity in which due respect is given to diversity, that is, a closely knit federation; a

politico-cultural entity where each constituent element contributes a distinctive and original party to the harmonized whole – a constitution is to the state what the soul is to man.[205]

As the transitional period was coming to a close, the KNDP was putting forward an earnest plea, that it was absolutely necessary to "re-examine our present constitution" in the light of the past three years and to refuse to do that would be the gravest error. Thereafter, the KNDP made six positive demands, namely: that discussion, negotiation and agreement should become the role in the coalition to ensure dignified participation in this government; a general framework policy and particular applications in diverse fields should be defined and adopted to give coherence and direction to all government action; a machinery should be set up at party and government levels for implementation of policies; that the constitution should be revised to provide for a council of ministers or for reinstallation of the principle that all government decisions are taken in council (cabinet system); the provision of an *ad hoc* committee to work out the details of these suggestions and finally, that these proposals should be studied, worked out and put into effect before the final close of the transitional period in 1966.

It is needless to add that not a single one of the suggestions made in the Fonlon KNDP memo was effected, meaning that for the entire existence of the UC-KNDP coalition from 1962 - 1966 not a single KNDP proposal was adopted. Moussa Yaya declared that it was a Presidential system with only one voice, the President's. However, it indicated the incompatibility of the two systems and deepened the dislike and distrust Ahidjo had for Foncha, who by this act had identified himself as the enemy within and an obstacle who had to be cleared off sooner rather than later. If anything, the KNDP stance hastened the introduction of the one party system (the CNU) but, first the KNDP had to be weakened, destroyed and put out of the way. Muna became the Judas Iscariot, Ahidjo and Moussa Yaya used to create the Cameroon united congress (CUC) so as to wreck the KNDP.

---

[205] Nalova Lyonga, ed. *Socrates In Cameroon, The Life and Works of Bernard Nsokika Fonlon*, Tortoise Books, 1989

All within four years Jua and Foncha were out, successively replaced by Muna. In fact, Ahidjo soon boasted that he had successfully shattered the disorderly so called parliamentary system. Democracy, the parliamentary system, federalism and sharing power did not exist in the Ahidjo Machiavellian mentality. The brutality meted out to the opposition leaders in East Cameroon had only been camouflaged and not abolished. Whereas in August 1964, Bernard Fonlon proudly declared that: "A constitution is to the state what the soul is to man", Justice Nyo' Wakai thirty years later, ably demonstrated that in Cameroon it was the exact opposite, as it is actually a door mat: used, abused and discarded as it suits the whims and caprices of the Head of State. This occurred countless times but most notably in 1972 and in 1984.[206]

As a testimony that no solid, progressive and democratic nation could be constructed on a policy of folly, falsehood and deceit by an unstable and untrustworthy character like Ahidjo, it is amazing and revealing that finally he either executed, imprisoned, exiled, sacked or politely dismissed without exception, his closest collaborators, the last of whom was his childhood and livelong collaborator, Moussa Yaya. He did this just before going on exile. No one was spared because he actually trusted none of them.

The concluding point in all of this is that, folly and deceit finally had become embedded and entrenched as party policy and ultimately dispensed as government and national policy. When the UC camouflaged into the Cameroon National Union (CNU) in September, 1966, practically nothing had changed as it carried with it the Maroua declaration of deceit and culture of lies. If anything, matters had only gotten worse as the CNU became the oracle of the Head of State, an instrument which recognised only his voice. So far, it has been demonstrated that the President violated all his major declarations especially those made on and, to Southern Cameroonians till he finally demolished the Federal Republic of Cameroon. National unity, progress and development constructed on a foundation of falsehood at best remains flimsy and can hardly endure the strains and stresses of the powerful winds of change that batter a world

---

[206] Nyo'oWakai, *Inside The Fence*: Bamenda: Patron Publishing House, Box 598, 31 Jan. 2000

that has become a global village.

That an open declaration by the Head of State could not be taken as a given was altogether strange to Southern Cameroonians, where leaders were *ipso facto*: magnetic, honest, dignified, personalities, role models and charismatic figures who strove to leave footprints on the sands of time for posterity. They were invariably admired not feared, respected and not dreaded, since they were heroes and role models to their people, who had elected them in the first place. Having to face power hungry, villainous, blood thirsty leaders with bad will and bad faith, to whom the constitution was a mere door mat and who were the first to violate the fundamental and supreme law of the land have been traumatic experiences in Anglophone Southern, West Cameroon, where the constitution and the rule of law always reigned supreme.[207]

For the parliamentary system to have been spurned and replaced with the '*List System*', where individual talents were suppressed in favour of factions and finally in the *One Party System* where the choice of the PM and other decisions rested with the Head of State (President) alone, whose decisions and appointments were not subject even to parliamentary scrutiny was far from democratic. This was the system Ahidjo celebrated and finally installed to replace the democratic West Cameroon Westminster Parliamentary system on which he poured scorn. With the CNU as his oracle '*Grand Camarade*', as his biographers maintain was imbued with the qualities of firm leadership, as he was: "iron willed, hard hearted" and "one who always obtained what he wanted".[208]

This practically meant that as: head of the CNU party, Head of State and Head of Government, all power and patronage radiated from him. No sane person dared contradict him and all citizens literally without exception "out of fear" were reduced to sycophants and praise singers. This is a situation not easy to configure in the comfort and peace of our homes and offices with relative freedom of speech, press, religion and all else. To

---

[207] Wakai, Justice Nyo', *Under The Broken Seal of Justice: The Law And My Times*, Bamenda: Langaa Research and Publishing, CIG, 2009.

[208] See *Afrique Biblio Club (ABC)*, France, *The History Of Cameroon, Once Upon A Time, Ahidjo*

the mass of Southern Cameroonians, who do not know or understand the history of reunification and, especially the role of the ruling francophone majority injected with indifference, bad faith and lack of political will, fingers will forever be pointed at those "who took us over there."

In fact, there are those who regard them as "sell outs" pure and simple. The straightforward explanation is that the Southern Cameroonian leaders were trusting people, who in all discussions and agreements took their Francophone compatriots with equal and total trust and faith but as exemplified by President Ahidjo nothing was guaranteed. This knowledge can only come from following the facts positively with open and tolerant minds. It can never be overemphasised that a solid Cameroon nation can only be built on democratic principles, truth, sincerity and dedication. Southern Cameroons leaders at all levels could be identified with honesty, diligence, resourceful, dedication and above all truthfulness. A leader's word was his bond. The deviants were few and far in between and mostly learnt their crafts after reunification.

## Southern Cameroons: Tough, Resilient Roots

"Anglophone" Southern Cameroonians as a people and a socio-cultural, geo-political entity have a powerful, incorruptible and enduring spirit, mostly born of sustained adversity and hardship, which may not immediately be apparent until critically examined. It has firm, radical roots buttressed by socio-cultural, economic, ethnic, linguistic and demographic tentacles developed over the past century of fusion and interaction, which historically go back to precolonial and pre-German times. More concretely, these roots are traced back to when as a unit; it was administered distinctively as "British Southern Cameroons" within the vast Nigerian Federation running through the stages of the Mandate and Trusteeship periods until it attained statehood.

Interestingly, though stifled and integrated within Nigeria, this spirit thrived, got strengthened by endurance in tough conditions and, with the rise of African nationalism found expression and leadership in: Paul M Kale, Dr. EML Endeley, NN Mbile and JN Foncha with scores of other compatriots under the standard of the Cameroon Youth League (CYL) in Lagos in 1940. At about the same time GM Mbene had instinctively responded to the same call back at home in Victoria and founded the Cameroon Welfare Union, (CWU) in 1939. This process underwent final gestation within the National Congress of Nigeria and Cameroons (NCNC), the first Nigerian political party created by Dr. Nnamdi Azikiwe in 1944. The addition of "Cameroons" to the name of the party was significant as it was maintained even after Southern Cameroons attained its Quasi Federal status indicating the prominence it enjoyed within the Nigerian Federation.

Eventually, in consonance with constitutional changes and the democratic ferment, elected members representing Southern Cameroons in Nigerian legislatures were rudely reminded of their innate "Cameroonian" identity with the eruption of the Eastern Regional Crisis in 1953. It was at this point that they rallied behind Dr. EML Endeley in response to the battle cry of "Benevolent Neutrality". They were determined to steer clear of Nigerian politics, while intensely focusing their attention on the "Southern Cameroons" homeland having as indicated undergone political tutelage within Dr. Nnamdi Azikiwe's NCNC within which they had a clear vision of their destination towards eventual political autonomy.

## The Search for a National Identity

This search for a national identity and a fatherland was partially achieved when after stringent mounting political pressure, Britain finally granted the then British Southern Cameroons a '*Quasi Federal Status*'. It was preceded and, actually brought about by what Dr. EML Endeley and his "*Benevolent Neutral*" colleagues had fought relentlessly for since 1953. Historically, this remarkable achievement was finally consummated on 26 October 1954, when the pioneer thirteen elected legislators as Members of Parliament (MPs) of the brand new State took up their seats in the *Southern Cameroons House of Assembly* in the State Capital at Buea. Having attained 'Home Rule', this occasion marked a great mile stone in their history as now they were taking responsibility for the management of their own internal affairs. In comparative terms, it deserves to be noted that French Cameroun only acquired this status four years later in 1957! That is to say, southern Cameroons enjoyed 'Home Rule' or Self Government for four long years before their Francophone brothers.

Though this was an important first step, there still remained the attainment of the final goal of full sovereignty or independence over which Southern Cameroonians were fraught with immeasurable and insuperable international intrigues and hurdles which blocked this most cherished option. This had been the objective for which they had battled all along: to stand alone as an independent unit or what was generally referred to as the missing "*Third Option*" in the plebiscite of 11 February 1961. To block this option, the British Government working in collaboration with the United Nations and other international groups mounted what Malcolm Milne, the Acting Commissioner appropriately described as "*inescapable traps*" for the Foncha Government,[209] *which demanded extended Trusteeship, independence and negotiated reunification terms with Republic of Cameroon*, both of which Britain, the Trusteeship Authority flatly rejected but turned round and awarded on a platter of gold to British Northern Cameroons, which did not even request for it.[210] Together with the questions: "Do you want to achieve independence by joining the Independent Federation of Nigeria" (integration), or "Do you want to achieve independence by joining the Independent Republic of Cameroon" (reunification)? However, the most desired and expected question was, or'; "*Do you want to remain as an independent State?*" was suppressed by a collusion of Great Britain and the UN.[211]

Somehow relevant here, is the 'bad blood', which developed between Malcolm Milne and Foncha. However, while Malcolm Milne's distaste for Foncha is on record, the reverse of Foncha for him is not so visible. While the latter had a penchant for making instant friendship with individuals as he did with Muna and Ahidjo, the same applied in the negative for Foncha for whom he developed deep 'hatred'. The root cause of which was the fact that he refused to abide by the demand of the British colonial masters for integration with Nigeria. To Milne, whatever originated from

---

[209] This is the substance of two publications bearing that title, by Anthony Ndi, *Southern West Cameroon Revisited, 1950-1972 : Unveiling Inescapable Traps* Vols One and Two

[210] ibid. vol. l.pp.110-113

[211] John Percival, *The 1961 Cameroon Plebiscite, Choice or Betrayal*, Bamenda, Langaa Research and Publishing CIG, 2008, p.32.

Whitehall was dogma and could not be contradicted, and Foncha fell into this category for backing reunification with Republic of Cameroon.

In his epic biography[212] he discloses that for that reason, British civil servants in Southern Cameroons with himself included, withdrew their 'supposed' loyalty to his government and more or less tended it to the opposition KNC/KPP alliance, which stood for integration or association with Nigeria. However, Foncha requested for Malcolm Milne, who openly and excessively displayed these tendencies to be withdrawn from the Southern Cameroons service. Though officially, these poor relations were soon patched, in practice they deteriorated even further as demonstrated in the nature of the reports Malcolm Milne and Johnson Field, the Commissioner wrote to the colonial office about Foncha and his cabinet. There was not a single positive word they said about Foncha, which led to a lot of misinformation about the territory. In the ultimate analysis it impacted massively on British attitude to Southern Cameroons

Even so, at this moment of grave frustration, Southern Cameroonians still found courage and, as a unit, voted by a crushing majority in the plebiscite of 11 February 1961 to vote for the next possible option to attain independence by reunification with their Francophone "brothers." This came after seven long years of internal autonomy during which they had distinguished themselves as a model state; hence the qualification for the appellation, the '*Golden Age*'. It was in recognition of their uniqueness and distinction, that at the Foumban Constitutional Conference, reunification was struck on the basis of: a "co-equal" bilingual, bicultural state by Southern Cameroons with their Francophone brothers of the Republic of Cameroon. Surprisingly these bright prospects at Foumban were soon again overtaken by: the absence of political will and bad faith with the introduction of tyrannical rule in the guises of the One Party State, the List System and megalomania exhibited by President Ahmadou Ahidjo.

## ST Muna in the Iron Grip of Ahidjo

These came in quick succession, manifested through the dismissal of

---

[212] Ibid., *No Telephone To Heaven*

AN Jua, the diehard federalist and democrat PM in 1968, followed by that of the VP, Dr. JN Foncha; the acknowledged Father of reunification in 1970. Both men were replaced by Mr. ST Muna with whose abiding support Ahidjo with little effort administered the final *coup de grace* on the Federal Republic of Cameroon, which all along had been a pain in his neck. He was most gratified with this achievement that he had finally done lasting irreparable damage to parliamentary democracy, which he considered a nuisance and imposed his personal, dictatorial and oppressive type of "Presidential rule". This was demonstrated by the fact that he ruled single-handedly by decree, that year as even the rubber-stamp parliament was suspended; hence he rightly christened this coup, the "*Peaceful Revolution*".

There are many analysts who hold Muna mutually, culpable with Ahidjo for this dastardly act. This arises from reflecting on his political record beginning from the Eastern Regional Crisis in Nigeria in 1953; the intrigues involved in his jumping ship from the KNC to the KNDP in 1957, after dilly dallying for two expectant years waiting for the winning side to throw in his weight; the nasty leadership tussle he ignited with AN Jua in the KNDP in which he was repeatedly trounced in open democratic elections, but the results of which he rejected while carrying out secret deals with Ahidjo to undercut the foundation of that party. This was followed by his jumping ship yet again from the KNDP to found the CUC prior to opening up his alliance with Ahidjo to back-stab and bring down the FRC. Putting these together political analysts have described him as an 'opportunist' and one who either sat on the pilot's seat or he was not part of any enterprise.

## Zombification and Sycophancy

Of course, all of this analysis should take into consideration, the fact that dealing with President Ahmadou Ahidjo was a totally strange and complex ball game. Once you got entangled with him there was no easy turning back as he brooked no opposition, and those who dared, paid heavily for it.²¹³ At a certain rally on Mankon Field in Bamenda, a bold inquisitive listener in the audience asked Muna why he did not resign if he could not oppose Ahidjo or change the course of events; caught off guard, he rhetorically retorted whether the questioner wanted him to have his head cut off. At the AAC I holding in Buea in 1993, the same question was put to him differently and he cited the allegory of using a long stick to prod when crossing a deep dangerous river to test its depth and pressure before deciding to back off.

It is extremely difficult in our present circumstance to remotely figure out, what life was like under the Ahidjo Regime with people simply disappearing, being held in underground prisons or made to face public executions after trumped up charges. The prevailing culture was one of '*zombification*' and sycophancy. The author was reliably informed that even after their dismissals, Jua and Foncha were made to go out on campaigns for the Unitary State of 20 May 1972. Not long after that it was falsely rumoured that Jua was planning to form an Opposition Party (which in any case was not forbidden in the constitution). Although, apparently not personally touched, a good number of people who were alleged to be involved in the process of forming the party were rounded up, questioned, detained and tortured.²¹⁴ All it sufficed was for a zealous CNU party militant to start the rumour mill and point a finger at an unfortunate individual, who was invariably taken care of by the gendarmes or any of the numerous security operatives. Once in the Ahidjo net, pulling out was not an option, you carried out his biddings.²¹⁵ An official could

---

²¹³ See Appendix II on the spurious circumstances surrounding the trial of Mgr. Albert Ndongmo.

²¹⁴ A number of prominent people were arrested in Bambui and Babanki, Mr. Anthony Abange, headmaster of St. Peter's Primary School, Bambui and Mr. Ntang, a Retired Veterinary Officer.

²¹⁵ There is the case of a young man who after his '*maitrise*' got employed in the public service as a secondary school teacher but later decided to become a priest and so, went to the St. Thomas Aquinas' Major Seminary, Bambui. He was pursued by the security forces to state why he had resigned from the public service, while his salary continued to be paid after he had explained that he had resigned. He sent the money back to the state treasury, but he was still suspected for years afterwards as having resigned for sinister anti-state motives.

be dismissed or sacked but was not allowed the 'privilege' and liberty to resign, thereby indicating that there was something wrong in the system. The state controlled everything and was all-powerful.

However, for the moment, Ahidjo had succeeded to set into full swing his plans for the complete assimilation of Anglophone Southern Cameroonians in the course of obliterating their Anglo Saxon heritage and values. With their backs to the wall, once again, the stoic Anglophone spirit was provoked and came to life in Yaoundé such that they rose and fought tooth and nail though battered by forces of law and order with water cannons, tear gas and police truncheons. Finally, they wrested the GCE Board and the University of Buea; the two key institutions considered bastions of their Anglo-Saxon heritage. The recent creation of the University of Bamenda is a welcome addition. However, what remains to be accomplished is the Anglo Saxon essence in these institutions.

## The All Anglophone Conference (AAC I), Buea

The All Anglophone Conference, (AAC I) which held at Buea from 2-3 April 1993, the first and only of its kind after the so called "Peaceful Revolution of 1972", when placed in historical perspective using the parameters of: necessity for the conference, its venue, timing, convenors, issues discussed, resolutions reached and their impact on the people, coupled with the number and calibre of delegates, who attended it, give AAC I a ranking rivalling that accorded to other earlier Anglophone or Southern Cameroons conferences such as: the two held at Mamfe; on 22-25 May 1953 at the instance of the "Benevolent Neutrality" group in Nigeria and the Plebiscite Conference of 10-11 August 1959, together with the Bamenda All Party Conference of 26-28 August 1961. However, AAC I further distinguishes itself in that, whereas all the other conferences were sponsored and presided over by the establishment for official purposes, AAC I was free range; a spontaneous, populist Anglophone outcrop held rather, in the teeth of government restrictions- a veritable vestige of the Southern Cameroons indomitable moral fibre.

With that spirit, they spoke out frankly and clearly, and again with one voice. During the Tripartite Talks in Yaoundé, they proposed a return to a modified version of the 1961 Federal Constitution as what could best keep Cameroon as a nation together in peace, harmony, progress and unity.

> The frustrations born of oppression, subjugation, marginalisation and neglect finally led some Anglophones in desperation to organize political dissent in May 1990, to which the Cameroon government responded by shooting dead six persons in Bamenda and telling Anglophones to go elsewhere. But Anglophones do not want to go anywhere else; their demand is for a return to the legality of the 1961 constitution of the Federal Republic of Cameroon.[216]

That its participants, who exceeded 5.000 in number were mostly elite of high calibre; cut across all divides: political, social, economic, religious, age, cultural and sectional, came from all over Cameroon; the US, Europe and Africa at great risk and at individual cost in the face of political and administrative intimidation – furthermore, that the conference produced the famous "Buea Declaration", which essentially called for a return to the legality of the Federal State, speaks volumes for the Anglophone ethos and will certainly enter the annals of history for this and other reasons. AAC I was followed by the "Bamenda Proclamation" after AACII, which intimated that if the government failed to address the anglophone problems, they would eventually rise and proclaim the revival of the independence and sovereignty of the southern Cameroons state with the readiness to secure, defend and preserve that independence.[217]

Remarkably, AAC I was graced with the presence of the two surviving anglophone political leaders: octogenarians, pioneers, icons and erstwhile political protagonists: Pa Foncha and Pa Muna; undeniably makers and shakers of Southern Cameroons and Cameroon history. At different times they had been political allies, then opponents but in the fullness of time, protagonists in typical Southern Cameroons spirit, when

---

[216] See Cameroon Anglophone Movement: "A Socio-Cultural Organization, Douala," 5 December 1991. Chief Dr. HNA Enonchong was its chairman.

[217] See, Ngoh, *History of Southern Cameroons Since 1800*, p.323ff. This may also explain why the government is so sensitive on the use of the appellation, 'Southern Cameroons', which immediately connotes southern Cameroons national council, which stands for secession.

responsibility called; they found common cause in defending the rights and privileges of Anglophone Southern Cameroonians for a return to legality; the federal system.

In 2014 there are frantic moves by the Government towards introducing "devolution", which was regarded as a great novelty by the rest of the nation who certainly would be experiencing it for the first time. Yet, the inhabitants of the North and South West Regions, as "Southern Cameroonians" had abundantly lived and experienced a better and more accomplished version under the guise of "Indirect rule" popularly known as Native Administration, (NA) through local autonomous Native Authority Councils. To them the devolution proposals did not amount to much. In fact, they were a parody of the reality they lived before the introduction of the United Republic of Cameroon in 1972.

Nonetheless, though spontaneous, AAC I was convened because the besieged Biya Administration in the wake of the political turbulence that had ravaged the country since 1990, rejected the calls for a "Sovereign National Conference" by the Coalition of Opposition Parties and instead, proposed a "National Debate on Constitutional Reform."[218] For the convenors: Mr. Ekontang Elad, Dr. Carlson Anyangwe and Dr. Simon Munzu and the participants at the Buea Conference, substance for discussion was readily drawn from the perennial stack of unheeded Anglophone complaints over the years, indeed since reunification. Anglophone complaints had thus festered, become chronic, endemic and taken the collective appellation "the Anglophone Problem". These combined socioeconomic, educational, legal, administrative and generalised malaise; all of which had radical political roots – hinged on the absence of a political will, a patriotic spirit, inate disdain for Anglophones and endemic failure to observe accords reached with them by successive administrations led by the ruling Francophone elite. Consistently, Anglophones had been excluded from top appointments in strategic ministries involved in decision making, marginalised and reduced to second class citizenry. Wherever Anglophones were appointed they were usually surrogates, stooges and quislings ready to do the biddings of their Francophone overlords. The

---

[218] ibid, Ngoh, p323ff.

hope therefore was that this forum would be used to constitutionally redress this grave imbalance.

## Foncha, Muna and Mukong: Ground Breaking Revelations

Contributions from the octogenarian leaders were most significant. Apparently Dr. John Ngu Foncha had lost none of his aura and charisma. As: "The first speaker on the second day of the Conference, when he rose to take the rostrum, he received a long standing ovation from the huge gathering." At 76 and speaking *ex-empore*, he proved to be still quite alert and opted to "clarify certain things that might not have been understood". The first of these was that "federation" was a *sine qua non* for reunificaation and secondly, that it was the UN Trusteeship Council that had to give independence to Southern Cameroons and not Great Britain, which was only an administering power.[219] The third significant point was that the Foumban accord was never ratified by the West Cameroon House of Assembly because, before this could be done, Ahidjo had rushed to have it approved by the National Assembly of the Republic of Cameroon, which endorsed it to become the constitution of the Federal Republic of Cameroon. He later on elaborated on these issues.

In all, Foncha made startling revelations especially about his frustrations with President Ahmadou Ahidjo. Attempts to bring him to book failed "because he bought over the opposition and even members of his own ruling KNDP". Foncha pointed out that this happened in 1964, when the KNDP Government of West Cameroon felt dissatisfied with the intrusion of Yaounde in the affairs of Buea and protested against this, but his attempts to bring Ahidjo to book failed for this reason. It was well known during Ahidjo's visit to Buea in 1962 that he held nocturnal discussions with Dr. Endeley on the formation of a single party on the basis of West Cameroon political parties dissolving and fusing with Ahidjo's UC even before the CNU. Ultimately however, his UC and KNDP as the ruling parties in West and East Cameroon formed a loose coalition at the central and federal levels prohibiting "interference in each others

---

[219] *The Herald No. 033*, Wednesday April 14,1994

sphere". Nevertheless, this did not stop the Ahidjo-Endeley overtures. The surprise however, came with Foncha's revelation that "Ahidjo bought over even members of his own ruling KNDP."[220]

All along, with the unfolding tussle for leadership of the party as Foncha prepared to take up his position as the VP of the FRC in Yaounde as required by the constitution, Jua and Muna competed to replace him. In this, Muna was abundantly defeated by Jua at two successive KNDP conventions holding at Bamenda and Kumba and again at a combined meeting of WC and Federal MPs at his own request. But Muna continued to reject the results, illogically arguing that only the President of the FRC could appoint the PM without respecting the standard convention of the WCHA, which pursued the Westminster Parliamentary system. However, Ahidjo succumbed to democratic pressure and appointed Jua in 1965 but three years later, he flung the system to the winds and appointed Muna.

Matters came to a head when Muna and nine dissident followers were dismissed from the KNDP for indiscipline and went ahead to form the Cameroon United Congress (CUC), which in every sense was the West Cameroon version of Ahidjo's UC. Judged by the public utterances made by Moussa Yaya in support of the CUC, it was generally conjectured that the new party which became the first to join the UC to form the CNU was an annex of the UC and the handiwork of Ahidjo but all of this was hypothetical until Foncha's open announcement at AAC I. Foncha's task had been made extremely difficult because the CPNC opposition and the KNDP dissidents joined forces with Ahidjo and so he could not be brought to book.

Thereafter, Ahidjo's audacity increased as he had both men, Jua and Foncha sacked and replaced one after the other by Muna with absolute impunity. It was also because of these invidious deals and support that Ahidjo had the Foumban Constitutional Conference accord single handedly ratified by the National Assembly of Republic of Cameroon. This was the beginning of the collapse not only of the KNDP, the formation of the CNU, the subsequent appointments of Muna to the combined posts

---

[220] ibid.

of PM and VP and finally the dismantling of the FRC.[221]

With regard to reunification, Foncha was adamant that he had done the right thing because reunification only came after firm agreements with the Ahidjo administration that it would be on the basis of federalism, equality and respect for Southern Cameroons' Anglo-Saxon culture. Having followed southern Cameroonians wishes and won overwhelmingly with a poll of over 70% in the plebiscite, he had nothing to apologise for and, that given another chance he would still go for reunification on a federal basis. Nigeria could never be an option, he repeated:

> We were working on the will of the people and the people are still in favour of reunification. …. Young men don't know what happened at that time. I will never apologise anything. I am still in favour of remaining a Cameroonian. That is what our forefathers believed and I want that federation to be democratic. The Anglophones have virtually been stopped from progressing.[222]

He added that his greatest disappointment was the failure of the federal system and if the need arose, he was ready to return to the UN to explain what happened as one who had lived the experience. On relations with Ahidjo, he pointed out that he did not like him; and he, Foncha; "Did not like working with somebody, who would not listen to me and who would use me as a tool, so the time had come and I decided to leave him".[223]

Foncha generally acclaimed as "one who pursued politics without bitterness", had this clearly demonstrated at AAC I in Buea as he and Muna sat together and had just returned from New York where both men went to fight for the Anglophone cause, a return to federalism, which paradoxically Ahidjo with the assistance of Muna had wrecked to pieces almost beyond repair. Significantly, Muna reported to have been wavery, openly

---

[221] This topic is a fertile and revealing area for research by budding historians and political scientists of Cameroon history with the perfidy perpetuated by Ahidjo and Muna.

[222] ibid.

[223] ibid.

admitted that: "He had no basic disagreement with Foncha's retale of the past". However unlike Foncha, "he delved into lengthy apologies saying" that "no one is intrinsically bad, only his acts can be qualified as good or bad." On the other hand, he offered to: "Show the new Anglophone leadership the ways and tricks that should lead them to the fulfilment of their goal for a return to federalism".[224]

The other notable elder statesman at the conference was Mr. Albert Womah Mukong of the *"Prisoner Without A Crime"* fame. He had suffered untold torture at the hands of President Ahmadou Ahidjo in several of his jails including underground dungeons for being outspoken against his tyrannical rule. Mukong's address titled:"Where things went wrong," was drawn from the substance of a book he earlier publihsed in 1985. Being a political activist and critic, among other issues, he hit hard on the British for abandoning their charge over Southern Cameroons and cited how:

> The British army on October 1 1961 at Tiko Airport, beat the retreat before a tattered undisciplined gang of Cameroon Republican soldiers as the Union Jack was lowered. The British officials serving the southern Cameroons government quit the country and even British Firms, the UAC, John Holt, Cadbury and Fry quickly wound up and left our land.[225]

Mukong noted with " horror and astonishment that neither Her Majesty's Government nor the UN's three advisers were present at Foumban to oversee the deliberations probably after a neocolonialist agreement with France over its empire." He equally criticised Foncha as PM and Endeley as Leader of the Opposition for not standing up to Ahidjo's outrageous behaviour and added that, "We sold our birthright when we bowed to the One Party idea in 1966 and so blest the violation of our constitution,"which cumulatively built up to the illegal coup d'etat in 1972 with Ahidjo's fake referendum. In further indictment of Francophone duplicity, he cited the example of Sengat Kuo, who personally boasted about his role in putting up the 1972 constitution but who since 1990 had

---

[224] ibid

[225] ibid, *The Herald*

joined forces with the "Union For Change" to fight the system. Mukong questioned what " change" could be fostered with such people. After running through a couple of similar Francophone examples, Mukong concluded by way of a warning: "They are all apostles for the destruction of our Anglo-Saxon culture and training. There is no sincerity in their hearts."[226]

He continued: "If we are keen on continuing the union, then the terms of union have to be negotiated now and the basis for any such negotiation may only be the two alternatives. This immediately compels the participation of the UN to attend to its unfinished job" and in sequence on a serious note warned: "The insult on us executed by the Biya return to the Republic of Cameroon and a bid to subjugate us to a colonial status must not be allowed to continue after this conference." Mukong was confident that if we take a just decision in the interest of our people, our collective will, will be able to effect it. Let us not fear because of our numerical minority. The hundreds of millions of Arabs have not yet succeeded to wipe out the State of Israel of under four million.[227]

Finally, glowing tributes were paid to late statesmen, who had led Southern Cameroons like EML Endeley, PM Kale, Chief Nyenti and others. Prophetic quotes, which painted a very realistic picture of what union with East Cameroon would mean for Southern Cameroons ascribed to Endeley were freely circulated.

## Consistent Tendency to Downgrade Anglophone Values

There has been a consistent tendency to down grade whatever originates from former Southern Cameroons for integration into the national system as inferior or is generally treated with scorn and ridicule. This is manifested in the manner in which the Anglophone sub-system of education as well as the legal practice are currently being treated. Nonetheless quite a number of changes such as with the police uniforms, car registration numbers, the one shift system of work and many more, have

---

[226] ibid.

[227] Ibid, *The Herald*

been adopted through the "backdoor" after years of relegation and 'panel beating' so as not to give credit to Southern Cameroons. Ordinarily, with a little openness, honesty and humility much could be adopted from the Anglophone sub-system for the mutual benefit of the nation at large. In Southern Cameroons, the system of the Native Administration through Native Authorities, ethnic groups and federations of clans already ran their own affairs with great accountability and efficiency. Crudely, that is what is being introduced afresh under the guise of 'devolution' or 'decentralization' and made to look as a great novelty.

The surprise is that its introduction is being made to look as some great reform or innovation in local administration, whereas the reality is that Southern Cameroons lived the full experience under the system of Native Administration through the creation of Native Authorities and Local Councils. In fact, these advanced to a level where by the 1950s the Native Authorities had coalesced into semi-autonomous 'Federations' managed their own affairs to the extent of handling projects such as the construction of clinics, schools, hospitals, roads and bridges in many cases supporting the central administration. This was precisely the case with the "Local Clan Councils of Kom, Wum, Bum and Beba-Befang," which pooled together their resources towards the construction of a hospital.[228] These were represented by Rev. Hon Jeremiah Chi Kangsen, one of the six NA Members of Parliament from Southern Cameroons in the East Region House of Assembly in Enugu, Nigeria.

Somehow, the Ahidjo administration nurtured the myopic and illogical feeling that a free and united Southern Cameroons would become a threat to the unity of the Republic of Cameroon and would cultivate a passion for secession and autonomy the reason why everything was done then and continues to be done to ensure that the two Regions are weakened and kept wide apart. In fact, within the FRC, Southern Cameroons was deliberately deprived of major revenue yielding services and burdened with

---

[228] See, JC Kangsen's letter of 13 May 1953 to the Clan Councils of Kom, Bum, Wum etc. whom he represented in the Eastern House of Assembly. Victor J Ngoh, *Constitutional Developments in Southern Cameroons*, 1946-1961, CEPER, Yaoundé, 1990 pp. 101-102. He was one of the six MPs who represented Native Authorities in parliament; for the names of the MPs, see appendix four.

those that needed heavy expenditure, a policy which rendered it weak and insolvent. Consequently, the State Government had to keep turning to the Federal Government for subventions to survive. It was for this reason that Southern Cameroons was stigmatised as being economically weak, indigent and insolvent, factors which became the major excuse for the abolition of the FRC. This was a repeat performance of the experience they had gone through while integrated within Nigeria.

Logically, therefore, with the discovery of huge oil and gas reserves in the *Bakassi creeks* of Southern Cameroons by **ELF SEREPCA**, a French oil prospecting company in 1967, the alleged problem of indigence would have been considered providentially solved. Paradoxically, it was now feared that Southern Cameroons generally regarded as insolvent with its erstwhile unexplored and underrated natural resources, of a sudden had turned out to be richly endowed with such vast reserves of oil and gas left loose within the FRC would contemplate secession and independence. On the other hand, it could not be left as a state to run the huge revenue derived from the oil enterprise without defined restrictions. Ahidjo's solution on directives from France was far from predictable–it was decided as soon as possible to abolish the FRC, split up West Cameroon into separate Provinces; possibly to weaken the relations between them so as to vitiate any powerful combinations that could arise to resist the intended radical changes or to contemplate secession.[229] The fear of secession has since then become the main bogey haunting the powers that be and yet mighty little seems to be done to avoid it happening.

Of course, there was the genuine need to ensure that the newly discovered wealth would serve the interests of the entire nation and not just the Anglophone Provinces. In fact, for many years, oil revenue remained a top state secret, the expenditure of which was reserved to the Presidency alone and never featured in the State budget. Discussion on oil revenue was considered a taboo subject.[230] Consequently, what took place in May 1972

---

[229] See OBB Sendze, *My Reflections On Southern Cameroons*, also Anthony Ndi, *Unveiling Inescapable Traps* vol. 1 p. 216

[230] Late Hon. Nwalipenja, MP for Ndian Division repeatedly told the story to whoever cared to listen of how he was shut up at the Presidency for having dared to openly raise questions about oil revenue. He was called up slapped by the president, given a

was a culmination of several factors but the most important of which was the oil discovery in the Bakassi Peninsula. Ironically, since the oil finds and revenue remained secret, the major reason proffered for the abolition of the FRC was that it was too expensive to run and particularly that Southern Cameroons needed heavy subventions all the time to balance its budget.

## "The 1972 Peaceful Revolution": A Charade

Returning from France, where he had visited President Georges Pompidou and a deal had been struck on the exploitation of the oil reserves in the Bakassi Peninsula; on 5 May 1972, President Ahmadou Ahidjo in his address to MPs the following day 6 May, unveiled a few utterances to corroborate the instructions he had received from France. In that address, he inadvertently assumed and declared the reality of the Unitary State even before the conduct of the Referendum had been launched, maintaining that: *"The Cameroon people have already sealed in deed their own unity and, on the other hand; the federal organisation is a stumbling block"*[231]. Simply put, the deal had been sealed well ahead of the conduct of the referendum! The institution of a Unitary State had become a matter of urgency with pressure from France and so everything had to be rushed to meet President Pompidou's expectations. This manipulation was a clear case of the President's use of folly and deceit as party and government policy, a practice which in time converted the masses into zombies and inculcated the policy of sycophancy which has become embedded in the psyche of the people manifested in motions of support and electoral fraud. In fact, it is responsible for much that is wrong in the country because after rigging at the elections and getting sycophants in parliament and government, there can be no contrary opinion from that issued by the top hierarchy.

Since it was a matter of grave urgency, barely one week later, precisely

---

huge bundle of money and told to go home and never again talk about oil money. The author personally heard him recount the tale in Buea Mountain Club in the early 70s.

[231] See, *The Post*, no. 01631 of Monday June o1, 2015. As a precondition, ELF SEREPCA, the French company needed to be assured that the Bakassi Peninsula was securely Cameroon territory before it could commence with the heavy investment in oil and gas exploration there. (Interpolation by Nfor N Nfor 11/08/16).

on Sunday 20 May 1972, Cameroonians on getting to the polling booths discovered that only two types of ballot papers were available bearing either the word, "**OUI**" or "**YES**" with no ballots bearing the word "**NO**". The outcome was that there was an overwhelming 99.97% "**YES**" vote. In everything he did the President was obstinately determined to obtain a 100% result. "For what reasons, we will probably never know. He filled prisons with people who did not think like him in the quest for unanimity. He did not tolerate any opposition views. In short, he was a tyrant to the core".[232] Paradoxically, after the sweeping victory of the **Yes** vote on Sunday 20 may 1972 the population was severely subjected to security checks, raids and roadblocks, while police cordons in the neighbourhood increased. Anybody who did not have a voting card in their pocket was arrested. It seemed as if he was punishing Cameroonians for taking part in his referendum.[233] This was exactly, administration through **'folly and deceit'**, which in this case was sheer forgery with the results, declared before the referendum was announced and the campaigns launched. A solid nation cannot be constructed on such a faulty and whimsical foundation.

## Integral Existence of Southern Cameroons Never in Dispute

A crucial point often ignored, when talking about "Reunification" is the fact that the integral existence of Southern Cameroons whether as a Region within the Federal Republic of Nigeria or as a State within an independent Republic of Cameroon its integral existence was never in dispute. This was preconceived at the UN and enshrined in the two alternatives for the 11 February 1961 Plebiscite organized by the United Nations. This resulted from the plebiscite questions, which simply and clearly stated: "Do you wish (Southern Cameroons) to achieve independence by joining the independent Federation of Nigeria?" or, "Do you wish (Southern Cameroons) to achieve independence by joining the independent Republic of Cameroon?" In other words, whether Southern Cameroons chose to integrate with Nigeria or to reunify with an

---

[232] See , *The Post*, no. 01631 of Monday June 01, 2015

[233] Ibid.

independent Cameroon Republic, it was to do so integrally, a condition further emphasized by Nigeria in supporting the CPNC option. If within the federation of Nigeria, with which it had been administered in the Anglo Saxon tradition for forty-five long years, sharing a common political system, Southern Cameroons was assured a distinct corporal identity, what logic can there be to justify the Unitary State system imposed on it in 1972 after ten short, transient years of basically trying to understand each other's geographical bearings? In simple comparative terms, even after close to three centuries Ottawa and Quebec are as far apart as they were at the Treaty of Paris in 1763! This mad rush could only have resulted from ill conceived; possibly selfish interests in sowing a whirl wind certain to reap confusion, agony and ultimate failure.

The deliberations at Foumban were to do basically with ***the nature of the "Federation"*** than with the choice of government. A ***"Unitary State"*** was totally out of the question and so was not even remotely considered, rather, there was talk of a ***"con-federation"***,[234] by some Southern Cameroon delegates and even referred to by Ahidjo himself as totally inadmissible. Prior to this, in all the discussions between President Ahidjo and Dr. Foncha as well as in all consultations, the focus was always on Federation. In the numerous public declarations made by Ahidjo beginning from his first reception at Tiko International Airport on 15 July 1960 till the Foumban Conference, there was never a shred of doubt on the issue of a Federation. Rather, all the discussions at the Foumban Constitutional Conference were centred on the nature of the Federal system and the inclusions and exclusions within it. In his opening address he had already circumscribed what had to be discussed on the basis of earlier agreements with Foncha; centralisation and confederation were totally excluded.

Finally, ***the Foumban Accord*** to make assurance doubly sure, entrenched for all times, the federal nature of the constitution. This was enshrined in **Article 47(1)** the first clause of which declared as follows: *"**Any proposal for the revision of the present constitution, which impairs the unity and***

---

[234] Interestingly, this extreme suggestion was made by ST Muna, who argued that the differences between the two systems were too wide to contemplate a basic federation. See reports of the Foumban Constitutional procedures in the Southern *Cameroons Information Bulletins.*

*integrity of the Federation, shall be inadmissible."* There was no provision for whosesoever and by whomsoever for the abrogation of the Federal Constitution. Thus, the referendum conducted by President Ahidjo on 20 May 1972 was an aberration, wholly uncalled for and illegal.

*Furthermore, the constitution deliberately did not provide for a referendum. Rather, it allowed in clause 3 of Article 47 for an amendment of the Constitution. All it stipulated was: "That, proposals for revision shall be adopted by simple majority vote of the members of the Federal Assembly provided that such majority includes a majority of the representatives in the Federal Assembly of each of the Federated States".* There was no advantage of size. Thus with a "Federal" Assembly of 50 members, ten of whom represented West Cameroon, if all 40 East Cameroonian Deputies voted for an amendment and six of the West Cameroon Deputies voted against it, the amendment was defeated. This clause safeguarded minority interest and rights. *It was a veto clause.* This is probably why Ahidjo chose to use a referendum, which of course was never *previewed* or provided for in the Federal Constitution.

## A Pointless and Flawed Procedure with a Hidden Agenda

The procedure Ahidjo adopted was a wholly unfathomable and bewildering window dressing intended for the consumption of the international community. It was on 6 May 1972 at 11 am that he informed the Political Bureau of the CNU that he intended abolishing the Federal system that had obtained since 1 October 1961. Henceforth, the process evolved at an incredible speed, after he addressed the National Assembly on 9 May. In that speech he recounted his experience and achievements over the past ten years of the Federal system and of reunification, which necessitated the abolition of the Federation. He then declared that he was taking his responsibility before history and destiny and had decided to consult the nation through a referendum as; "masters of their destiny on the institution of a unitary state".[235]

Very like in George Orwell's *Animal Farm*, immediately, political stalwarts were dispatched to all regions of the Federation preaching the

---

[235] Ibid, *The Post*.

new doctrine of the "*referendum*" and the "**Unitary State**" scheduled for 20 May 1972. Thus, in less than a fortnight, the Referendum was enacted; the FRC was relegated to the dustbin of history while the **URC** was born. The Federated States, their parliaments and the West Cameroons House of Chiefs were abolished, declared anathema and henceforth regarded as having been a source of waste and unnecessary duplication. All the energies invested in the exercise that yielded the Federation beginning with meetings at the UN, consultations, debates conferences and tense atmosphere among the various political parties, traditional rulers; the time, the cost and expectations reaching their peak at the Foumban Constitutional Conference were simply cast down the drain as so much rubbish by the ambitions of an individual into whose hands all power and authority had been consolidated or had been arrogated by him to himself.

Both in retrospect and in perspective, the 1972 Referendum was bizarre and irredeemably flawed in diverse dimensions but especially with the secrecy, haste and total unpreparedness with which it was executed. In comparison, the 11th February 1961 Plebiscite involving only Southern Cameroons, geographically constituting less than 20% of the Federal Territory had taken the all-powerful United Nations with its enormous human, material and financial resources some six months to organize. The two Provinces of Southern Cameroons were divided into twenty-six Electoral Districts manned by as many highly qualified officials internationally appointed by the UN with scores more of support staff. Transport, communication sensitization and other necessary logistics were carefully put in place and an electoral roll established to certify how many people were actually involved in the exercise: these had first to be ascertained before actual polling could take place. And of course gathering the results, counting and tallying them was another delicate process which took time.

In simple comparative terms to the 1961 UN organised Plebiscite in Southern Cameroons, the sickening feat of that in 1972 covering the entire territory of the FRC, five times the size of Southern Cameroons with difficult terrain during the rains coupled with poor communications and transportation network took less than two weeks to accomplish, with imponderable results. Interestingly this was the length of time it took in 2008, thirty-six years later with greatly improved circumstances (roads communications network etc.) to merely compose results for the parliamentary elections in the tiny Santa Special Constituency in the North West Region! The other pertinent question begging to be answered is why the participants of the Foumban Constitutional Conference of 17-20 July 1961, many of whom were still alive in 1972 were not invited to participate in the deliberations reversing the earlier historic decision.

With hindsight and in comparative terms, the Plebiscite of 11 February 1961 had concerned only Southern Cameroons, which was faced with the crucial options of attaining independence either by integration with Nigeria or by reunification with Republic of Cameroon. The stakes were therefore obviously grave and the choices neatly cut. However, in May 1972, the entire national territory was inexplicably involved, while the stakes for East Cameroon were not obvious. Even if the entire Southern Cameroons electorate with less than 20% of the total population voted against the option in the Referendum it would not have caused a dent in the 99.97% declared results. Much of what took place during the entire process was shredded in mystery. For example the UN organized plebiscite in Southern Cameroons eleven years earlier had stipulated qualifications for voters, the electoral lists were posted at all polling stations for a considerable period; in fact, much longer than it took to conduct the entire 1972 Referendum and it was finally possible to declare that: there were 331.312 registered voters, with a turn-up of 94.75%; with 70.49 % or that 233.971 voted for "reunification with Republic of Cameroon" and 29.51% or 97.741 voted for "integration with Nigeria". All of this was transparent, conducted and observed by the international community as acknowledged by the UN Plebiscite Commissioner Dr. Djalal Abdoh in his letter of congratulations to the "nice" people of Southern Cameroons. In all the process took over six months to accomplish compared to two weeks or a fortnight that was taken for the peaceful revolution of 1972, covering a territory several times the size and population of Southern Cameroons.

On the other hand, the most that is known of what took place in *the 1972 Referendum* is that 99.97% voted for the abolition of the Federation and that there were *3.179.634 "Yes" and 176 "No" votes* without any of the stringent formalities observed in the 1961 plebiscite. It is apparent that the so called 'no' votes in the circumstance would have been the equivalent of spoiled ballot papers by those who deliberately opted to show their disapproval or simply by those who did not know what to do as interestingly the choice was between "*Oui*" and "Yes". In any case, all of this was inconsequential except to demonstrate to the world that the Cameroonian electorate had options and actually exercised their democratic rights.

How these lofty statistics were arrived at without any verifiable figures of those who actually registered and the number who finally voted is all a matter of conjecture. The trend was the same with 97.68% for the Presidential election of March 1970, while the single Party List of May 1973 for the Legislative Elections yielded **99.98%.** With these imponderable statistics; the *CNU Secretary General, Mr. Victor Ayissi Mvodo openly boasted that it was "one of the very few political parties in the world that have managed to make reality of this dream"*.[236] In this sense therefore the process was appropriately daubed a "*Peaceful Revolution*", for even the most advanced democratic states are yet to achieve this feat.

However, to any keen analyst of the Cameroon political scene, the developments of May 1972 were basically a logical sequence to all that had been unfolding since Ahidjo's call for a '*Grand National Party*" in 1962 and the evolution of *the Cameroon National Union (CNU) in September 1966,* the replacement of Jua with Muna in 1968 and finally of Foncha with Muna as a running mate and Vice President to Ahidjo in 1970. The deposition of Jua began with Ahidjo's introduction of the *List System* in West Cameroon for the Legislative elections of December 1967. They were filled with his supporters. The crafted dented political image of Prime Minister Jua [237] made it easy for Ahidjo to nominate Muna as PM in 1968. He was the right person in the circumstances, totally subservient to the President and ready to carry out his wishes.

To begin with, unlike the democratic procedures engaged for electing *Jua as PM* in 1965, *Muna* was personally handpicked by Ahidjo in 1967 without any clear prior consultations with the West Cameroon legislators and politicians. By a subsequent modification of the constitution in 1969

---

[236] Victor Ayissi Mvodo, Report on CNU Congress, Douala 10-15 Feb. 1975 p. 20 *Gaullist Africa* P.189).

[237] See Joseph Richard p. 88 for unproven Financial Scandals with which Jua was associated.

the West Cameroon State Legislative Assembly was finally deprived of the right to choose its Prime Minister. This prerogative was restricted to the President alone who was further conceded powers to intervene in any affairs of the West Cameroon House of Assembly as he deemed fit. In time it became clear that he hated the 'Westminster parliamentary system' in which most of the procedures were based on democratic procedures as even ministers first had to be elected members of parliament from among which the leader of the party with most MPs, was called up to form the cabinet and the government. Even appointments to top administrative and managerial positions had to undergo parliamentary vetting and not limited merely to presidential appointments. In other words the system greatly limited presidential interference and powers. Ahidjo beat his chest when he finally dismantled what he described as the so called chaotic and disorderly parliamentary system'.

That the 1972 fast - track Referendum, inexplicably was extended to include the entire Federal Republic of Cameroon originally not part of the 1961 event and attained such an unimaginable and hard to believe "success rating" was a feat only possible in Ahidjo's Cameroon. This was all the more startling as this was taking place with nonexistent or poor logistics: in the heart of the rainy season with impassable roads, untrained personnel, absence of electoral rolls and all else. On the overall, therefore, it probably deserved the metaphorical caption which President Ahidjo its creator, chose to christen it: the "Peaceful Revolution" especially as there were no "registered" protests, incidents of opposition, and only a minute handful of absentees.

Of course, in the dreadfully intimidating, dense and tense climate, which the President had instituted; suspending Parliament and mounting his personal rule for twelve months, the press gagged with all demonstrations banned; what prevailed was immense fear and trembling as even "walls had ears". No one could raise a finger against Ahidjo and hope to survive and so it was a cowed and heavily subdued electorate that supposedly went to the polls; and the statistics officially delivered were exactly or even higher than those officially desired, sometimes exceeding

100%.²³⁸ In a significant number of cases results were declared without as much as opening the ballot boxes. Subsequently, this was the trend for all elections in the country. Perhaps, the greatest point to note as indicated is that the President ruled throughout 1972 by decree. Consequently, on record, it was "absolute victory" for him on all counts since this was what he desired, it was therefore what was delivered.

### The "Peaceful Revolution": Ironical Implications

In fact, all the moves of the "Peaceful Revolution" were geared towards this objective - "absolute victory". The rhetorical question is why it was so called, as if the President expected a revolution or opposition of sorts which failed to happen. Others interpret it to mean "conquest" since there was no open contention to his declaration by Southern Cameroonians, meaning, he had successfully captured them. Whenever pertinent studies would eventually be conducted on this sordid topic there would be fascinating revelations demonstrating as, Albert Mukong put it; "How it happened that a nation of seven million intelligent people could have been reduced to zombies and mesmerized hand clappers."²³⁹ What logic can there be to explain the fact that in big towns like Kumba and Victoria in the South West Region of Cameroon for example, there were less than twenty people who voted against the single question referendum in 1972. It was totally absurd that people went out to vote for a Unitary State constitution copies of which were hardly available. The few people in Kumba who dared to have voted against the proposition can actually be traced out in the National Archives at Buea, as they were objects of police and gendarme investigations, arrests and possible torture.²⁴⁰

It is intriguing to imagine that the road and air links between the

---

²³⁸ In fact, there were some of the elections in those days, where the percentage of those who polled superseded the number of those who had registered or practically those who went to the polls! Presidential elections hardly dropped below 99.99% and unconvincing complicated statistical explanations were given to justify such situations.

²³⁹ Albert Mukong, *The Case For Southern Cameroons*, CAMFECO, USA nd.

²⁴⁰ The author cursorily examined some of these files.

North and South West Regions were deliberately left to fester in a state of total disrepair and ceased to function after the abolition of the FRC, while other measures were subtly entrenched to keep the peoples of these Regions apart as a matter of covet government policy.[241] There is any amount of information to demonstrate that President Ahidjo was allergic to democracy, federalism and even worse, sharing power with anybody. He was innately megalomaniac. A reluctant and late convert to the ideology of reunification and even independence; it was actually imposed on him by his French mentors as a precondition for sponsoring his candidature as PM against Andre Marie Mbida.

## Charles Assale: Contemptuous of West Cameroons

Owing to the key positions he held and the very signifcant role he played in the history of Southern and later, West Cameroon, as Prime Minister of East Cameroon and the abhorrent statements he made about

*Fig. 39 Prime Minister, Charles Assale.*

[241] The ongoing construction of the Mundemba-Mamfe-Kumba road as well as the Bamenda-Mamfe-Ekok road net-work is a byproduct of the Green Tree Agreement concluding the Cameroon-Nigeria conflict over the Bakassi Peninsula.

West Cameroon, an introductory note needs to be sounded on who was. Born and bred in Ebolowa, the capital of the Southern Region of Cameroon, Charles Assale participated in the formation of some the early tribal and political groups and finally led the *Mouvement d'Action Nationale Camerounaise* (MANC), which he dissolved to join Ahidjo's *Union Camerounaise*.[242] As compensation, Ahidjo made him PM, an important appointment which balanced the representation of Christian South from which he came with Moslem North, Ahidjo's own home region (East Cameroon) under the umbrella of the UC. This therefore gave the *Union Camerounaise* a truly national image, internally and internationally. He served as the first PM of East Cameroon under President Ahidjo from 1960-1972 besides holding other important positions such as Mayor of Ebolowa.

Thus, Charles Assale worked very closely with, and provided backbone support to Ahidjo's Administration notably in affairs concerning Southern and later West Cameroon. For example, he accompanied President Ahidjo during his maiden visit to Southern Cameroons (14-17 July 1960) and was by his side when he made his historical declarations at Tiko, Buea and Victoria. In the wake of that visit, he was member of a powerful committee set up by the Foncha and Ahidjo Governments comprising top ministers which met thrice, worked strenuously and produced two draft federal constitutions which notably were jointly signed by President Ahmadou Ahidjo, Charles Assale and John Ngu Foncha. The next occasion and easily the most significant was at the Foumban Constitutional Conference from 16 -21 July 1961 to which President Ahmadou Ahidjo and Charles Assale led the East Cameroon delegation to meet with their West Cameroon counterparts led by Foncha and Endeley. He was equally present at the Yaounde Tripartite Conference, which gave final legal touches to the Foumban Constitutional Conference.

True enough at this conference Charles Assale is not on record for having made any addresses or declarations, nor was this necessary since President Ahidjo his boss was present. However, as demonstrated above,

---

[242] Gardinier, Cameroun p. 107; quoted in 'Federalism in a One Party State' by Mbu Ettangondop, in, *Cameroon From A Federal To A Unitary State*, Ngoh ed.

Charles Assale fully participated in all the activities as well as listened to the numerous speeches, declarations and far reaching promises made by his mentor. The paradox and utter embarrassment is that when interviewed over CRTV as quoted in *Le Temoin* and *Le Patriote*, he arrogantly and shamelessly maintained in part that:

> Ahmadou Ahidjo was never interested in reunification ... French Cameroun became independent without reunification and assumed sovereignty on 1 January 1960 to become Republic of Cameroon .... The 1961 United Nations plebiscite, which resulted in the Cameroon union, did not involve Republic of Cameroun. Of their own accord, Anglophones unilaterally opted to achieve independence by joining the Cameroun republic. Reunification was not an imposition from the Republic of Cameroun[243].

Actually, Assale says nothing new but essentially confirms all the measures taken by his mentor, President Ahidjo, who reneged on all agreements earlier reached over Southern Cameroons without blinking. He made repeated references and emphasis on: fraternity, federation and equality of the two brotherly territories, which he added were a debt owed to 'our ancestors'.

Above all, asked to state the stance of Republic of Cameroon as Southern Cameroons prepared for the plebiscite of 11 February 1961, Ahidjo unequivocally declared that he "had no intention of promoting the type of integration capable of sounding the death knell of the hopes of Southern Cameroons." He then concluded:

> **We do not wish to bring the weight of our population to bear on our British brothers. We are not annexationists ... if our brothers of the British zone wish to unite with an independent (French) Cameroun, we are ready to discuss the matter with them, but we will discuss it on**

---

[243] See Nicodemus Fru Awasom, "The Reunification Question In Cameroon History", in *Africa Today*, vol. 47, no. 2. Generally, the Francophone political elite and public at large are not versed in the Anglophone woes or even in the basic facts of reunification. This largely affects their unsympathetic attitude towards the situation.

a footing of equality.²⁴⁴

For both men to turn round and say that reunification was an entirely Southern Cameroons affair and that the Southern Cameroonians imposed themselves on Republic of Cameroun is most unfortunate; meaning that Assale like Ahidjo, basically played mere lip service and did not believe in the declarations that they made or the agreements that were reached among them: Ahidjo, Foncha and himself (Assale) in consolidating reunification.²⁴⁵ When "trusted" leaders like Ahidjo and Assale openly renege on solid declarations they had made and agreements they reached with others with such barefaced disregard, the bases for constructing a solid nation cease to exist as nothing then is certain. A leader should be a dependable person, one who leads by example and by precept, is honest, sincere and committed, has the welfare of his people at heart and whose word is his bond. This was the quality of leadership understood in Southern Cameroons for the most part.

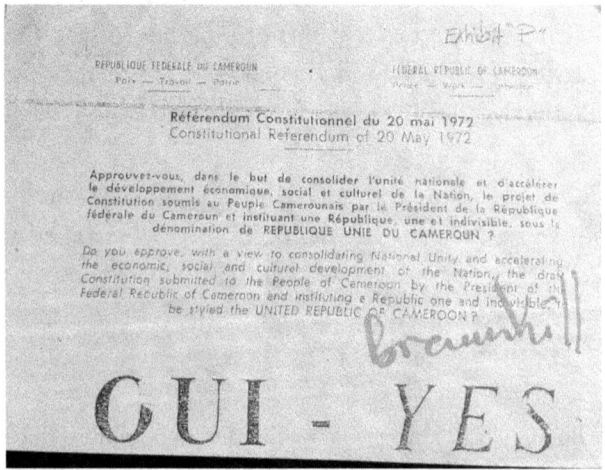

*Fig 40: The double-faced ballot paper for the 20th May Referendum in 1972. It yielded 99.9% approval for the unitary state and brought about the famous Peaceful Revolution.*

---

²⁴⁴ UNGA A/C.4SR:846 25 feb.1959

²⁴⁵ Ibid., Nicodemus Fru Awasom.

## Chapter Seven

# IRONIC OUTCOME OF MARGINALISATION: AN INVINCIBLE SPIRIT

## Deepening Marginalisation Causes Groundswell of Revulsion

In the course of the Spring months of May, June and July 2015, out of a sudden, a generalized feeling of disgust and malaise gripped certain professional groups and individuals in the North and South West Regions spontaneously and variously. Interestingly, acting in unison as if there had been prior agreement reached among them; educationists, lawyers, the South West Chiefs Conference, Christian Cardinal Tumi and Hon Cyprien Awudu rose separately in a common reaction to what had become a chronic, deepening culture of disregard, bad faith and absence of political will by the ruling Francophone elite characterized by; unrelenting broken agreements and promises, paying lip service and the excessive and ever increasing marginalisation of Anglophone Cameroonians. A point had reached, where spontaneously these groups felt that 'enough is enough' and fiercely and openly expressed their feelings independently but with the same objective and reaching the same conclusion of a return to the 1961 Federal agreement.

This generalized groundswell of revulsion and malaise was aptly captured by an editorial in the *Eden newspaper* famous for its perceptive articles, in its issue of Monday 20 July 2015 fittingly entitled: "*Fifty–Four years after Derailed Dreams of the Foumban Conference*," in July 1961. This was a moment that every Cameroonian, especially the English speaking Cameroonians thought: "The dream of living together with our brothers was going to usher in a new nation – one that promised justice and fair play, mutual respect, freedom and growth within an environment, where people were going to be judged not by their colonial lingo –cultural heritage but by the content of their character".²⁴⁶ The commentary succinctly continued:

> After a vital segment of this bicultural African experiment is only questioning whether it wasn't a *faux pas* from the onset. The new dawn that was expected to come out of the Foumban Conference ... is having a sour taste. To many the new dawn has not arrived: in its place retrogression, repression and glaring marginalisation are the order of the day. After the bells toll on the fifty-fourth anniversary of what was supposed to be a historic conference, the cries of a failed enterprise, a dream that never was, or is yet to be realized , and of a well intentioned initiative that has gone adrift are only growing, signalling disappointment and, failure stemming from sheer deceit and greed.²⁴⁷

In conclusion, the paper declared constructively, logically, hopefully and with extraordinary optimism that:

> The Cameroon bicultural project could and should be put back on its rails and all that is required is the will to accept the reality of the facts of history, the history agreed upon at Foumban in 1961, no matter how imperfect it was, demands that the Cameroonian train returns to its rails and retakes off from there.²⁴⁸

On the other hand, Mwalimu George Ngwane²⁴⁹ poignantly and squarely addressed the Anglophone Diaspora specifically, maintaining that as a keen political observer, he has watched them engage in picketing, hold conferences, present memos, indeed take every available constructive politi-

---

²⁴⁶ *Eden* no. 914 Monday, 20 July 2015

²⁴⁷ Ibid.

²⁴⁸ ibid.

²⁴⁹ He is a renowned socio-political analyst and winner of; the Chevening Peace Fellow - 2010; Rotary Peace Fellow -2015 and author of two new books "Rebranding Cameroon" and, the "Cameroon Condition".

cal action to regain a paradise lost. He further points out that they have made the Anglophone problem one of Cameroon's greatest democratic challenges and hopes the guiding spirit of history and the optimistic tenet of human nature would galvanize the Cameroon Diasporas into pursuing this constitutional goal using political means.[250] After bewailing the almost irredeemable ills that have befallen all illustrious Southern Cameroonian entrepreneurs, businessmen the airports, road infrastructure, parastatals and the fact that it is almost at the point of losing hope as well, this is where he steps in and invites the Cameroon Diaspora to turn homewards for all sorts of activities and investments. He concludes, from a global dialectics of history that "An interface between the Anglophone Cameroon Diaspora and their geopolitical territory on cultural entrepreneurship is a vital ingredient in the political search for constitutional redress."[251]

## Christian Cardinal Tumi

*Fig 41. Christian Cardinal Tumi; outspoken on issues of human rights and the marginalization of Anglophone Cameroonians.*

In May, the distinguished outspoken and intrepid Christian Cardinal Tumi, whose views are thoroughly and widely respected and to whom at crucial moments in the history of the Cameroon nation, people of all walks of life across the political, linguistic and religious divide have turned to, for leadership, gave an explosive interview in which he expressly pointed out

---

[250] Ibid, *Eden.*

[251] Ibid.

that: "If a referendum is organized to determine the views of Anglophones of the North and South West Regions about the continued union with the Francophones, they would vote to quit."[252] This was a simple, objective and altruistic observation but it: "Angered his Francophone critics, who maintain that Cameroon is one and indivisible" against the equally logical and powerful argument by others that great federations such as the USA, Canada and Germany are no less, 'one and indivisible' and even reference made to President Paul Biya's Fiftieth Anniversary celebration speech at Buea in which he referred to Cameroon as a nation united in diversity. As for the Cardinal's utterances, he was not saying anything new, as he has expressed these views openly and repeatedly in his speeches and works.[253] And indeed as a flash back to the Foumban constitutional conference of 1961, just before the conclusion of the procedures, the Anglophone or the southern Cameroons delegation complained against the use of the phrase, 'one and indivisible' proposed by the Republic of Cameroon delegation and President Ahidjo, the Chairman, asked for it to be struck off from the record pure and simple, there and then[254]. It was therefore not supposed to appear in the constitution.

Of course, he spoke for many as rejoinders and commentaries in the same vein have continued to be expressed in the private press and over the mass media. He does not even spare the Catholic Church, which he heads in Cameroon. Recently, he declared in another interview with *L'Effort Camerounais*, that it was the failure to implement bilingualism in the Catholic University of Central Africa (UCAC) Yaoundé, which led to the creation of an Anglo-Saxon Catholic University; the Catholic University of Cameroon, (CATUC) Bamenda. This was in spite of the fact that he was founder-creator and Chancellor of UCAC, which is owned

---

[252] See, *The Independent Observer*, issue no. 065 of July 02 2015 p.2 on Anglophone marginalisation

[253] See, Tumi, *The Political Regimes Ahmadou Ahidjo And Paul Biya And Christian Tumi, Priest*, MACACOS SA, 2006 Such as was the case in 1990, when there was a resonant call for a National Conference, all eyes turned on him.

[254] This can be found in the minutes and reports of the Foumban Constitutional Conference. In fact it was about the last entry to be made.

by the six Francophone Central African Dioceses for sixteen years.²⁵⁵ Obviously, he had not been able to impose his personal feelings on the top heavy Francophone leadership. As a consequence, foreign students from several English-speaking countries who had rushed to register at UCAC with the assurance and expectation that bilingualism was going to be implemented expectedly regrettably withdrew. This cannot be to anybody's credit.

## Hon Cyprian Awudu Mbaya: Anti-Lip Service Bilingualism

Barely a fortnight after the encounter with the Cardinal, precisely on Wednesday 27 May 2015, it was reported that Hon Cyprien Mbaya Awudu, a Social Democratic Front (SDF) opposition MP, declaring, "Enough is enough" of "The imperialism of the French language over the English language even on Anglophone territory" had gone on rampage at the government owned *Ayaba, Hotel,* where he was staying in Bamenda. Enraged, he brutally tore down all sign posts, notices and pieces of information which were boldly written exclusively in French. As well, the management and staff for the most part were Francophone. The MP considered this an unacceptable provocation in the heartland of Anglophone Cameroon in supposedly bilingual Cameroon. He was ready to carry the battle further even to parliament though threatened that criminal action could be taken against him in breach of Section 2 of the new terrorism law. However, soon after that the notices had all been redone in impeccable English and French.²⁵⁶ He has been hailed all over in the mass media and interviewed over the national radio, programme, "Cameroon calling" as championing the cause of marginalised Anglophones.

---

²⁵⁵ *L'Effort Camerounais* no. 609(154)058 of July – August 2015.

²⁵⁶ See, *The Guardian Post,* no. 0749 of Friday 29 may 2015. The MP, Hon. Cyprien Awudu Mbaya an SDF parliamentarian is *Questo*r and represents Nkambe Central in Donga – Mantung. The manager, Mr. Doume' Zacharie and his assistant Ondoua Francoise were both Francophones.

## Trends to Wipe Off the Common Law System: Reaction

In its edition of 1 June 2015, *The Post* newspaper declared that: "*It had evidence of a systematic trend to wipe off the civil law system*" and, "*proof of a conspiracy to subjugate the Common Law*". It went ahead to provide what it described as "cast iron evidence" of a systematic trend to wipe off the Common Law system, which Anglophone lawyers are in a desperate fight to keep alive.[257] The paper cited the fact that the decree creating the University of Buea in 1993 as an Anglo-Saxon institution of higher learning intended that it would cater for the less dominant Anglophone subsystem of education but over the years, a systematic effort has been deployed to undermine the specificity of that university. As part of this process, the Ministry of Higher Education convened a meeting on 6 May 2015 to discuss harmonization in the University of Buea starting with Law, Political Science and Management, pointedly decided that Common Law should be scrapped from the syllabus at the undergraduate level with wide ranging ramifications.[258] Furthermore, of 148 magistrates in the SWR, 58 were Francophones while of 30 new Bailiffs appointed in 2014, 28 were Francophones with only two Anglophones. The NWR statistics were even worse as of the 128 magistrates, 67 were francophone while all the 21 new bailiffs were Francophone! Worse still, judgments in the courts in the two Anglophone Regions are expected to be delivered in French! In other words, matters are only getting worse for the Anglophones in the system.

## Reaction of South West Chiefs and Lawyers

As a follow up to the resolutions taken by the Bar Association of all Anglophone lawyers at an earlier meeting in Bamenda, Barrister Felix Agbor Nkongho, President of the Fako Lawyers Association, affirmed among other demands: a return to the Federal system for the country

---

[257] *The Post* newspaper no. 01631 of June 01, 2015. Actually, they have staged a match to the authorities in Yaoundé to see the authorities concerned to make their point.

[258] ibid.

as obtained before 1972, protection for the Common Law subsystem, respect for the bi-jural system; and above all, protection of the Anglo-Saxon educational system in the North and South West Regions.[259] Next, after the meeting of the lawyers and University of Buea lecturers, the Conference of the South West Chiefs with powerful voices like those of Senator, Nfon Victor K Mukete better known for their moderation and support for the Yaoundé regime through motions of support, this time loudly decried "*The Rape on Anglophone Heritage*", once again recalling the glorious days of Southern Cameroons and the FRC.[260] However, Senator, Chief Nfor Tabetando took a different view from that of the Chiefs Conference Meeting in Kumba and: "Advised the people not to believe in prophets of doom, who have had successful careers as top civil servants and high class diplomats but are now promising a new country". Taking advantage of the exception made by Senator, Chief Nfor Tabetando, Barrister Felix Agbor Nkongho, President of the Fako Lawyers Association addressed an even more serious outstanding issue concerning the culture of sycophancy among leading politicians. Arguing deductively, he pointed out squarely that:

> If there is one group of persons, who manipulate people in this country it is politicians. And Chief Tabetando is a politician. They are the people who have been manipulating people in this country by selling falsehood. They are sycophants, they preach hatred and they are the ones who are deceiving the Head of State by not telling him the truth.[261]

In an editorial captioned "Anglophone plight in Cameroon: time to stop infighting and face the common enemy", The Times Journal of Monday April 13 2015, chastised Anglophones of the North and South West Regions. To this effect, it commented:

> Today the talk of the day is about the divide between Southern

---

[259] ibid.

[260] See, *The Horizon* no. 237 of Monday 8 June 2015.

[261] *The Post* Newspaper No. 01631 of June 01, 2015.

Cameroonians from the North West and those from the South West; they are at daggers drawn over the sharing of the crumbs from the table of the authorities of *La Republique du Cameroun* to the point that instead of addressing their common daily problems and focusing on whoever is depriving them of the right to effective citizenship, they spend time blaming each other. *And from all indications, this is the picture most enjoyed by the Yaoundé regime that wastes no time in pushing it with the divide and rule approach.*[262]

It points out to the blatant lies perpetrated by selfish elite to earn political and other personal gains going back to fairy tales of how in Southern Cameroons people of the North West cheated and sidelined those of the South West – charges that have proven to be baseless and senseless.[263] The paper laments the disappearance of the leadership and unity that obtained during AAC I and II and, as the way forward, stresses the fact that: "In unity we shall become a block that is taken seriously with the fear that we can bark and bite but in division, no one fears us as they find it easy to use some of us to thrash the others."[264] Finally it emphasised that such unity is possible and all that is required is to give it a try.

## Unity of Anglophone Trade Unions

The *Times Journal* further reported on the threatened strike action by Anglophone Civil Society Organizations (CSO) over the heavily flawed

---

[262] *The Times Journal* vol. 03 No. 145 of Monday April 13 2015. Taking the same line, introspectively: in an editorial, The *Guardian Post*, no. 0783 of Wednesday 19th. August 2015 identifies (SCAPO) the Southern Cameroons People's Organisation as the 'Judas Iscariot of the Anglophone struggle, which wants to metamorphose into a political party to fight the Yaoundé Administration, when its case with the same Yaoundé Administration at the African Commission on Peoples and Human Rights at Banjul is pending judgement.

[263] The examples quoted ad nauseam, cite two Bakweri early graduates from London, Efange and Quan, who were allegedly dismissed by the Foncha Administration for backing the opposition although they were later reinstated the criticisms persisted.

[264] Ibid.

entrance exam into the Police College with poorly translated questions that gravely disfavoured Anglophone candidates given that they could never find any sensible answers to the boggled questions to be able to successfully write the exam and pass. Since this is a recurrent problem, frustration is mounting among members of the Anglophone civil society across the board, who feel that their elite in government have betrayed them. Consequently, the Commonwealth Journalists Association(CJA-Cameroon) with the four Teachers Trade Unions: the Presbyterian Authority Teachers' Trade Union (PEATTU), the Catholic Education Workers'Trade Union (CEWOTU) and the Teachers' Association of Cameroon ((TAC) followed by the Cameroon Teachers'Trade Union (CATTU)have sworn that they would not accept the results of such a heavily flawed exam. The paper notes that much as these organizations are spoiling for street protests, the authorities appear unperturbed because of the existence of the "Obnoxious Anti – Terrorism law." Nevertheless put together, these civil society organizations are a potent force and constitute a serious challenge to the powers that be either now or later.[265] Increasingly they are realising the power that emanates from united action in a situation where, forever, the government manipulates the various factions in a bid to play the divide and rule game.[266] All put together, this gives an aggregate of the totality of the escalating Anglophone mood of discontent. The powers that be ought to give these complaints the serious attention they deserve in the shortest run possible to avoid incalculable damage in the long run.

True to their word, the four Anglophone Teachers Trade Unions and Unions of Parent Teachers' Associations (PTAs) on 4 November 2015 came out with an even more incisive and pungent three page memo addressed

---

[265] Ibid.

[266] As part of this game during the past couple of years, a series of top notch appointments have been made from among the Bakweri of the South West Region ethnic group. These include: two PMs; Chief Ephraim Inoni, Peter Mafany Musonge in a row; three female Vice Chancellors: Profs. Dorothy Njeuma, Nalova Lyonga, and Joyce Endeley; Humphrey Monono, Registrar of the GCE Board, and the CDC General Managers, Njalla Quan among others, all out of proportion to the size of the ethnic group in the Region. At other times it was meant to pit up the North and Southwest Regions against each other, but here the objective is not so obvious; rather it causes jealousy within the South West Region.

to the Head of State on Anglophone marginalisation and permissive unethical admissions particularly in the University of Bamenda created by Decree No. 2011 /045 of 8 March 2011 as the second Anglo-Saxon institution of higher education after the University of Buea inaugurated a decade earlier. The combination of trade unions came out with a litany of grave irregularities backed by amazing statics of how the Decree had been openly violated as that university had been, "Flooded with a plethora of Francophone lecturers with no smattering of English to teach in an Anglophone university". Even worse, was the massive admission of Francophone students in the Higher Teachers Training College hitting figures as high as: 100% in the Mechanical Design Department and 70-95% in others like Air Conditioning and Design on the false pretext that Anglophones are not interested in technical education.[267]

In conclusion, they pointed out that this marginalisation is designed to deny Anglophones from the former West Cameroon the training and employment quotas that are their deserved heritage. They asked for: The "shameless perpetrators of these ignominious acts to be brought to book and that forums for sincere nation building and for dialogue between the peoples of the two States, who deliberately opted for reunification in 1961 in the wake of the plebiscite to pre-empt the indignation that has been building up in Anglophone Cameroons. Because their previous correspondence had not received any reaction, they declared: "We will give this letter the widest publicity. We are convinced that you have been kept in the dark about such efforts to keep a portion of your people sidelined from nation building and to institutionalise mediocrity for personal gain at the expense of meritocracy."[268] The baton stick was next taken over by the Cameroon branch of the commonwealth journalists association. Meeting in Limbe on 5 December 2015, "They joined the bandwagon of lawyers, teachers, and traditional rulers of Anglophone extraction among

---

[267] See "Memo to HE The President Of The Republic By Anglophone Parents And Teachers Trade Unions About Anglophone Marginalisation…'signed by the various Trade Union Leaders and forwarded by Mr. Ngen Sylvester Yengo, secretary.

[268] It is far from being a mere coincidence, that barely three weeks later, precisely on Friday 27 November 2015, the Vice Chancellor and some top officials of the University of Bamenda were replaced.

others fighting for the rights of people who hail from the erstwhile British Southern Cameroons territory, which include cultural and educational systems, which are being assimilated by their francophone counterparts." Mwalimu George Ngwane of Africaphonie avowed that Senator Nfon Victor Mukete should not be talking alone about the marginalisation of Anglophones in Cameroon, while Chief Nkemayang, President of CJA-Cameroon further declared, "We would not be strangers if we take certain lines of action".[269] Consequently, the struggle is unrelenting.

*Fig 42. Independence Day celebrations in Buea with Cecil King, the British Ambassador to Cameroon reading the Queens speech*

## Collusion between Britain and Republic of Cameroun

When in mid June 1960, the British colonial masters were preparing for the organisation of the plebiscite the following year as well as to pack out bag and baggage from Southern Cameroons and requested President Ahidjo to "foster" the Territory, he turned down the offer; maintaining that he had neither the economic nor military means to undertake that task. Mr. Patrick Johnston the British Ambassador to the Republic of

---

[269] *The Post* no. 01684 of Monday December 2015

Cameroun accordingly reported to the Governor General of Nigeria as follows:

> *The defence question is obviously the most difficult and a great deal depends on the length of time the present disturbances continue.* I did not understand Mr. Ahidjo to say in Buea, as Mr. Field reports that the Camerounian Government could not accept responsibility for internal security in the British Cameroons. Certainly Mr. Foncha would wish to keep the police in his own hands... because (soldiers of Republic of Cameroun) as a result of French training and as the result of the emergency are inclined to methods which we consider rather deplorable.[270]

This came up again in the course of the clash Ahidjo had with Foncha at the Buea Tripartite Conference of 14-17 May 1961. Commissioner, JO Field had first reported on the conditions which Nigeria had clearly declared as the propositions for Southern Cameroons if in the impending plebiscite it decided for 'integration' way back in 1968. They declared it would be on the basis of equal Regional status for Southern Cameroons with the other three existing Regions in the Federation: the Northern, Eastern and Western Regions of Nigeria enjoying internal autonomy or "Home Rule." These were exceedingly attractive propositions. However, on Cameroon JO Field reported that:

> Immediate re-unification is demonstrably impracticable and a separate existence must, therefore intervene ... Furthermore, Ahidjo bluntly declared that – *'The Cameroon Republic cannot undertake the defence of Southern Cameroons, nor provide the financial and technical assistance necessary for the replacement of the agency services and development of the territory's economy'.*[271]

---

[270] See CO554/2249 XC 3406, Patrick Johnston to the governor general of Nigeria. However, in further correspondence, Ahidjo promised to give Southern Cameroons top priority after clearing existing problems.

[271] CO55/2258 XC 4122 See also, Southern *Cameroons Revisited*, Vol. 1 pp.210 -211

It was explicit and, that this yawning gap was all of a sudden sufficiently narrowed and bridged at the Tripartite Conference to warrant an agreement between Britain and Republic of Cameroon over such thorny issues was a marvellous feat. Other than the high suspicion that there was collusion between the British delegates and those of the Republic of Cameroun, attendance at the conference was equally unbalanced comprising: Britain, France, Republic of Cameroon and Southern Cameroons, fielding some twenty delegates only four of whom represented Southern Cameroons with the three other partners frequently combining to impose on the Foncha cabinet. This became so flagrant that *Foncha was obliged to politely point out to a barefaced collusion that had developed between Britain and Republic of Cameroon over several issues* especially concerning defence and where he was suspected of nurturing communist sympathies because he dared to suggest reconciliation between Dr. Felix Roland Moumié and other UPC members with the Ahidjo Regime.

## Foncha: Branded Leftist and Communist-Anathema

To Foncha, the moment when forces were gathering momentum for reunification and independence between Republic of Cameroon and British Cameroons, a cause for which the UPC had fought so valiantly, was the right time to mend fences. Because of this and the fact that he was known for being sympathetic towards Patrice Lumumba and Pan-Africanism, in the *Cold War* political climate of the time, he was daubed a communist. This fact deserves a certain measure of emphasis because this was in that context, a stigma, which further strengthened the British Colonial Administration's extreme dislike for him. Nor can this be disassociated from their decision to withdraw British defence forces from the Territory at its most vulnerable point especially as Ahidjo had declared that he had neither the means to foster Southern Cameroons' economy or defence. In fact, the Ahidjo cabinet declared that if Moumie dared step his foot on Cameroon soil, he would be arrested right at the Airport.[272]Interestingly, it is precisely at about this moment that Foncha

---

[272] See Appendix 1, No. 21; also, Ndi, *Southern West Cameroon Revisited*, Vol. 1

was 'suspected' of having done a deal with Ahidjo for positions in his pre-unification cabinet for Muna and himself.

In fact this is best presented in the words of Patrick Johnston, the British Ambassador to Republic of Cameroun. Together with Malcolm Milne and JO Field, the Deputy Commissioner and Commissioner Of Southern Cameroons respectively, the trio did all in their power fair or foul to get the territory stay in Nigeria and because Foncha and his KNDP stood for reunification with Republic of Cameroon, he was persona non grata and they made life difficult for him. In his highly confidential report widely circulated to: Her Majesty's Ambassadors in Paris and Dakar, the UN Permanent Delegate in New York and HE the Governor General of Nigeria, Johnston had the following report to make about Foncha. There was genuine fear by the Governor General Sir James Robertson, that Foncha would turn to Nkrumah or even to the Communist Bloc for assistance available neither from Britain nor the Republic of Cameroon since Ahidjo was sceptical. Johnston notes:

> I cannot believe that M. Ahidjo could contemplate a federation so loose that such a step would be permitted. If there are differences between M. Ahidjo and Foncha, they lie precisely in the fact that Mr. Foncha is inclined to the "LEFT" and towards pan-Africanism or the Nkrumah – Sekou Toure' – Lumumba brand, which is anathema to the Cameroun Government. I cannot think that Mr. Foncha's recent attempts to mediate between Dr. Moumie and Ahidjo have been very much to the latter's liking. If moreover, Mr. Foncha is going to start *playing with fire* in a Camerounian Federation, he is just as likely to do so in a Federation of Nigeria[273].

To be branded "Leftist" or a "Communist" in the Cold War era was not a stigma to be taken lightly imagining that it led to the assassination of Patrice Lumumba and several others. For that reason, Southern

---

pp.226-229

[273] See CO 554/2249 XC 3406 Report by Patrick Johnston to Governor General of Nigeria, April 1960

Cameroons which was considered of strategic importance in the cold war struggle mattered even much more to Britain and the West than it did to Ahidjo. Consequently, Foncha was not only a security risk to Ahidjo but to the British as well and Nkrumah's visit to Southern Cameroons in 1959 only added fuel to the fire. Johnston's report written in April 1960 was re-enacted on the floor of the Buea Tripartite Conference, where Foncha was literally isolated by all the parties and provided material for the black mail by the trio named above against him. This was the framework within which Foncha organised the Bamenda All Party Conference and proceeded to the Foumban Conference. How was he able to do this after the disagreement with Ahidjo? One wonders whether, in earnest Ahidjo later vested confidence in Foncha as a political partner and whether indeed there was ever any genuine confidence and love lost between the two men.

JO Field and Malcolm Milne spared nothing to humiliate and discredit Foncha and his cabinet, and so the announcement of the withdrawal of the British Armed Forces just before the Bamenda All Party Conference of 26 -28 June 1961 was appropriately timed to do maximum damage - stir up discontent and disaffection first, within the KNDP against its leadership and, opposition to Foncha by a combination of the delegates assembling for the Bamenda All Party Conference: the One Kamerun party the CPNC and Traditional Rulers, possibly leading to a civil war in the country. This was intended to punish Foncha and bring down his Government as insinuated by Malcolm Milne in his report to the Colonial Office. Together, JO Field, Malcolm Milne and CE King, the British Ambassador to Cameroun had earlier done all in their power to buy over KNDP MPs to cross the carpet to Endeley's CPNC opposition.[274] Again, in this case, they failed woefully, as instead, the Bamenda All Party Conference preparing for the Foumban Constitutional Conference was a resounding success and came out with unanimous endorsement of the KNDP proposals for Foumban. Ironically, they issued a powerful condemnation of the British Administration for their announcement to withdraw their army from the Trust Territory at such a very precarious

---

[274] ibid, the woman MP referred to is Mrs. Josepha Mua, On this score, it should be noted that Foncha was never found fit for decoration by the queen.

moment in its history, leaving it totally defenceless. Back in London in the House of Commons, Sir Hugh Fraser, the British Under Secretary of State for Colonies was taken to task for this grave betrayal of trust and found speechless. There is little doubt therefore, that Malcolm Milne finally apologised in his autobiography and personally confessed to those Cameroon Anglophones he met after his retirement in London.[275]

This was the most trying period in Foncha's political life. With looming threats of a civil war overflowing from Republic of Cameroon into West Cameroon, Foncha's assurances that peace would prevail fell on deaf ears as some British citizens and missionaries of all denominations decided to leave the country.[276] For one thing, at the conference, Ahidjo wanted all power to devolve on his person during the interlude between independence and setting up the federal structures. Precisely this was what the British finally did mostly out of spite for Foncha who had favoured reunification against their best advice, which was integration with Nigeria.[277] For that reason, they withdrew all their defence forces even before Ahidjo could send in his troops whom Foncha regarded as 'uncouth.' As an alternative, he asked the British to repatriate the Southern Cameroonian soldiers, they had deployed in the Nigerian army to form the nucleus of a West Cameroon defence force to no avail. This indeed is one of the most sordid chapters of Cameroon history needing thorough investigation and explanation. The deal the British and Republic of Cameroun Governments struck over Southern Cameroons is most likely a significant cog in the "inescapable traps" with which Foncha was threatened by Malcolm Milne.[278]

In fact, more like a bully or a spoilt kid, not used to being contradicted or opposed, President Ahidjo absconded the Buea Tripartite Conference

---

[275] He did this in his personal contacts formally at conferences and informally as well, with Professors; Verkijika GF and Mathew Gwanfogbe in London.

[276] Among these were the Mill Hill Missionary Sisters, who opened up and ran the famous St. Francis GTTC, Fiango, Kumba. IT was difficult to replace them.

[277] See Appendix 5.

[278] Malcolm Milne, *No Telephone To Heaven; The Inescapable Traps Vols* 1 and 2 by Anthony Ndi.

mid way leaving his Minister of Foreign Affairs, Charles Okala to "wrest as much power for him" in the negotiations as he could. Consequently, after the deal was struck between the Republic of Cameroun and Great Britain, the transfer of power ultimately passed straight from the Queen to President Ahidjo and not to Foncha or, to "a body representing" both states as previewed in the UN agreement. Subsequently, on the eve of independence on 1st October 1961, Sir Hugh Fraser, British Under - Secretary of State for Colonies formally informed the House of Commons that Southern Cameroons had been transferred to President Ahidjo.[279] Her royal Majesty the Queen's speech was rendered that evening at Buea Mountain Hotel by the British Ambassador to Cameroon, CE King. It explicitly read:

> On the occasion of ending the British Trusteeship in Southern Cameroons, I send Your Excellency my sincere good wishes for the future of the united territories over which you now preside. I am glad that friendly cooperation between our countries should have made it possible for the Southern Cameroons to attain independence in accordance with the results of the February plebiscite. I look forward to the continuation of our cordial relations in the future.[280]

The deal, the Anglo-Cameroun authorities had struck for this fostering process, given that Ahidjo had earlier declared that he could not handle the economic and defence responsibilities for Southern Cameroons requested by Great Britain can only be conjectured. However, the radical change of mind and attitude could not have been for trifles as Foncha suspected at the Buea Tripartite Meeting. However, Mr. Iain Macleod, the Secretary of State for the Colonies on the same occasion, that evening addressed a separate message to Foncha, the PM of Southern Cameroons noting:

---

[279] See, Carlson Anyangwe, *Betrayal of Too Trusting A People – The UN, The UK And The Trust Territory of Southern Cameroons,* Langaa Research and Publishing CIG, Mankon, Bamenda, 2009, p. 54

[280] ibid. p. 233

> As the period of our Trusteeship comes to an end and your country takes its place with the Republic of Cameroun in the new federation, I should like to send you my best wishes for the future to yourself and your countrymen. We look forward to maintain with the Federal Republic of Cameroon the happy ties of friendship which have linked us with Southern Cameroons for over forty years.[281]

This version of the address was read by Malcolm Milne, the Acting Commissioner of Southern Cameroons; actually, his very last official engagement in that capacity. It was in the course of writing his report on the events of that day that a miraculous transformation happened, opening his eyes to the incalculable damage the British had wrought on Southern Cameroons. He regretted and confessed profusely, poetically noting in his own words how:

> That afternoon of 30th September had been exceptionally brilliant. There weren't many days in the year Ambas Bay could be like that. But I for one – and I think others of my colleagues as well – felt that the beauty of the scene was an ironic comment on what we'd been up to rather than a sign of approbation for what we'd done. May be we'd let these nice little people down 'and one day would rue it'[282].

This heavily loaded quotation speaks volumes as Malcolm Milne further regrets that Whitehall had treated Southern Cameroons with levity and that the British colonial establishment had made a mess of their watch over the Trust Territory after forty years of administration. Thus, his regrets and apologies were not only on his own behalf but for the entire British Colonial Administration.[283] He continued even more remorsefully and intimately:

> We'd come to the end of a pretty sorry saga. We had obedient to orders

---

[281] Ibid, Anyangwe p. 233.

[282] Malcolm Milne, *No Telephone To Heaven*. 447

[283] ibid.

## IRONIC OUTCOME OF MARGINALISATION: AN INVINCIBLE SPIRIT

– given away what once we'd been charged with constructing. On the other hand, none of us felt competent to question the orders coming from cabinet level, our experience had always been that such orders based upon all the facts were correct, infallible.[284]

Malcolm Milne together with his boss, Johnson O Field, the Commissioner of Southern Cameroons, had been the main executors of British colonial policy and had been responsible for the sad state in which they were abandoning the Trust Territory, which they had grossly mismanaged. Finally, they robbed the people of their well deserved qualification for independence as was the case with the Gambia, Gabon, Equatorial Guinea, Ceylon and even other smaller and poorer states than Southern Cameroons. Taking Malcolm Milne's predictions, in fact, prophecy, there is a chance that alive to the facts of history, logic, law and equity with the example of what recently took place in Kenya, with belated apologies and reparations over the *Mau Mau* colonial atrocities: The wrongs done by the British Government to Southern Cameroons ought legally in the logic of history, in simple justice and equity to be corrected else they would certainly "rue it" in Malcolm Milne's words.

Among other reasons the French colonial masters saw Ahidjo at independence as a more likely leader to handle the UPC rebellion, which was sapping away all their human, financial and material resources without let off than the Andre Marie Mbida incumbent. In fact, reunification would only have been meaningful to Ahidjo if British Northern Cameroons voted for it but with their loss, he was most upset. Consequently, he fought hard to have the results of the Northern Cameroons Plebiscite reversed. He lost the fight first, at the UNTC and, then again at The Hague and immortalized his disgust by declaring a day of national mourning.

### Malcolm Milne's Penchant for President Ahidjo

As for Malcolm Milne's expression of unmitigated spite for Foncha and spontaneous admiration for Ahidjo, this happened precisely on 30

[284] ibid.

September 1961 after the President had presided over the ceremonies marking the independence of Southern Cameroons at the Tiko International Airport that afternoon. It was Malcolm Milne's last day in office and, he had the privilege of driving the President in the Commissioner's land rover from Tiko to Buea. He honestly described it as his most pleasant and fulfilling experience, expressly as Ahidjo's presence in Buea would even for that brief period "put Foncha out of the limelight". This was because Foncha's charismatic personality impulsively magnetized adulating crowds wherever he appeared in public. As it turned out Foncha's popularity greatly hurt and upset Malcolm Milne, and he was outspoken enough to declare this in his autobiography. Put together with quite a few similar instances, his dislike for Foncha was as boundless as it was baseless, meanwhile, by the same token he openly declared his esteem for Ahidjo; the well cultured, conservative, Moslem, Fulani Northerner. Thus Malcolm Milne's love for Ahidjo as for Muna was spontaneous.[285] Consequently, at the Buea Tripartite Conference, Ahidjo easily emerged as *L'enfant Cherie*, having earlier won French approval against André Marie Mbida as PM, this time he added the British Deputy Commissioner and probably more, to the list of his admirers.

It was apparent that to Ahidjo, unification with only Southern Cameroons without British Northern Cameroons with its Fulani Moslem population to counterbalance it was something of an unnecessary burden and not worth the bother. Hence, the severance of links between the North and South West Regions was part of deliberate government policy, to mutilate these Regions, disrupt their solidarity, in short, take the sting out of them so that they could become demoralized, weakened and malleable bits to control and assimilate as factions in the guise of the Unitary State. At one point soon after 1972, there were feelers sent out suggesting that some of the government services in these Regions would have their headquarters transferred to Douala for the South West Region and Bafoussam for the North West Region, but these received very hostile responses from these Regions and were quietly withdrawn. The idea of course was to dismember them and eventually create new latitudinal rather

---

[285] *No telephone* p.447. Also *Southern Cameroons Revisited* p.320

than the existing conventional longitudinal North-South West Anglophone connections and loyalties. Indirectly, this was partially achieved through the back door simply by leaving the North West – South West road and air links to get into a state total disrepair thereby forcing commuters between the two Regions to do so circuitously only through the West and Littoral Regions.

*Figure 43. André-Marie Mbida; First Prime Minister of French Cameroun*

## Fuel for Breeding Anglophone Resentment

Curiously, this policy has become exactly counterproductive as instead it is breeding spontaneous and unfettered resentment, hostility, rejection and opposition, while continued suppression has over time driven simple, honest, law-abiding Anglophone Southern Cameroonians, who repeatedly have declared that their one wish is the re-establishment of the Federal State, where they can live in peaceful co-existence with their Francophone brothers to contemplate extreme militant measures even of secession from a State they willing opted to create. This of course is totally inconsistent with the Southern Cameroonian ethos of peace, respect for law and order, loyalty, harmony and accommodation. Reviewing the plight of Southern Cameroonians at the hands of the rather insensitive successive Francophone dominated Administrations and the fact that the apparent divisions between the North and South West Regions result from direct government policy; Dr. JN Foncha reiterated in his letter of resignation in 1990, what he had decried repeatedly:

> The Anglophone Cameroonians, whom I brought into the union have been ridiculed and referred to as; Les Biafrais, Les Enemies Dans La Maison, Les Traites, etc and the constitutional provisions which protected this Anglophone minority have been suppressed, their voices drowned, while the rule of the gun has replaced the dialogue which the Anglophones cherish very much.[286]

And concretely referring to the source of the official support for factious divisions between the Anglophone Provinces, he noted how; "The national media has deliberately been used by the government through people, who never voted for reunification to misinform the citizens from Bamenda (and vice versa the coastal region)".[287] Such thoughts clearly in the absence of any meaningful dialogue are an imposition as most Southern Cameroonians favour peace and believe as repeatedly stated right back in July 1960 by Ahidjo himself that "Cameroon is ancestral patrimony and so belongs in equal measure to all of us", Anglophones, Francophones, North Westerners and South Westerners alike.

The ruling elite ought to realise that the Southern Cameroons Anglophone ethos is irrepressible as many historians and political analysts and journalists have painstakingly demonstrated and, above all as borne by numerous examples in history.[288] In any case, the distinction between Southern Cameroonians craving for a return to the FRC, re-enacting their existence as a State and the demand for secession by certain factions among them as a consequence of despair from failure by the ruling

---

[286] Foncha's Letter of Resignation from the CPDM, 9 June 1990.

[287] Ibid.

[288] For penetrating articles on this issue, see: Professor Martin Njeuma; *Introduction to the History of Cameroon in 19th & 20th centuries;* Professor Tazoacha Asonganyi: *Southern West Cameroon Revisited* Vol 11, post script pp. 163 – 173; *Eden Xtra Magazine No. 001, Oct. 2011*, "Setting the record straight".

Francophone elite to listen to their woes; are two distinct options. The latter is a demand for "unity in diversity" acknowledged by President Paul Biya in his address during the Golden Jubilee celebrations at Buea, while the others are being forced to contemplate extreme action void of violence by repression and the refusal to dialogue. When powerful insiders like former Minister Mbombo Njoya and Emah Basil, Delegate to the Yaoundé City Council described Anglophones in awful derogatory expressions such as: 'enemies within the house', 'strangers' or are asked to 'go elsewhere' and the national media is made to chant false messages as happened when the SDF was launched in 1990 with six youth shot in broad day light in cold blood by zealous trigger happy soldiers but reported by the official press as having been trampled underfoot during a stampede; and that Ni John Fru Ndi was seen escaping to Nigeria or, that Nigerians were involved in the launching and sang the Nigerian national anthem,[289] no right thinking people and not only Anglophones could be expected to be indifferent to such flagrant falsehood. No successful and progressive nation can be groomed on the foundation of deceit and falsehood.

## Unity and Strength Brewed from Adversity: Historical perspectives

This invincible Southern Cameroons spirit was largely demonstrated against British colonial attempts to Nigerianise them through implanting Ibo hegemony, which backfired and finally, instead resulted in the "intimidating" results of the 11 February 1961 plebiscite in favour of reunification, exactly the opposite of what the British had expected through their manoeuvres. This was in spite of the fact that at the time the Republic of Cameroon was experiencing the worst *maquisards-terrorist* attacks – "It was raining fire and brimstone!" *This was a mark of the iron will of the people, who united, knew exactly what they wanted against the worst odds. Over the years, this unyielding will power has gained strength and resilience from being ignored and marginalised and is unlikely to succumb to intimidation, which is*

---

[289] Victor Julius Ngoh, *History of Cameroon Since 1800*, Presprint, Limbe, 1996, p.308; SDF at 25.

*undoubtedly responsible for the extreme options indirectly imposed on militant Southern Cameroons groups such as: the SCNC, SCARM, SCAPO, SCYL and Ambazonia*, simply because they are neither given a chance for dialogue, a listening ear nor room to vent their feelings and their grievances.[290] If the British with all their might as a colonial master totally failed in their attempt to yoke "British Southern Cameroons" to Nigeria, after forty-five years of manoeuvres, the present authorities need to review the one track policy being pursued to avoid possible collateral damage.

Notable for his capacity to double talk, President Ahidjo in his ultimate address abolishing the FRC, on 6 May 1972, when introducing the Unitary State, reiterated that the Federal structures were adopted at Reunification in order to assure the Southern Cameroonians that the heritage which they were contributing to the nation would not be ignored: "But would be taken into consideration within the framework of a bilingual multicultural state".[291] In other words, even as he was abolishing the Federal Republic of Cameroon, he nevertheless emphasised its bilingual and multicultural character, which of course is ambiguous and contradictory in terms as these were the major reasons for the creation of the FRC in the first place.

## "Unitary State" Reverted to "Republic of Cameroon"

President Ahidjo's reassurance notwithstanding, by a simple decree in 1984 President Paul Biya changed the constitution, abolished the Unitary State, and reintroduced the name "Republic of Cameroon" by which French Cameroun had been christened at independence on 1 January 1960. The document primarily altered articles 1, 5 and 7 of the previous constitution. Article 1 renamed the country the "Republic of Cameroon", while Article 7 recognized the Speaker of the National Assembly as the

---

[290] See, "Setting the record straight" in *The Guardian Post* of 19 Dec 2014 article "SCNC activists boycott gathering for fear of anti-terrorism law." There are in-depth articles in there on the election of Hon. Paul Ayah as SCNC President as leader to revive the Southern Cameroons struggle on p.11

[291] See Resolutions Made by the Inaugural All Cameroon Common Law Lawyers" Conference Held at Bamenda in the North West Region of Cameroon, 9 May 2015; Courtesy of Barrister Harmony Bobga.

Presidential successor....²⁹²" In part, this was reversing the alteration made by President Ahidjo to the unitary constitution in 1979 specifically paving the way for Biya, then as PM, to eventually replace him as his successor. This was a comic situation as it followed the tussle that had taken place between the two men in the aftermath of the failed coup. However, theologically legal, historical and political implications for Southern (West) Cameroon carried another message, especially bearing on its deliberate ambiguity. According to François Mattei, "Biya thinks that Cameroon must not be seen as federation of provinces but as a unique global entity to be able to exist, last, give birth to a national identity.²⁹³ Unfortunately, this philosophy emphasises the ephemeral rather than the essence and deals with the smoke instead of the fire at the base.

It was, and continues to be subject to varying interpretations including in the first place; that Southern Cameroons had been liberated since by that single Act, Republic of Cameroun had seceded from the Unitary State; or, that Southern Cameroons had finally been "absorbed, integrated or assimilated" into the Republic of Cameroon. This seems to be the case, despite Ahidjo's own assurance and declaration on introducing the United Republic of Cameroon to replace the FRC in 1972, that the bilingual and multicultural status would be maintained. Of course, this has not been supported by what is taking place with regard to the Anglophones in the country, let alone openly calling the name, "Southern Cameroons", a solid and inexorable fact of history, which seems to have become a taboo appellation.

Over time, even fifty years later, as the *Golden Jubilee of Southern Cameroons* independence was being celebrated at Buea in 2014, there continued to resonate complaints of *'assimilationist'* and discriminatory propensities in the system. These abound in the spheres of: education, the judiciary, administration and employment, while it was pointed out that only mere lip service is paid to bilingualism which originally was

---

²⁹² Emmanuel Y Sobseh, *Rethinking Citizenship: Towards A Better Future*, Global Press, 2012, p.113. as Mattei describes it.

²⁹³ See François Mattei, p. 277. Within context, this is seen as provoked by the Ahidjo rebellion, but how the change of name fits into the puzzle.

instituted as a crucial tool for national integration.²⁹⁴

*Some historical and political analysts think that the Southern Cameroonian or Anglophone situation within the Republic of Cameroon is worse than what obtained in South Africa under the system of apartheid given that even "Black South Africans could freely scream, dance in the streets and thus draw world attention to their plight compared to the policy of zero tolerance faced by Southern Cameroonians."* They dare not openly express their dissatisfaction and demand equal fundamental rights and privileges as provided for in the constitution, a return to the FRC or much worse, voice out their frustration by craving for secession seeing the union as unworkable. This is the perspective for Southern Cameroonians in a celebrated 21ˢᵗ century; free, democratic Republic of Cameroon and not in 19ᵗʰ century apartheid-ridden South Africa. Consequently, either out of despair, frustration, self interest or sheer opportunism:

> As a people divested of their political heritage, status and lands, they cowardly plead political evolution seeking refuge in atomised and doubtful apolitical associations - Chief's Conferences, Fons' Unions, elite associations etc. engage the deaf (Francophone leadership) from their strongholds in a monologue of petitions, communiqués, motions of support²⁹⁵

Careful note should be taken between the present strenuous efforts being made towards devolution and the system that obtained under the Federal Republic of Cameroon, which was a union of two vastly asymmetrical, socio-cultural and political systems, respecting these differences as those that exist between a man and woman that enable them to live together in harmony. Devolution, on the other hand, while largely containing some of the positive qualities found in a federation is limited to facilitating administration and socio- economic development of the nation. In other words, devolution stays at the surface and does not cater for the

---

²⁹⁴ ibid.

²⁹⁵ S Takang Mainyu: "The Southern Cameroons Question, Where Tetchiada Had Left Off", A terse response to an article in *Cameroon Panorama*.

foundation: in fact, the 'soul' that constitutes the very essence, identity and innate qualities inculcated and deeply entrenched in the psyche of the people over forty years of Anglo-Saxon upbringing of "Southern Cameroonians." The palliative measures being dished out through devolution, would only intensify the quest for a political solution to what has become an intractable predicament, "the Anglophone problem". The best wine cannot quench the thirst for common water.

## The Southern Cameroons on Point of Legality

Interestingly at the international level, the African Commission on Human and Peoples' Rights (ACHPR) of which Cameroon is a bona fide member and signatory, in its powerful ruling on Communication 266/2003 of 2009, confirmed and upheld the distinctiveness of Southern Cameroons. This as lucidly expressed in its Article 179, states in a few simple penetrating, far reaching words:

> The Commission finds that the people of *Southern Cameroons* qualify to be referred to as a 'people' because they manifest numerous characteristics and affinities which include a common history, linguistic tradition, territorial connection and political outlook. More importantly, they identify themselves as a people with a separate and distinct identity. Identity is an innate characteristic within a people. It is up to other external people to recognise such existence but not to deny it[296].

The last sentence of this quotation perfectly addresses the gullibility of the Cameroon public reminding them that the affirmation of the appellation "Southern Cameroons "is an indelible cultural, legal and historical fact and so is not optional. It is only of recent that the names 'Ni John Fru Ndi 'and that of the first President of the Republic, 'Ahmadou

---

[296] The Commission came into existence with the coming into force, on 21 October 1986, of the African Charter (adopted by the OAU on 27 June 1981). Although its authority rests on its own treaty, the African Charter, the Commission reports to the Assembly of Heads of State and Government of the African Union (formerly the Organisation of African Unity)

Ahidjo' have been rehabilitated and are back in full currency once again in the country. Otherwise, a couple of years back, they were wholly anathema and calling them was tantamount to sedition. One cannot point out precisely as to why, when and how this came about but, together with the habitual "Motions of Support" this can easily be put down to the culture of *zombification* and sycophancy by fanatical party stalwarts. This is generally carried out by individuals and groups in a stupefied, zealous competitive bid to indicate the degree of their particular attachment to the *deified* Head of State and support for the ruling party.

Consequently, many political zealots, both of the CPDM and SDF parties were genuinely petrified, if not scandalised that President Paul Biya and Ni John Fru Ndi, the SDF opposition leader shook hands and were publicly seen sitting and chatting amicably together before the glare of TV cameras during the President's visit to Bamenda in 2014 as part of festivities marking the Golden Jubilee celebrations of Southern Cameroons independence. It easily brought to mind, President Paul Biya's dramatic conversion to multi-partyism and his declaration in favour of open competition, when CPDM party stalwarts and zealots were still marching and dancing in the streets throughout the country in defence of the One Party system and vehemently protesting against any attempt to reintroduce multiparty politics in the 1990s.[297]

This is precisely what is referred to as "*zombification*" because after that it was the self-same party activists, loud-mouthed individuals and groups, who barefacedly moved nauseating motions of support and congratulations to the Head of State for his clairvoyance and declaring him "Father of democracy". This of course, totally ignored the heroic launching of the SDF at the cost of the lives of six youth shot in cold blood by trigger happy troops; followed by the state of emergency imposed on Bamenda Town.[298]

---

[297] The popular example usually cited is the famous, '*Dimabola*' demonstrations organized in the streets of Kumba by the erstwhile Minister of Justice and CPDM big wig, Justice Benjamin Itoe.

[298] Foreword by Ni John Fru Ndi, SDF at 25, 1990- 2015: *The Struggle For Democracy And Good Governance*, Presbyterian Printing Press, Limbe, 2015, Pp16-17: *the six young SDF supporters killed were: Asanji Christopher Fombi, a student; Fidelis Chosi, a corn mill operator; Juliette Sikod, a student; Nfon Edwin Jatop, a tailor; Tifuh Mathias Teboh, a student*

Cameroon history will have to be written and rewritten especially as the people seem to be very slow learners, forever oblivious of the reality that with the fast evolving technology, the world is an infectious shrinking global village and, they either have to move with the tides or be swept by them as has happened in other countries.

The acknowledgement that Southern Cameroons is a *de facto* socio-cultural and political entity by the ***African Commission on Human and Peoples' Rights*** (ACHPR) in itself carrying the weight of international law and recognition, tallies in whole with the expression by Malcolm Milne, the Acting Commissioner of Southern Cameroons, who concluded that the British Government owes an obligation to right the wrong they did to the nice, honest, loyal, "little," people of Southern Cameroons, whom they literally dumped at independence in 1961.[299] This is equally the conclusion that has been reached by two luminaries: Professor Martin Njeuma, a highly rated, seasoned teacher and erudite historian, who actually lived the experience together with Professor Tazoacha Asonganyi, a renowned political analyst, who after independent critical analyses jointly concluded that peace, harmony and unity in Cameroon are dependent on how well the "Anglophone problem" is managed by the ruling Francophone elite. Interestingly, the editor of the *Eden Xtra Magazine*, Chief Zachee Nzohngandembo in its analytical editorial No. 001 of October 2011, entitled: "Setting the Record Straight" approximately reached the same conclusion adding that it will take an interaction of History and Law to resolve the Southern Cameroons problem.

In the meantime, if this had merely been an aspiration in 2011 when Chief Zachee Nzohngandembo, made his forecast, interestingly, the lawyers of the Cameroon Bar Association of the Common Law Extraction of the North and South West Regions of Cameroon, spontaneously reached such a resolution in their meeting of 9 May 2015 at Bamenda. They were reacting some forty-three years after the acclaimed "Peaceful Revolution

---

*and Toje Evaristus Chatum, a student.*

[299] Historically, after serious analysis Professor Martin Njeuma concluded like Professor Tazoacha Asonganyi that peace and harmony in Cameroon are dependent on how the Anglophone problem is handled.

of 1972", to the deepening and unheeded complaints of marginalisation of the Anglophones in nearly all aspects of national life citing a litany of violated national and international agreements, covenants and failed promises. These included: the famous ***General Assembly Resolution 1608 (XV of 1 April 1961*** on the future of the Trust Territory of Southern Cameroons Under the United Kingdom Administration; the United Nations International Covenant on Social, Economic and Political Rights; the African Charter of Human and Peoples' Rights; the Constitution of the Republic of Cameroon itself together with a number of abnormalities in the administration of justice in the country. Consequently, after, 'carefully and assiduously deliberating on a wide range of issues affecting the nature and quality of the administration of justice and the rule of law in Cameroon, as they negatively impact on the minority English speaking members of the bi-cultural, bi-jural and bilingual nation, they reached several resolutions. They profoundly regretted and noted with deep disappointment:

> We have observed with utter dismay that there has been and continues to be a lack of protection with regard to the rights of the minority (Anglophones) as provided for in the constitution of this, bi-jural, bilingual, bi-cultural nation. It is obvious that the rights of the Anglophones in Cameroon in the spheres of education, socio-cultural values, administrative set-ups etc. are continuously and systematically being eroded with a view of imposing the socio-cultural and administrative views of the French or civil heritage of the majority Francophone Cameroon.[300]

In winding up, they further emphasized that the State should exercise its constitutional duty to protect the Anglophone minority: their history, heritage, education and cultural values. Above all, *"For the better protection of the minority Anglophone Cameroonians and the common law heritage, we*

---

[300] Resolutions made at the Inaugural All Cameroon Common Law Lawyers Conference Held at Bamenda in the North West Region of Cameroon 9 May 2015; Courtesy of Barrister Harmony Bobga.

*strongly demand a federation.*"[301]

Earlier, the point had emphatically been made about the invincible spirit of Anglophone; Southern Cameroonians whose morale toughens the more they are suppressed. This is a lesson that is taking the authorities that be, far too long to learn to nobody's credit. The nation is most likely to make better and greater progress in diversity than in compulsory uniformity.

## Decisive Lessons of History: Divine Retribution

The historian's mission unlike that of the journalist is not towards writing a "balanced account" of anything, but rather, he is "obliged" to report as authentically as possible backed by supporting evidence; to bring out the good, the bad and the ugly in any work. His real task is to interpret the past generation to the present without adulteration; basically, to tell the story as analytically as it happened regardless whose "ass is gored." He does not set out to write a balanced account in the sense of pleasing all the parties concerned, but renders an analytical depiction of the situation as he finds it. His task is to interpret the past to the present without adulteration. Thus he carries a grave burden as the "world" depends on him for the "truth" as far as possible in matters of the past, as he passes judgement over those who can no longer resurrect to defend or explain themselves, mindful that historical facts forever evolve.

History abounds with lessons of what happens when the liberties of a people are systematically trampled upon or muffled and freedom of expression and dialogue gagged. This is much like adding steam to a pot while pressing hard on the lid the result of which is predictable - an explosion. Crudely put; those who prevent subtle evolution open the flood gates for revolution. For that matter, revolutions are ugly and unpredictable things because once started they carve their own paths, destroying everything blocking their way. The French revolution is a typical example, as many of those who supervised the guillotines eventually were guillotined themselves. On the other hand, the fruits of freedom and liberty are boundless

---

[301] ibid.

as in the example of the momentous and predictive, inaugural address made by Brigadier EJ Gibbons, the first Commissioner of Southern Cameroons, on the occasion of launching the first session of the Southern Cameroons House of Assembly on 26 October 1954; part of which reads:

> The lesson of history has been that if any people persists steadfastly in this line of conduct (freedom and welfare of the common man and woman, who dig the beloved soil of our country) however poor and small it may be, however humble its origins, in the end it will succeed and there will be added to it prosperity and honour and respect of the world.[302]

What makes this speech pertinent is the fact that it was not delivered by a Southern Cameroonian political leader but by the representative of Her Majesty, the Queen of England. He utterly identified himself with the plight of the Territory, the welfare of the people as a whole and, especially the responsibilities of the newly elected Members of Parliament. Nothing could have been more inclusive and prophetic than this address as the Southern Cameroons State turned out to be exactly ideal. Still inbuilt in the address is the prediction that steadfast to its principles of defending the freedom, welfare and rights of its peasant masses it could never fail. It is regrettable that his successors did not follow his example and ended up limply regretting and apologising for the misuse of their tenure of office.

Suppression of this principle in the present circumstances is counterproductive as it only reinforces the irresistible determination of the people. In the State of Southern Cameroons for all its existence, even during the most turbulent period, there was never recourse to violence or much worse, shedding the precious blood of a single citizen on the altar of political discord. This was an indelible record, a brilliant report card forever to be proud of. The lesson the authorities ought to imbibe is the reality from history that the tide of nationalism is irrepressible and generally thrives and blossoms on repression, suppression, oppression and intimidation regardless of the shape, manner or form this takes.

---

[302] Ibid, Nfor Ngala Nfor.

## Chapter Eight

# THE LAST LINES: AHIDJO-BIYA TUSSLE

### Transition from "Illustrious Successor" to "Illustrious Predecessor"

Earlier in this work I pointed out that it is unlikely that President Ahmadou Ahidjo read Machiavelli's treatise: "The Prince,"[303] an exposition in the perfidious art of the acquisition and callous exploitation of power for egotistic ends and, that he could well have written an autobiographical masterpiece on the subject himself. This intriguing melodrama is neatly epitomized in his tussle to regain power which he had of a sudden, as if hypnotized,[304] graciously relinquished to President Paul Biya, his anointed successor. It graphically exposes his innate disposition towards duplicity, egomania, rank nepotism, intrigue and the callous institution of fear and ruthlessness as tools for manipulating the population into a mass of unthinking individuals - simply sycophants and zombies dedicated to singing his praises - something of a demigod such that ultimately, he came to incarnate "Cameroon" and, his name became synonymous with the entire "Cameroon nation".[305] Regrettably, this is a disgusting heritage

---

[303] See Niccolò Machiavelli (1469-1527), Italian historian, statesman, and political philosopher, whose amoral, but influential writings on statecraft have turned his name into a synonym for cunning and duplicity. Microsoft ® Encarta ® 2009. © 1993-2008 Microsoft Corporation. All rights reserved.

[304] In fact, one of the French papers, *La Croix* described him as" clinically mad." See, Francois Mattei, *The Biya Code*, Balland, Paris, 2009 p.149.

[305] The big joke is made that, when the news of the change was broken to his mother,

that has literally taken the Cameroonian political elite including celebrated intellectuals hostage, long after the departure of President Ahmadou Ahidjo from the political scene. It has become a political culture within which all manner of vices are accepted and openly practised since, "politics is a dirty game" in which the end justifies the means.

This tragic story vividly began unfolding on the fateful evening of Thursday 4 November 1982 as the news time on the National Radio was deliberately, unduly delayed being delivered at 8.23 PM instead of 8.00 PM. Naturally, this caused suspense and raised great expectations. The announcement over the air carried the familiar, resounding voice of President Ahmadou Ahidjo, only this time it sounded graver, measured and unduly tired, when he solemnly declared: "Ladies and gentlemen, fellow citizens, I have decided to resign from my functions as the President of the United Republic of Cameroon. This decision shall take effect on Saturday 6 November 1982 at 10.00am."[306] He then invited all Cameroonians to give full support to "his constitutional successor Mr. Paul Biya", who deserved the trust and confidence of every Cameroonian within and without the country.[307] To say the least, the entire nation was dazed and shocked with disbelief, especially as it was not preceded by rumour as usual, or by any semblance of a credible clue.

The choice or better still, the confirmation of Paul Biya as his 'heir apparent' came after fierce debates within the Ahidjo inner circle comprising: his wife, Germaine Habibah and close associates: Moussa Yaya, Sadou Daoudou, Sengat Kuoh, Samuel Eboua and Ayissi Mvodo, all of whom individually and collectively had a very low opinion of Paul Biya. Collectively, they all regarded him as "conceited and essentially inefficient" bate within the Ahidjo inner circle.. But Ahidjo alone, firmly stood his ground based on 17 years of keen observation, rating him as; "indolent"

---

that her son Paul Biya had become President of Cameroon, she translated it as: "Do you mean he has become Ahidjo"; to be able to fully grasp it. See, also Albert Mukong. *The Case for Southern Cameroons*. Enugu: CAMFECO, 1990

[306] See, Francois Mattei, *The Biya Code*, Balland, Paris, 2009 p.153.

[307] Repeated on a panel discussion over CRTV Cameroon on the eve of 6 November and the following morning over Cameroon calling on 7 November, 2015

and one who would take instructions without questioning; simply a "smart nobody". It was crystal clear to President Ahidjo as regards whom he wanted to succeed him as President. He did not have to be a contender with a strong will power, but simply a gullible and acquiescent pushover, who could be bullied into submission as the occasion arose. However, François Mattei adds: "They only saw a lamb but were to discover a fox, a snake, crocodile, gazelle, boa or laughing monkey, whenever he wants to".[308]

On being sworn in on 6 November 1982, Paul Biya as could be expected, over and over again paid glowing tribute to his mentor; his: "Illustrious predecessor, a giant in the history of Cameroon and of history in general." And, indeed, it was exceptional in Francophone Africa, the only other example being President Leopold Sedar Senghor of Senegal, who quietly handed over power to Abdu Diouf and retired into a lofty life of writing and academic bliss.[309] For President Ahidjo at this early stage, it was not clear how he hoped to fill in his time as apparently, he had no other hobby than playing politics. As he took off on a short break prior to commencing on his well-deserved anticipated retirement; waiting ministers and crowds at the airport openly shed genuine tears at the departure from office of the 'Father of the nation'. Still gripped in this effervescence, in mid-November, Ahidjo was awarded: the "1982 World Merit Award" followed by the "Dag Hammarskjöld Award," and in December, the "Man of the Year 1982 Award by the National Press of Cameroon. By this one noble, distinguished and highly cherished act, he had become a highly acclaimed national and international celebrity and, had endeared himself to friend and foe alike.

The future looked really glorious and promising. Without in any way alluding to retribution, triumphalism or staging a swan song, but just for the record, as an exemplification of what history is about, an analogy could be taken from the manner in which President Ahmadou Ahidjo rounded off his life. It would have been to his eternal credit and glory that after twenty-two years of absolute tyrannical rule, he abruptly, but graciously

---

[308] Ibid. p. 145.

[309] He was member of the *Academie Francaise*, and had invitations to international conferences, university seminars, cultural expositions etc.

handed over power to his anointed heir, PM, Paul Biya. He would have been absolved from the indelible stains of the totalitarian brutality that epitomised his "reign" as a "reincarnated" leader, whose main aspiration indeed had always been peace, development, national integration and national unity for which such sacrifices were a cruel necessity. In actual fact, this is the conclusion reached by some of his biographers.[310] Still basking in the euphoria following his resignation and with the generous facilities at his disposal coupled with undefined power in his hands, the former President undertook a nationwide tour from, 23-29 January 1983 ostensibly to canvass support for his illustrious successor, Paul Biya.

In actual fact, he used that opportunity to bolster his position as the CNU, Party Chairman in which capacity, President Biya was introduced as a Vice Chairman. He continued to grant press conferences and make authoritative pronouncements as previously over the radio, such as that carried by *Cameroun Tribune* of 30 January 1983 in which he further emphasized the primacy of the CNU, which alone retained the responsibility of defining guidelines for national policy for the government.[311] In reaction, seeking support for himself, President Paul Biya also undertook a tour of the nation leaving noteworthy messages as he went. Starting in Bamenda, which he declared his "second home", he concluded in Centre Province in June 1983 declaring that although born there, he was President of all Cameroonians. In the North and South West Provinces, he made significant announcements at Buea, where, he said that he was born a Cameroonian and would always be a Cameroonian; while in the North Province, Ahidjo's region of origin, he made it known that no ethnic group could claim to dominate the others. It was only much later that, analyzing these quotable quotes in contrast and in context that their full import was driven home.

Moussa Yaya, who was delegated by Ahidjo, CNU Chairman to explain the important changes that had just taken place, convincingly to the Bamilekes instead seized the opportunity to project his own image. He

---

[310] See, *Afrique Biblio Club* (ABC), France, *The History of Cameroon, Once Upon A Time, Ahidjo*. Afrique Biblio Club, 1980.

[311] Ibid, Mattei, p177

maintained that both Ahidjo and Biya were national traitors and counterfeit leaders with little appreciation for the enormous contributions made by the industrious Bamilekes and Foulbes (like himself) to the national economy. He also tried to incite the northern Lamidos to revolt against Ahmadou Ahidjo. Above all, he claimed equal patent rights with Ahidjo to the founding of the UC, parent to the CNU and, the right to its leadership as well. In typical fashion, Moussa Yaya re-enacted the dubious role he had played in 1964 in wrecking the KNDP to create the CUC for Muna which became the staging post for the dismissals of Jua and Foncha and finally, the dismantling of the FRC.

Unfortunately, these were vastly changed times and circumstances as during the CNU Executive Committee Meeting of 10 January 1984, an enraged Party Chairman, Ahmadou Ahidjo ordered for his instant expulsion from the CNU and deposition from all other posts he held together with his collaborators for trying create a parallel political party. This clearly demonstrated Ahidjo's brutality and callousness and that he would not brook anyone, who brazenly crossed his path, when it came to political power, not even his subaltern and most trusted childhood and life time friend Moussa Yaya.[312] At another level it was an act of divine retribution and a sign of worse things still to follow, for both men as their past was finally catching up with them in vindication of the adage, that: "the evil that men do lives after them" or that, "by their fruits we shall know them".

## Who really is in Charge?

For months, while his Lake Side residence underwent a befitting face lift, former President Ahidjo was President Biya's guest at Mont Febe Hotel; feted with a fleet of cars, a helicopter and planes generally attached to presidency at his disposal, for national and international trips. For what looked like endless months, the portraits of the two men continued to hang in offices, halls and public places, with that of former President Ahidjo glistening above that of the current president. No one felt courageous or

---

[312] See, Victor Julius Ngoh, *History of Cameroon Since 1800*, Presprint, Limbe, 1996, pp 281-2.

bold enough to rectify this anomalous situation. Acting as a "Patriarch" or an "Ayatollah" of sorts, he arrogated to himself the authority to dictate policy for execution by the State President as previously. In fact, the situation worsened as on public occasions, protocol was openly reversed as President Biya would arrive at the venue before the CNU Party Chairman, Ahmadou Ahidjo, and rise to cheer and receive him.

Appointments to ministerial and top managerial positions in the Biya Administration continued to be a monopoly of the Party Chairman, Mr. Ahidjo. This situation became so worrisome that President François Mitterrand dispatched Guy Penne on a mission to offer President Biya security experts, a situation which confirmed Ahidjo's original suspicion now mingled with fear, anger and bitterness arising from the way things were unfolding blinded his reasoning or, was he really getting "clinically mad" as disclosed by *La Croix*?[313] If indeed he had been tricked into resigning for purely health reasons in France, Ahidjo was now undeceived; as instead he was regaining his health and vitality – hence, he intensified his plots to regain or 're-conquer' the position he had let go so easily, to continue to cling to the reins of power one way or the other. Herein lies the clue to the unfolding tragedy. To capture the spirit of the moment, *Jeune Afrique* ran a caption: "Ahidjo runs Biya" and continued piercingly:

> Ahmadou Ahidjo does not only control the party but also all the elected members, all executive members or high ranking officials previously appointed by him. For nearly a quarter of a century, he has inspired fear that is still present – most if not all of the strategic posts are filled by his supporters.[314] My emphasis.

The hitherto rumoured rift between the two men broke into the open when in a minor cabinet reshuffle of April 1983, Biya hesitated to fire Paul Desire Engo as desired by Ahidjo. In an answer to a question in another interview with Jeune Afrique, he burst out in angrily and retorted: "Paul

---

[313] *La Croix in Mattei, p.149*

[314] *Jeune Afrique*, quoted In Mattei, p.184.

Biya is doing the exact opposite of what he is told to do.[315] His vaulting ambition for power, 'megalomania' had broken loose.

## The Looming Nightmare

This rigmarole could not go on ceaselessly and finally Biya muscled up courage and in his first radical cabinet reshuffle, sacked prominent Ahidjo barons[316] though still retaining Bouba Bello Maigari, the PM and Abdoulaye Maikano, Minister of Armed Forces on 18 June 1983. The *die* was cast and Ahidjo got the message which he understood to mean a declaration of war and immediately summoned two secret meetings that same day; one of all Northern ministers and top personalities and the other of top military officers from that region, who were requested to write collective letters of resignation. Matters deteriorated quickly as President Paul Biya, alerted of a planned assassination against him, excused himself from attendance at an Executive CNU meeting convened by Ahidjo for the following day, 19 June 1983. One month later, precisely on 19 July, the Ahidjo family left Cameroon after his requests for the presidential plane and allowances had been turned down. These were the deplorable conditions and sad memories that marked the ultimate exit of the acclaimed "Father of the nation" as he quit the country he allegedly had founded and never again stepped on Cameroon soil before his "unannounced" demise on 30 November 1989 in Dakar, Senegal.

The saga of the former and current Presidents continued smouldering the symptoms of which were expressed in President Biya's address to the nation on 22 August 1983, when he publicly declared that the National Security had arrested people whose mission was to destabilize the state. His next cabinet reshuffle carried more far-reaching changes as even Bouba Bello Maigari and Maikano Abdulaye; the PM and Minister of Armed Forces respectively and the rump of the Ahidjo barons in the Biya government were given the boot, while General Semengue was named the

---

[315] ibid.

[316] These comprised: Victor Ayissi Mvodo, Samuel Eboua, Mustapha Hamadou and Sadou Daoudou.

new Head of the Armed Forces. There were territorial alterations as well; as the former monolithic North from which Ahidjo drew strength and used as a shield was dismantled and carved out into three distinct entities; the Far North Province with its Headquarters at Maroua, the Northern Province with its Headquarters at Garoua and Adamawa Province with its Headquarters at Ngaoundere. To counterbalance this, the Centre South was also split into two Provinces with capitals at Yaoundé and Ebolowa.[317]

## Ahidjo: Absolute Double Talk

While he perpetually preached national unity and national integration to every other community and ethnic group,[318] Ahidjo exhibited some of the worst practices of sectarianism and nepotism,(based on geography, religion and ethnicity) in favour of "Northerners," who finally, were on the whole, over-represented in the political, administrative and executive arms of government as well as in the armed forces."Northerners" indeed, were special and their appointments and recruitments based on quotas hardly ever respected merit or normal standards which applied to all the other ethnic groups in the country.[319] Ahidjo's concept of "Cameroon" ultimately was articulated around that one vast and monolithic Northern Province, which he preserved as his personal fief, while the South until 1984 comprised six Provinces. As Mattei best puts it, this was the blackmail he continuously used as a comprehensive insurance to stay in power for as long as he did.[320]

Interestingly, Ahidjo himself points out that as far back as 1958, when he was Vice Prime Minister and Minister of Interior in the Mbida Government, he was entrusted with the implementation of the law setting up a Province of North Cameroon with its own Local Assembly but realizing that such a measure would jeopardize the country's unity, he managed to

---

[317] See Mattei. pp. 252-3

[318] see Ahmadou Ahidjo, *Contribution To National Construction*, Presence Africaine, Paris, 1964 p. 18

[319] Ibid, p, 202.

[320] Ibid, p. 206

postpone it.³²¹ However, after his "Peaceful Revolution" in 1972 and the abolition of the FRC, he hastily, mutilated the already "tiny" West Cameroon by dividing it yet into the "North and South West Provinces" leaving the impression that such division had punitive or negative imputations. Put in proper perspective, this was the epitome of his policy to divide, weaken, confuse and assimilate the Anglophone political entity. On the other hand, the vast monolithic North and the rest of Cameroon remained intact and untouched until after the putsch in 1984, when curiously for "administrative" reasons; President Biya applied his administrative axe mostly on that region, confirming the impression that such divisions were punitive. Generally, Ahidjo preserved and used his Northern bastion as a bogey, which he frequently brandished, would secede without him holding the delicate balance between Northern and Southern eastern Cameroon.

Long after the division of West Cameroon into North and South West Provinces, these remained the only remarkable territorial alterations on record in the 22-year history of the nation under President Ahmadou Ahidjo. Interestingly, in the wake of the 1984 changes, President Biya was flooded with endless motions of support from the same quarters who had declared untainted loyalty to Ahidjo. In sequence, *Le Combatant*, exposed the shady deals with which the Ahidjo regime had been riddled. Aware that he had lost all credibility and support even from the CNU sycophants, Ahidjo in exile pointlessly resigned his chairmanship of the party on 27 August 1983 and Biya was unanimously elected to replace him on 14 September 1983. Ahidjo was so infuriated that he defiantly predicted the outbreak of a civil war between Christian South and Muslim North³²².

## The Five Day Epic Trials

This process was logically followed by the epic five day public trials of

---

³²¹ See, *As Told By Ahidjo*, p. 14.

³²² If because of Biya's division of his monolithic north into three provinces Ahidjo predicted a civil war between Christian south and Muslim north, did he by the same inference expect the Anglophones of the North and South West Provinces to rise in revolt after he Balkanized them in 1972; the reason why he termed his conquest: "The peaceful revolution"? These puzzles need further investigation by budding scholars.

former President Ahmadou Ahidjo, who together with Salatou Adamou, his Aide de Camp and Commandant Ibrahim Oumarou, his *Intendant*, were collectively arraigned before the Yaoundé Military Court on Thursday 23 February 1984 and charged with plotting assassination and revolution. Of course, Ahidjo was tried in absentia. High ranking witnesses mostly Northerners were called in to testify to the regionalist attempt to overthrow the government during the crucial months of June, July and August 1983, with spotlights on the secret meetings of 18 June. Ahidjo's criminal intentions were made manifest and irrefutable. The open trial concluded with hard verdicts as the prosecution demanded: death sentences by firing squad for Ahidjo and his collaborators, confiscation of property and a fine of 20 million francs. Ahidjo was further deprived of the very elaborate and cosy advantages he had allocated to himself as President, when he would go on retirement.[323] Ironically, this time, unlike when he crafted the draconic measures against his opponents in 1962, Ahidjo bitterly refuted the charges and vigorously denounced the trials ranting that the judges had been bought.

Finally, an international warrant was issued for his arrest and, until his death in Dakar, Senegal on 30 November 1989; he was categorized as a fugitive from justice. However, by a Presidential reprieve of 9 March 1984, Ahidjo and his collaborators were freed, precisely what he himself had denied to his countless opponents and victims especially *Upcistes*, many of whom suffered innocently and faced public firing squads. Tragically, and paradoxically Ahidjo and his cohorts were tried by the Military Tribunal which had specifically been set up by Ordinance No. 62/OF/18 of 12 March 1962, personally enacted by Ahidjo for the trial of his political opponents all of whom were invariably found guilty, fined, incarcerated or publicly executed. This special Military Tribunal heard cases transferred to it from civilian courts on Ahidjo's request and the judges were

---

[323] By a Decree dated 10 September 1981, a former president is granted a retirement free of tax equivalent to 2/3 of his civil list as president. He also enjoys office premises, two chauffeur driven cars and two servants, one head of mission, an executive secretary, two secretaries, two *aides de camp* and eight bodyguards. His medical fees and those of his wife are paid for by the state. See Mattei, p. 165.

substandard military recruits.[324]

## The Failed Coup d'état and Ramifications

Rationally, one would have expected that after the trials and the presidential reprieves, there would be a return to calm, reconciliation and normalcy but ironically the trials instead provided a launching pad for the events of Friday 6 April 1984. President Biya had transferred all the Presidential Palace guards, who mostly came from Ahidjo's predominantly Muslim north having been alerted of a coup plot involving dissident elements among them. It was they who promptly reacted against the transfer orders by rebelling against Biya. They launched a *blitzkrieg* from Obili; overran the army headquarters, took some top officials hostage, captured the National Radio Station, the Telecommunications Centre as well as the Airport and within hours were capable of announcing "The liberation of Cameroon by the *National Armed Forces* from the Biya gang," over the National Radio.[325]

In the meantime, on being interviewed over *Radio Monte Carlo* in France, whether he backed the rebels, Ahidjo's response was typically defiant. He held that if they were his supporters, he believed they would win. In any case, the rebel victory was pretty short-lived, as by the following evening President Paul Biya solemnly and triumphantly reassured the stunned nation: "Once again Cameroon has experienced a delicate period in its history. Yesterday, elements of the Republican Guard embarked on an attempted coup." He paid tribute to the units of the armed forces for their commitment and attachment to the law of the Republic. The Minister of Armed Forces, Mr. Gilbert Andze Tsoungui directly accused Northern businessmen of financing the coup and by 9 April, the rebels with their leader, Colonel Ibrahim Saleh were securely under arrest. Again, the repercussion was swift as on 11 April President Biya dissolved the

---

[324] See Appendix IV; Richard Joseph, *Gaullist Africa, Cameroon Under Ahmadou Ahidjo*, also, Victor Julius Ngoh, *History of Cameroon Since 1800*, Pp.289-291.

[325] Fortunately, the technicians had tactfully disconnected the radio from national and international networks so that the announcements were limited to Yaoundé.

Republican Guards as a unit. Officially, seventy deaths were reported but the private press suggested that over a thousand lives were lost.

Consequences of the attempted coup were dire and far reaching as by a cosmetic constitutional amendment, the name of the country was changed from the URC to RC with Present Biya arguing that: "Cameroon must not be seen as a federation of provinces but as a unique global entity, to be able to exist, last and give birth to a national identify".[326] The Presidential axe next landed on the CNU, Ahidjo's mouthpiece and "executioner", created in September 1966. It was now described as an anachronistic and illegal imposition, since President Ahidjo and his Vice President John Ngu Foncha set it up either freely or extorted through violent agreements with other parties to form, the single party.[327] In simple terms, the CNU was now largely a forceful imposition on the other parties by Ahidjo and Foncha, His Vice President.[328] Furthermore, it was described as a "political monopoly" and, at the Bamenda CNU Congress of 21-24 March 1985, it was voted out of existence by a thunderous and standing acclamation and replaced with the Cameroon Peoples' Democratic Movement (CPDM), with President Biya as its Chairman and Foncha as the Vice Chairman, while the Motto became: Unity, Progress, Truth and Democracy; the middle two words of the appellation and the last two of the motto were drawn from Foncha's Kamerun National Democratic Party (KNDP).[329] Precisely this was old wine in a new container as practically, other than the name, motto and leadership, all else remained intact.

---

[326] See Matei, p.276.

[327] Ibid, p. 313. The translation is not clear but sense is that it was an imposition.

[328] However, the KNDP at its 10th Convention violently rejected the invitation to join the new party especially as the CUC which joined forces with the UC as a nucleus of the new party was extracted through intrigues by Ahidjo and Moussa Yaya working with Muna to wreck the KNDP, which had become a stumbling block to Ahidjo's plans for a new single party.

[329] The author was present in the hall during that CNU congress, meeting in Mankon, Bamenda in March 1985.

## A Totally Rundown and Crumbling Economy

There is a strong argument that while not contending the alibi of ill health, President Ahidjo fully well knew the awful mess into which he had put the economy of Cameroon and did not want it to crumble in his hands. All along, he had lavishly squandered the income from the oil boom making the country's economy nationally and internationally credible and praiseworthy. Cameroonians were told to concentrate their attention on agriculture, and President Ahidjo actually launched the "Green Revolution" for which he was highly applauded. He advised Cameroonians to take their eyes off the oil revenue because it was transient and deceitful, oil issues were a taboo and the President alone knew and disbursed income accruing from the 'black gold'. In fact, until the rise of his 'illustrious successor' oil revenue did not feature on the national budget. Yet, given the heavy suppression under his rule, nobody could ask the burning questions about oil money; how much came in, where it was kept and more crucially, how it was spent and by whom. What is further telling is that the region from which the oil was exploited in former West Cameroon was and still is the most undeveloped, while West Cameroon for its entire existence was never able to balance its budget and needed subventions from the President's black account, very likely the oil revenue to survive. But this was only a fraction of the story.

## Likelihood of a Planned Abdication

Consequently, Ahidjo more than anybody else knew just how totally run down the economy of the country he was handing over to his "illustrious successor" was, certainly the reason for which he was specially chosen. François Mattei amply demonstrates how: Chronic ineptitude, nepotism, innate cronyism and self deceit had literally brought the state economy to its knees. The Chief Executive Officer (CEO) of *Societe Camerounaise de Banque* (SCB) was dismissed because he insisted that the colossal sums of money owed that establishment alone estimated at 100 billion francs by the President's cronies should be repaid. To make matters worse, the CEO had the guts to stress that Ahidjo should resign before the scandals became public. This was considered arrogant and inadmissible and so the CEO had to go but the hour of reckoning remained on course as at about the same time, the case came to light of the President's close friends who were racketeers engaged in illegal importation of rice besides the bankruptcy of two state companies. These economic criminals were never made to face the law, while the country's economy bled white.

Therefore, the issue of the President's desire to resign, on second thought was not altogether new. Earlier, at one of the CNU congresses in the mid-70s, a pungent rumour to the effect that President Ahidjo indicated that he did not intend to put up his name for re-election was whispered and spread like wild fire. This set the party zealots throughout the nation organizing motions of support and appeals for him not to consider such an 'abomination', because as: 'Father of the nation', its very existence was inconceivable without him. Since in Cameroon it is well known that even the most important decisions begin as 'rumours', it is equally conjectured that it originated from the inner circles of the Ahidjo Regime to test his popularity in view of the fact that he was very conscious of his personality- egomania.[330]

In 1983 he wanted to retain the reins of power from the background, the reason for which he so well crafted the CNU with himself projected as a Patriarch or an "Ayatollah" responsible for issuing dogmas or instructions and in turn, answerable to nobody. This way, he had everything in place and was confident that with Biya as the nominal head, with his numerous cronies strategically and firmly planted in government, he would be securely protected. Towards this objective, he had taken a long shot, first by the appointment of Biya, whom he had studied in detail as PM in 1979 with the new clause to succeed him in any eventuality instead of the President of the National Assembly. This was followed by the very juicy package which he crafted for himself by a Decree of 10 September 1981 barely a year to his resignation. By it:

> A former president is granted a retirement free of tax equivalent to 2/3 of his civil list as president. He also enjoys office premises, two chauffer driven cars and two servants, one head of mission, an executive secretary,

---

[330] This was likely at the CNU Congress of maturity which held at Douala.

two secretaries, two aides de camp and eight bodyguards. His medical fees and those of his wife are paid for by the state.[331]

However, the plan went berserk because, Biya unexpectedly cracked out his cocoon and asserted unpredicted signs of autonomy. This he began to do by sacking the Ahidjo henchmen from the strategic positions where he had installed them and, finally introduced the policy of "Rigour and Moral Rectitude." By Ahidjo's reckoning all these measures were intended to ridicule and discredit him by exposing the racket and embezzlement entrenched in the gross mismanagement of state companies, and scandalous state award of bank loans to his cronies. This was the point at which he got terribly irritated and publicly proclaimed that: "Biya was not doing what he was told to do".[332] Instead of the docile, harmless lamb, his illustrious successor became a lion with the qualities of a fox and totally upset all the egomaniac wiles Ahidjo had carefully strategized. Fortunately for Ahidjo, on assuming office, Biya had more than a full plate and did not bother to explode the ineptitude, mismanagement, embezzlement, corruption and, above all, the fact that he was taking over a totally rundown economy from his "illustrious predecessor." More or less Biya is remembered for asking people to "tighten up their belts" sometime after Ahidjo's abdication, which was understood more, as resulting from the international economic depression.

All being equal, given his intellectual claims and his lengthy exposure in office, Ahmadou Ahidjo is supposed to have known and done better having ruled contemporaneously with former African heads of state with whom he interacted variously, and who preceded him to abysmal deaths, considered good riddance, un-mourned and un-loved. These included: kleptocrats, tyrants and brutes like: Joseph Mobutu Sesseko of Zaire, Mohammed Sani Abacha of Nigeria, Idi Amin Dada of Uganda, Jean Bedel Bokossa of Central African Republic and Macias Nguema of Equatorial Guinea, all of whom concluded their lives in a most despicable manner, lonely, despised by the people they robbed and whose lands

---

[331] See Matei. p.165.

[332] ibid., p295

they devastated. Ahidjo, whose speeches were endlessly quoted and who is reputed to have authored several political works, and in this connection, the bombastic philosophical and historical discourses quoting *Cheik Anta Diop* on African hospitality or the one he delivered on the occasion of opening the UC party building in Yaoundé in 1964 mercilessly lampooning the brutality and callousness of "Benevolent Despotism" in eighteenth century Europe.

Therefore, with hindsight, he deserved to have been better informed[333] except as usual he was always playing to the gallery, so much double talk and little or nothing to be taken seriously. Equally, if he failed to learn from them, it was largely because they were to different degrees his ego image. His ambitions were encapsulated in the words, "egomania" and "megalomania," consequently, he attempted to recreate the mighty Cameroon Nation with an inestimable life span after his limited mortal image, which unfortunately extended to a meagre sixty-five years ending on 30 November 1989 in Dakar, Senegal. Typically, like his predecessors and contemporaries or like the French monarchs of old, he certainly had: "Learnt nothing and forgotten nothing," and consequently suffered the verdict of history which does not forgive those who do not learn the lessons of history.

### Demand for Return of Remains and State Burial

As of December 2014, twenty – five years after his death in exile, the wrangling over the remains of the late President continued to rage without any let-off directed by his widow, Mrs. Germaine Ahidjo. She robustly argued that the remains of her husband should be repatriated to Cameroon and that she should accompany them: "A special amnesty should be granted unambiguously to her late husband and the organisation of a State Funeral must be made public."[334] In response to this request and mildly veiled threats, Mr. Isa Tchiroma, the Cameroon Communication Minister gave a straightforward reply at a Press Conference on 26

---

[333] See. *As Told By Ahmadou Ahidjo*, pp. 90- 93.

[334] *Eden Newspaper* No. 880 Monday 01 December 2014, p.4.

November 2014 in which he characterised Mrs. Ahidjo's comments as manipulative and that she had employed inaccurate historical facts. The Minister maintained that:

> President Paul Biya promulgated in 1991, a law in parliament to grant amnesty to everybody (including late President Ahidjo) who had at one stage gone against state institutions. The Head of State has indicated his government's readiness to bring back the remains under the approval and coordination of the former leader's family.[335]

Though not much may be read into any political statement, especially a controversial one like this, it is clear that the late President enjoys a general amnesty with others of that category, while the repatriation of his remains is essentially an affair of the Ahidjo family with the government only stepping in to assist. There is nothing alluded to a state burial in the statement. On the other hand, the passing on of the Ahidjo's political victims like: Mr. Augustine Ngom Jua, the PM, whom he outrageously dismissed in 1968 and Dr. John Ngu Foncha, his Vice President, whom he causelessly sacked and placed under house arrest for over a year in 1970[336] remained very popular heroes among the masses and were accorded outstanding state burials full of grandeur and colour.

In point of fact, the Foncha State Burial of 10 April 1999, which occurred ten years after Ahidjo's demise was exceedingly popular and oversubscribed in a variety of ways: the sheer, size and texture of the population who attended it from all over the country, as well as from abroad, honours by the state (military), traditional dances and above all the church rituals. The occasion in every detail was a grand jamboree that brought together sons and daughters of Southern Cameroon in their numbers and in great unison. Besides this, the spiritual, traditional and secular touches were remarkable. Continuous daily celebrations lasted a whole month and several months later different groups from across the nation continued to trickle in intermittently. In retrospect, Foncha remained as charismatic

---

[335] Ibid; *Eden Newspaper* No. 880

[336] Pius Soh, his biographer, describes him as being 'caged like a rat'.

and popular in death as he had been in life.[337] Reporting the event in: The History of St. John the Baptist's Parish, Foncha Street appropriately named after him, the editors captured the spirit of the moment and, put it simply but graphically and briefly:

> The death of Dr. John Ngu Foncha in 1999 was an event that shook the State and the Church in and out of Cameroon and brought people from all over to St. John's Church and his compound became too small for the crowds that came continuously for over a month. He is buried in a simple grave behind the church in St. John's. It is our wish that someday, the cause of his canonisation shall start even in our life time.[338]

The editors speaking for the parishioners and public at large were asserting the fact that Dr. JN Foncha was not only a popular, charismatic and successful political leader, he was even more profoundly an active and effective Catholic Christian who deserves a place in heaven for the holistic life he lived here on earth, thus reflecting the Latin adage, *Vox populi, vox Dei*. (The voice of the people is the voice of God.)

Jua and Foncha like Muna, who worked "amicably" with Ahidjo till the end, rest peacefully in their graves at "home", respectively in Njinikom, Nkwen and Ngyenmbu, where their tombs continue to be visited by family members, relatives and friends from home and abroad. Some of these are literally budding into shrines with the passage of time. In historical perspective together with those of other ancestral Southern Cameroonian icons such as: **Dr. EML Endeley, Paul M Kale, Nerius N Mbile** and several others, like good wine mature with time and are liable to become genuine historical pilgrimage sites. The challenge is for nascent historians to ensure that the marvellous deeds attained by these heroes (and heroines) are not left to fester and wither with their bones in a nation like Cameroon lacking role models for the youth to emulate.

---

[337] See Lantum, Daniel N. Prof. *Tribute to Dr. John Ngu Foncha*, Yaoundé, 1999.

[338] Ambe, Bosco John, Fondzenyuy Mariana and Verhoeven, Arnold, *For The Record: St John The Baptist's Parish, Foncha Street – Nkwen*, Peaceberg Printers, Bamenda, June 2015, p.10.

# EPILOGUE

In a strange way, the rise and demise of the State of West Cameroon constructed on the foundation of Southern Cameroons is inextricably yoked to the life of President Ahmadou Ahidjo. It is therefore essential to make a flash back to his political career especially as he epitomised the Cameroon Nation during his twenty-two year "majestic reign" (1960-1982) which for the most part demonstrates the essence of the common English proverb that: "Power corrupts and absolute power corrupts absolutely." When of a sudden on 4 November 1982, he declared his irreversible decision to resign and peacefully handed or better still, "surrendered" power to his 'anointed heir,' Paul Biya, whom he had apparently appointed in 1979 as PM for this purpose[339], the entire nation was genuinely stunned. This was because, at least there had been one false alarm before, when at the CNU "Congress of maturity"[340] at Douala in 1975 "trial" rumours had been circulated that, President Ahmadou Ahidjo, "Father of the Nation" intended to resign. This threw the entire nation into frenzy as party zealots loudly crisscrossed the country campaigning against an act that would spell calamity to the nation and to be sure, drew endless motions of support for him not to contemplate such a disastrous action.

Remarkably, to the enlightened population, there was a mighty sigh of relief in 1982 for the simple reason that by 'abdication', he had done the one great deed for which history would forgive him and learn to forget all the abominations he had committed on the balance and, that; he had

---

[339] This is most probably the reason for which he changed the constitution in June 1979, altering succession to the Presidency from the President of the National Assembly to the PM see Sobseh, *Rethinking Citizenship, p134*. Probably too; he had misjudged the potency of the PM expecting that he would be docile, a simple walk over.

[340] This congress held from 9-15 February 1975. Ahidjo was "persuaded" to accept another five year term of office as President of Cameroon.

done so as maintained by his biographers, in the supreme interest of: "national unity".[341] This was a situation where he had literally reigned as a ruthless and brutal dictator, Head of State and Chairman of the CNU for twenty-two years. Under him the constitution in effect had become a mere doormat, largely irrelevant as the Fundamental Law of the Land, after numerous radical and cosmetic changes, while elections under the One Party, Single List system were at best symbolic and hardly ever scored anything less than 99.99%.[342] In this context, as the alpha and omega, how else was he ever to evacuate office?

Furthermore, when it was later disclosed that he had firmly stuck to the post of Chairman of the CNU, the party oracle which he had scrupulously structured to serve as his personal mouthpiece; it was clear that he had simply gone out by the front door and was staging a re-entry by the back door almost instantly and violently. This time the world was undeceived: they saw him for who really he was; in fact, that nothing had practically changed in the tyrant and that he had not sincerely meant to hand over power.[343] The tiger had merely camouflaged the black spots on his body, while sharpening his claws and his fangs. The next thing was that he had by his obduracy self-exile, followed by the attempted coup d'état led by his erstwhile Presidential Guards, cast the nation into total confusion. Clearly, he had learnt no lessons from those leaders around him, who had clung to the reins of power until they were overthrown by revolutionary uprisings. In turn, he stubbornly glued to power until it abysmally jettisoned him in justification of the dictatorial style he had used in administering the nation he is assumed to have created.

Nevertheless, President Ahidjo is credited with the fact that he made

---

[341] See Afrique Biblio *Club* (ABC), France, *The History of Cameroon, Once Upon A Time, Ahidjo.*

[342] Ibid., See, Justice Nyo' Wakai. *Under The Broken Scale of Justice: The Law and My Times.* Bamenda: Langa Research and Publishing CIG 2009.

[343] See, Appendix IV The Ndongmo Trial. It is credibly held that, his French doctor on directives from President François Mitterrand whose socialist political party was at variance with Ahidjo a Gaullist had tricked him to believe that he had a terminal disease and was advised to retire as the weight of office was the source. Even worse, President Ahidjo had blocked him from coming to defend Mgr. Ndongmo in 1970.

## EPILOGUE

national unity his clarion call and throughout, strenuously maintained that 'Cameroon ancestry belongs to all Cameroonians.' In actual fact, it was the pivot of his UC party aimed at uniting the northern groups, then the Moslem North and the Christian south and, finally East and West Cameroon. This emphasised the fact that all rights and claims to Cameroonian nationality derive from the Treaty signed by German firms with Kings Bell and Akwa on 12 July 1884 in Douala, and the Protectorate declared by Dr. Gustav Natchigal over Cameroon two days later on behalf of the Imperial German Government with the Wouri Estuary as the beachhead of the territory that became German Kamerun. It brought under one imperial flag, the multitude of ethnic groups that comprise today's Cameroon state on the path towards nationhood. The famous Douala Treaty together with the partition of Kamerun between Britain and France after German defeat in World War 1 was subsequently recognized and ratified at the Paris Peace Treaty, the League of Nations and other international bodies notably: the UN General Assembly and Trusteeship Council in 1946, independence and reunification in October 1961, right up to the recent Green Tree Agreement of 12 June 2006 between Nigeria and Cameroon over the Bakassi Peninsula – the fulcrum, remained 'German Kamerun".

All through, the history of Cameroon, the reference point remains "German Kamerun", a fact which President Ahmadou Ahidjo repeatedly chanted in his "passionate" appeal for the reunification to Southern Cameroons at Douala, Buea and Victoria during his maiden visit in July 1960. He maintained that "Reunification was a debt which all Cameroonians owe to our ancestors" and that this was to be done on the footing of equality.[344] Unfortunately, likely blinded by egomaniac and other tendencies, he blundered irredeemably after reunification had finally been achieved, but all the same it remains on record as an indelible fact of history which he played in laying the foundation of the Cameroon nation.

Logically, this imputes that Cameroonian citizenship belongs in equal measure to all citizens of this country regardless of: geographical location, political ideology, religious beliefs, linguistic orientation, ethnic origin

---

[344] 'This was during Ahidjo's maiden visit to Southern Cameroons from 14-17 July 1960 and he repeated this statement in his three addresses at Tiko on arrival, Buea and then at Victoria.

or social status since by the constitution, everybody from the President of the Republic right down to the lowest peasant enjoys the common franchise of one person, one vote. However, there are significant deviants, who arrogate a false superiority complex on the basis of: geographical location, language, political position, numerical strength and regard other compatriots as 'strangers'; call them derogatory names and ask them to go 'elsewhere'.[345] The perpetrators of such philosophies and practices, who generally wield their authority in a manner to denigrate, marginalize and deprive Anglophone Cameroonians of meritorious positions, should rightly face the wrath of the law as happens in other countries.[346] This is all the more ironical as such exclusivist "jingoists" turn round and accuse the Anglophone 'victims' of exhibiting secessionist tendencies, which is much like the logic in the reversion from the "United Republic of Cameroon" to "Republic of Cameroon" in 1984. Born and bred within this Triangle, no one can be more Cameroonian than the other.

After forty-five years (1916-1961) of cruel and brutal colonial separation, Southern Cameroonians freely and willingly entered the union with their Francophone "brothers" of the Republic of Cameroon, absolutely in good faith, with zeal, trust, determination, great hopes and expectations. The 1961 plebiscite which brought the union into being itself was the culmination of a colossal political decision taken after protracted consultations at all levels; local, national and international. It involved the grass roots of the North and South West Regions, coupled with conferences and consultations held at: Mamfe, Bamenda, Buea and internationally in New York, London and finally was sanctioned by the overwhelming approval of the Southern Cameroons electorate in the 1961 plebiscite. This is to say that it was both a bold political as well as a popular grass-roots decision and any attempts to resolve the situation must take these facts into consideration. Any attempts to down grade this process and belittles its significance is playing the ostrich and may succeed for a while but not for too long.

Tragically, today Southern Cameroons has been downgraded and

---

[345] See Foncha's Letter of Resignation from the CPDM in 1990

[346] Pretty often surrogate Anglophones are engaged to undermine fellow Anglophones.

# EPILOGUE

classified together with ethnic, 'tribal' and cloistered groups, all of which demonstrates the depth of bad faith, disregard for history, the absence of political-will, impunity and insensitivity on the part of the ruling majority Francophone elite. Historical accounts abound with how attempts to stem the tide of nationalist aspirations have invariably failed at great material and human cost to all concerned. In some cases this has taken several centuries as was the case with Britain stifling the national aspirations of the Irish and Scottish people. Conscious that this is the 21$^{st}$ century with the world daily shrinking into a global village, awash with terrorist gangsters[347] prowling for flash spots wherein to fester and plunder, should alarm leaders who have the genuine interests of their people at heart.

*Fig 44. The Green Tree Agreement; Presidents Paul Biya of Cameroon and Obasanjo of Nigeria shake hands as Kofi Anan, former Secretary General of the UN looks on*

Throughout the North and South West Regions, the masses appropriately hold 'Reunification' responsible for their mounting woes. For this, they logically castigate and curse their leaders, who carried out "the

---

[347] *'Boko Haram, Anti-Seneca'* and others allied to 'al Qaeda' groups are good examples.

negotiations at Foumban", unaware that their problems arise from the consistent violation of every single agreement reached with their Francophone brothers in the union at Foumban and elsewhere, followed by obstinate deafness to Anglophone complaints against the interminable and mounting problems of marginalisation, second class citizenship and assimilation. The tragedy is that the bad faith and absence of political will persists and is intensifying even with a more 'enlightened' leadership, who continue to negate the agreements solemnly reached at Foumban and entrenched in the Federal Constitution employing the time-worn irrelevant and ineffective colonial tactics of: scorn, superiority complex, suppression, oppression and of divide and rule on an intelligent, sensitive, highly enlightened and politically advanced community.

Without any exaggeration, the defunct State of Southern Cameroons enjoyed 'home rule' or 'internal self government' to the full, in accordance with the Westminster parliamentary democratic system of administration. There was an Executive Prime Minister, who presided over a Council of Ministers, all of whom were elected Members of Parliament (cabinet), with an Upper House (House of Chiefs[348] or Senate). Next, there was an independent Judiciary headed by a Chief Justice, thus exhibiting the inestimable virtues of the balance of power with 'checks and balances' among the Executive, the Legislative and the Legal arms of government, none of which overruled the others.

Everybody was subject to, and equal before the law. There was a vibrant, efficient and reliable civil service largely corruption free; as was freedom of speech, religion and of the press, which made for a robust, vocal Fourth Estate. Frequently, individuals, especially journalists had to defend their utterances on charges of perjury before the courts. In the same vein there were commissions of inquiry which impeached those in high positions, who fell foul of the law, the recommendations of which were published and scrupulously implemented. Leadership in Anglo-Saxon tradition was one of service coupled with transparency and high moral values. All correspondence emanating from the PM concluded with; 'Your humble

---

[348] It is noteworthy that, while a Senate or Upper House already existed in Southern Cameroons, it was only recently, more than half a century later, introduced in Republic of Cameroon.

servant', a pattern that applied to ministers and heads of service. Employment, promotion and award of medals were by merit and in recognition of outstanding service.

Leadership at all levels comprised dignified individuals, who had appropriately distinguished themselves by probity, character and diligence, devoid of conspicuous consumption and amassing of wealth. They led by example and not by precept; their word was their bond, hence they built a high level of trust and were respected by those for whom they were responsible.

Finally, a self-evident *democratic culture* flourished from 1954 to 1961 and even up till 1965, exemplified in the conduct of six general elections including the 1961 Plebiscite organised by the UN, all of which by and large were declared free, fair and transparent. There were no cases of violence, bloodshed or loss of life. Above all, there was peaceful transfer of power from one political leader and party to the other. In other words, on record, and as amply demonstrated, in this exposition, the Southern Cameroons State attained an advanced and clearly demonstrable democratic culture. This, of course, is still possible within the larger Republic of Cameroon as all the ingredients to regenerate it are still in place.

What basically is required is genuine introspection, an inward journey that could bring about a radical change of mentality making for a firm political will, openness to dialogue with all groups coupled with a genuine patriotic spirit and willingness to democratize. The challenges remain enormous having to do with a thoroughly corrupt, system clogged and choking with sycophants and zombies shielded beneath a veiled One Party system, but these have to be tackled sooner than later as is being done in other countries. On the whole, nothing needs to be imported from anywhere or re-invented to construct a new plural, bilingual, multicultural, self contained democratic Cameroon, which providence has endowed with an abundance of exceptionally talented human and natural resources. However, it must be repeated that a radical change of mentality is a prerequisite to resuscitate the socioeconomic and political leadership, who selfishly continue to regenerate themselves and block the democratic process while lavishly squandering the human and natural resources. Such indifferent and insensitive leadership as demonstrated inevitably, sooner or later would face the wrath of history, which does not forgive those who neglect to learn its lessons, that those who make evolution impossible make revolution inevitable.[349] Cameroon has much to learn from its own past.

## Ahidjo: the Nemesis of Southern Cameroons

This brief introductory study has been able to confirm from a historical standpoint that former President Ahmadou Ahidjo did a commendable job in galvanizing the various ethnic and political fragments in 'Moslem' Northern Cameroon into a political unit under the umbrella of his *Union Camerounaise*. By the same token he is also credited with having brought this 'Moslem' Northern Cameroon and Christian Southern Cameroon together in French Cameroon. However, his positive contribution to the process of bringing together French and British Southern Cameroons is doubtful. This was certainly not part of his political agenda, but was extensively the UPC ideology, a nationalist party which since 1948, had passionately canvassed for 'immediate independence and reunification' of the two fractions of German Kamerun and, for the expulsion of French colonialists from Cameroon as a consequence. This helps to throw light on the hostility between France and the UPC and Ahidjo's foot dragging when it came to reunification between French and British Southern Cameroons since he was a late convert to the idea and even worse, for reconciliation with the UPC nationalists.

Generally, Moslem Northerners distrusted and disliked Christian South for their religion and radicalism. This was further worsened by the fact the south harboured the UPC 'terrorists' and having to add British Southern Cameroons, another largely Christian unit was inconceivable, but hopefully tempered by the expectation that British Northern Cameroons with its Moslem population would tilt the balance. However, when they

---

[349] Currently, in addition to ***Samuel Doe*** of Liberia, ***Laurent Gbagbo*** of Ivory Coast and ***Bosco Ntaganda*** of Congo at the International Criminal Court; ***Hissene Habre*** after forty years of dictatorship and brutality in Chad and ***Blaise Compaore*** of Burkina Faso are on trial in the Extraordinary African chambers in Senegal in Africa. Furthermore, the maximum detention cells in Yaoundé and Douala can be visited to see the dozens of top Cameroonian mostly political leaders awaiting trial or actually imprisoned there for various crimes involving embezzlement, misappropriation or outright theft. All these are wrapped up one way or the other in the wheels of historical justice.

voted to stay within Nigeria, this made the situation wholly untenable and Ahidjo seriously began doubting the wisdom of such a venture. This was when he informed JO Field the Commissioner of British Southern Cameroons that he could afford neither the military protection nor the economic means to sustain Southern Cameroons, thus discarding the idea of reunification.

This came after the same question had earlier been put to the Nigerian political leaders as a precondition for the choices that Southern Cameroons had to make between Nigeria and Republic of Cameroon at the plebiscite of February 1961. Incidentally, the Nigerian leaders had a quick and ready response, if Southern Cameroons voted for integration with them: they were to be accorded a regional status with equal rights and privileges to those of the three existing Regions; Eastern, Western and Northern, all of which already enjoyed "Internal self government". This was a most palatable offer compared to the negative response given by President Ahidjo.

It is not clear how this gap was finally bridged, but after the plebiscite, and, as the Southern Cameroons delegates prepared for the Foumban Constitutional Conference in July 1961, the British loudly declared the withdrawal of their soldiers from Southern Cameroons leaving the fragile Territory totally without any defence. This came after Foncha had accused Ahidjo and the representatives of the British Government at the Buea Tripartite Conference of blatant and open collusion against Southern Cameroons. When British Northern Cameroons finally voted to stay with Nigeria, Ahidjo's disappointment was massive, the depth of which could be measured by the extent to he went in trying to reverse the plebiscite results of British Northern Cameroons. First, he dispatched his foreign minister to fight the issue at the level of the UN, where he is said to have harangued the members for hours on end on the issue, and failing there, the matter was taken to The Hague, where again he lost. Grieving over this tragic situation was sufficiently heartrending for Ahidjo hence he declared First June a Day of National Mourning, when all flags were flown at half mast, what became an annual event. It is maintained that he finally fired his Minister of Foreign Affairs, Charles Okala because, he thought, he had not fought the battle hard enough.

Consequently, Ahidjo's dealings with Southern Cameroons and its leadership were always, half hearted, dubious and even vindictive. It is therefore, hardly surprising the way and manner in which he sacked Jua and Foncha, diehard federalists, and handpicked Muna, who had repeatedly been defeated by Jua in open competition for KNDP party leadership. He was first appointed PM of West Cameroon to replace Jua, the popularly elected candidate and two years later he was again promoted and appointed Vice President to replace Foncha, posts he held concurrently. Thus he set the carefully constituted Westminster parliamentary system of government into total disarray. Like in a game of chess, these were tactical moves towards the ultimate goal, which was the brutal ambush of article 47/1 of the Federal constitution, which totally forbade any alterations that could impair the Federal status of Cameroon. This happened within another lapse of two years in 1972, when within a space of less than a fortnight (May 7-20 1972) without freedom of speech and in the heart of the rainy season, Ahidjo staged a fake referendum in which voters had to choose between "Oui" and "Yes," the result of which was a resounding 99.99%. Thus fortified he felt sufficiently emboldened to declare his 'Peaceful Revolution'; dismantled the FRC and laid the foundation for the perennial woes that have beset the Anglophone population for the past fifty-four years mounting in magnitude and literally leading to despair. In other words, Ahidjo's "Peaceful Revolution" after which the state of West Cameroon was split in two clearly marks the Anglophone Waterloo.

Put together, Ahidjo's detest for Southern Cameroons and its leaders was immense and the damage he did is incalculable, nearly irreparable and, that he finally openly boasted that he had destroyed, what he described with disdain as: "The disorderly, so called, parliamentary system" directly referring to what obtained in West Cameroon is one of the criminal deeds for which he will forever stand accused before the judgment of history. Consequently, there is practically little that he can be credited for as what he positively did for the State of West Cameroon or the Anglophones.

It is fairly obvious that Ahidjo's attitude towards Southern Cameroons was prompted by his blind obsession for "egomania", religious bias and his innate dislike for democracy and federalism. But then with a more enlightened leadership, matters seem to have gone even worse, when President Paul Biya of a sudden abolished the URC and reinstated the Republic of Cameroon, (RC) discarded at Reunification and Independence in 1961.

This ambiguous act has been subjected to countless interpretations. It was certainly influenced by the threat of civil war in the wake of President Ahidjo's resignation, but has continued to worsen with the passage of time, which calls for serious rethinking of this very nasty problem. For that matter, the majority of Anglophones are not asking for anything new or extraordinary but simply for a return to the drawing board; in fact, to the original agreement, one from which both parties would draw strength, peace, progress and prosperity devoid of friction, name calling, finger pointing, prosperity and recrimination.

On the other hand, the Biya Administration is by far more enlightened and capable of seeing beyond the immediate horizon into the far future especially as, when carefully analysed there is everything to gain and nothing to lose. Already on record as the harbinger of democracy to Cameroon, Biya could by the same logic, for the very serious reason, that this would restore hope, happiness and prosperity to an indestructible political unit on the edge of despair. This would not entail the importation of any foreign ideas but merely, another nod of the head for a return to the drawing board like at Foumban in 1961, taking precautions from the failed experiences over the past fifty- four years. The proper adage is that if keeping too close results in friction, irritates and hurts, then for everybody's interest, it is best to allow elbow room between former "East" and "West Cameroon" to move to their previous, well known positions to better stay cordially, connected, each side benefitting from the other in a truly win – win situation. Since the ultimate aim of all good governance, is providing the greatest happiness to the greatest numbers, Francophones and Anglophones severally and collectively, the welfare of its citizens lies in federalism, which is not the same thing as devolution. At the end of the day, this would be the most practical expression of bringing administration closest to the people respecting and embodying their familiar and accustomed systems, values, structures, environments, history and traditions with which they are most comfortable and identify. All that is called for is firm political determination, good will and openness to dialogue wrapped up in the original fraternal democratic spirit.

# Appendix I

## Southern Cameroons Elections (1951- 1961)

The 1951 Legislative Elections: Six Divisions of the Cameroons and Bamenda Provinces

    1. Victoria Division:    Dr. E. M. L. Endeley
                                         Mr. P. N. Motomby-Woleta

    2. Kumba Division:     Mr. N. N. Mbile
                                         Chief R. N. Charley

    3. Mamfe Division:     Mr. S. A. George
                                         Mr. M. N. Forju

    4. Bamenda Division:  Mr. S. T. Muna
                                         Mr. V. T. Lainjo

    5. Wum Division:       Rev. J. C. Kangsen
                                         Prince Sama Ndi

    6. Nkambe Division:   Mr. J. T. Ndze
                                         Mr. A. T. Ngala

*Observation*: The 1951 General Elections were the first democratically organized on the elective principleby throughout the six divisions of Southern Cameroons in accordance with the *Macpherson Constitution*. As yet, there were no local or national political parties in the Territory with only the National Council of Nigeria and Cameroons (NCNC) of Dr. Nnamdi Azikiwe in Nigeria. The elections marked a clean break with the traditional appointments made by the colonial administration with

APPENDIX I

the electorate exercising their franchise.

## *The December 1953 Legislative Elections*

Victoria: Dr. E. M. L. Endeley
Mr. E. K. Martin
Chief J. Manga Williams (NA Member)

Kumba: Mr. F. N. Ajebe-Sone
Mr. J. M. Bokwe
Mr. H. N. Mulango (NA Member)

Mamfe: Mr. S. A. George
Mr. S. E. Ncha
Mr. S. A. Foto (NA Member)

Bamenda: Mr. J. N. Foncha
Mr. S. T. Muna
Mr. V. T. Lainjo
Mr. Morju (NA Member)

Wum: Rev. J. C. Kangsen
Mr. J. N. Nkwain
Mr. A. N. Jua (NA Member)

Nkambe: Mr. J. T. Ndze
Mr. J. N. Nsame
Chief Nformi (NA Member)

*Analysis*: Only two parties the KNC led by Dr. E. M. L. Endeley and the KPP led by Mbile contested in the elections but the KNC won all the seats.

## *The 1957 Legislative Elections*

There were 13 seats contested by the KNC, KPP and KNDP
Victoria North: Dr. E. M. L. Endeley (KNC)

APPENDIX I

Victoria South:        Mr. P. N. Motomby Woleta (KPP)
Kumba East:            Mr. F. N. Ajebe-Sone (KNC)
Kumba West:            Mr. N. N. Mbile (KPP)
Mamfe South-East:      Mr. Ambrose Fonge (KNDP)
Mamfe North-East:      Mr. S. A. Arrey (KNC)
Bamenda East:          Mr. V. T. Lainjo (KNC)
Bamenda West:          Mr. S. T. Muna (KNC)
Bamenda Central:       Mr. J. N. Foncha (KNDP)
Wum South:             Mr. A. N. Jua (KNDP)
Wum North:             Mr. P. N. Mua (KNDP)
Nkambe North-East:     Rev. Ando She (KNC)
Nkambe South-East:     Mr. J. N. Nsame (KNDP)

\* *The analysis was as follows:*
KNC:     6
KNDP:    5
KPP:     2

\*The KNC and the KPP of Endeley and Mbile formed the KNC/KPP alliance in parliament. On 15 May 1958 Dr. E M L Endeley formed the first truly Southern Cameroons Government as the first Premier

### The 1959 Legislative Elections

The Elections were keenly contested by Endeley's KNC, Foncha's KNDP and Mbile's KPP

Victoria:
North-West:    Dr. E. M. L. Endeley;           KNC
South-West:    Mr. P. N. Motomby-Woleta;       KPP
North-East:    Mr. M. N. Ndoke;                KNDP
South-East:    Mr. Mbua Monono;                KNDP

Kumba:
North-West:    Mr. N. N. Mbile;                KPP
South-West:    Mr. J. N. Nasako;               KPP
East:          Mr. F. N. Ajebe-Sone;           KNC

293

| | | |
|---|---|---|
| West: | Mr. J. M. Bokum; | KNDP |
| Central: | Mr. J. E. Sona; | KNDP |

Mamfe:
| | | |
|---|---|---|
| North: | Mr. S. E. Nam; | KPP |
| West: | Mr. W M N O Effiom; | KNDP |
| East: | Mr. P. M. Kemcha; | KNDP |
| South : | Mr. D. N. Frambo; | KNDP |

Bamenda:
| | | |
|---|---|---|
| Bafut East: | Mr. J. N. Foncha; | KNDP |
| West: | Mr. S. T. Muna; | KNDP |
| North: | Mr. V. T. Lainjo; | KNC |
| Ndop West: | Mr. J. H. Nganje; | KNDP |
| South: | Mr. W. S. Fonyonga; | KNDP |

Wum:
| | | |
|---|---|---|
| East: | Mr. A. N. Jua; | KNDP |
| West: | Mr. J. M. Boja; | KNDP |
| Central: | Rev, J. C. Kangsen; | KNC |
| North: | Mr. S. N. Nji; | KNDP |

Nkambe:
| | | |
|---|---|---|
| North: | Rev. J. Ando Seh; | KNC |
| South: | Mr. J. N. Nsame; | KNC |
| Central: | Mr. S. N. Tamfu, | KNC |
| East: | Rev. D. Y. Nyanganji; | KNC |

*Analysis*
* There were a total of 26 seats
* Three parties competed:
  - Dr. E. M. L. Endeley's KNC won 08 seats
  - Mr. N. N. Mbile's KPP won 04 seats
  - Mr. J. N. Foncha's KNDP won 14 seats
*The KNC (Endeley) and KPP (Mbile) formed the KNC/KPP Alliance with 12 seats.

*After the defection of Hon. J. M. Boja, the KNDP Representative of Wum West to the KNC, Parliament was stalemated at 13:13.

*Another attempt by Hon. David M. Frambo from Mamfe South Constituency to cross the carpet from the KNDP to the KNC/KPP Alliance in April 1960 got botched up; when he declared that he had been forced to sign the resignation papers at gun point by Dr. E. M. L. Endeley and Mr. N. N. Mbile. Thus the parties continued to be stalemated at 13:13 in parliament although the KNDP under Mr, J. N. Foncha formed the Government. The 1961 Elections were contested by the KNDP and the CPNC parties into an enlarged thirty-four-member parliament

## *The 1961 General Election*

These were contested by the KNDP and the CPNC parties into an enlarged thirty-four-member parliament.

Victoria:
| | | |
|---|---|---|
| Victoria South West: | Lifio Carr; | KNDP |
| Victoria South East: | M. M. Monono; | KNDP |
| Victoria North East: | M. N. Ndoke; | KNDP |
| Victoria North West: | Dr. E. M. L. Endeley; | CPNC |

Kumba:
| | | |
|---|---|---|
| Kumba West: | J. M. Bokwe; | KNDP |
| Kumba East: | F. N. Ajebe-Sone | CPNC** |
| Kumba South East: | H. N. Elangwe; | CPNC |
| Kumba North East: | E. E. Ngone; | CPNC** |
| Kumba Central: | J. E. Sona; | KNDP |
| Kumba South West: | D. B. Monyongo; | CPNC |
| Kumba North West: | N. N. Mbile; | CPNC |

Mamfe:
| | | |
|---|---|---|
| Mamfe South: | Nzoh Ekha-Nghaky; | KNDP |
| Mamfe North: | J. C. Lekunze; | KNDP |
| Mamfe East: | P. M. Kemcha; | KNDP |
| Mamfe West: | W. N. O. Effiom; | KNDP |

| | | |
|---|---|---|
| Mamfe North West: | S. E. Ncha; | CPNC** |

Bamenda:
| | | |
|---|---|---|
| Bali: | A. W. Daiga; | KNDP |
| Bafut East: | J. N. Foncha; | KNDP |
| Bafut West: | M. M. Fusi; | KNDP |
| Ngie Ngwo: | Z. A. Abendong; | KNDP |
| Lower. Ngemba: | Chief Angwafor III; | Independent |
| Upper Ngemba: | Sam Mofor; | KNDP |
| Menemo: | S. T. Muna; | KNDP |
| Moghamo: | L. M. Mdamukong; | KNDP |
| Ndop East: | J. F. Nyoh; | KNDP |
| Ndop West: | J. H. Nganje; | KNDP |
| Nso North East: | B. T. Sakah; | KNDP |
| Nso North West: | J. Tatah; | KNDP |
| Nso South: | J. Lafon; | KNDP |

Wum:
| | | |
|---|---|---|
| Wum East; | A. N. Jua; | KNDP |
| Wum West: | E. A. Mendi; | KNDP |
| Wum North: | S. N. Nji; | KNDP |
| Wum Central: | P. Mua; | KNDP |

Nkambe:
| | | |
|---|---|---|
| Nkambe Central: | S. N. Tamfu; | CPNC |
| Nkambe South: | J. Nsame; | CPNC** |
| Nkambe North: | Docta Ndongo; | KNDP |
| Nkambe East: | S. G. N. Yoh; | KNDP |

**Defectors from the CPNC to the KNDP Analysis: Of the 36 seats contested the KNDP won 27 and the CPNC won 9 and one "Independent" candidate. However, 4 of the CPNC candidates crossed the carpet to the KNDP leaving only 5 CPNC members in the opposition. This situation facilitated the move towards the one party system.

# Appendix II

*February 11 1961 Plebiscite Results*

*Fig 45. Plebiscite Results*

# Appendix III

## The Civil Service as I Knew It

This was a service with standards. The Civil Servant was really a servant. Letters to the Public were usually concluded, no matter the rank of the officer, with the words "Your Obedient Servant". All permanent staff were employed through the Public Service Commission. The Secretary for the Public Service kept a record of all personnel in service. This record contained all information about an officer, and this information was updated as one's status changed. The record showed date of employment, date of promotion, salary, increments, and disciplinary actions if any, date of leave, marital status, birth of children etc. Towards retirement, your record was available, from which you were given notice to retire and your pension was accordingly calculated and paid out on your leaving the Service.

Every year, a staff list was gazetted; you knew your position in the service. You lost this position only on disciplinary grounds, thus a junior could never boss his pier or senior. And so there was discipline with no question of intrigues to ascertain progress. Meritorious service resulted in promotion and rise to responsible positions in the service. All Civil Servants knew their functions and every Head of Service had to defend their requests for extra staff. All Civil Servants had their names in the Budget provision for the Department or Ministry. There was consequently no chasing of dossiers, and no one in authority had to run around ensuring that officers high and low were at work.

### *Accountability*

Ministers defended their Budgets before Parliament, which had to be satisfied with the defence before passing the item. The Auditor General at the end of every year published government's income and expenditure for the attention of the public. State Auditors called on Vote Holders without advanced notice. Any shortage resulted in a query and punishment if fault was discovered. There was the case of an officer who through intent or carelessness was found short of funds placed at his disposal. He, not only soon after that lost his job, but spent 20 years in jail, for chicken feed, compared to what disappears these days.

Every office, every residence had an inventory of state property kept therein. These were checked and taken over on change of office. Files contained all in-coming and out-going letters. Every page was numbered. If a document was removed or transferred to another file, this was indicated. Each state vehicle had a Log Book, which carried the performance of the vehicle. Amongst these were fuel supplied, mileage covered, route, purpose. All these were controlled on a regular basis. Mission orders covered vehicle movements.

Nick Ade Ngwa.

## Appendix IV

### The Ndongmo Trial

The alleged coup planned by Mgr. Ndongmo was a ridiculous allegation supported by the production by the Government of eight old and rustic guns with cartridges that could not be used in those guns. These were alleged to be the arms that were to be used for the coup d'Etat. Government officials posing to act as agents of Ahidjo, notably Sabal Leco, then as Prefect of Nkongsamba, Sadou Daoudou Minister of Defence and some others who induced Ndongmo to attempt discussions for peace with Ernest Ouandié were not allowed to come to the Military Tribunal even after we requested their presence. It was these contacts by Mgr Ndongmo to try and persuade Ouandié and his group to lay down their arms that was now used against him as if these contacts were unilateral.

The BMM had trumped up evidence through torture and other methods to implicate the Bishop at all costs and during the trial the victims of these tortures showed their scars to prove this but the carefully selected military tribunal ignored this useful evidence. During the trial, which commenced on a Sunday, the National Radio claimed that Ndongmo had confessed to the offences and was asking for pardon, and this provoked our withdrawal from the defence if there was no apology, correction and an undertaking to give accurate report.

Ahidjo was so scared by our withdrawal and its impact on his international image which he treasured so much that he invited Fon Dinka and myself to the Presidency to persuade us to go back to Court as several international observers (Amnesty International, *Pax Romana* etc) were following the proceedings and he was anxious to show that Cameroon respected the rule of Law.

Our suspension of participation was a major incident and until we got assurance from the President of the accuracy of the reports and of the fact that nobody was going to do anything against us for doing our job as advocates, the military tribunal was in suspense and confusion until we returned to continue the proceedings.

The President of the Military Tribunal at the time, Captain Njock was a Military law student in the University, while one of the military assessors who was a semi illiterate hardly understood what was going on. Forchive kept a close tab on our movements and many Anglophones were scared to be seen in our company except late Akum Fomum who took us around and some people alleged, he was a secret agent for the Government.

In spite of the description of the trial as a farce by a French Lawyer Orcel, who immediately withdrew, the proceedings went on and the French Lawyers of Ouandié and others were refused admission into Cameroon - We learnt one of them was Francois Mitterrand.

Ndongmo had to be condemned to death by the carefully composed military tribunal in order to put Ahidjo in a position of strength to negotiate his ouster from the country as a compromise to his execution. By so doing, he watered down the impression that he was hostile to the Catholic Church. After all, had he not stopped the execution of a Catholic Bishop while executing his accomplices?

Fon Dinka and myself were briefed to appear for Mgr. Ndongmo by the Council of Bishops of Cameroon and the job we did was quite risky as anyone who wanted to cash in on the situation in order to curry favours of the Ahidjo Regime had to denounce and ostracize us. In fact Bishops Peeters and Verdzekov, plus Siam of Nkongsamba at the time were the Clerics who actually collaborated fully with us and were deeply committed to saving Ndongmo from the trumped up charges of Ahidjo's agents.

Barrister Luke K Sendze
May 3, 2005.

# Appendix V

## Selected Declassified British Secret Documents

*Pertinent Excerpts on the Foncha Administration and Southern Cameroons. (The numbering is basically for easy reference and convenience and has no bearing to the original arrangement.)*

1. "Our policy remains strongly against a separate Southern Cameroons state … if Cameroons political parties combine to take action to establish an independent state, this would place us in a very embarrassing position. With support of moderate Afro-Asians and others, we have always argued that separate independence would produce an entirely unviable state." (***Sir Andrew Cohen in a secret Brief of 11 October, 1960 to the secretary of state at the Foreign office).***
2. "What would worry me is if a sequel to the Southern Cameroons' try for independence was that the Northern Cameroons went the same way. That would really, I think, upset our relationship with Nigeria as a whole and for which we must, at all costs, avoid. The Southern Cameroons and its inhabitants are undoubtedly expendable in relation to this"(Lord Perth, British Minister of state at the colonial office in a minute of 12$^{th}$ October 1960 to Sir John Marten of the same office.)
3. One question was always asked. This was "why have we not had a third choice? …Why can we not stand alone? Why should a poor man sell his independence to join with bigger and richer men? …. There was widespread ignorance of what exactly the Republic of Cameroon was; particularly in the remote area". Mr. K. Lees, Plebiscite Supervisory Officer, Bamenda, in a Report on the first

APPENDIX V

plebiscite Enlightenment Campaign dated 28th October, 1960, to the Deputy Plebiscite Administrator, Buea.)

4. "We are as anxious as the French that the Southern Cameroons should join the Cameroun Republic effectively on 1st October 1961… the French may be right that we should not give the Southern Cameroons authorities too much reign." (Mr. E.B. Booth by, in a confidential Memo of 4th July 1961, to the British Permanent Under- Secretary)

5. In particular we must be very careful about independence and temporary sovereignty lest Northern Cameroons is likely influenced not to join Nigeria. This, I believe is the overriding consideration so we must be more or less tough with Foncha that joining Cameroun Republic does not allow sovereignty for a term (sic) of years and then a Federation,"

6. "Mr. Hammarskjöld was afraid lest a difficult security situation should arise and was anxious to avoid any thing in the nature of a "contest between two independent states" (Nigeria and Cameroun Republic) he was wondering therefore whether it would not be a good thing for him to summon about March a "round table discussion" between Ahidjo, Foncha, Endeley and representatives of Nigeria. It might then be possible to work out a formula, which would avoid the necessity for any plebiscite. The formula could however be tested by a plebiscite if the United Nations so wanted. We criticized this idea rather sharply."

7. "First of all I take it that objections hitherto seen as establishment of a separate Southern Cameroons state remain as strong as ever." … I am therefore assuming in what follows that our policy remains strongly against such a solution. If Southern Cameroons political parties did combine to take action envisaged in paragraph 2 of telegram under reference, this would place us in a very embarrassing position. With support of moderate Afro-Asians and others, we have always argued that separate independence would produce an entire unviable state. We have supported a unanimous resolution prescribing plebiscite which involves choice between Nigeria and Cameroon Republic."

8. "There is an increasing movement in the Southern Cameroons in

APPENDIX V

favour of a third choice in the plebiscite. Total independence with United Kingdom aid or continued United Kingdom Trusteeship. We have not supported this proposition."

9. "I realize of course that the Cameroons question is of such a nature that whatever line we take, we must make enemies. This is recognized in paragraphs 10 and 11 of brief for Colonial Secretary enclosed in Greenhill's letter of 17th November. This being so instead of trying to please everyone and failing might it not be worth while trying to please one side viz Nigeria? If we try to be impartial, both Nigeria and Afro-Asian bloc will believe that our real aim is to keep Southern Cameroons as a colony and military base. By coming down firmly against the "third question," we will keep Nigeria as a friend and blunt any teeth of our enemies."

10. "When I wrote my letter 1519/166/60 of June 7 about the Southern Cameroons, I had not seen Halls letter1847/s.6/112 of May 25 to Kale about the third question. The terms of the last sentence of that letter cause me some concern. It seems to me that they amount to a statement that the United Nations, may well be prepared to reconsider its decision on the choices if a majority of the Southern Cameroons assembly wishes to do so. This seems to me likely to encourage Foncha, if he wants to ask for the questions to be changed, to come to the United Nations and do so. It is impossible to predict what reception he would in fact get there if he did any such thing. I think it quite likely that he would fail to secure the necessary two thirds majority but in the process, United Kingdom and the United Nations generally would be placed in an exceedingly difficult position, and need not elaborate on the possible complications for our relations with both Nigeria and the Cameroun. I must reiterate therefore what I said in my letter of June 7, that I think we ought now to use all our influence to prevent this third question idea being raised at the United Nations. This may mean saying publicly that we can see no likelihood of United Nations agreeing to changing its position on this matter."

11. I think it is important that we should not allow this matter to slide as may happen if we are not sufficiently firm with Foncha and perhaps also with Field about the "third question" matter

APPENDIX V

movement. I believe a firm attitude on this now may save us a great deal of trouble later and think that H.M.G's position should be made abundantly clear to Foncha in an effort to scotch tendencies towards the third question."

12. "Can one argue the terms of the question; "Do you wish to attain independence by joining the Republic?" allow for an interim period during which the Southern Cameroons will virtually have its own separate and independent existence while, the terms of reunification with the Republic are being worked out? The words "by joining the Republic" taken literally appear to rule this out. But it may be that Foncha will seek to argue that if his solution having been argued to by Ahidjo is not opposed by the U.K, the U.N may be induced to wear it. There would be the better grounds for this if Endeley were prepared also to agree to this interpretation of the question. We do not like this at all. But we kike the alternatives even less. To go for complete independence or to seek to insert a third choice in the plebiscite would create major difficulties."

13. But from the point of view of our relations with Nigerian delegation and of getting the most satisfactory result, it seems to us essential that, when we discuss tactics with them, they should be left in no doubt not only that we disagree with Foncha's interpretation of the second question but that whatever tactics we adopt, our objective in Assembly discussion will be to secure that question is not redefined as Foncha proposes, or changed, or supplemented by a third question. That does not mean of course that we would not accept Assembly decision to redefine the second question. It would mean that we should pursue tactics to prevent this."

14. "Our trusteeship over the Southern Cameroons is due to terminate on October 21(sic) upon the Southern Cameroons joining the Cameroon Republic." These last words are taken from the UN General Assembly resolution and are read by the Cameroon Government as implying that sovereignty over the Southern Cameroon Republic on October I, and that a federal constitution should be worked out after wards. The Southern Cameroons view is that it has always been recognized that the association between the two territories would be a federal one and that it was on this basic that

APPENDIX V

the people of the Southern Cameroons elected to join Cameroun. They think that, on October 1, they should transfer their sovereign powers to an organization representing the federation rather than to the Cameroun Government itself.

15. The problem in quite a complicated one, from a legal point of view and no doubt it is possible to hold different views about it. But from preliminary examination the Deputy legal Adviser thinks that the Southern Cameroons has quite a strong case. At the end of 1960 President Ahidjo of Cameroun and Prime Minister Foncha of the Southern Cameroons, subscribed to communiqués which emphasized that a federal state would be created and requested that "immediately after the plebiscite and in the event of the people voting for unification with the Cameroun Republic, a conference should be held attended by representatives of the Cameroun Republic and the Southern and Northern Cameroons… which…would have as its aim for the transfer of sovereign powers to an organization representing the future federation." We are as anxious as the French, that the Southern Cameroons should join the Cameroun Republic effectively on that date. But it could be argued that we have a responsibility to the Southern Cameroons to that before we relinquish our trusteeship there is a provision for carrying out our engagement to which the two leaders subscribed before the plebiscite.

16. We very much hope that Foncha and Ahidjo will eventually reach an agreement on the question and save us the, embarrassment of taking a definite line on it ourselves. We have no intention of making things difficult for the Cameroons Government, so long as they can carry the Southern Cameroons authorities with them. But it would be difficult for us to approach the matter in the same black and white way as the French and the Cameroonians. Apart from legal difficulties, there is the question of what sort of tactics are likely to have the best effects on Foncha. We are afraid if he is pressed too hard, opposition from certain circles in the Southern Cameroons might prevent the federation from taking place at all. This is a matter of guess work and the French may be right that we should not give the Southern Cameroons authority

APPENDIX V

too much reign".

17. Independence for the Southern Cameroons would face us with considerable problems. They would expect financial support from us up to the tune of perhaps one million pounds a year and also that we should leave our troops in the country to defend them. If we met these requests it would be expensive for us financially and militarily and we would be accused of "neo- colonialism." If we refused the requests, Ghana, Guinea or the Russians would, no doubt, be only too pleased to help. In short this is not a course which we should at all encourage Foncha to adopt.

18. The department is strongly of the opinion that we should not encourage Foncha to go to the U.N. at all. In the telegram authorized by the African Committee, we have in fact said that "H.M.G. considers that this (ending of Trusteeship on 1st October.) must be regarded as final decision by the U.N. and will not be able to support any proposal for extension of U.K Trusteeship or any other arrangement other than that the Southern Cameroon joins the Cameroun Republic on October 1st. The French would be most strongly opposed to any approach to the U.N. M. Gorse repeated this to our Ambassador on Saturday and we should antagonize them if they thought that we were supporting it.

19. The Cameroon Government appear seriously worried about the possibility that Foncha or Jua may appeal to the United Nations for a ruling that reunification should come about on the terms set out in the joint communiqué and declarations issued on December 10th and used in the pre-plebiscite enlightenment campaign. At a farewell luncheon given for me by Mr. Okala, two members of the ministry of foreign Affairs, one of them in charge of U.N. Affairs pressed a member of my staff to indicate the line that would be taken by the United Kingdom delegation if the matter came up for debate in the United Nations. This impression has been confirmed by the American Embassy who have told us that the Secretary General of the ministry of foreign Affairs agrees with the view expressed in paragraph 2 of your telegram to Paris No. 2472 saying that the Southern Cameroons would have quite a respectable legal case for opposing an unconditional transfer of

sovereignty. In accordance with your telegram No. 197, we have been stressing that as far as we are concerned sovereignty will be transferred to the Republic on October 1 and that it is up to the Cameroonians to reach an agreement among themselves".
20. "Foncha is due to see Ahidjo again this week. The main purpose of the visit this time is to get Ahidjo's support for an economic mission to tour the capitals of Europe between now and October to get aid for various development projects after independence. I can't see Ahidjo being very enthusiastic about such a jaunt on the eve of unification but one never can tell and if he doesn't shoot it down, I suppose I shall be writing to you about it before long. I have naturally thrown what cold water I can on the idea at this stage." " I agree generally with paragraphs 5 and 6 of your letter to the effect that if the southern Cameroons so chooses, sovereignty will have to be handed over to the United Kamerun when Trusteeship Agreement is terminated, and that this will involve the new federal Government having from the outset the necessary powers in foreign affairs. Otherwise Foncha might apply for U.N; membership? In other words Foncha will have to be told that the point in paragraph 6(4) of Milne's dispatch personal No.6 of October 18 is not possible. This is in accordance what I said in my telegram Brief 154 to John Martin. I of course, appreciate the need to drive Foncha back to no plebiscite and separate independence.
21. "You asked me to discuss with Field the possibility of requiring the woman member to resign so that Foncha would no longer have a majority I find the situation here has changed. There now seems a distinct possibility that Government and Opposition may combine together to urge H.M.G to use their influence with the U.N to cut out plebiscite, and secure immediate independence for the Southern Cameroons on its own leaving the question of union with either of their neighbour over for settlement later. Field will be writing dispatch explaining background to this."
*Reasons are:*
- Realization by Endeley and co the vote is most likely for Nigeria.
- Doubts by all parties as to capacity of Republic to replace

Nigeria federal services and provide financial and economic support."

22. "I referred to the possibility of some positive and success full action to sway Cameroons to choose other than to rejoin Nigeria."

    "Most people in the Southern Cameroons do not want to be administered by the Republic; they do not want to have anything to do with French army or police (which they fear.) They do not want a French system of law, they do not the French language, they do not want to risk being pushed around by French officials and they do not want policy dictated to them by Republic politicians. Least of all they do not want the British connection to be completely severed or to be cut off from British help… They fear being pushed into Nigeria as much as they fear being pushed into the Republic."

23. "Her majesty's Government position should be made abundantly clear to Foncha in an effort to scotch tendencies towards the third question. The policy of Her Majesty's Government is to discourage any tendency towards a "third question" very strongly".

24. "The Southern Cameroons is a frontier exposed….to communism–inspired influence which can become a danger of serious magnitude. This reason not to speak of its great potentialities makes the Southern Cameroons an area of serious concern for the United States. The present government in the Southern Cameroons made up of almost totally inexperienced and naïve ex-primary school teachers with good intentions is incapable of grappling with the tremendous problems which face it. Leadership in the Southern Cameroons is inexperienced, untrained and naïve……. The logical conclusion would seem to be that the Southern Cameroons with its remoteness from Lagos, its complexities and its vulnerability, deserves increased attention on the part of the United States."

## Interviews and Written Notes

- Mrs. E M Chilver: Discussions and copious notes, August-November, 2004
- Rev. Fr. William Neba: Valuable documents
- Rev. Fr. Jules Peeters: Discussions and documents
- Rev. Fr. Clemens Ndze: Discussions and notes
- Dr. Elias M Nwana: Discussions over several months in 2005
- Mr. John I A Foleng: Discussions and written notes February-March, 2005
- Mr. Nick Ade Ngwa: Discussions, Documents and Photographs Bamenda, March-June 2005
- Mr. Peter N Eba: Discussions and written notes, December 2005
- Mr. Henry Fonge: Discussions and written notes, January - February, 2005
- Mr. James Tangiri Ndi: Discussions, March 2005.
- Mr. David Ngiewi Asunkwan: Discussions and notes, November 2004 - January 2005.
- Mr. Luke Sendze: Discussions and written notes, March - May, 2005.
- Mr. John Mofor Ndi: Discussions and copious documents, March - April 2005.
- Mr. Stephen N Nfor: Proof reading and Discussions, April 2005.
- Mrs. Esther Ngala: Discussions, April 2005
- Mr. Johnson T Muluh: Discussions, April 2005
- Mr. Fidelis Afuba: Discussions, April 2005
- Mr. Francis T Nkwatoh: Discussions, written notes and documents, April 2005
- Archival Reports and Articles
- Annual Report by Trusteeship Council 4th session 27/1/49, BA Ba 1947/4

- Arnett, E J. "Native Administration: A Comparison of French and British Policy" in Journal of the African Society. 1933 XXXIIE
- Bayart, J F. "The Neutralization of Anglophone Cameroon" in Gaullist Africa: Cameroon Under Ahmadu Ahidjo, Richard Joseph ed., Fourth Dimension Publishers, 1978
- Director of Audit, Federation of Nigeria. Federation of Nigeria, Report of the Director of Audit on the Accounts of the Government of the Southern Cameroons for the Year ended 31st March, 1959. Buea: Government Press, 1960
- West Cameroon. Report of the Director of Audit on the Accounts of the Government of West Cameroon for the Year Ended 30th June, 1965Buea: .Government Printer, 1967
- West Cameroon. West Cameroon Report of the Director of Audit on the Accounts of the Government of West Cameroon for the Year ended 30th June 1970. Buea: Government Press, 1970
- Foncha, J N Dr. "A Memorandum on the Return to Federalism in Cameroon, to All Patriotic Cameroonians", Nkwen, Bamenda 20 Dec.1991
- Fossung, Henry, Ambassador. "A Tribute to Late Hon. S T Muna by theSouthern Cameroons People's Conference", 28/1/2002, Bamenda
- Jackson, HOH Vernon. "A chronology of the History of Academic Education in Cameroon 1844-1940."Abbia, September 1963, No 3
- Nasah, Prof Boniface T. "The Role of Students and Student Associationsin the Political Struggle for Independence and Reunification of Cameroon", CP, No 539 Vol. IX Sept. 2002
- Nfor N Susungi, The Crisis of Unity and Democracy in Cameroon, 1991
- Nkuo, George, Rev. Fr. "Homily for the Funeral Mass of Pa Ernest Kalla Lottin at St. Anthony's Parish Church, Buea Town, Saturday 13/11/04"
- The Cameroons Under United Kingdom Administration: Report by Her Majesty's Government in the United Kingdom of Great Britain and Ireland to the General Assembly of the United Nations for the year 1960. London: HMSO, 1960
- The UN Plebiscite Commissioner's Report to the General Assembly, 1961, Addendum to agenda, item 13. Trusteeship Council AR 1947,

BA 1947/2

***Websites***
http://lucy.ukc.ac.uk/Chilver/Paideuma/paideuma-Indirec-2.html

# BIBLIOGRAPHY

*Published Sources*

Ardener, E W. Historical Notes on the Scheduled Monuments of West Cameroon: Government Printer, Buea, 1965

Afrique Biblio Club (ABC), France, The History Of Cameroon, Once Upon A Time, Ahidjo. Afrique Biblio Club, 1980.

Aka, Emmanuel A. The British Southern Cameroons 1922-1961; A Study in Colonialism and Underdevelopment. Madison: Nkemnji Global Tech, Platteville, 2002.

Ambe, Bosco John, Fondzenyuy Mariana and Verhoeven, Arnold, For The Record: St John The Baptist's Parish Foncha Street – Nkwen, Foncha Street – Nkwen: Peaceberg Printers, Bamenda, June 2015

Ardener, E W. Historical Notes on the Scheduled Monuments of West Cameroon Buea: Government Printer, 1965.

Cullompton. "Talk to the Probus Club, The Early Days in the Cameroons". 1982, nd

Elango, Lovett Z. The Anglo-French Condominium in Cameroon 1914-1916, History of a Misunderstanding. Limbe: Navi Publications, 1987

Epale, Simon J. Plantations and Development in Western Cameroon, 1885-1975: A Study in Agrarian Capitalism. New York: Vantage Press, 1985

Eyongetah, T. and Brain, R. A . History of Cameroon. London: Longman. nd

Flannery, Austin ed. Vatican Council 11, The Conciliar and Post Conciliar Documents

Fonlon, Bernard N. A simple Story Simply Told or The Rise of Dr. Pavel Verkovsky, First Archbishop of Bamenda. Yaoundé: CEPER, 1983

Fiona Bowie et al, Eds. Women, Missions: Past and Present: Berg, Providence, OxfordInstitute, 1956

Johnson, Willard R. The Cameroon Federation, Political Integration in a Fragmentary Society. New Jersey: Princeton University Press, 1970

Joseph, A Richard. Radical Nationalism in Cameroon: Social Origins of UPC Rebellion.: Oxford at the Clarendon Press, 1977

Killingray, David and Rathbone, Richard eds. Africans and The Second World War: MacMillan Press Ltd, 1986

Lantum, Daniel N. Prof. Tribute to Dr. John Ngu Foncha. Yaoundé, 1999

Lugard, Lord. The Dual Mandate in British Tropical Africa. London: Frank Cass 86 Co. Ltd., 1965.

Mason, R J. British Education for Africa. London: OUP, 1959

Milne, Malcolm, No Telephone to Heaven- From Apex to Nadir- Colonial Service in Nigeria, Aden, The Cameroons and The Gold Coast, 1961. Meon Hill Press, 1999.

Mbile, N N. Cameroon Political Story; Memories of an Eye-Witness. Limbe: Presbyterian Printing Press. 1999.

Mukete E, Victor. My Odyssey – The Story of Cameroon Reunification. Yaoundé: SOPECAM, 2013

Mukong, Albert W. Prisoner without a Crime. London: Editions Nubia, 1990

_____ed. The Case for Southern Cameroons. Enugu: CAMFECO, 1990

Nalova, Lyonga ed. Socrates in Cameroon, The Life and Works of Bernard Nsokika Fonlon, Tortoise Books, 1989

National Episcopal Conference of Cameroon. Pastoral Letter of the Bishops of Cameroon About Catholic Education to All Christian Communities and to All Men of Goodwill. Yaoundé: SOPECAM, January 1989

New Webster's Dictionary. The New Webster's Comprehensive Dictionary Encyclopedia Deluxe Edition: Trident Press International, 1998

Newington, W F. West Coast Memories: London: 1993

Ndi, Anthony. Mill Hill Missionaries in Southern West Cameroon, 1922-1972- Prime Partners in Nation Building: Paulines Publications, Africa 2005.

Ndi, Anthony. Southern West Cameroon Revisited, 1950-1972, Vol One, Unveiling Inescapable Traps: Paul's Press, Bamenda 2013, pp. 301-308.

_____Southern West Cameroon Revisited, 1950-1972, Vols One and Two: Paul's Press, Bamenda 2013

Ndi, Anthony Ed. *A Concise Centenary History of The Catholic Church: Archdiocese of Bamenda, 1913 -2013:* Archdiocesan Information Services

Ndi, Ni John Fru. SDF at 25, 1990- 2015: The Struggle for Democracy and Good Governance: Presbyterian Printing Press, Limbe, 2015

Nfor, Nfor N. The Southern Cameroons: The Truth of the Matter: Bamenda: 2003

Nfor N Susungi, The Crisis of Unity and Democracy in Cameroon, 1991 nd

Ngoh, Victor Julius. Constitutional Developments in Southern Cameroons, 1946 - 1961, Yaoundé: CEPER, 1990

_____The Untold Story of Cameroon Reunification, 1955-1961: Presprint Plc, 2011.

_____History Of Cameroon Since 1800: Presprint, 1996

Ngwafor, E N. Ako-Aya (An Anthology). London: Institute of Third World Art 86

_____Literature, 1989.

Nicolson, I F. The Administration of Nigeria, 1900-1960. Oxford: The Clarendon Press 1969

Nwana, E M. Tracing My Roots Through the Njuh Vaatkuna and Mfum Wadinga Family Lines. London: Adelphi Graphics Ltd, 2004

Nyamndi, Ndifontah B. The Bali Chamba of Cameroon, A political History. Paris: Editions CAPE, 1988

Oake, Mary Elizabeth. No place for a White Woman. Edinburgh: Neill and Co. Ltd nd

Okoye, Mukwugo. The Growth of Nations. Enugu: Fourth Dimension Publishers, 1978

Percival, John. *The Southern Cameroons Plebiscite, Choice or Betrayal:*Langaa Research and Publishing CIG, Mankon, Bamenda. Pp.77-78

Political Bureau of the Cameroon National Union (CNU). As told by Ahmadou Ahidjo, 1958 –'68: Paul Bory Publishers, Monaco. 1968

Samah, Albert. Nation Building, Governance and Human Rights: Wivans

Publishers, March, 2010

Sobseh, Y. Emnanuel. Rethinking Citizenship, Politics and Governancein Cameroon. Bamenda: Global Press 2012

Soh, Pius B. Dr. John Ngu Foncha, The Cameroonian Statesman. Bamenda: Centre for Social Sciences, 1999

The Government of Southern Cameroons. Introducing the Southern Cameroons. Lagos: Federal Information Service, 1958

The Ministry of Information and Tourism. The Federal Inspectorate of Western Cameroon-The Federal Republic of Cameroon

The New Webster's Comprehensive Dictionary, Deluxe Encyclopedic Edition. Trident Press International, 1998

Toh, Peter Njah Rev. The Anglophone Problem. Bamenda: 2001

Victoria Centenary Committee, Victoria, Southern Cameroons 1858-1958. Victoria: BM Book Depot, 1958

Wakai, Nyo'o. Inside The Fence. Bamenda: Patron Publishing House, Box 598, 31 Jan. 2000

_____Justice Nyo'. Under The Broken Scale of Justice: The Law and My Times. Bamenda: Langaa Research and Publishing CIG 2009

Welch, C E. ed. Dream of Unity: Pan Africanism and Political Unification in West Africa. Ithaca: Cornell University Press 1966

*Journals*
*Cameroons Champion.*
*Cameroon Information Bulletin*
*Cameroon Panorama*
*Cameroons Star*
*Cameroon Times*
*Catholic Information Bulletin*
*Daily Times [Nigeria]*
*Eden Group of newspapers*
*Jeune Afrique Economie*
*The Horizon*
*Kamerun Times*

*Life Time*
*The Cameroon Voice*
*The Horizon* no. 237

**Unpublished Sources**

Kiawi, Paul Tuh. "The Germano-Kom War Tactics" An MA Dissertation in the Faculty of Arts, University of Buea, Dec., 2001

Ndi, Anthony. "Alfred Saker, The Mission to Cameroons and the Founding of Victoria Colony," MA Dissertation, SOAS, University of London, 1977

Ndi, "Mill Hill Missionaries and the State in Southern Cameroons, 1922-1972," A Thesis Submitted in Partial Fulfilment for the Doctor of Philosophy (SOAS) University of London, 1983

Neba, Judith Ngum. "The Evolution of Secondary Education Under the Basel Mission and PCC 1949-1991." MA Dissertation Dept. of History, University of Buea, 1998

Newington, W F. "West Coast Memories", 1993, an unpublished autobiography.

Ngoh, Victor J. "The Origin of the Marginalisation of Former Southern Cameroonians (Anglophones), 1961-1966: A Historical Analysis", An Address at Buea University, nd.

Thomas, Guy Alexander. "Why do We Need the Whiteman's God? African Contributions and Responses to Formation of a Christian Movement in Cameroon, 1914-1968." Ph.D. Thesis SOAS, University of London, 2001.

Wache Francis, "Parliamentary Eloquence: The First Assembly of West Cameroon Democracy", Cameroon *Life*, Vol II, No 3, 1992

# Index

Abacha, Sani xxxviii, 275
Abakpa Market 82
Abdu Diouf 263
Achirimbi II, Fon of Bafut xii, 99, 102
Administrative Officer 56
adulteration, of palm wine
  Ibo 82
African Commission on Human and Peoples'
  Rights
  ACHPR 255, 257
African union 188
Agbor Nkongho, Barrister Felix 234, 235
Ahidjo, Ahmadou ix, xii, xiii, xiv, xix, xxvi,
  xxvii, xxxvii, 5, 7, 8, 14, 19, 23, 25, 27,
  28, 73, 83, 91, 113, 116, 117, 119, 120,
  121, 128, 137, 138, 142, 143, 151,
  152, 153, 154, 155, 156, 158, 159,
  160, 161, 162, 163, 164, 165, 166,
  167, 170, 172, 173, 175, 176, 179,
  180, 181, 182, 185, 186, 187, 188,
  189, 190, 191, 192, 193, 194, 195,
  196, 197, 198, 199, 200, 202, 203,
  204, 205, 206, 209, 210, 211, 212,
  214, 215, 216, 218, 219, 222, 223,
  225, 226, 227, 228, 232, 239, 240,
  241, 242, 243, 244, 245, 247, 248,
  250, 252, 253, 256, 261, 262, 263,
  264, 265, 266, 267, 268, 269, 270,
  271, 272, 273, 274, 275, 276, 277,
  278, 279, 280, 281, 286, 287, 288,
  289, 301, 302, 304, 306, 307, 309,
  312, 315, 317
Ahidjo favoured Muna 158
Ahidjo, Mrs. Germaine 276
Ahidjo's fake referendum 212
Ajebe Sone, Hon. SN 126, 155, 175
Aka, Emmanuel 156

All Anglophone Conference
  AAC I 206
Amin, Dada Idi xxvii, xxxviii, 275
Anglo-German boundaries 82
Anglophone Problem xxv, 318
Anglophone Resentment 249
Anglophone Southern Cameroonians xxx,
  206, 208, 249. *See also* Southern
  Cameroonians
Anglo-Saxon xxv, xxvi, xxxv, xxxvi, 10, 34, 39,
  44, 52, 54, 59, 61, 74, 104, 105, 138,
  156, 206, 213, 232, 234, 235, 238,
  255, 284
Anglo-Saxon culture xxvi, 44, 59, 74, 213. *See
  also* Anglo-Saxon outlook
Anglo Saxon outlook 68. *See also* Anglo-
  Saxon
annexationist tendencies xxx
Anyangwe, Dr. Carlson 208, 245, 246
Aquinas, St. Thomas Major Seminary
  STAMS xv, xviii, 205
Arab Spring xxxviii, xxxix
argument of force 25, 113
Article 47(1) of the Federal Constitution
  185
Assale, Charles xiii, xiv, 117, 118, 193, 194,
  225, 226, 227, 228
assimilation xxx, xxxii, 34, 38, 40, 54, 56, 158,
  174, 187, 206, 284
Assisted Mission Schools 47
Asunkwan, Mr David Ngiewi xv, 45, 311
Awa, Mgr. Pius Suh, Bishop of Buea Diocese
  74
Awudu, Hon Cyrpien Mbaya 229, 233
Axis Powers 58
Ayandele, Professor 111
Azikiwe, Dr Nnamdi xi, xviii, 10, 19, 87, 201,

Bafia 82
Bakassi Peninsula xxxix, xl, 147, 177, 216, 225, 281
Bakweri, people xix, 79, 80, 84, 144, 236, 237
Bakweri women 80
Bali i, xi, xii, xiii, 21, 29, 30, 36, 37, 48, 81, 86, 115, 124, 144, 145, 296, 317
Bamenda All Party Conference xii, 6, 27, 97, 113, 115, 121, 137, 206, 243
Bamenda Division xxxiv, 56, 63, 103, 104, 291
Bamenda Grasslanders combining forces with their Bamileke kith and kin, 152
Bamenda Grasslands 29, 33, 40, 63, 79, 80, 83, 107, 126, 131, 144
Bamenda Proclamation 207
Bamileke 152
Banyo 29, 82
Baptist Mission xviii, 47, 65, 66, 85, 108, 109, 123. *See also* Cameroon Baptist Mission
Baptist Missionaries 39, 51, 56, 63, 106
Baptist Teacher's Training College, Great Soppo, Buea 86
Basel Mission xviii, 47, 56, 85, 123, 319
Baseng 40, 41, 64, 107
Bayart, JF 152, 156, 157, 159, 312
Beba-Befang 37, 214
Ben Bella, nationalist leader 188
Benevolent Neutrals 18, 157
Benign British Neglect 101
BGS. *See also* Bilingual Grammar School
bicultural state 203
Bishop of Kumbo xxxiii
Biya, President Paul ix, xiv, xxvi, 182, 208, 213, 232, 251, 252, 253, 256, 261, 262, 263, 264, 265, 266, 267, 269, 271, 272, 274, 275, 277, 279, 283, 288, 289
black imperialist 79
Bodleian, Library xv
Boja, Hon JM 99, 126, 294, 295
Bokassa, Jean Bedel xxxviii
Boko Haram, insurgency xxxviii, xxxix, 127, 128, 283
British Colonial Administration 63
British Mandated and Trusteeship periods 77
British Mandate of the League of Nations 77
British Northern and Southern Cameroons 82
British Northern Cameroons xvii, 78, 83, 128, 152, 202, 247, 248, 286, 287
British policy of underdevelopment 94
British secret files
 on the Trust Territory of Southern Cameroons 95
British Trust Territory 77
Buea Declaration 207
Buhari, Retired General Mohammadu xxxix, 127, 128
Bum xxxv, 37, 100, 104, 135, 214

Calabar 59, 77, 83, 85
Cameron, Sir Donald 45
Cameroon Baptist Convention xviii, xxxiv, 70, 74, 147, 149. *See also* CBC
Cameroon College of Arts Science and Technology
 Bambili 86
Cameroon GCE Board 74
Cameroonisation of the Southern Cameroons Civil Service 88
Cameroon Protestant College, Bali 86, 124
Cameroon United Congress xix, 25, 161, 210
Cameroon Youth League 20, 78, 112, 200
cannibalism
 Ibos accused of cannibalism 80
Catholic Church xviii, xxxiv, 35, 40, 41, 64, 107, 124, 147, 148, 170, 171, 172, 232, 302, 317
Central African Republic xxxviii, xxxix, 275
character above wealth xxxiii
Chilver, Mrs Elizabeth M xv, xliii, 30, 43, 82, 177, 311, 313
Christian conduct and influence 65, 109
Christian spiritual contributions 66
Christian teaching 61, 103
Christian values 104
Christian Villages 41
Christo-centric 44
Civic knowledge xli
civilizing and educating mission 79
civil service xii, xvi, xxxiii, xxxiv, 4, 5, 13, 14, 49, 50, 59, 71, 74, 84, 87, 133, 134,

154, 284
Cold War political climate 241
Collusion between Britain and Republic of Cameroun 239
commissions of inquiry 284
Communist-Anathema 241
Congo 31, 144, 286
corruption free 4, 128, 139, 284
Côte d'Ivoire xxxviii
Crimea xxxix
Cross River 83
cross the carpet 153
culture of truth 44

Dag Hammarskjöld Award 263
Day of National Mourning 152, 287
Democratic Culture ix, 123
didactic material xli
Dinka, Fon Gorji 173, 301, 302
dismantling of the KNDP 159
District Heads and Notables 40
Divine Retribution 259
Doe, Samuel xxxviii, 286
Douala xviii, xli, 10, 16, 74, 82, 124, 146, 147, 158, 170, 174, 207, 222, 248, 274, 279, 281, 286
Dual Mandate 33, 35, 40, 68, 105, 316

East Cameroon xi, xxii, xxvi, 34, 54, 56, 70, 134, 155, 156, 167, 168, 176, 187, 191, 192, 193, 198, 209, 213, 221, 225, 226
Eastern Regional House of Assembly 37
Eba, Mr Peter N xv, 311
Ebu, Mr Cyril xvi, 45, 96, 134, 173
Economic Commission of West African States xix. *See also* ECOWAS
economic exploitation
  Ibos 80
ECOWAS xix
Education Code of Nigeria 68
Education Rating 47
Efik
  Traders 83
Elad, Mr. Ekontang 208
embezzlement xxxiii, xxxv, 10, 64, 107, 275, 286. *See also* corruption

Emir of Sokoto 96
Endeley, Dr. EML xii, 13, 20, 21, 89, 112, 116, 129, 131, 136, 155, 200, 201, 278
Enduring German influence 60
Enugu 4, 6, 18, 37, 77, 139, 174, 214, 262, 316, 317
Enugu, Southern Cameroons under purview of 77
erosion of the ethical values 74
Essimbi 37
Europe xxxv, xxxix, 1, 58, 103, 191, 207, 276, 309
Executive Secretary of the Cameroon Baptist Convention. *See also* Rev. Samuel Ngum
Eyidi, Bebey 151, 194

Fako Lawyers Association 234, 235
Fatherland xxxiii, 10, 19
Federal Inspectorates 167
Federal Republic of Cameroon xi, xiii, xvii, xxii, xxxi, 5, 6, 7, 23, 54, 61, 94, 129, 157, 158, 168, 175, 176, 181, 188, 198, 204, 207, 209, 223, 246, 252, 254, 318
Federation of Nigeria xxxi, 5, 35, 59, 88, 202, 217, 242, 312
Field, Johnson O xii, xiii, 13, 14, 53, 72, 89, 95, 98, 119, 156, 203, 205, 240, 242, 243, 247, 287, 305, 309
  Commissioner of Southern Cameroons 242
Final Act 164
Foncha Administration 47, 87, 133, 135, 154, 303
Foncha, Dr. John Ngu xvii, xxx, xxxi, 20, 24, 30, 56, 58, 62, 67, 83, 88, 89, 99, 102, 110, 112, 131, 132, 151, 152, 171, 185, 187, 189, 286
Foncha State Burial 277
Fonlon, Professor Bernard Nsokika 99
force of argument 25, 113
Forces Vive de l'Opposition 151
Foumban Constitutional Conference xxix, 6, 23, 27, 53, 97, 113, 121, 137, 138, 157, 161, 178, 185, 186, 187, 190, 195, 203, 210, 218, 220, 221, 226, 232, 243, 287
Foumban talks 179

**323**

Francophone Cameroonians 44. *See also* French Cameroon
Francophone elite xxx, 208, 229, 251, 257, 283
French Cameroon xvii, xxx, xxxi, 20, 24, 30, 56, 58, 62, 67, 83, 88, 89, 99, 102, 110, 112, 131, 132, 151, 152, 171, 185, 187, 189, 286
French Sacred Heart Fathers 63, 106
Funeral Mass
  See Funeral Mass of Pa Lottin xxxiii, 312

Galega I, Fon
  Bali xiii, 144
Galega II, Fon xi, xii, 21, 36, 37, 89, 115
GCE Ordinary and Advanced Level 74
George Orwell's Animal Farm 219
German 56
German-aligned, nationals 62
German Army, the 58
German Colonial Impact 55
German Kamerun xii, xvii, 29, 30, 60, 78, 82, 90, 281, 286
German Protestant missionaries 63
German Reich 60. *See also* German
Ghana xli, 10, 50, 98, 134, 135, 144, 308
Gibbons, Brigadier EJ xi, 8, 21, 91, 153, 260
Gifford, Dr. Paul xv
Godwin, Mr 56
Gold Coast 13, 14, 31, 144, 316. *See also* Ghana
Golden Age i, iii, v, ix, xxv, xxvi, xxvii, xxix, xxxi, xxxii, xxxiii, xxxvii, xxxviii, 1, 2, 3, 5, 8, 9, 13, 30, 31, 50, 128, 129, 132, 147, 178, 192, 203, 226, 228, 258, 260, 276, 278
Golden Age, Southern (West) Cameroon. *See* Golden Age
Golden Fleece 77
Gongola State 128
Government Assisted Schools 68
Government Bilingual Grammar School BGS 70
Government Gazette 140
Government Residential Areas 17, 104
Government Technical College, (GTC) Ombe 86
Governor General of Nigeria, the xii, xiii, 44, 45, 59, 72, 91, 92, 119, 240, 242

Grand Unified Party 152, 153, 163, 166
Gray, Professor Richard xv, xliii
Green Tree Agreement xiv, xxxix, xl, 225, 281, 283
Gwellem, Mr. Jerome 141

Hanrahan, Father Noël 103
heroines xxxv, xli, xlii, 278
heroes xxxv, xli, xlii, 278
Hitler, Adolf xxxviii, 58
Home Rule 21, 201, 240
Human Rights 100, 317
Human Rights Abuse in Republic of Cameroun 100

Ibo back-yard
  Southern Cameroons 79
Ibo domination 84
Ibo hegemony 88
Indirect Rule xvii, xxvi, 33, 34, 40, 41, 43, 53, 59, 63, 107, 123
Inoni, His Excellency, Chief Ephraim xvi, xxxiv, 237
Inviolable Federal Constitution ix, 185
ISIL xxxix
Islamic State of Iraq
  ISIS xxxix. *See also* ISIL

Jantzen xii, 29, 60, 144
Jihadist Islamic movement xxxix
Johnson, Willard 156
Jonathan, President Goodluck xxxix, 127, 128
Joseph Merrick Baptist College 86, 124
Joseph, Richard xii, xiii, 30, 51, 61, 71, 78, 79, 81, 82, 86, 100, 119, 124, 131, 152, 156, 157, 159, 169, 171, 176, 189, 194, 222, 271, 275, 312, 316
Jua, Mr. Augustine Ngom 141, 277
Jua, Prime Minister xi, xii, xiii, xix, xxvi, 9, 11, 24, 28, 73, 89, 97, 115, 117, 118, 121, 129, 130, 138, 141, 153, 156, 158, 159, 160, 161, 162, 163, 164, 165, 166, 168, 169, 175, 178, 192, 198, 204, 205, 210, 222, 265, 277, 278, 288, 292, 293, 294, 296, 308. *See*

*also* Augustine N. Jua

Kale, Mr. Paul M. xi, xviii, xix, xxvi, 9, 11, 19, 20, 24, 89, 112, 130, 166, 200, 213, 278, 305
Kamerun xi, xii, xvii, xix, 6, 8, 15, 19, 20, 22, 24, 29, 30, 38, 58, 59, 60, 61, 78, 82, 89, 90, 92, 96, 112, 126, 133, 144, 152, 168, 169, 196, 243, 272, 281, 286, 309, 318
Kamerun National Congress xix, 19, 20, 22, 112, 126
Kamerun People's Party xix, 8, 19, 20, 112
Kamerun United National Congress KUNC xix, 20, 112
Kamerun United Party KUP 89
Kame, Samuel 193
Kangsen, Rev. Jeremiah C 9, 37, 74, 89, 92, 126, 214, 291, 292, 294
Keandie, Brother Justin 172
Kenyatta, Jomo xli
Kisob, Mr. Jack A 88
KNC/KPP Alliance 24, 89, 126, 178, 294, 295
KNDP xii, xiii, xix, xxxii, 6, 13, 14, 19, 22, 24, 25, 27, 58, 59, 72, 88, 89, 97, 98, 99, 121, 126, 127, 130, 131, 132, 136, 138, 140, 153, 154, 155, 158, 159, 160, 161, 162, 164, 165, 166, 167, 174, 179, 192, 195, 196, 197, 198, 204, 209, 210, 242, 243, 265, 272, 288, 292, 293, 294, 295, 296
KNDP Convention 160
KNDP Memorandum of Protest to Ahmadou Ahidjo 196
Kom xxxv, 37, 40, 63, 64, 107, 214, 319
Kumba xii, xix, xx, xxxv, 30, 38, 46, 64, 68, 69, 80, 81, 84, 86, 103, 107, 124, 131, 132, 141, 142, 143, 146, 210, 224, 225, 235, 244, 256, 291, 292, 293, 295
Kumba, GTTC 68
Kumbo xviii, xxxiii, xxxiv, xxxv, 40, 48, 64, 80, 81, 86, 103, 107, 148
Kumengisa, Richard 80

labour raids 145

Lady MP 98
League of Nations 16, 30, 77, 78, 92, 93, 127, 281
Lees, Mr. K. 101
Lennox-Boyd, Mr. Allan 98
Liberia xxxviii, 31, 144, 286
List System 156, 199, 203, 222
Lottin, Pa Ernest Kalla xxxiii, 312
Lubich, Chiara 124
Lugard, Lord 30, 34, 35, 68, 82, 91, 98, 316
Lump Sum 47

Maa Agatha 99
Machiavelli's treatise 261
main line Missions 65, 108
Mambila 66, 109
Mamfe xviii, xix, xxxv, 20, 30, 40, 63, 64, 80, 81, 84, 85, 86, 87, 89, 107, 112, 126, 131, 132, 137, 146, 148, 169, 206, 225, 282, 291, 292, 293, 294, 295, 296
Mamfe All Party Conference 20, 112
Mamfe Plebiscite Conference 89
Mandela, Nelson xli
Manga Bell, Rudolph Douala xli
Man O' War Bay 70
Marginalisation ix, 169, 229, 238, 319
Mariapolis 124
mass media xli, 74, 128, 139, 145, 232, 233
Mbile, Mr. N. N. xi, xiv, xviii, xix, 6, 7, 8, 9, 11, 19, 20, 25, 37, 59, 84, 95, 112, 113, 126, 130, 131, 138, 141, 142, 153, 154, 156, 161, 162, 163, 166, 168, 176, 180, 200, 278, 291, 292, 293, 294, 295, 316
Mediterranean Sea xxxix
Mill Hill, Archives xv
Milne, Malcolm xi, xiii, xxxvi, 12, 13, 14, 15, 22, 50, 87, 119, 135, 202, 203, 242, 243, 244, 246, 247, 248, 257, 309, 316
Milosevic, Slobodan xxxviii
ministers and directors of parastatals behind bars 74
Mission culture in Southern Cameroons 108
Mission Station 65, 108
Mobutu, Joseph Desiré xxxviii
Moderator, Presbyterian Church 74
monolithic North 268, 269
moral degeneracy 74
moral lessons xli, 141

**325**

Moran, Father Michael 103
Motherland xli
Moumié, Félix Roland xli, 188, 241
Mua, Mrs. Josepha 98
Mukong, Albert Womah xi, xix, 24, 174, 209, 212, 213, 224, 262, 316
multiparty democracy 126, 132
Muna, Solomon Tandeng xi, xii, xiii, xiv, xix, xxvi, 8, 9, 11, 25, 79, 89, 92, 97, 115, 116, 117, 118, 126, 130, 138, 141, 153, 158, 159, 160, 161, 162, 163, 164, 174, 175, 176, 178, 179, 192, 193, 197, 198, 202, 203, 204, 205, 207, 209, 210, 211, 218, 222, 242, 248, 265, 272, 278, 288, 291, 292, 293, 294, 296, 312
Mungo River 83
Munzu, Dr. Simon 208
Mussolini, Benito xxxviii

National Archives xv, 187, 224
national consciousness xli, 18, 37, 149
National Integration 123, 143, 147
nationalism xxv, xli, 15, 31, 66, 67, 110, 111, 123, 200, 260. *See also* patriotism and nationalism
Native Authorities xi, 33, 34, 36, 40, 63, 80, 107, 123, 137, 214
Native Courts xxxv, 35, 41, 123
Native Quarters 104
Nazi 55, 60. *See also* Nazi leadership
Nazi leadership 60
Ncha, Hon SE 126
NCNC xviii, 19, 37, 79, 87, 201, 291
Ndi, Mr John Mofor xvi
Ndongmo Affair xvi, 170, 171, 172
Ndongmo, Mgr. Albert xiv, xvi, 170, 171, 172, 173, 205, 280, 301, 302
Ndongmo Treason Trial 172
Ndze, Mons Clemens xv, 291, 292, 311
Nemesis of Southern Cameroons 286
NEPAD xix
New Partnership for African Development xix
Nfi, Joseph 78, 79, 81, 82, 84
Ngoh, Mr. Jean Claude, the Federal Inspector of West Cameroon 167
Nguema, Marcias xxxviii, 275
Ngum, Rev. Pastor Samuel 74, 319

Nigerian civil servants 47, 87
Nigerianisation 88
Nigerian teachers 85
Nigerian Youth League 20, 112
Njinikom 40, 41, 62, 64, 86, 107, 148, 278. *See also* Kom
Nkrumah, Kwame xi, xli, 10, 18, 242, 243
Nkuo, Rev. Fr George xvi, xxxii, xxxiii, xxxiv, 312
No bill to amend the constitution may be introduced 185, 188
North-South West balance 125
North West Region xvii, xxix, xxxiii, xxxiv, 148, 221, 248, 252, 258
nostalgic era 8
Nyerere, Julius xli
Nyo'Wakai, Justice 158, 175, 198, 280
Nzohngandembo, Chief Zachee 257


Officer of the British Empire 155
Okala, Mr. Charles 152, 194, 245, 287, 308
One Party State 121, 203, 226
open letter to the KNDP 153
Operation Antelope xxxiv
Organisation of African Unity xix, 47, 255. *See also* AU
"Oui" and "Yes" 176, 222


patriotism and nationalism xli, 67
PCC xv, xviii, 139, 147, 148, 149, 319
Peeters, Bishop Jules 94
penitentiary services xlii
Percival, Mr. John
  Plebiscite officer 100, 104
Phillipson Report, unfounded 83
Plebiscite Conference 87, 89, 137, 206
politics is a dirty game 262
POWERCAM xxv, 141, 146
premature demise of the FRC 121
Presbyterian Church in Cameroon xv, xviii, xxxiv, 147, 148. *See also* PCC
Presbyterian Secondary School, Besong Abang, 86
Presbyterian Secondary School, Kumba 86
Priso, Soppo 151
Proto-Nationalism 111
Public Record Office xv

Quasi Federal status  6, 21, 24, 66, 85, 86, 109, 112, 126, 201
Quasi Federal status in 1954  85
Queen of the Holy Rosary College  85, 124

Referendum  157, 176, 180, 216, 220, 221, 223
Regina Pacis College, Bonjongo  86
Regional Major Seminary for West Cameroon  103
Religious and Moral Education  68
Religious Knowledge  xxxvi, 68, 70, 71
Republic of Cameroon  xi, xiii, xvii, xxii, xxvi, xxxi, xxxii, 5, 6, 7, 10, 13, 15, 23, 28, 54, 61, 67, 91, 94, 99, 110, 121, 128, 129, 132, 136, 157, 158, 168, 175, 176, 177, 179, 181, 183, 188, 198, 202, 203, 204, 207, 208, 209, 210, 213, 214, 217, 221, 223, 227, 232, 241, 242, 244, 246, 251, 252, 253, 254, 258, 262, 282, 284, 285, 287, 288, 303, 318
Republic of Cameroun  xvii, 6, 53, 88, 100, 161, 181, 196, 227, 228, 239, 240, 241, 242, 244, 245, 246, 253
Retirement  134
revolutions  191, 259
Rio Del Rey Basins  83
rise and demise of the State of West Cameroon  279
Rogan, Bishop Peter  xii, 41, 43, 45, 69, 85, 139
role models  xxxv, xli, 66, 109, 199, 278
Roman Catholic Mission
  RCM  xviii, 40, 42, 47, 48, 63, 64, 65, 85, 107, 108, 123. *See also* Catholic Mission

Sacred Heart College
  Mankon  85, 172
Saker Baptist College  85, 124
Samba, Martin Paul  xli
Sardauna's Province  83, 128
Sasse, St Joseph College  xii, xvi, 51, 71, 86, 124, 139, 140, 141
second class citizenship  xxx, 284

Second World War  15, 20, 39, 54, 55, 58, 59, 60, 62, 92, 112, 316
Self-Government  xxx, 94
self-reliance  33, 36, 53
Sendze, Barrister Luke K  xvi, 35, 170, 173, 192, 215, 302, 311
Senghor, Leopold Sedar  xli, 10, 263
Senior Service (SS) Clubs  104
Shisong  xxxiii, xxxiv, 40, 41, 48, 64, 107
Sierra Leone  xxxviii, 31, 50, 144
single party dictatorship  132
small things, honesty  xxxiii
SOAS
  School of Oriental and African Studies  xv, 57, 319
Soh, Pius  81, 82, 87, 176, 180, 277, 318
Somalia  xxxviii, xxxix
South Africa  xli, 105, 254
Southern Cameroonians  xxvi, xxx, 8, 9, 18, 20, 28, 33, 36, 38, 39, 44, 53, 54, 55, 59, 61, 80, 86, 88, 99, 112, 121, 133, 134, 169, 198, 199, 200, 202, 203, 206, 208, 224, 228, 235, 249, 250, 252, 254, 255, 259, 282, 319. *See also* Southern Cameroons
Southern Cameroons  i, iii, v, ix, xi, xii, xiii, xvi, xvii, xxii, xxiii, xxv, xxvi, xxvii, xxx, xxxi, xxxii, xxxiii, xxxv, xxxvi, xxxvii, xxxviii, xliii, 3, 4, 5, 6, 7, 8, 9, 10, 12, 13, 14, 15, 17, 18, 19, 20, 21, 22, 23, 24, 25, 26, 27, 28, 30, 31, 33, 34, 35, 36, 37, 38, 39, 41, 43, 44, 47, 48, 50, 51, 52, 53, 54, 55, 56, 57, 58, 59, 60, 61, 62, 63, 64, 65, 66, 67, 68, 69, 71, 72, 77, 78, 79, 80, 81, 82, 83, 84, 85, 86, 87, 88, 89, 90, 91, 92, 93, 94, 95, 96, 98, 99, 100, 101, 102, 103, 104, 105, 106, 108, 109, 110, 111, 112, 113, 116, 119, 121, 123, 124, 126, 127, 128, 129, 130, 131, 132, 133, 135, 138, 139, 141, 146, 149, 151, 152, 153, 155, 157, 161, 174, 176, 178, 179, 180, 181, 183, 185, 186, 187, 190, 200, 201, 203, 206, 207, 208, 209, 211, 212, 213, 214, 215, 216, 217, 218, 220, 221, 224, 226, 227, 228, 229, 235, 236, 239, 240, 241, 242, 243, 244, 245, 246, 247, 248, 250, 251, 252, 253, 254, 255, 256, 257, 258, 260, 262, 276, 278,

279, 281, 282, 283, 284, 285, 286, 287, 288, 291, 293, 303, 304, 305, 306, 307, 308, 309, 310, 312, 315, 316, 317, 318, 319
   a "colony of a Region" of a Colony of Nigeria" 78
Southern Cameroons Culture 52, 61, 62, 106
Southern Cameroons House of Assembly 85
Southern Cameroons Public Service Commission 88
Southern Cameroons state structures 106
southern region of former French Cameroon 151
Southern Sudan xxxviii
Southern (West) Cameroon xxix, 50, 51, 61, 89, 131, 141, 151, 253
Southern-West Cameroon civil service 134
South West Chiefs Conference 229
South West Province xvii
spearheaded a moral crusade
   Tataw Obenson 141
State of West Cameroon 47, 61, 70, 132, 156, 158, 167, 168, 174, 192, 193, 279, 288
St. Augustine's College 86
St. Bede's College 86
St. Peter's College, Bambui 86, 124
Sudan xxxviii
Sydney, Sir Philippson's Report 83, 87

Tabetando, Nfor, Chief, Senator 235
Tanjong Mixed Commission 141
Tataw Obenson, Mr. Patrick 140, 141, 178
Teacher Training Centres 46
the 1972 debacle xxx
The 1972 Referendum 219
The Five Day Epic Trials 269
The Ibo Vector 78
the Renaissance 1
Third Option of independence in the plebiscite 102. *See also* Third Option
"Third Option" Saga 90
"Third Question" 95, 99
Thormalen xii, 29, 60, 144
Traditional Establishment xxxiii, 63, 107
Transparency International 74
transparent, elections xxv, xxxi, xxxix, 4, 23, 132, 137, 221, 285
Treaty of Versailles 77, 78, 82, 92

tribal Ibo flag 87
Tripartite Talks in Yaoundé 206
Truth and Reconciliation Commission xli
TTC, Batibo 86
TTC Kake 86
Tumi, Christian Cardinal xiv, 229, 231, 232

UC party 28, 121, 276, 281
UC political platform 195
Ukraine xxxix
Um Nyobé, Nyobé xli, 24
Union Camerounaise
   UC xix, 151, 161, 162, 192, 193, 196, 226, 286. *See also* UC
Union Jack, the 14, 59, 212
Unique Public Service 132
Unitary State 157, 161, 181, 205, 216, 218, 220, 224, 226, 248, 252, 253
Unity and Strength 251
Unity of Anglophone Trade Unions 236
UN Trusteeship Agreement 93, 101
UN Visiting Missions 46, 100
UPC xviii, xix, 16, 24, 27, 38, 67, 110, 113, 137, 151, 152, 157, 170, 171, 172, 188, 191, 193, 194, 241, 247, 286, 316

Verdzekov, Mgr. Paul
   Bishop of Bamenda Diocese 74, 170, 173, 302
Voluntary Agencies xxxvi, 34, 47, 65, 69, 108
Voluntary Agency schools 47

wealth xxxiii, 9, 10, 85, 215, 285
West Cameroon Development Agency 146
West Cameroon Educational Policy Investment 69
West Cameroonian culture 103. *See also* Anglo-Saxon outlook
Williams, Chief Joanes Manga xi, 4, 36, 37, 292
winds of change 198
wisdom xxxv, xxxviii, xl, 143, 152, 287
Woermann xii, 29, 60, 144
Women's Special Representative. *See also* Mrs. Josepha Mua
Wum xxxv, 37, 48, 100, 104, 126, 131, 135,

146, 214, 291, 292, 293, 294, 295, 296

Yabassi 82
Yaya, Moussa xiii, xix, 117, 164, 193, 195,
    197, 198, 210, 262, 264, 265, 272
Young Moslems 151

Zintgraff xiii, 29, 144

## Praise for *The Golden Age of Southern Cameroons*

"...In quick succession, Prof Ndi is churning out mouth whetting chunks of its history. The inescapable attraction of this volume is the erudite verve, scintillating language and the engaging style which he employs to tell his story."
—**Prof. Canute A Ngwa, Dean, Faculty of Arts, University of Bamenda**

"... It is an outstanding publication that breaks 'new grounds' and lays the foundations for a comprehensive and more open consideration for constructing a new society. In a way the author demonstrates a Cameroon Nation envisioned by the founding fathers as the political laboratory of African integration and unity which has today succumbed to a failed democracy."
—**Prof. John W. Forje, ARAD, Bali, Cameroon**

*"The Golden Age of Southern Cameroons: Prime Lessons* is a historical masterpiece for nation building. It pricks the conscience of those who have glossed over the Southern Cameroonian dedication to the values of patriotism, liberty, diligence, honesty, and search for peace, truth and justice. The volume serves as an inimitable moral compass for national unity in diversity; a companion for all patriotic Cameroonians.
—**Confidence Chia Ngam, Lecturer/Researcher, University of Bamenda, History of International Relations and Social Sciences**

"Cameroon is a complex geopolitical entity, where contradictory variables exist in inexplicable harmony; a marriage of two former self determining UN Trust territories; French and English-speaking with the former today crying wolf about shabby treatment. While some become emotional about facts, which they hardly master, Prof Anthony Ndi has taken a more academic approach to state historical facts that are difficult to contest. *The Golden Age of Southern Cameroons* is a work that should tickle scholars and provoke a rethink among others."
—**Fr Tatah Mbuy, Director of Communications, Archdiocese of Bamenda.**

"Auspiciously, historical facts are irrepressible and sooner or later rebound. Professor Anthony Ndi's *Golden Age of Southern Cameroons* is a glorious wakeup call for a nation in deep stupor."
—**Prof. Simon Tata Ngenge, Head of Department, History, University of Bamenda**

### The SCHLOSS (Cover Photo)

The SCHLOSS as the residence of the German Governors situated in Buea, the former capital of German Kamerun, became the residence of the Vice President of the Federal Republic of Cameroon and Prime Minister of West Cameroon (1961-1965), then subsequent Prime Ministers of the State of West Cameroon (1965-1972). Thus the Schloss symbolises the one unchanging historical rock that runs through the German colonial period up to 1916, the British colonial period as the residence of the Residents and Commissioners of the British Southern Cameroons (1916-1961), residence of the Prime Minister and Vice President of the Federal Republic of Cameroon, (1961-1965), residence of the Prime Ministers of West Cameroon (1965-1972), residence of the President of the United Republic of Cameroon (1972-1984) and residence of the President of the Republic of Cameroon since 1984).